Rethinking the 1990s

Rethinking the 1990s

Liberal World Order-Building in the Aftermath of the Cold War

Edited by
G. JOHN IKENBERRY
PETER TRUBOWITZ

OXFORD
UNIVERSITY PRESS

Oxford University Press is a department of the University of Oxford.
It furthers the University's objective of excellence in research, scholarship,
and education by publishing worldwide. Oxford is a registered trade mark of
Oxford University Press in the UK and in certain other countries.

Published in the United States of America by Oxford University Press
198 Madison Avenue, New York, NY 10016, United States of America.

© Oxford University Press 2025

All rights reserved. No part of this publication may be reproduced, stored in a retrieval system, transmitted, used for text and data mining, or used for training artificial intelligence, in any form or by any means, without the prior permission in writing of Oxford University Press, or as expressly permitted by law, by license or under terms agreed with the appropriate reprographics rights organization. Inquiries concerning reproduction outside the scope of the above should be sent to the Rights Department, Oxford University Press, at the address above.

You must not circulate this work in any other form
and you must impose this same condition on any acquirer.

CIP data is on file at the Library of Congress.

ISBN 9780197813102

ISBN 9780197813096 (hbk.)

DOI: 10.1093/9780197813133.001.0001

The manufacturer's authorized representative in the EU for product safety is Oxford University Press España S.A., Parque Empresarial San Fernando de Henares, Avenida de Castilla, 2 – 28830 Madrid (www.oup.es/en or product.safety@oup.com). OUP España S.A. also acts as importer into Spain of products made by the manufacturer).

Contents

List of Contributors	vii
Preface and Acknowledgments	ix

1. Making Sense of the 1990s: Choices, Pathways, and Missed Opportunities   1
   G. John Ikenberry and Peter Trubowitz

PART I: BRAVE NEW WORLD: LIBERAL CONSOLIDATION OR TRANSFORMATION?

2. How Recursive Is Global Governance? Revisiting the Ordering Choices of the Nineties   25
   Daniel W. Drezner

3. That Faustian Decade: The Financialization of the American Economy   49
   Jonathan Kirshner

4. When Hegemony Mostly Worked: U.S. Relations with Europe and Japan during the 1990s   77
   Michael Mastanduno

5. Responsible Sovereignty and Individual Accountability: Liberal Internationalist Aspirations from the 1990s   107
   Jennifer M. Welsh

PART II: TAKING STOCK: WESTERN SUCCESSES AND FAILURES

6. Populism and the Durability of the Liberal Order in Eastern Europe: EU and NATO Enlargement Reconsidered   141
   Hilary Appel

7. Who Lost Russia? The 1990s Revisited   169
   Michael Cox

8. Reconsidering Engagement with China: Authoritarian Power and International Order 195
 Miles Kahler

9. The Return of/to Europe and the New Politics of Globalism 227
 Harold James

PART III: FALSE DAWN: WESTERN OVERREACH OR UNDERREACH?

10. Ever Deeper and Wider? The Globalization of the Liberal International Order and the End of the Cold War 257
 Tanja A. Börzel

11. The Liberal Order Reconsidered: Europe, the United States, and the Missteps of the 1990s 281
 Charles A. Kupchan

12. Mistakes Were Made: Revisiting the 1990s from the EU's Immediate Neighborhood 309
 Ayşe Zarakol

13. On Breakthroughs, Deadlocks, and Rose-Gardens Lost in Between: The Failed Promise of North-South Cooperation 327
 Amrita Narlikar

Index 355

List of Contributors

Hilary Appel is the Podlich Family Professor of Government and George R. Roberts Fellow, Claremont McKenna College.

Tanja A. Börzel is Professor of Political Science and Director of the Center for European Integration, Freie Universität Berlin.

Michael Cox is Emeritus Professor of International Relations, London School of Economics and Political Science.

Daniel Drezner is Distinguished Professor of International Politics, The Fletcher School at Tufts University.

G. John Ikenberry is Albert G. Milbank Professor of Politics and International Affairs and Co-Director of the Center for International Security Studies at Princeton University and a Global Eminence Scholar at Kyung Hee University, South Korea.

Harold James is Claude and Lore Kelly Professor in European Studies and Professor of History, Princeton University.

Miles Kahler is Research Professor-in-Residence and Distinguished Professor Emeritus, American University and Senior Fellow for Global Governance, Council on Foreign Relations, Washington, DC.

Jonathan Kirshner is Vincent Q. and Mary Ann Giffuni Professor, Political Science and International Studies, Boston College.

Charles A. Kupchan is Professor of International Affairs, Georgetown University and Senior Fellow, Council on Foreign Relations, Washington, DC.

Michael Mastanduno is Nelson A. Rockefeller Professor of Government, Dartmouth College.

Amrita Narlikar is Distinguished Fellow, Observer Research Foundation, Delhi; Honorary Fellow, Darwin College, University of Cambridge.

Peter Trubowitz is Professor of International Relations and Director of the Phelan US Centre, London School of Economics and Political Science and Associate Fellow at Chatham House.

Jennifer M. Welsh is Canada 150 Research Chair in Global Governance and Security and Director of the Max Bell School of Public Policy, McGill University.

Ayşe Zarakol is Professor of International Relations and Politics Fellow at Emmanuel College, University of Cambridge.

Preface and Acknowledgments

"There are decades where nothing happens; and there are weeks where decades happen." This remark, often attributed to Vladimir Lenin, reminds us that history unfolds in uneven, unexpected ways. Sometimes it is in bursts of rapid, transformative change, such as the 1990s following the sudden collapse of the Soviet Union and end of the Cold War. Yet even in such instances, the rapid change we experience often stems from longer, deeper sequences of events, contingencies, and choices that go undetected for years or whose potential impact is underappreciated by those living in the moment. At a time when the liberal international order is under extreme stress and the future direction of international politics is uncertain, this volume casts a wide historical net to consider the choices and pathways that brought the world to this unsettled moment.

In the spring of 2022, we brought together a group of leading historians and political scientists to look back on the liberal international order of the 1990s and reimagine what went right and what went wrong in light of what we know today. We were interested in rethinking the 1990s on two separate, yet related levels: at the level of policy and events, and at the level of what we as scholars thought at the time. We invited scholars who had written on themes related to the liberal order and were thus well positioned to enrich our understanding of the 1990s. Our purpose is not to re-litigate the past, but to use it to deepen our understanding of the liberal order's fissures and to inform our thinking about the contemporary challenges we face, from great power rivalry to reactionary nationalism to global inequality. As we go to press in Summer 2025, the stakes seem even higher.

At each stage of this collective endeavor, we have benefited from the comments, suggestions, and insights of other workshop participants: Jan-Ole Adolphsen, Daniel Deudney, Elizabeth Ingleson, Woojeong Jang, James Morrison, Inderjeet Parmar, Or Rosenboim, Matias Spektor, Helen Thompson, Leslie Vinjamuri, and Odd Arne Westad. We would also like to thank Sophie Kaldor, Tolya Levshin, and Jacklyn Majnemer for their clear-eyed summaries and thoughtful commentaries on the discussions we held at the

London School of Economics and Political Science in June 2022 and at Princeton University in October 2022.

Our meetings were made possible by the generosity of the John and Amy Phelan Foundation and the program on Reimagining World Order at the Princeton Institute for International and Regional Studies. We are also grateful to Ms. Adeola Akande Pierre Nöel at the Phelan US Centre at LSE and Ms. Nikki Woolward at the Reimagining World Order program for their indispensable support in organizing the conferences that resulted in this volume. At Oxford University Press, we wish to thank David McBride for his sound advice and encouragement. The volume also benefited from Sarah Ebel's attention to detail during the production process.

G. John Ikenberry and Peter Trubowitz
May 2025

1
Making Sense of the 1990s
Choices, Pathways, and Missed Opportunities

G. John Ikenberry and Peter Trubowitz

The fall of the Berlin Wall in 1989 and the collapse of the Soviet Union two years later brought to a sudden end four decades of superpower conflict. The old bipolar order disappeared, and a new distribution of power appeared. The United States and its allies claimed victory, while the Soviet Union and its allies either collapsed or fell into disarray. The ensuing decade opened up new hopes and new possibilities. At first, the world looked like it had become a single global system, with societies and peoples everywhere seeking new opportunities to trade, invest, develop, and integrate into larger political and economic realms. The twentieth-century upheavals of two world wars and the Cold War were now over. With Western democracies in ascendance, the great ideological conflicts between fascism, communism, and liberalism appeared settled. The direction of "modernity" seemed clearer than it had for decades. History, in some profound sense, seemed to have spoken. Politicians, diplomats, and scholars advanced and debated grand ideas about the future of world politics.

Globalization, integration, and democratization were the watchwords of the post–Cold War liberal order. Trade and investment boomed in the 1990s, as markets expanded globally and regionally, becoming more integrated than ever before. Washington, Paris, Berlin, and other Western capitals launched new multilateral projects to deepen their economic ties as well as their reliance on international institutions. NATO and the European Union expanded. The World Trade Organization (WTO) was created, while regional free-trade agreements proliferated. Democracy and the rule of law spread. Countries in Eastern Europe, East Asia, and Latin America undertook difficult economic and political transitions to become more closely tied to this expanding order. By the end of the 1990s, the United States and most of its allies and partners had reason to see their post–Cold War efforts at liberal world-order building as a major accomplishment.

Today, three and a half decades after the end of the Cold War, the excitement and anticipation that marked this global transition have vanished. The 1990s look like a different era. The liberal international order, which became a capacious global presence in the 1990s, has weakened and started to unravel in the face of mounting geopolitical and domestic pressures and cross-pressures. Great power competition has returned. Economic nationalism has resurfaced. Ideological extremism has reappeared. Talk of a new Cold War between the West and Russia and China is rife. From today's vantage point, the 1990s look less like a great triumph for liberal democracy and Western modernity than like a decade in which post–Cold War optimism and designs obscured a slowly gathering global storm.

This volume brings together a group of scholars who look back on the 1990s to identify choices and pathways that have brought the world to this unsettled moment. Looking back, could the United States and other countries have made choices in the 1990s that would have garnered greater "buy-in" internationally and domestically and placed the world order then envisioned by Western policymakers on firmer foundations? What do the foreign policy choices that liberal democracies and other states made then tell us about the pressures and cross-pressures fracturing the liberal order today? Where did understandings and predictions about the liberal order's future go wrong, and why? How might global politics look today if Western leaders had not bet so heavily on globalization, supranationalism, and democratization? Were judgments about how China, Eastern Europe, and other emerging economies would integrate into the liberal order hopelessly naïve, or reasonable given the novelty of the moment? What other viable strategies were on offer to manage relations with these nations, and why were they disregarded?

In weighing these questions, our authors revisit the intellectual debates of the period. In the 1990s, realists and liberals, nationalists and globalists, scholars and commentators engaged in wide-ranging deliberations about how benign or rivalrous world politics would be. Many predicted heightened competition within the West for economic advantage.[1] In the absence of Cold War barriers to trade and investment, they predicted that new geoeconomic blocs would form in Asia, Europe, and North America. Other analysts argued that the post–Cold War world would be one of increased military and security competition: that Japan and Germany would become formidable great powers, that NATO would weaken and break up, and that alliance commitments would be more fluid and shifting.[2] The end of bipolarity, they predicted, would usher in a return to traditional multipolar great power politics.

These things did not come to pass, at least not in the early decades of post–Cold War politics. Western economies became more, not less, integrated. Security cooperation within the West deepened.[3] Countries once excluded from the Western "club" for geopolitical or economic reasons, or that had opted out of their own volition, sought to become attractive destinations for Western investment and trade. This is not to suggest that liberal scholars and analysts who believed that democracy and free markets had tamed the forces of illiberalism and nationalism were right.[4] If realists and nationalists underestimated Western democracies' ability to continue to cooperate in the absence of a common Soviet-style threat, in time it would become clear that liberals and globalists had overestimated the liberal model's international appeal and immunity to domestic opposition.[5]

In this introductory chapter, we lay out the analytic framework for this volume. We start by looking at the "mixed outcomes" that emerged out of the 1990s. These are the choices, successes, and missed opportunities that our chapters explore—and seek to explain. After this, we introduce the volume's core themes and summarize the essays. While all the authors explore each of these themes, we have organized the essays to highlight key features of liberal order-building in the 1990s, as well as areas of agreement and disagreement over what was achieved and at what cost. We conclude by considering the volume's implications for understanding the challenges that China, Russia, and the antiglobalist backlash within the West pose to the liberal order today.

The 1990s Reconsidered

The debate on the legacies of the 1990s is lively and profound.[6] The questions themselves—were mistakes made, were opportunities missed in the 1990s?— are fraught with a sense that missteps were made. The contributors to this volume offer a variety of answers. In some respects, the United States and the other states that emerged with power and agency after the Cold War did open their Cold War system of "embedded liberalism" to the wider world. Countries once on the periphery of the liberal order were brought into the system, at least on terms that the Western states offered. China and Russia, at least initially, were engaged by Western governments. China did not evolve in the direction of liberal democracy, but it did experience stunning growth, lifting hundreds of millions of people out of poverty. The United States, Europe, and Japan—the core of the old Western system—renewed and expanded their working relationships.[7]

During the 1990s and even into the next decade, the world experienced widespread economic growth, a surge in institutionalized cooperation, and an expansion of liberal democracy. Policy changes along with declining shipping costs fueled global economic growth. These developments were reflected in the ratio of world trade to global GDP, a widely used measure of international openness and global integration. During the 1990s and 2000s, that ratio soared, reaching unprecedented heights before leveling off after the 2008 global financial crisis.[8] As part of this global liberalizing movement, Western governments also deepened their commitment to regional integration and free trade agreements (FTAs). Once considered anathema to trade liberalization, by the 1990s regional integration and FTAs were now widely viewed as engines of growth and stepping stones to greater liberalization.[9]

In the 1990s, Western democracies' commitment to institutionalized political cooperation also gained new momentum.[10] In Europe, the Maastricht Treaty of 1993 formally established the European Union, including a new European Central Bank and a new common currency, the euro. In North America, the Canada-U.S. Free Trade Agreement was expanded to include Mexico, resulting in the 1994 North American Free Trade Agreement. In Asia, the Asia-Pacific Economic Cooperation forum expanded its goals, calling for free and open trade in the Asia-Pacific region by 2010 for the region's more advanced economies and 2020 for its developing economies. Meanwhile, a host of new global issues—from human rights to climate change—were thrust onto the international agenda by progressive voices in the developed and developing worlds. The result was a rapid expansion in the number of international institutions. Between the mid-1980s and the late 2000s, the number of international government organizations more than doubled globally, from 3,546 in 1985 to 7,459 in 2008.[11]

As the number of international institutions expanded, so too did their functional authority. Governments began delegating more sovereignty at the international level. Countries' motivations for doing so ranged from gaining access to larger markets and capital to harmonizing tax, regulatory, and social standards to neutralizing contentious domestic issues by going beyond national borders. These efforts did not go unchallenged, internationally or domestically. Domestically, public worries about democratic accountability, political intrusiveness, and social protection quickly surfaced in party platforms and public deliberation—itself an indication of just how far-reaching and invasive the changes were. In Western democracies, the demands for social redress were most forcefully pressed in the case of the European Union and the WTO, but similar concerns figured in international demands emanating from the Global South to reform the International Monetary Fund and the World Bank.

In the 1990s, the liberal order's security architecture was also reshaped and updated. In Europe, Germany was reunified, and the former Warsaw Pact states and Soviet Baltic republics were integrated into NATO. In Asia, Washington and Tokyo reaffirmed their alliance commitments. As liberal democracies' conception of security broadened, so did the range of missions they were prepared to support. Democratic enlargement, democracy promotion, humanitarian intervention, and the responsibility to protect increasingly vied with more traditional conceptions of national interest and international security such as balance of power, collective security, and extended deterrence. At the United Nations, international peacekeeping expanded dramatically. In the 1990s, the Security Council authorized new peacekeeping missions in Somalia, Haiti, Rwanda, Bosnia, East Timor, and elsewhere. With the creation of the Office of the High Commissioner for Human Rights and the Office of the Coordination of Humanitarian Affairs, the UN's remit for security and development was widened to include human rights and humanitarianism.

The 1990s also witnessed a surge in the pace of democratization globally. Spurred by the velvet revolutions in the former Soviet bloc between 1989 and 1991, a growing number of countries in Africa and Central Asia expanded rights to political participation and to freer political exchange. The surge of political liberalization in the 1990s eclipsed earlier democratic waves in the twentieth century, including the postwar boom and the democratic wave of the 1960s, 1970s, and 1980s in Africa, Latin America, the Asia-Pacific, and South Asia.[12] At a time when the number of sovereign states was increasing rapidly, the end of the Cold War created opportunities and incentives to democratize by weakening the ties that many military and one-party dictatorships previously enjoyed with one of the superpowers. Of course, political liberalization did not spread everywhere—the Middle East and North Africa lagged behind. Some countries only partially democratized, while others did become more democratic, only to reverse course. Even before the 1990s were out, autocracy was gaining ground.

If the 1990s were a decade of achievements, they were also a time of missed opportunities. As the chapters show, Washington and other Western capitals often misjudged developments, squandered opportunities, and overestimated support. Several of the chapters argue that the Western democracies entered and exited the 1990s brimming with overconfidence in the power of liberal political and economic ideas. Great hopes were pinned on the promise of a more open, integrated, neoliberal world order and America's capacity to consolidate, protect, and extend democracy and markets across the globe. The "liberal bet" on China also failed: as China got rich, it did not become a more open, democratic, and status-quo power. A wide debate continues over whether a better relationship between Russia and the West could have been salvaged from the ashes of the Cold War and whether the seeds of Vladimir Putin's war on Ukraine were sown in decisions by America and its European allies to expand NATO and the European Union eastward. Meanwhile, antiglobalist opposition to this more expansive liberal international agenda took root and spread within the Western democracies themselves.

The sequence of steps and missteps—by Western and non-Western states—were many and are scattered across the past thirty years. Perhaps the most consequential international missteps manifested long after the 1990s. The failure to find a way to reform the United Nations, expand cooperation with the Global South, and build new capacities to confront climate change, health pandemics, and nuclear proliferation also led to questions about whether all the post–Cold War opportunities for building new forms of cooperation were fully seized. In these various ways, the "victory" in the Cold War led to reassessments of the trajectories of modernity in the 1990s that turned out to be incorrect. The expansion of the liberal order after the Cold War also had the ironic effect of planting the seeds for later conflicts and eroding the liberal order's international *and* domestic foundations in ways that are now too obvious to ignore or wish away. We must also factor these longer-term effects into any assessment of the 1990s and its impact on world politics.

Themes and Points of Departure

In reassessing the 1990s, three analytic themes figure prominently in the volume's essays. One has to do with the scope of change ushered in by the 1990s. Is the period best understood as one when Western democracies sought to transform the liberal order's architecture and rules, or as one when the West was focused principally on consolidating gains that the end of the Cold War made possible? A second theme concerns success and failure. To what extent should Western democracies' efforts to promote greater international openness and institutional cooperation in the 1990s be judged a success? In what ways did the choices Western leaders make result in failure? Questions of success and failure raise other issues, about whether Western leaders were too optimistic about the liberal order's future or too cautious. Did they overreach by misreading what was politically possible in an anarchical world of sovereign states? Or should the period be read as one of underreach, when Western policymakers collectively failed to address looming global challenges (e.g., climate change, nuclear proliferation, demands of the Global South)? The essays that make up the volume explore these themes across a variety of geographic and functional settings.

In exploring these themes, the authors also consider whether there were junctures, choice points, or opportunities in the post–Cold War era that might have led to alternative outcomes in the areas they are writing about. Put another way, were there roads and pathways not taken that, for better or worse, might have produced a different result? Each of the chapters offers a view on this basic question. In effect, the authors in this volume premise their argument on a counterfactual claim: if Western leaders had made different choices or valued some policies differently, the subsequent flow of events would have resulted in different outcomes.[13] By doing so, the authors help us isolate key variables and drivers of Western policy and better understand the causal reasoning underlying contentious, and often competing, arguments about the wisdom, or folly, of policies Western leaders advanced in the post–Cold War era.

Liberal Consolidation or Transformation?

The end of the Cold War evoked comparisons to past postwar ordering moments: 1815, 1919, and 1945.[14] On these occasions, great power war left an old order shattered and discredited. Victorious states emerged from conflict with opportunities to shape the peace. New ideas and projects for organizing international relations were on offer. Out of the momentary upheaval of these postwar "switching points," a new set of rules and institutions were hammered out to guide the next era of global order.

Such comparisons were apt, up to a point. Like these earlier ordering junctures, the post–Cold War moment offered an opportunity for the United States, the West, and other peoples and societies around the world to debate and set the terms of global order. Yet in one crucial respect the post–Cold War period was decidedly different from past international ordering moments. It did not involve the creation of a new international order whole cloth out of the remnants of the older order, but rather a rapid expansion, functionally and spatially, of the existing order. International relations scholars have characterized this shift in different ways: as "global neoliberalism," "liberal internationalism 3.0," and "postnational liberalism" to distinguish it from earlier iterations of liberal internationalism—Wilsonian liberal internationalism after World War I and the liberal internationalism of the Cold War era—and to highlight the continuities and correspondences.[15]

What these labels leave open to interpretation and debate is whether the patterns and outcomes that emerge during the post–Cold War period are best understood as a story of consolidation or one of transformation. As the chapters by Daniel Drezner, Jonathan Kirshner, Michael Mastanduno, and Jennifer Welsh suggest, to some extent the answer depends on the historical baseline or reference points one uses to size up the 1990s as a turning point. As their accounts of the post–Cold War ordering moment suggest, analytic judgments about the scale of change can also vary cross-sectionally: that is, in terms of how widely and evenly new ordering ideas and agendas are projected and consummated, spatially and functionally.

In his chapter, Daniel Drezner argues that the 1990s is a story of consolidation rather than transformation. In contrast to previous ordering moments following World War I and World War II, the end of the Cold War legitimated rather than discredited the existing order. Instead of being destroyed or delegitimized by the Soviet Union's collapse, existing liberal global governance structures were strengthened and expanded. This was especially true in the realm of political economy, where Western democracies encouraged developing and transition economies to join Bretton Woods institutions such as the International Monetary Fund, World Bank, and

WTO. In Drezner's account, the recursive power of existing global governance structures precluded the kind of "clean slate" or "de novo" option for the post–Cold War era that Western leaders attempted unsuccessfully in 1918 and again in 1945, with considerably greater success. In the 1990s, the issue was not so much that there was no alternative. It was that Western policymakers saw no need to search for one, doubling down instead on the existing institutions and rules.

In his chapter, Jonathan Kirshner views the 1990s less as a switching point and more as a "gathering storm." Focusing on "the great American financial liberalization project" that began as early as the 1980s, Kirshner argues that the crucial transformative moment came in the 1990s, when liberal political elites acquiesced and embraced the conservative agenda of Wall Street and, more specifically, the financial services sector. In retelling the story of American political and business elites' departure from the postwar bargain of "embedded liberalism," Kirshner reminds us of just how incompatible unbridled finance was with the "middle way" path that successive administrations embraced during the second half of the twentieth century and, also, how much the antiglobalist backlash we see today in the United States and elsewhere is rooted in the decisions taken in the 1990s to liberalize finance and deregulate the banks. He argues that it didn't have to be this way, that U.S. policymakers could have recommitted to the Keynesian strategy of embedded liberalism that guided and sustained the liberal order during the Cold War. In Kirshner's account, questions about roads not taken loom large in our understanding of what came after the floodgates of 2008 opened up.

Michael Mastanduno's analysis of American relations with Europe and Asia in the 1990s also takes up the issue of consolidation versus transformation. He argues that U.S. policymakers tried to do both in the 1990s, with mixed success. They succeeded in the consolidation project by preserving and strengthening America's Cold War–era security alliances at a time when many leading international relations scholars and foreign policy commentators were predicting that Germany and Japan would exit the American hegemonic order and revert to more traditional great power roles. In explaining the persistence and, indeed, strengthening of U.S. relations with Europe and Japan after the Cold War, Mastanduno turns to the realist theory of hegemony, illuminating the incentives that a hegemonic state like America and would-be challengers such as Germany and Japan had in bolstering their respective leading and subordinate roles in the existing order. Yet, as he notes, Washington's efforts to extend American hegemony beyond its Cold War boundaries was a transformational project that failed. For Mastanduno this is a dilemma inherent in a liberal international project that sought not only to anchor liberal allies but to incorporate illiberal adversaries as well.

Jennifer Welsh's chapter rounds out this part of the volume by examining the ways in which the 1990s were a decade of innovation in global norms, particularly in the area of human rights. As Welsh shows, the transnational social movements that were forged across East and West during the late stages of the Cold War provided a network of activism that inspired the post–Cold War consummation of global human rights norms. She explores this remarkable "soft revolution," demonstrating that the 1990s were a fertile moment for the notion of "sovereignty-as-responsibility," that is, the twin ideas that sovereign rights were conditional upon states fulfilling their core responsibilities to their citizens and that individuals who commit egregious violations of human rights should be held accountable, regardless of status or official function. As significant as these innovations were, Welsh argues, more could have been accomplished if the United States, the most powerful advocate of liberal ideas in the decade, had been more committed to turning these liberal imaginings of the 1990s into concrete achievements.

Western Successes and Failures

One of the challenges in assessing the Western liberal order's performance is gauging the appropriate time frame for taking stock. As the widening disconnect between Western governments' international *and* domestic policies suggests, policy choices and strategies that are widely deemed successful at one point may, in the fullness of time, be judged disappointments.[16] It can take time for policy contradictions to become manifest and for those who find themselves consistently on the losing side of policy choices to make their voices heard. Judgments about relative success and failure can vary depending on where one stands geographically, too. The eastward expansion of NATO which began in the 1990s offers an illuminating if contested illustration of this point. Much of this debate has focused on whether NATO enlargement led to the decline of the West's relations with Russia and, more recently, contributed to Putin's decision to invade Ukraine. Countries that lie close to Russia's borders find arguments about Western provocation less persuasive. There is a difference between those on the front line and those who enjoy the advantages of distance.

The uneven geographic effects of trade and financial liberalization offer another telling example. There is mounting evidence of the long-term effects of trade and financial liberalization on income inequality, economic growth, and social stability in Western democracies. Yet the rapid integration of China, the former Soviet bloc countries in Eastern Europe, and many other developing economies in Africa, Latin America, and South Asia into the world economy enabled countries once on the periphery of the world economy to grow more rapidly than they did during the Cold War. The most successful went far in catching up to the higher income levels long enjoyed in the advanced industrial economies. To be sure, the fruits of globalization were not shared evenly within these emerging economies. Publics in some countries that raced to join the West have come to express resentment about the hardships, corruption, and inequities that often accompanied market-induced liberalization.[17] Even so, as developing countries around the globe reduced their trade barriers and adopted market-oriented policies to attract foreign capital and investment, global poverty dropped sharply. Between 1981 and 2015, the share of the world's population living in extreme poverty fell from 42 percent to 10 percent.[18]

There is also the challenge of explaining failures. As America's forever wars in Afghanistan and Iraq reveal, rarely is there only one explanation for strategic failure. In Afghanistan and Iraq, ideology, power, and interest all had a hand in the disaster.[19] Some international relations scholars root these outcomes in a failure of the marketplace of ideas in the preceding decade that did not weed out unfounded, misleading, or self-serving foreign policy arguments. Others attribute the failure to unbridled American power. From this vantage point, unipolarity and an arrogance of power led to strategic failures in the Middle East and elsewhere. America intervened, the argument goes, because it could. And still others place the blame on the outsized influence of powerful domestic interests that hijacked the American national security apparatus following the September 11 attacks, advancing narrow parochial interests at the expense of the national interest.

Hilary Appel, Michael Cox, Harold James, and Miles Kahler all consider the choices and strategies pursued by Western policymakers, where they succeeded or failed, and what alternative futures might have been possible. In her chapter, Appel analyzes the incorporation of Eastern European states into the EU and NATO and the subsequent rise of Euroskepticism and illiberalism in the Visegrad countries. Appel examines how Poland and Hungary, two of the most promising early cases of political liberalization in Eastern Europe following the collapse of communism in 1989, had to satisfy broad membership conditions to join the EU and NATO. While acknowledging that Western leaders could have shown greater care and concern for Eastern European citizens in setting conditions of EU and NATO membership and buffering them against the pain of transition, Appel argues that the rise of antidemocratic leaders and illiberal regimes in the 2010s are not the product of the inclusion of these countries in multilateral institutions in the 1990s. She suggests that we need to look well beyond enlargement programs of the 1990s and early 2000s to understand the resentments and insecurities that have fueled antiglobalism and illiberalism in Central and Eastern Europe and, instead, examine domestic and international challenges arising in the 2010s.

Michael Cox's essay takes up the question of whether Western leaders mishandled post–Cold War Russia, creating the conditions for Putin's aggression against Ukraine and, more generally, Russian revanchism and opposition to the liberal international order. For Cox, the pivotal question is whether there was ever a serious chance of Russia becoming a stable liberal polity or living within a rules-based Western-led system of relations. In his view, the "weight of history" in the former USSR was against such a post–Cold War transformation. To be sure, Cox argues, the United States and its Western partners made mistakes that undercut the prospects for a liberal democratic transition in Russia, most notably by pushing NATO expansion in Moscow's "near abroad" and promoting economic "shock therapy" within Russia. However, he argues that the causes of Russia's failure to reinvent and reinvigorate itself owe more to classic problems of disintegration and fragmentation that flow from the breakup of imperial orders. Cox's analysis of the West's inability to integrate Russia into the liberal order suggests that the West's "failure" says at least as much about the limits of Western influence as it does about the dangers of Western overreach.

If Western leaders should have tried harder to integrate Russia into the liberal order, when it comes to China many scholars claim that they tried too hard to do so. Miles Kahler takes up this question in his analysis of American efforts to engage and integrate China into the liberal international order. As he notes, the mix of U.S. policies that fall under the heading of "engagement" shifted over the course of the 1990s, as Washington dialed down its concerns about Beijing's human rights abuses and expanded its interest in

China's potential as a market for U.S. exports and, importantly, a destination for U.S. foreign investment. He argues that counterfactual claims that America's strategy of engagement was based on false optimism about China's ambitions or, alternatively, that the United States and China were destined to become adversaries do not hold up to closer examination. Kahler argues that a more plausible explanation for the subsequent deterioration in U.S.-China relations is domestic politics—in the increasingly fraught interaction between their respective internal politics. These domestic dynamics have only accelerated in recent years. Barring unlikely political change in China, Kahler concludes that Western leaders must now contend with a major economic and military power that, for purely pragmatic reasons, will continue to pursue à la carte support of the international liberal order.

Harold James's essay on Europe's new politics of globalism in the 1990s also paints a picture of mixed success. He argues that the collapse of communism in 1989–1991 opened the door to a radically new view of politics and especially of what the state could do. In its extreme form, it presented politics as having "no alternatives." This approach was especially influential in Europe, where it drove public debate about the obsolescence of the nation-state and Westphalian notions of sovereignty, as well as a new burst of thinking about reducing government's role as a public goods provider and social equalizer. James argues that this new approach gained considerable momentum in the 1990s and 2000s. The problem is that it tended to sweep away tough political choices (e.g., class compromises) that would come back in 2008 to haunt Europe in the form of an intensifying antiglobalist backlash. The outcome, James argues, might have been different if the Soviet Union had not collapsed. If the Cold War had not ended with the collapse of communism, neither such a full-throated commitment to globalism nor the subsequent nationalist backlash against it would have materialized.

Western Overreach, or Underreach?

The end of the Cold War left the United States and its liberal democratic allies in a commanding position to shape the terms of order-building to follow. The dramatic geopolitical collapse of the Soviet Union was also an ideological collapse of the last great rival to Western capitalism and liberal capitalism. At this juncture, liberal internationalism and the Western liberal project were in full bloom. Western leaders and intellectuals made sweeping judgments about the direction of history and the power of ideas. Most famously, Francis Fukuyama argued that the great centuries-old contest over what form of political rule was most viable and legitimate was now over.[20] Liberal democracy was left standing. American leaders in the 1990s likewise saw the stature of the United States tied not just to its power but also to the success and appeal of the Western liberal model.

Looking back, it is easy to conclude that American and Western leaders were too confident about the power and appeal of liberal political and economic ideas. Whether and how their overconfidence led to overreach at the level of policy is more contested. On the one hand, Western leaders and thinkers were overly optimistic about the possibilities for political transitions to liberal democracy. Here, the United States especially overreached in its efforts to push and pull the world in its direction. To be sure, the security and economic institutions that defined the "free world" during the Cold War were opened up to new members. However, Western ambitions and expectations about how much cooperation and consensus institutionalized forms of partnership would yield exceeded what was delivered. On the other hand, America and its democratic partners also underreached in critical ways. In contrast to other historical switching points in world order, the rules and institutions of the post–Cold War global order were not fundamentally rethought or renegotiated. In various ways, countries in the non-West were kept on the outside looking in or systematically disadvantaged for the benefit of the West. The UN Security Council was not re-formed, and new cooperative efforts for tackling the global problems of the future—such as climate change and public health pandemics—were not programmatically pursued.

In retrospect, it is also evident that Western governments' commitment to globalization exceeded what their publics were willing to support. Much of the debate over the West's weakening commitment to the liberal order focuses on recent developments: Donald Trump's "America First," "Brexit," and the spread of populism in France, Germany, Italy, and other Western democracies. But the antiglobalist pressures we see today cannot be easily divorced from decisions Western governments took to liberalize international markets earlier. In doing so, they relaxed the social bargains that formed the bedrock of the postwar compromise between free-market capitalism and social democracy. Domestic battles over globalization and neoliberalism in the 1990s (e.g., the Battle of Seattle against WTO policies in 1999) were harbingers of the antiglobalism we see across the West today.

If Western governments significantly underestimated international opposition to their efforts to promote democracy, they also greatly overestimated the extent to which their own publics would back their efforts to liberalize the world economy and weaken economic security at home.

The chapters by Tanja Börzel, Charles Kupchan, Amrita Narlikar, and Ayşe Zarakol explore the issue of Western overreach and underreach, among other issues. In her chapter, Börzel makes a case for Western overreach through a longitudinal analysis of membership in liberal international institutions. Instead of using the post–Cold War moment to bring non-Western nations into the liberal-order tent on terms that were inclusive and nonobtrusive, as core Western states did in the postwar era, the West sought to leverage its extraordinary power after the Soviet Union collapsed to impose a "postnational liberalism" that was more intrusive. This was especially so in the areas of political and civil rights involving the rule of law, democracy, and freedom of movement. This triggered a "wave of contestations" from outside the West by Russia, China, and others, but also by populist, antiglobalist parties within the West. The United States and its Western allies thus succeeded in making the international order more liberal by implementing reforms that expanded the liberal content of international institutions and strengthening their political authority. However, Börzel argues, those efforts led Russia and other countries to push back against the liberal order by withdrawing from it and, later, attacking it.

Charles Kupchan's chapter also focuses on problems of liberal overreach. He makes two related arguments: first, that the liberal order's woes today spring from overconfidence in the 1990s in liberalism's international appeal, and second, that the United States and the United Kingdom were the main sources of liberal overreach; the EU, much less so. In his view, the United States spent more effort seeking to expand the Western liberal order than in protecting and nourishing its own liberal institutions and practices. These mistakes had a double-edged effect. Efforts to globalize the liberal order provoked resentment and pushback by countries outside the West. Meanwhile, inside the West the hollowing out of the embedded liberal order led to an erosion of political support for liberal internationalism. This trend, Kupchan argues, was strongest in the United States and United Kingdom, which were at the vanguard of the effort to spread democracy outside the West. By contrast, European states spent the first decade of the post–Cold War era focused principally on strengthening and deepening its institutions, capped by the launching of the European Union. As a result, Europe's commitment to building a stronger union has put it in a comparatively stronger position than its Anglo-American counterparts to defend the liberal, rules-based international order.

In her chapter, Ayşe Zarakol explores the post–Cold War relations between the Western liberal powers and semi-peripheral countries, finding a mixed and shifting record. Some countries gained quick acceptance into the Western-led liberal order and went on to undermine it. Others were jilted by the West but continued to pursue membership in the liberal club. Zarakol examines this variegated record, highlighting mistakes the West made in the 1990s. Specifically, she argues that extending membership recognition to states where it was not deserved was doubly mistaken because it fueled resentments by others in the queue while emboldening those who received the recognition to act out. Zarakol unpacks this story by analyzing three semi-peripheral countries that were partially included but treated mostly as outsiders: Russia, Turkey, and Ukraine. The last, until recently, was the least recognized in some ways but, ironically, the most pro–liberal Western order. She also considers three semi-peripheral countries that were given almost full membership in the liberal international order and mostly treated as insiders: Hungary, Poland, and the Czech Republic. Zarakol's comparative analysis shows that there are two sides to the story: (1) the choice among Western states to open up and expand the liberal order in the 1990s and (2) the reasons "status-seeking" states on the periphery sought access to the order only to attack it once they were brought into the tent.

Amrita Narlikar's concluding chapter also takes up the question of inclusiveness and whether the 1990s constitute a "missed moment" for improving North-South relations more broadly. She argues that the end of the Cold War provided a "refreshing context" for improvement in relations between the West and the Global South. The expansion of markets within and across regions, the emerging multipolarity of the distribution of power, and the evolving system of multilateralism all provided opportunities for new bargains and relationships across the North-South divide. However, looking at this period of opportunity from today's advantage point, the 1990s underperformed. Shortly after the decade ended, disillusionment and disappointment had set in on both sides, although the specific experiences differed across issue areas and regions. Narlikar singles out the WTO as a prime illustration of this pattern. It did expand its membership and reform its agenda in response to the growing demand from non-Western states to gain access and authority within international bodies. Yet formal expansion of membership and institutional reforms were not enough to ensure successful cooperation across North and South.

Takeaways and Implications

In undertaking this collective enterprise, we encouraged our colleagues and contributors to reflect on conflicting claims about the impact and significance of the 1990s as a world-historical moment. From the very start of the project, three critical questions stood out: What kind of historical juncture or breakpoint was it? Were choices and pathways available after the Cold War that might have prevented the subsequent breakdown in the West's relations with Russia and China and its estrangement from the Global South? And what can the 1990s—the strategic choices, political trade-offs, and lost opportunities—tell us about the West's own increasingly fraught commitment to the liberal international order that it did so much to create and sustain during the long Cold War? In this concluding section, we reconsider each of these questions in light of what the chapters, taken together, offer by way of answers and insights.

First, while the end of the Cold War has evoked comparisons with the postwar moments of 1815, 1919, and 1945, we have seen that it was different in important ways. The destruction of societies and regimes came from the collapse of the Soviet Union and not from the violence of war. Only part of the post–World War II order—the bipolar order—was destroyed by the dramatic events of 1989–1991. The order among the democratic industrial powers was still intact. Indeed, many Americans and Europeans were quick to argue that the Soviet collapse amounted to a triumph for Western institutions and policies. After past great wars, the old international order lay destroyed and discredited, opening the way for sweeping negotiations over the basic rules and principles of postwar order. In contrast, after the Cold War, Western leaders were more likely to argue that the international order was working just fine. Western policy toward the Soviet Union had been vindicated, and the organization of relations among the industrial democracies remained stable and cooperative.

In this sense, the end of the Cold War was a "conservative revolution," leaving the core Western political, security, and economic institutions and arrangements largely intact, with countries on the outside making choices about whether and how to operate in a world with only one ideological, economic, and geopolitical pole. The breakpoint of past postwar moments was more profound in that the violence and destruction left the old order in ruins, and the war itself discredited the ideas upon which the prewar order was based. The liberal order was not only left standing; it was widely seen in Western capitals as a political formation that should be preserved and even celebrated.

Yet, as several of the chapters emphasize, there was still a lot of contingency and choice in the first years after the end of the Cold War. After all, the breakup of the Soviet Union and the end of bipolarity did amount to a sudden, dramatic shift in the distribution of power. New asymmetries of power were exposed. The former Soviet Union faced a more powerful West, and Europe and Japan faced a more powerful America. As we have seen, the way the post–Cold War world would evolve and operate was not obvious. While liberals argued that a new liberal democratic world era had dawned, realists expected a "back to the future" return of geopolitics. Others argued that the world would break into civilizational groupings or geo-economic blocs.

The 1990s historical breakpoint was not a tabula rasa, where the United States and its allies were forced to rethink the fundamental questions of world order. Instead, they found themselves in a position to try to hold on to those parts of the surviving Cold War order that seemed to offer the greatest promise of a future of global peace and prosperity. It was a breakpoint in the sense that Western leaders looked back to the past for lessons. This was especially true around matters of security, where most leaders sought to build on rather than discard the post-1945 Western logic of order that got them to where they were. As in the past, the upheavals and breakdown in the international order created great political openings and uncertainties, which in the 1990s drove efforts by Western leaders to consolidate and expand institutions and relationships that worked in the past.

What was less clear to Western leaders in the 1990s was how the rest of the world would react and adjust to the collapse of the great alternative to Western liberal democracy and to the liberal international order. It was also unclear how Western governments would sustain support for the liberal internationalist project in the absence of a common, unifying geopolitical and ideological adversary like the Soviet Union. When Bill Clinton blurted out, "Gosh, I miss the Cold War," he said aloud what many Western leaders at the time were thinking privately. In a world defined by bipolar superpower rivalry, the international rules of the road were clearer and the task of coalition-building between and within liberal democracies was easier. A big, outstanding question is whether the Western democracies need a foreign enemy to foster social coherence and common purpose. This brings us to the matter of China and Russia and who is to blame for the sharp breakdown in relations decades later with the West.

The chapters do not settle this question, and so the debate continues. They do make clear that American and European leaders did seek to build a post–Cold War order that was "one world" in character, open to Russia and China, at least on Western terms that did not entail negotiating away their hegemonic position on the overall order. Still, the question remains whether Western leaders could have taken more seriously the option of building a trans-European security order that included Russia. This issue turns on judgments about whether NATO could have remained a stable source of security for Europeans without expanding its membership to Central and Eastern European states that were eager to join. The Clinton administration's strategy of "enlargement" saw NATO as a means to bind post-Soviet states to the West and reward and reinforce their domestic reforms and democratic transitions, leaving Russia out in the cold. Meanwhile, Western leaders might have eschewed neoliberal "shock therapy" and worked harder to encourage post-Soviet Russia to reform politically and economically in ways that left it less humiliated and less ready to embrace Putin's neo-imperial and anti-Western agenda.

With China, the question is not whether the West could have done more to accommodate its rise, but whether it did too much. A succession of American post–Cold War presidents sought to engage China and make it a "responsible stakeholder" in the liberal international order. The Americans bet that Chinese integration into the Western capitalist system would create knock-on pressures and incentives for Beijing to open up, reform, and take its place within the existing order. Here, too, the question is whether other strategies were available to the United States that would have altered the long trajectory of China's rise from a peripheral developing country at the end of the Cold War to a global geopolitical rival. There is very little evidence that Washington could have thwarted and constrained the rise of China. But that leaves open and unanswered whether there were diplomatic opportunities to negotiate a more managed integration of China into the world trade system, starting with China's WTO membership, and whether alternative U.S. economic policies could have reconciled China's economic development with the needs of American industries and workers imperiled by its growth.

Finally, did the leaders who navigated the 1990s have choices and options that would have put the liberal international order on a stronger domestic footing? Several chapters emphasize the fateful significance of the West's "neoliberal" turn in the 1980s and its consolidation in Western political economies after the Cold War. As the United States and the other advanced industrial democracies opened up, deregulated, and privatized their economies, the older postwar system of "embedded liberalism" weakened and the long-standing consensus around economic openness and multilateral liberalization of the world economy broke down. A sequence of policy choices was made that set the stage for the backlash against economic globalization that accelerated in the wake of the 2008 financial crisis. In this sense, today's decline in the stability and functioning of the liberal international order can be traced to domestic policy choices over many decades. As several of our authors make clear, the problem was less the absence of a single breakpoint that might have led Western democracies to change course than the domestic political and economic incentives that pushed and pulled them along the same misguided path. Looking back at the 1990s is important not only because it presented an "opportunity" for the reordering of global relations but also because it reveals how contingent grand international designs ultimately are on the practical realities of domestic politics.

Notes

1. Thurow 1992; Garten 1992; Huntington 1993; Wallerstein 1993. For a survey of these debates, see Mastanduno 1999.
2. Layne 1993; Mearsheimer 1990; Waltz 1993.
3. Ikenberry 1996.
4. Friedman 1999; Fukuyama 1989; Ōmae 1992.
5. Trubowitz and Burgoon 2023.
6. See Anderson 2024; Gavin 2021; McTague 2020; Thompson 2019; Von Eschen 2022.
7. Ikenberry 2020.
8. Irwin 2022, 2.
9. Frieden 2006, 383.
10. The description of developments in the 1990s here draws on Trubowitz and Burgoon 2023, 38–41.
11. Bloodgood 2016.
12. Boese et al. 2021, 1206.
13. On the strengths and limitations of counterfactual analysis, see Van Evera 1997; George and Bennett 2005; Goldgeier and Shifrinson, 2022; Tetlock and Belkin 1996.
14. Ikenberry 2001.
15. See, Ikenberry 2009; Slobodian 2018; Börzel and Zürn 2021.
16. Levshin 2022.
17. Krastev and Holmes 2020.
18. See https://data.worldbank.org/topic/poverty; Irwin 2022, 25.
19. See, for example, Lieberfeld 2005; Hinnebusch 2007; Harvey 2011.
20. Fukuyama 1989.

References

Anderson, Terry H. 2024. *Why the Nineties Matter*. Oxford University Press.
Bloodgood, Elizabeth. 2016. "The Yearbook of International Organizations and Quantitative Non-State Actor Research." In *The Ashgate Research Companion to Non-State Actors*, edited by Bob Reinalda. Routledge.
Boese, Vanessa A., Staffan I. Lindberg, and Anna Lührmann. 2021. "Waves of Autocratization and Democratization: A Rejoinder." *Democratization* 28 (6): 1202–1210.
Börzel, Tanja A., and Michael Zürn. 2021. "Contestations of the Liberal International Order: From Liberal Multilateralism to Postnational Liberalism." *International Organization* 75 (2): 282–305.
Frieden, Jeffry A. 2006. *Global Capitalism: Its Fall and Rise in the Twentieth Century*. W. W. Norton.
Friedman, Thomas. 1999. *The Lexus and the Olive Tree: Understanding Globalization*. Anchor Books.
Fukuyama, Francis. 1989. "The End of History?" *National Interest* 16: 3–18.
Garten, Jeffrey E. 1992. *A Cold Peace: America, Japan, Germany, and the Struggle for Supremacy*. Times Books.
Gavin, Francis J. 2021. "Learning from the Big, Bold 1990s over the Post–Cold War World." *Engelsberg Ideas*, February 22. https://engelsbergideas.com/notebook/learning-from-the-big-bold-1990s-debates-over-the-post-cold-war-world/.
George, Alexander L., and Andrew Bennett. 2005. *Case Studies and Theory Development in the Social Sciences*. MIT Press.
Goldgeier, James, and Joshua R. Itzkowitz Shifrinson. 2022. "Evaluating NATO Enlargement: Scholar Debates, Policy Implications, and Roads Not Taken." *International Politics* 57 (3): 291–321.
Harvey, Frank P. 2011. *Explaining the Iraq War: Counterfactual Theory, Logic and Evidence*. Cambridge University Press.
Hinnebusch, Raymond. 2007. "The US Invasion of Iraq: Explanations and Implications." *Critique: Critical Middle Eastern Studies* 16 (3): 209–228.
Huntington, Samuel P. 1993. "The Clash of Civilizations?" *Foreign Affairs* 72 (3): 22–49.
Ikenberry, G. John. 1996. "The Myth of Post–Cold War Chaos." *Foreign Affairs* 75 (3): 79–91.
Ikenberry, G. John. 2001. *After Victory: Institutions, Strategic Restraint, and the Rebuilding of Order after Major War*. Princeton University Press.
Ikenberry, G. John. 2009. "Liberal Internationalism 3.0: America and the Dilemmas of Liberal World Order." *Perspectives on Politics* 7 (1): 71–87.
Ikenberry, G. John. 2020. *A World Safe for Democracy: Liberal Internationalism and the Crises of Global Order*. Yale University Press.
Irwin, Douglas A. 2022. "The Trade Reform Wave of 1985–1995." Working Paper No. 29973. NBER.
Krastev, Ivan, and Stephen Holmes. 2020. *The Light That Failed: A Reckoning*. Penguin Books.
Layne, Christopher. 1993. "The Unipolar Illusion: Why New Great Powers Will Rise." *International Security* 17 (4): 5–51.
Levshin, Anatoly. 2022. "Report on the LSE-Princeton Conference, June 10–11, 2022."
Lieberfeld, Daniel. 2005. "Theories of Conflict and the Iraq War." *International Journal of Peace Studies* 10 (2): 1–21.
Mastanduno, Michael. 1999. "A Realist View: Three Images of the Coming International Order." In *International Order and the Future of World Politics*, edited by T. V. Paul and John A. Hall. Cambridge University Press.
McTague, Tom. 2020. "Remember the '90s, Don't Long for a Return." *The Atlantic*, August 20. https://www.theatlantic.com/international/archive/2020/08/brexit-trump-china-90s-golden-era/615406/.

Mearsheimer, John J. 1990. "Back to the Future: Instability in Europe after the Cold War." *International Security* 15 (1): 5–56.

Ōmae, Kenichi. 1992. *The Borderless World: Power and Strategy in the Interlinked Economy.* HarperCollins.

Slobodian, Quinn. 2018. *Globalists: The End of Empire and the Birth of Neoliberalism.* Harvard University Press.

Tetlock, Philip E., and Aaron Belkin. 1996. *Thought Experiments in World Politics: Logical, Methodological, and Psychological Perspectives.* Princeton University Press.

Thompson, Helen. 2019. "The Illusions of the 1990s have been Shattered but the Decade Is Still Distorting World Politics." *New Statesmen*, August 28. https://www.newstatesman.com/politics/uk-politics/2019/08/illusions-1990s-have-been-shattered-decade-still-distorting-world-politics.

Thurow, Lester C. 1992. *Head to Head: The Coming Economic Battle among Japan, Europe, and America.* William Morrow.

Trubowitz, Peter, and Brian Burgoon. 2023. *Geopolitics and Democracy: The Western Liberal Order from Foundation to Fracture.* Oxford University Press.

Van Evera, Stephen. 1997. *Guide to Methods for Students of Political Science.* Cornell University Press.

Von Eschen, Penny M. 2022. *Paradoxes of Nostalgia: Cold War Triumphalism and Global Disorder since 1989.* Duke University Press.

Wallerstein, Immanuel. 1993. "The World-System after the Cold War." *Journal of Peace Research* 30 (1): 1–6.

Waltz, Kenneth N. 1993. "The Emerging Structure of International Politics." *International Security* 18 (2): 44–79.

PART I
BRAVE NEW WORLD
Liberal Consolidation or Transformation?

2
How Recursive Is Global Governance?

Revisiting the Ordering Choices of the Nineties

Daniel W. Drezner

To paraphrase Yogi Berra, hindsight is hard, especially about the past.[1] The premise of this edited volume is that by examining the first decade of the post–Cold War era, one can assess the counterfactual worlds that might have led to a more robust liberal international order.[2] The implicit critique behind this exercise, replete in a considerable amount of current commentary, is that at least one of these counterfactuals would have produced a longer-lasting order than what our actual history has produced.

There is no denying that from the perspective of the 2020s, that order is graying and fraying badly. Over the past decade the world has experienced a series of discrete shocks, ranging from a global pandemic to the largest war in Europe since 1945; the responses from the liberal international order to these shocks have ranged from fair to middling. There are deeper trends—democratic recession, geo-economic fragmentation, persistent climate change, and the greatest number of state-based conflicts since the end of the Second World War—that demonstrate the erosion of the depth and breadth of the rules-based international order.[3]

The blame game for the fraying of global order has been in full swing. U.S. policymakers from both parties have roundly criticized the policy choices made during the 1990s; since 2016, strategy documents from both the Trump and the Biden administrations have criticized the global governance choices of the 1990s.[4] Both diplomatic historians and security scholars have posited that the United States doubled down too much on Cold War institutions like NATO, laying the groundwork for a revanchist Russia. Prominent economists and political economy scholars have decried the neoliberalism of the Washington Consensus, arguing that it facilitated hidden and visible shocks. China's entry into the World Trade Organization (WTO) had devastating effects in some parts of the developed world. Capital account liberalization facilitated the buildup of imbalances that led to the 2008 financial crisis, which in turn created the permissive condition for the Troubling Twenties.

To the extent that there is a conventional hindsight wisdom, it is that the U.S. hegemonic order sowed the seeds of its own destruction. Alternative arrangements, grounded in more inclusive institutions, might have led to a more sustainable order. These critics raise valid questions that merit further exploration: Why did the United States fail to create a more sustainable system of multilateral cooperation? Were there preventable mistakes? As the global hegemon, did the United States do anything right after the Cold War ended?

This chapter stands athwart this historical revisionism and yells "Stop!" No doubt, the governance choices of the past are partly responsible for today's policy challenges. Far too many critics, however, exaggerate the U.S. freedom of action at the end of the Cold War. In doing so, they make a category error when thinking about the post-1991 world, equating the end of the Cold War as a constitutional ordering moment akin to 1917 or 1945.[5] While 1991 was an ordering moment, it was not one where preexisting institutions were rendered obsolete. Indeed, if anything, the opposite was true: the peaceful collapse of the Soviet bloc further legitimized the institutions that defined the Cold War liberal international order. An institutionalist approach demonstrates that the costs of switching away from international governmental organizations like NATO or the Bretton Woods structures would have been high. The recursive power of global governance made it far more attractive for the United States to bolster existing institutions than create new ones. The global governance decisions of the 1990s seem hubristic only in retrospect. To the extent that there was space for alternative decision-making, that space was far more fertile at the domestic level than the systemic level. To put it more concretely: the fateful decisions of the 1990s that led to subsequent instability had more to do with domestic politics than international politics.

In reaching these conclusions, this chapter offers some straightforward responses to the key themes of this volume as expressed in the introduction. First, the 1990s are clearly a story of consolidation rather than transformation. The success of liberal global governance structures during the Cold War meant that all of them were strengthened rather than replaced during the post–Cold War era. Second, given U.S. policy preferences at the end of the Cold War, one would have to judge their global governance choices during the decade of the 1990s as a success. The United States and its allies successfully converted governance structures that had been partial into more universal institutions. Indeed, it was precisely because institutions like NATO and the WTO were viewed as successful that so many countries were clamoring to join them. Finally, while it would be easy to conclude that the United States overreached in extending the mandate of these international institutions, one could argue that the problem was one of domestic policy underreach. The error was extending the scope of global governance without developing the necessary compensatory mechanism at the domestic level. Whether that was due to excessive ambition at the systemic level or lethargy at the domestic level is an exercise best left to the reader.

The rest of this chapter is divided into four sections. The next section reviews the critical autopsy that scholars have performed on the global governance decisions of the 1990s in order to understand their preferred counterfactual history. The third section assesses these arguments and analyzes the assumptions underlying them. It then applies an institutionalist lens to explain why these critical assumptions are flawed. The fourth section suggests that the biggest governance failure occurred at the domestic level rather than the systemic level. The constraints of American politics restricted U.S. policy responses to globalization far more than international politics did. The final section summarizes and concludes.

The Critical Autopsy

To distill the dominant critique of 1990s-era global governance down to a single sentence, the United States was too exclusive in its post–Cold War security architecture and too inclusive in its post–Cold War economic architecture. These choices were made during a critical ordering moment in which a welter of governance possibilities lay before Washington; other governance choices could have led to a more sustainable international order. As Steven Weber and Bruce Jentleson put it, the "arrogant triumphalism of the 1990s" meant that "the international institutions that were an important part of the American world order had their own overpromise and underdeliver pathology."[6] According to this argument, different governance arrangements would have bred less revanchism within Russia, less power within China, and less populist nationalism within the advanced developing countries.

As the Cold War was winding down, Mikhail Gorbachev and other Soviet leaders were searching for novel security arrangements that could promote a Kantian pluralistic security community. In this view, NATO and the Warsaw Pact were security doppelgängers, creatures of bipolarity that had no place in the post–Cold War order. At the same time, dormant postwar security architectures had the potential to be more functional in a world devoid of Cold War tensions. Within Europe, the Conference for Cooperation and Security in Europe (CSCE), created during détente and inclusive of all European countries, was viewed by many as a possible mechanism for creating a common European security home. Soviet and Russian diplomats embraced the CSCE as their preferred focal point for the Eurasian security order.[7]

At the global level, the collapse of the Soviet Union potentially unlocked the United Nations system to be a more useful regulator of global order. During the Cold War, superpower rivalry effectively hamstrung the UN's security architecture for all but the most anodyne tasks. As great power tensions lessened, the UN Security Council's pivotal role in responding to Iraq's August 1990 invasion of Kuwait seemed to presage a new world order based on collective security. Scholars and policymakers began to research the role of the UN's Military Staff Committee, hoping that it could begin to function as originally intended in the 1940s. One observer suggested in 1993 about the Military Staff Committee, "[F]or the first time since 1948, the political context has returned to that envisaged by the UN's founders. . . . [S]pecific points of disagreement that prevented constructing a working system then are much less likely to cause problems now."[8]

Instead of these possibilities, the United States and its key allies pursued a different course of action. They reinforced and expanded NATO's role on the European continent and elsewhere.[9] The end of the Soviet threat did not eliminate the need for NATO in the minds of its members. Instead, according to NATO's own narrative of events, the alliance was still needed after the collapse of the Soviet Union "to deter the rise of militant nationalism and to provide the foundation of collective security that would encourage democratization and political integration in Europe. The definition of 'Europe' had merely expanded eastward."[10]

The critiques of this approach are well known. In prioritizing NATO expansion over all other security arrangements, the United States ostensibly paved the way for Russian revanchism. Joshua Shifrinson concludes that the rejection of alternative security structures laid the groundwork for Russian bellicosity in this century: "NATO expansion nullified the assurances given to the Soviet Union in 1990.... Baldly stated, the United States floated a cooperative grand design for postwar Europe in discussions with the Soviets in 1990, while creating a system dominated by the United States."[11] Mary Sarotte is equally severe in her judgment: "[I]t is hard to escape the fact that one particular U.S. policy added to the burdens on Russia's fragile young democracy when it was most in need of friends: the way that Washington expanded NATO."[12]

The autopsy of post–Cold War global economic governance reads somewhat differently. In the realm of security, the hindsight narrative is that the post–Cold War institutions were insufficiently inclusive; in the realm of political economy, the claim is that they were too inclusive. The collapse of centrally planned economies and the failures of import substitution and industrialization buoyed proponents of the "Washington Consensus" to promote neoliberal policies as a template for transition economies as well as the Global South.[13] These economic ideas were diffused through a welter of different causal mechanisms, including the training of economic advisors in the Global South.[14] These policies were easier to advance as the United States encouraged developing and transition economies to join the Bretton Woods institutions: the International Monetary Fund (IMF), World Bank, and WTO. These expansion efforts were particularly concentrated in the 1990s. The General Agreement on Tariffs and Trade (GATT) had fewer than a hundred members as the Cold War was ending. By the end of 2000 an institutionally stronger WTO had added an additional forty-five members—and China entered final negotiations for membership.[15] The IMF and the World Bank engaged in a similar expansion in the 1990s, adding thirty-five and thirty-two members, respectively, during that decade.[16] These organizations transformed themselves from club membership institutions to more universal membership structures.[17]

The United States did not merely expand the power and scope of the Bretton Woods institutions; it actively discouraged the creation of structures that might be viewed as substitutes. During the early stages of the post–Cold War era, France and the EU proposed the creation of an "Economic Security Council," an idea that died without U.S. support. When Malaysia proposed the creation of an exclusive East Asian economic grouping, the United States moved quickly to nudge the idea into the more inclusive Asia-Pacific Economic Cooperation forum.[18] During the depths of the Asian financial crisis, Japan floated the idea of an "Asian Monetary Fund." U.S. officials strongly discouraged the idea, and it went nowhere as a result.[19] When other countries proposed economic clubs that could compete with the Bretton Woods institutions, the United States acted as the veto player.

The economic and geopolitical indictments against this U.S. strategy have coalesced into a clear and compelling narrative. The content of neoliberal policies led to a dramatic increase in economic volatility and economic inequality. Capital account liberalization helped trigger the so-called tequila effect in Latin America following the Mexican peso crisis of 1995; the Asian financial crisis of 1997–1998, with knock-on effects ranging from Russia to Brazil; and, most important, the 2008 financial crisis. At the same time, economic inequality increased in every major economy during the two decades of hyperglobalization.[20]

The biggest mistake, according to both economic and geopolitical critics, was the acceptance of China into the global economy. The Clinton administration began its first year in office by attempting to link China's most-favored-nation status to its human rights performance; by the end of his second term, Clinton was forcefully advocating for China's admission into the WTO. Rana Foroohar describes that decision as "a seismic shift that removed the guardrails from the global economy."[21] While economists hailed the policy at the time, follow-on work suggests that the "China shock" in the Global North was quite real.[22] In the United States, geographic regions vulnerable to import competition were hit hard. In those localities, exposed workers experienced higher rates of unemployment, greater job churn, and lower wages than expected. These regions also suffered from reduced labor-force participation rates and lifetime income streams over time. It is not difficult to trace the political effects of the China shock through to the wave of populist nationalism in the developed world over the past decade, as well as a post-neoliberal retreat from globalization in economic policymaking.[23] For many observers, it represented the twenty-first-century equivalent of Karl Polanyi's "double movement."[24]

Realists have been equally critical of accepting China into the international economic order because of its geopolitical implications. In *The Tragedy of Great Power Politics*, John Mearsheimer argued in 2001 that "the United States has a profound interest in seeing Chinese economic growth slow considerably in the years ahead." Warning that China would become neither democratic nor a status-quo power, he concluded, "[T]he U.S. policy on China is misguided."[25] Twenty years later, he asserted in *Foreign Affairs*, "Engagement [with China] may have been the worst strategic blunder any country has made in recent history: there is no comparable example of a great power actively fostering the rise of a peer competitor. And it is now too late to do much about it."[26]

A Morbidity and Mortality Assessment of the 1990s

The critical analyses cited in the previous section resemble a morbidity and mortality conference after a patient dies. As with such exercises, a crucial assumption undergirding this analysis is that different treatment choices were available and preferable. The collapse of the communist bloc ostensibly created a constitutional ordering moment. During these critical junctures, alternative governance arrangements are more viable than during routine moments in world politics. The United States and its security allies and economic partners are judged to be negligent because, had different governance choices been made, perhaps the rules-based international order would not be fraying so badly in the 2020s. In other words, this autopsy rests crucially on the assumption that the governance choices of the 1990s were mutable.

This perspective is consistent with how international relations theorists have viewed constitutional ordering moments. In *After Victory*, G. John Ikenberry explicitly characterized these critical junctures as "rare," "unusual," and "extraordinary," explaining that "the most consequential reordering moments in international relations have occurred after major wars."[27] In both that work and in follow-on research, Ikenberry categorized the end of the Cold War as an ordering moment akin to postwar critical junctures.[28] Indeed, in the introduction to this volume Ikenberry and Peter Trubowitz characterize 1991 as a historical juncture that "evoked comparisons to past postwar moments: 1815, 1919, and 1945." In failing to choose an alternative governance path, critics argue that the United States damned itself to a fleeting moment of unipolar dominance at the price of domestic and international instability.

It is worth discussing the necessary conditions for constitutional ordering moments to exist, however. For scholars researching hegemonic orders, the conclusion of great power wars is the most propitious time for such a moment.[29] This is for two reasons. First, the end of a large-scale war provides a clarifying moment for the international distribution of power. Great power wars reveal each actors' relative strength, and that information becomes common knowledge diffused throughout the international system. When the great powers know each other's relative capabilities, it is possible (though far from guaranteed) for these actors to fashion an institutional bargain acceptable to key stakeholders.[30]

Second, the end of a great power war provides a clean slate for surviving actors to erect new international structures because the existing global governance structures have either been destroyed or delegitimized. For example, the League of Nations was disbanded as the Second World War raged, easing the creation of the United Nations. As Ikenberry notes, "[T]he destruction caused by war and the breakdown of the old order provide opportunities to establish new basic rules and organizing arrangements that are likely to persist well into the future."[31] Note that the institutionalist logic places great weight on these constitutional ordering moments precisely because institutions are designed to be long-lasting.[32] In the absence of great power war, institutional arrangements are extremely sticky. Other severe shocks, like financial crises or pandemics, are not necessarily disruptive enough to wipe the slate clean in the modern state system.[33]

The end of the Cold War satisfied the first necessary condition to produce an ordering moment. The crackup of the Soviet Union clarified the distribution of power for all observers.[34] The United States was left as the last superpower standing, characterized as a "hyperpower" by its allies and adversaries alike. It is the second necessary condition where 1991 deviates significantly from prior constitutional ordering moments, however. The Cold War contained some draining conflicts involving the superpowers, such as Korea, Vietnam, and Afghanistan. Nor was the end of the Cold War free of violence, as the citizens of Bosnia, Kuwait, and Tajikistan could attest. Nonetheless, a fundamental stylized fact remains: the end of the Cold War was largely nonviolent. The Soviet Union collapsed primarily because of its internal contradictions.[35] The international institutions created by the USSR collapsed along with it, even as Western structures endured.[36] Compared to the state of play after the end of both world wars, most international institutions of any significance were still standing after 1991. In other words, while the end of the Cold War led to an undeniable shift in the global distribution of power, the slate remained decidedly unclean.

Seen in this context, it becomes more difficult to posit that the end of the Cold War represents an ordering moment akin to 1917 or 1945. The United States became the undisputed hegemon as the USSR disintegrated. The institutional order that the United States helped create after 1945 remained decidedly functional. Indeed, GATT, NATO, and the European Union performed extremely well compared to structures like the Warsaw Pact or the Council of Mutual Economic Assistance—so much so that most of the transition economies clamored to join these Western structures as quickly as possible. Existing U.S. allies also strongly preferred the preservation of those institutions. European countries viewed NATO and the EU as key pillars to prevent the emergence of an independent Germany; U.S. allies also viewed the Bretton Woods institutions as offering vital technical assistance for transition and emerging economies. Even non-allies were keen to join many of these global governance structures. The third wave of democratization created an influx of new regimes with neoliberal economic policy preferences, eager to join the WTO, IMF, and World Bank.[37]

It is worth remembering that the immediate end of the Cold War was an uncertain moment when many observers were predicting economic competition and violent conflict on the European continent.[38] Choosing that moment to eliminate binding, functional institutions would have been odd to say the least. As Joseph Nye noted at the time, a key component of U.S. soft power was the competent exercise of policy.[39] The U.S.-created institutional order was the most obvious manifestation of those policies; to abandon them would have meant leaving ample amounts of soft power on the table. This helps to explain why the George H. W. Bush administration adopted a grand strategy of reintegration to replace the containment policies of the Cold War, and why the Clinton administration reframed it as enlargement. The strategic idea was that more countries could join the Kantian triad of democracy, economic interdependence, and membership in the rules-based international order.[40]

As long-standing hard law structures, institutions such as the IMF, World Bank, GATT, European Union, and NATO were desirable clubs; democratizing and liberalizing states aspired to membership. All of these international institutions met Ikenberry's criteria for a constitutional political order: they reflected a shared agreement over ordering principles, they set binding limits on the unilateral exercise of power, and they were "entrenched in the wider political system and not easily altered."[41]

That last criterion is worth stressing, because much of the criticism of the governance choices of the 1990s emanates from realists. The modal realist perspective on institutions is that they are epiphenomenal, merely reflecting fluctuations in the distribution of power.[42] Therefore, realists would expect that a pronounced shift in the distribution of power should have triggered a concomitant shift in global governance structures.[43]

In contrast, every variety of institutionalism argues that once institutions are created, they are difficult to obviate. Whether rational, sociological, or historical, these approaches posit a wide array of causal mechanisms that generate recursive power within preexisting institutions. Institutions possess path-dependent properties, making it more difficult to change future orders due to decisions made in the past. The transaction costs of maintaining existing institutions are inherently smaller than the transaction costs of creating new structures. For many institutionalist approaches, the utility of their existence generates network externalities and increasing returns for their ongoing use. Ikenberry's more historical institutionalist approach further observes that as institutions persist, they create stakeholders with a vested interest in preserving the ongoing existence of those structures.[44] This is particularly true if those institutions generate assets that are useful for purposes beyond their initial motivation. As Celeste Wallander observed, "[I]f the marginal costs of maintaining an existing institution outweigh the considerable costs of creating an entirely new set of norms, rules, and procedures, states will choose to sustain existing arrangements rather than abandon them."[45]

All of the institutionalist logics in the above paragraph operate at the systemic level. It is worth noting, however, that the domestic politics of the hegemonic actor also plays a role. Even given the switching costs delineated above, it was theoretically possible for the United States to have pushed for de novo global governance structures. For new governance structures to supplant existing treaty organizations, however, they would have needed a similar hard law status.[46] In requiring a two-thirds supermajority for treaty ratification, however, the U.S. Constitution invests significant veto power in the Senate. Rising levels of political polarization—a trend that predated the end of the Cold War by a generation—made it difficult to achieve the necessary bipartisan support for any treaty ratification.[47] Even if treaties secure bipartisan support, the opportunity cost of Senate floor time often leads the United States to delay ratification.[48] As a result, the U.S. ranking for treaty ratification during the immediate post–Cold War era was mediocre at best.[49] The United States was an active player in several high-profile 1990s multilateral agreements—including the Comprehensive Nuclear-Test-Ban Treaty, the Kyoto Protocol, and the Rome Statute of the International Criminal Court—that it never ratified.

The governance choices of the 1990s were not quite as elastic as contemporary critics have suggested. In a counterfactual world, the United States could have created more de novo institutional arrangements; it certainly had the power to do so. However, between the cost of creating new institutions and the ease of relying on the preexisting panoply of global governance structures, the latter was the more rational institutional choice. This helps to explain why the growth rate of intergovernmental organizations (IGOs) was at a low ebb during the late 1980s and 1990s.[50] This preference for persisting with existing global governance structures holds with even greater force when considering the additional cost of terminating international organizations.[51]

Another sign of the recursive power of U.S.-led international institutions is that all of them—not just NATO and the WTO—saw their power and remit augmented after the end of bipolarity. Beginning in 1990, the CSCE created a permanent administrative infrastructure, including a secretariat, a conflict-prevention center, and an office to monitor free elections. This led to its 1994 renaming as the Organization for Security and Cooperation in Europe (OSCE). Miriam Sapiro noted at the time, "[T]he change in its name reflected both its evolution into a more established structure, and the expectation that it would play an even greater role in regional conflict prevention, crisis management and dispute settlement."[52]

A similar dynamic played out at the United Nations Security Council (UNSC). Deadlock between the United States and the Soviet Union guaranteed that the UNSC played, at best, a marginal role in the global security order during the Cold War. That changed dramatically during the 1990s. This can be seen in its authorization and implementation of economic and military statecraft. During the Cold War, the UNSC authorized thirteen peacekeeping missions. From just 1989 to 1994, it authorized an additional twenty operations encompassing nontraditional peacekeeping missions. In the process, the UN raised the number of peacekeepers from eleven thousand to seventy-five thousand. UN peacekeepers took on more ambitious tasks in the 1990s as well, ranging from state building to election monitoring.[53]

The pattern of UN economic sanctions follows a similar arc in the 1990s. During its first forty years, the UNSC authorized economic sanctions only twice. In the 1990s, it became a much more active sender, approving sanctions against twelve different targets. Furthermore, the UN took the lead in refining best practices for economic statecraft. The UNSC switched from comprehensive to targeted economic sanctions, reducing humanitarian suffering by focusing on arms embargoes, travel bans, and asset freezes. The UNSC also authorized the creation of sanctions monitoring committees and expert panels to better enforce their mandates.[54] This increased activity at the UNSC did not necessarily translate into greater effectiveness.[55] Nonetheless, it was indisputable that the UNSC was a far more active and powerful security institution at the end of the 1990s than at the beginning.

Beyond the UN's economic statecraft, Russia and China were also invited into numerous multilateral export control regimes. Russia joined the Missile Technology Control Regime and the Wassenaar Arrangement, the successor to the Coordinating Committee for Multilateral Export Controls. China joined the Nuclear Suppliers Group. Membership in these organizations socialized these countries into using export controls as a means of ensuring nonproliferation.[56] The Nuclear Non-Proliferation Treaty was renewed indefinitely in 1995. The result was a successful decade of nonproliferation, as countries ranging from Argentina to Ukraine scuttled their nuclear programs.

The post–Cold War pattern in global economic governance echoes the pattern in the security realm, in that all preexisting institutions were bolstered. All three of the Bretton Woods institutions played an important role in post–Cold War global governance. This did not preclude the strengthening of regional institutions as well. The North American Free Trade Agreement was being negotiated as the Cold War was ending; it was signed and ratified in the mid-1990s. The European Community transformed into the European Union. In the 1990s the EU's twin focus was on strengthening its internal institutions and enlarging the body to include countries from Eastern Europe.[57] The United States augmented the power and influence of a welter of G-7 emanations, ranging from the Basel Committee on Banking Supervision to the Financial Action Task Force, during this period as well.[58]

None of this is to deny that institutions like NATO and the WTO were also strengthened, or that they played a more pivotal role within the post–Cold War liberal international order. Indeed, Russia's disillusion with the OSCE in this century came about because they recognized NATO as the more important focal point for the Eurasian security order.[59] The point is that *all* of the U.S.-supported extant governance structures were strengthened after the Soviet Union collapsed. That is more consistent with an institutionalist account than a realist one.

The Hidden Hand of the Second Image

As noted in the previous section, the exceptional nature of U.S. domestic politics was one factor among many in explaining why the United States did not opt for the creation of new global governance structures after the end of the Cold War. Domestic politics, however, was a more powerful factor when examining a different causal mechanism. The primary importance of American and European domestic politics to this story was the failure of domestic institutions to respond to second image-reversed effects from the global economic governance of the 1990s.[60]

An assumption made throughout this volume is that the United States created a liberal international order after its own image as a means to advance its material interests and political values. As a first cut, that is a plausible assumption. But there are two complicating factors that also need to be acknowledged. First, no foreign economic policy will produce overwhelming domestic assent. Any international economic policy yields domestic distributional effects. Those who lose out on policy choices have reason to fear for their ability to affect future public policy choices. These sectors will often face waning economic clout and political lobbying capacity, triggering a negative feedback effect on their future influence.[61] For any hegemon to support a sustainable global order, domestic constituencies that resist the order require some form of accommodation.

Distributional issues can be ameliorated through global governance; it is not hard to envision a hegemonic actor attempting to ensure special treatment for all its citizens. This runs into the second complicating factor, however: even a liberal hegemon is constrained in its ability to use global governance structures to satisfy every domestic interest. As Ikenberry and others have noted, the very appeal of a liberal order is that the hegemon agrees to binding constraints as a means of credibly committing to the rules of the game. Such constraints reassure other actors in the system that the constitutional order will not just be an imperium in disguise. Hegemons therefore cannot rely on international institutions to assist in their domestic distributional issues. This was certainly true of the Bretton Woods institutions at the time. Indeed, Judith Goldstein and Lisa Martin warned in 2000 that creating hard law through WTO adjudication would make it increasingly difficult for governments to exercise any policy autonomy through the use of escape clauses, safeguards, and other means of protection.[62]

Without domestic policies to ameliorate those distributional issues, there is no global economic order that will please all citizens all of the time. Paul Musgrave notes that when an open global order is dependent on the support of a hegemonic actor, the domestic politics of that hegemon are critical to the sustainability of the order: "As relative bargaining power shifts among the hegemon's domestic groups, and between the core and the rest of the hegemonic order, some groups within the hegemon may feel sufficiently excluded from the bargain, or insufficiently rewarded by their status within the leading state, that they will clamor for revisions. If the international bargain cannot easily be redone to accommodate those demands, these groups may seek to force revisions in their favor by breaking that bargain, straining or breaking the order."[63] The domestic politics of globalization in the 1990s confirms that the crucial failure was not at the systemic level but at the domestic level in the advanced industrialized economies.

The economic logic behind neoliberalism was that an open global economy would promote greater static and dynamic efficiency within the global economy. The price of that efficiency and dynamism would be greater distributional churn within each national economy. The consensus among economists was that further liberalization would be a Pareto-improving move for the United States—provided that the winners were able to compensate the losers.[64] This could have taken the form of a stronger safety net more generally, more investments in public goods that could have promoted greater labor mobility, or more aggressive forms of trade adjustment assistance.

In theory, this was the essence of the "Third Way" championed by Bill Clinton and Tony Blair during the 1990s: to expand public investments as a means of permitting greater globalization.[65] These kinds of economic ideas had the potential to entice transnational capital while still providing benefits to citizens.[66] In practice, this was not how Third Way policies were implemented. Both Blair and Clinton were operating in challenging political environments during the 1990s; to accommodate those political realities, they prioritized fiscal rectitude over public investment.[67] Flavio Romano points out, "[T]he Third Way sacrificed its programme of public investments to adhere to its neoclassical programme of 'sound' public finance.... The key macroeconomic policy effect of the Third Way may be summarized as fiscal austerity through reduced public expenditure. Thus, the Third Way is not third at all but the first (neoclassical) way."[68] In the United States, rising levels of political polarization prevented the Clinton administration from securing any significant increase in trade adjustment assistance. Blair enacted similar austerity measures in the United Kingdom. Even in continental Europe, government after government scaled back social protection programs in an effort to qualify for the Maastricht criteria and enter the eurozone.

The inability of Third Way politicians to enact the necessary compensatory mechanisms for an open global economy was bound to affect the long-term stability of the global economic order. The failure to ensure that globalization was Pareto-improving for all U.S. citizens contributed to an inevitable public backlash against globalization.[69] Public attitudes toward free trade soured soon after China was admitted into the WTO and did not reverse course for much of the next decade. In the wake of the 2008 financial crisis, policymakers from both parties increasingly blasted the trade liberalization of the 1990s as an example of prioritizing market efficiency over other considerations. In 2023, National Security Advisor Jake Sullivan acknowledged, "[F]rankly, our domestic economic policies also failed to fully account for the consequences of our international economic policies. For example, the so-called 'China shock' that hit pockets of our domestic manufacturing industry especially hard—with large and long-lasting impacts—wasn't adequately anticipated and wasn't adequately addressed as it unfolded."[70]

The contemporary takeaway from the China shock has been that integrating China into the global economy was a policy mistake, making the United States worse off. The bipartisan U.S. consensus has been that these policies strengthened China and weakened the United States. This accords with the post-neoliberal analysis suggesting that greater trade liberalization should be subordinate to targeted industrial policies.[71]

Almost all of these post-neoliberal analyses cite the China shock to justify their policies. But it should be noted that even the authors of the groundbreaking China shock paper reject the idea that admitting China into the WTO was a mistake. In a follow-up paper they concluded, "[W]e are aware of no research that would justify ex-post protectionist trade measures as a means of helping workers hurt by past import competition."[72] Their point was not that admitting China into the WTO was a net economic negative for the United States; it was that the failure to bolster the domestic social safety net prevented China's entry from becoming a Pareto-improving policy: "Few economists would interpret our empirical results as justifying greater trade protection. As expected, quantitative models indicate that U.S. aggregate gains from trade with China are positive. Yet the fact that the losses from trade are regionally concentrated and long lasting suggests that existing policies failed to insulate workers from the disruptive impacts of globalization."[73]

The neoliberal policies of the 1990s undeniably contributed to the populist blowback decades later. The interesting counterfactual is whether such blowback would have occurred if the United States had made greater public investments and implemented stronger social safety nets. At a minimum, the blowback might have been more muted, minimizing the post-2016 disruptions to the liberal international order.

The Churchillian Successes of the 1990s

To use the language of Rodrik's "governance trilemma," a quarter-century ago it looked as though states were willing to sacrifice national sovereignty in return for greater globalization and democratic politics. It now appears that most states are sacrificing hyperglobalization in return for retaining national sovereignty and popular democracy.[74] Perhaps better choices at the dawn of the neoliberal age would have led to a more sustainable order. Those mistakes were rooted in domestic policy choices far more than global governance structures, however. In other words, the flaws with the liberal leviathan lay within American politics, not international relations.

Winston Churchill famously said that "democracy is the worst form of government—except for all the others that have been tried." For social scientists engaged in hindsight, the meaning of this aphorism should be clear: counterfactual choices might have led to even worse outcomes than the current status quo. This seems particularly true with respect to the proposed realpolitik alternative of containing China from the end of the Cold War onward. The preferred realist post–Cold War approach to China would have been a variation of containment, restricting trade and exchange with China to maximize relative gains. Mearsheimer argued that U.S. leaders should have "negotiated a new bilateral trade agreement that imposed harsher terms on China. They should have done so even if the agreement was also less favorable to the United States."[75]

Would such an approach have actually deferred Chinese economic growth, however? There are two reasons to doubt this assertion. First, the bulk of China's economic progress since 1978 has been due to domestic institutional changes.⁷⁶ More restricted access to global markets would have slowed Chinese economic growth, but not by much. Even Mearsheimer acknowledges that, "[g]iven its market reforms and latent power potential, China would still have risen despite these policies." Second, a unilateral containment approach would have been unsuccessful. Again, as Mearsheimer acknowledges, "if the United States had played hardball on trade and investment, China would surely have turned to other countries for help."⁷⁷ The only way such a strategy could have worked would have been if the United States had pressured all of its allies to agree to a containment strategy. This would have triggered a reprise of Cold War disputes between the United States and its allies about how much to trade with the Soviet bloc. During that era, the United States consistently preferred a more expansive list of restrictions on trade, while its European allies preferred a much narrower list. In the 1980s, U.S. pressure failed to move European allies on this issue despite the Soviet invasion of Afghanistan and the declaration of martial law in Poland.⁷⁸ The idea that a similar U.S. approach toward a more geographically distant and less bellicose China would have succeeded in the 1990s is risible at best.

Finally, if the United States had tried this approach, the end result would have been the rise of a resentful China far less interdependent with the global economy. As Stacie Goddard has noted, China's rise within the liberal international order has enabled it to engage in some revisionist actions, but its interdependence with the rest of the world has also generated constraints on that revisionism.⁷⁹ The evidence that China seeks to upend this order wholesale remains scant. Iain Johnston observed, "It is problematic to claim that China is less economically open to trade today than in 1997, or less supportive of the arms control regimes it has joined than in 1997, or less committed to global counterterrorism today than in 1997, or less committed to dealing with greenhouse gases today than in 1997."⁸⁰ If anything, in recent years the United States has engaged in more revisionist actions than China.⁸¹ A powerful China untethered to the global economy would have been a much greater security threat than the current iteration of China.

The actual governance choices of the 1990s might have led to a lousy, rotten form of global order—except when considering the alternatives. This is particularly true given how that decade played out in terms of global order. There was a marked decline in interstate violence in the decade after the Cold War ended.⁸² There was a further reduction in other forms of violence, such as civil war and extrajudicial killings. Global military expenditures declined dramatically as well. At the same time, the third wave of democratization was entering its full flower.[83] Most of Eastern Europe consolidated their democracies during this period. Finally, the 1990s marked the beginning of the greatest acceleration of global poverty reduction in world history.[84] Correlation does not equal causation, and global governance was not the primary factor for all of these trends. Nonetheless, those trendlines suggested that the post–Cold War international institutions were exerting a largely benign effect. The internal contradictions and flaws were not apparent at the time.

In the modern history of international relations, there have been policy choices that were quickly viewed as catastrophic.[85] The governing choices of the 1990s do not fall into that category. It would be more accurate to characterize the neoliberal age as akin to the "embedded liberalism" era that lasted from the late 1940s to the early 1970s.[86] The Bretton Woods era collapsed under the weight of its own contradictions after a quarter-century. If one dates the end of the post–Cold War era as the twin 2016 shocks of Brexit and Trump, then the neoliberal epoch lasted about as long.

Within the developed world, current discourse about the Bretton Woods era has been tinged with nostalgia for a time when the domestic political economy was perceived to be more stable and equitable. Such nostalgia badly distorts the past—but also reflects a desire to revisit the perceived strengths of that bygone order. It will be unsurprising if, going forward, a similar nostalgia develops about the governing choices of the 1990s. Gideon Rachman echoed Churchill's dictum when he recently considered the governance choices of the 1990s: "For all the discontents that hyperglobalization has created, I suspect that, in decades to come, the period from 1989 to 2022 will come to be seen as a golden age of peace and prosperity. The world may soon discover that globalization is the worst possible system—apart from all the alternatives."[87] Dev Patel, Justin Sandefur, and Arvind Subramanian concur: "[T]he era of convergence that began around 1990 stands out for its ubiquity of remarkable growth, extending to a plurality of developing countries. As a group, they started reversing their previously bleak economic fortunes."[88] This perspective may also distort the past—but it might reflect an appreciation for the strengths of the neoliberal world order that are currently out of fashion. It will be interesting but unsurprising if, by 2050, public commentary produces a similar wave of nostalgia for neoliberalism.

Notes

1. Previous iterations of this chapter were presented at Princeton University and the University of Amsterdam. I am grateful to John Ikenberry, Jonathan Kirshner, and Peter Trubowitz for their feedback. Brian Burgoon, Matias Spektor, Harold James, Charles Kupchan, Miles Kahler, Tanja Börzel, Tolya Levshin, Hilary Appel, Sitara Srinivas and the two anonymous reviewers provided useful suggestions on an earlier draft. The usual caveat applies.
2. See the introduction to this volume by Ikenberry and Trubowitz.
3. See Diamond (2021) and Lindberg et al. (2023) on the democratic recession, Aiyar et al. (2023) on geoeconomic fragmentation, and Palik et al. (2022) on the surge in state-based conflict.
4. For the Trump administration, see the December 2017 National Security Strategy at https://trumpwhitehouse.archives.gov/wp-content/uploads/2017/12/NSS-Final-12-18-2017-0905.pdf. For the Biden administration, see Jake Sullivan, "Renewing American Economic Leadership," White House, April 27, 2023, at https://www.whitehouse.gov/briefing-room/speeches-remarks/2023/04/27/remarks-by-national-security-advisor-jake-sullivan-on-renewing-american-economic-leadership-at-the-brookings-institution/.
5. On ordering moments, see Ikenberry 2001.
6. Weber and Jentleson 2010, 125, 127.
7. Zellner 2005.
8. Grove 1993, 172, 182.
9. Space constraints prevent a fuller discussion of post–Cold War choices in the Indo-Pacific region, but it is worth noting that, as in Europe, the United States retained status quo policies. This meant the continuation of the hub-and-spoke alliance system across the Pacific Rim.
10. NATO 2022.
11. Shifrinson 2016, 11.
12. Sarotte 2021, 24–25.
13. Yergin and Stanislaw 1998; Williamson 2004.
14. Chwieroth 2007; Abdelal 2007.
15. Calculated from WTO websites https://www.wto.org/english/thewto_e/gattmem_e.htm and https://www.wto.org/english/thewto_e/whatis_e/tif_e/org6_e.htm, accessed April 2023.
16. Data calculated from https://www.imf.org/external/np/sec/memdir/memdate.htm and https://www.worldbank.org/en/about/leadership/members, accessed April 2023.
17. See Drezner (2007, ch. 3) on the distinction.
18. Ikenberry 2001, 243.
19. Blustein 2001. The United States also opposed the creation of the China-led Asian Infrastructure Investment Bank in 2015 but was unable to prevent its creation. Summers (2015) characterized the birth of the bank as "the moment the United States lost its role as the underwriter of the global economic system."
20. See Tooze (2018) for the most accessible version of this critique.
21. Foroohar 2022, 140.
22. Autor et al. 2016.
23. See Tooze (2018) on the rise of populism, and Foroohar (2022) on the post-neoliberal retreat from globalization.
24. Polanyi 1944. For a recent applications of Polanyi, see Martin 2013.
25. Mearsheimer 2001, 402.
26. Mearsheimer 2021, 50.
27. Ikenberry 2001, 8.
28. See, for example, Deudney and Ikenberry 2009.
29. Gilpin 1981; Ikenberry 2001.
30. Ikenberry (2001) notes that the hegemon has other ordering options, including imperialism and disengagement.
31. Ikenberry 2001, 50.
32. See also Olson 1982.
33. See Drezner (2014) on financial crises and Drezner (2020) on pandemics.
34. It is worth noting that this clarifying moment was sorely needed. In the decade prior to the end of the Cold War there were multiple geopolitical assessments that the United States was in hegemonic decline; see Gilpin 1981; Kennedy 1987. This suggests that the expert consensus at the time exaggerated U.S, decline and misperceived the relative balance of power.

35. Miller 2016. See Bartel (2022) for an important and interesting dissent.
36. Furthermore, by 1991 the alternative governance choices supported by the developing world during the Cold War had largely fallen by the wayside. Both the New International Economic Order and the Non-Aligned Movement ceased to be relevant after the early 1980s. See Krasner (1985) on this point.
37. See Mansfield et al. 2002.
38. See, for example, Mearsheimer 1990; Garten 1992.
39. Nye 1990.
40. Suri 2009.
41. Ikenberry 2001, 31.
42. See, for example, Krasner 1991; Mearsheimer 1994–1995.
43. This argument highlights an internal contradiction within the realist critique: that the United States should have been far-sighted enough to generate a global order that did not trigger any security dilemmas, even though abstaining from the exercise of hegemonic power contradicts ontological assumptions within the realist paradigm. See Oren (2009) on this tension between realism as a scientific paradigm and as policy praxis.
44. Ikenberry 2001. See also Fioretos 2011.
45. Wallander 2000, 706.
46. This also explains why most of the key post–Cold War structures created by the United States were soft law groupings rather than treaty bodies. While a thicker institutional environment can allow for great powers to engage in more realpolitik approaches to global governance (Drezner 2009), the asymmetry in legal standing made wholesale forum-shopping more difficult.
47. Jeong and Quirk 2019.
48. Kelley and Pevehouse 2015.
49. Elsig et al. 2011.
50. Eilstrup-Sangiovanni 2020, 353. It is also worth noting that the 1990s stood in sharp contrast to both postwar decades, when the rate of IGO creation was significantly elevated. See also the chapter by Tanja Börzel in this volume.
51. The more likely path to IGO desuetude is through organizational drift into "zombie" status. See Gray 2018.
52. Sapiro 1995, 636.
53. Yilmaz 2005.
54. See Biersteker et al. (2016); Jentleson 2022, ch. 8.
55. UN institutions devoted to sanctions and peacekeeping suffered from myriad scandals during the 1990s. There were multiple sexual abuse and exploitation scandals in the UN peacekeeping missions of the 1990s. UNSC sanctions exacted an enormous humanitarian toll, particularly in Iraq, while also being an engine for corruption in the Oil for Food scandal.
56. See Johnston 2001; Hurd 1999.
57. See the chapter in this volume by Hilary Appel.
58. See Drezner 2007, ch. 5.
59. Zellner 2005.
60. Trubowitz and Burgoon 2023. The domestic politics of the post–Cold War security architecture are thin and unremarkable. NATO was popular with the American public. There were ethnic communities in the United States that supported NATO expansion and no ethnic groups that were opposed. That said, Clinton administration officials have denied that domestic politics played a significant role. See Goldgeier 1998.
61. Hathaway 1998.
62. Goldstein and Martin 2000, 619.
63. Musgrave 2019, 458.
64. See Rodrik 2011.
65. Ironically, within U.S. domestic policy discourse, some of these ideas were also called "neoliberal." See Peters 1982; Reich 1991.
66. See Bell (2012) on the ability of economic ideas to constrain the structural power of capital.
67. Woodward 1993.
68. Romano 2006, 8.
69. Walter 2021.

70. Sullivan, "Renewing American Economic Leadership."
71. Foroohar 2022; Harris 2025.
72. Autor et al. 2021, 47.
73. Autor et al. 2021, 4.
74. Rodrik 2011.
75. Mearsheimer 2021, 51.
76. Brandt et al. 2014.
77. Mearsheimer 2021, 52.
78. Jentleson 1986.
79. Goddard 2018.
80. Johnston 2019b, 102.
81. See Drezner 2019; Johnston 2019a.
82. Mueller 2009; Themnér and Wallensteen 2012.
83. Huntington 1991.
84. Deaton 2013.
85. Drezner and Narlikar 2022.
86. Ruggie 1982.
87. Rachman 2022.
88. Patel et al. 2024.

References

Abdelal, Rawi. 2007. *Capital Rules: The Construction of Global Finance*. Harvard University Press.

Aiyar, Shekhar, Jiaqian Chen, Christian H Ebeke, Roberto Garcia-Saltos, Tryggvi Gudmundsson, Anna Ilyina et al. 2023. "Geoeconomic Fragmentation and the Future of Multilateralism." IMF Staff Discussion Note SDN/2023/001. https://www.imf.org/en/Publications/Staff-Discussion-Notes/Issues/2023/01/11/Geo-Economic-Fragmentation-and-the-Future-of-Multilateralism-527266.

Autor, David, David Dorn, and Gordon Hanson. 2016. "The China Shock: Learning from Labor-Market Adjustment to Large Changes in Trade." *Annual Review of Economics* 8: 205–240.

Autor, David, David Dorn, and Gordon Hanson. 2021. "On the Persistence of the China Shock." Working Paper 29401. NBER, October. http://www.nber.org/papers/w29401.

Bartel, Fritz. 2022. *The Triumph of Broken Promises*. Harvard University Press.

Bell, Stephen. 2012. "The Power of Ideas: The Ideational Shaping of the Structural Power of Business." *International Studies Quarterly* 56 (4): 661–673.

Biersteker, Thomas, Sue Eckert, and Marcos Tourinho, eds. 2016. *Targeted Sanctions*. Cambridge University Press.

Blustein, Paul. 2001. *The Chastening*. PublicAffairs.

Brandt, Loren, Debin Ma, and Thomas G. Rawski. 2014. "From Divergence to Convergence: Reevaluating the History behind China's Economic Boom." *Journal of Economic Literature* 52 (1): 45–123.

Chwieroth, Jeffrey. 2007. "Neoliberal Economists and Capital Account Liberalization in Emerging Markets." *International Organization* 61 (2): 443–463.

Deaton, Angus. 2013. *The Great Escape: Health, Wealth, and the Origins of Inequality*. Princeton University Press.

Deudney, Daniel, and G. John Ikenberry. 2009. "The Unravelling of the Cold War Settlement." *Survival* 51 (6): 39–62.

Diamond, Larry. 2021. "Democratic Regression in Comparative Perspective: Scope, Methods, and Causes." *Democratization* 28 (1): 22–42.

Drezner, Daniel W. 2007. *All Politics Is Global*. Princeton University Press.
Drezner, Daniel W. 2009. "The Power and Peril of International Regime Complexity." *Perspectives on Politics* 7 (1): 65–70.
Drezner, Daniel W. 2014. *The System Worked*. Oxford University Press.
Drezner, Daniel W. 2019. "Counter-Hegemonic Strategies in the Global Economy." *Security Studies* 28 (3): 505–531.
Drezner, Daniel W. 2020. "The Song Remains the Same: International Relations after COVID-19." *International Organization* 74 (S1): E18–E35.
Drezner, Daniel W., and Amrita Narlikar. 2022. "International Relations: The 'How Not To' Guide." *International Affairs* 98 (5): 1499–1513.
Eilstrup-Sangiovanni, Mette. 2020. "Death of International Organizations. The Organizational Ecology of Intergovernmental Organizations, 1815–2015." *Review of International Organizations* 15 (2): 339–370.
Elsig, Manfred, Karolina Milewicz, and Nikolas Stürchler. 2011. "Who Is in Love with Multilateralism? Treaty Commitment in the Post–Cold War Era." *European Union Politics* 12 (4): 529–550.
Fioretos, Orfeo. 2011. "Historical Institutionalism in International Relations." *International Organization* 65 (2): 367–399.
Foroohar, Rana. 2022. "After Neoliberalism." *Foreign Affairs* 101 (6): 134–145.
Garten, Jeffrey. 1992. *A Cold Peace: America, Japan, Germany, and the Struggle for Supremacy*. Crown Books.
Gilpin, Robert. 1981. *War and Change in World Politics*. Cambridge University Press.
Goddard, Stacie. 2018. "Embedded Revisionism: Networks, Institutions, and Challenges to World Order." *International Organization* 72 (4): 763–797.
Goldgeier, James. 1998. "NATO Expansion: The Anatomy of a Decision." *Washington Quarterly* 21 (1): 83–102.
Goldstein, Judith, and Lisa Martin. 2000. "Legalization, Trade Liberalization, and Domestic Politics: A Cautionary Note." *International Organization* 54 (3): 603–632.
Gray, Julia. 2018. "Life, Death, or Zombie? The Vitality of International Organizations." *International Studies Quarterly* 62 (1): 1–13.
Grove, Eric. 1993. "UN Armed Forces and the Military Staff Committee: A Look Back." *International Security* 17 (4): 172–182.
Harris, Jennifer M. 2025. "The Post-Neoliberal Imperative." *Foreign Affairs* 104 (3): 94–107.
Hathaway, Oona. 1998. "Positive Feedback: The Impact of Trade Liberalization on Industry Demands for Protection." *International Organization* 52 (3): 575–612.
Huntington, Samuel. 1991. *The Third Wave: Democratization in the Late Twentieth Century*. University of Oklahoma Press.
Hurd, Ian. 1999. "Legitimacy and Authority in International Politics." *International Organization* 53 (2): 379–408.
Ikenberry, G. John. 2001. *After Victory*. Princeton University Press.
Jentleson, Bruce. 1986. *Pipeline Politics: The Complex Political Economy of East-West Energy Trade*. Cornell University Press.
Jentleson, Bruce. 2022. *Sanctions: What Everyone Needs to Know*. Oxford University Press.
Jeong, Gyung-Ho, and Paul J. Quirk. 2019. "Division at the Water's Edge: The Polarization of Foreign Policy." *American Politics Research* 47 (1): 58–87.
Johnston, A. Iain. 2001. "Treating International Institutions as Social Environments." *International Studies Quarterly* 45 (4): 487–515.
Johnston, A. Iain. 2019a. "China in a World of Orders: Rethinking Compliance and Challenge in Beijing's International Relations." *International Security* 44 (2): 9–60.
Johnston, A. Iain. 2019b. "The Failures of the 'Failure of Engagement' with China." *Washington Quarterly* 42 (2): 99–114.

Kelley, Judith, and Jon Pevehouse. 2015. "An Opportunity Cost Theory of US Treaty Behavior." *International Studies Quarterly* 59 (3): 531–543.
Kennedy, Paul. 1987. *The Rise and Fall of the Great Powers*. Vintage.
Krasner, Stephen D. 1985. *Structural Conflict: The Third World against Global Liberalism*. University of California Press.
Krasner, Stephen D. 1991. "Global Communications and National Power: Life on the Pareto Frontier." *World Politics* 43 (3): 336–366.
Lindberg, Staffan, Felix Wiebrecht, Yuko Sato, Marina Nord, Martin Lundstedt, and Fabio Angiolillo. 2023. "State of the World 2022: Defiance in the Face of Autocratization." *Democratization*, 30 (5): 769–793.
Mansfield, Edward, Helen Milner, and B. Peter Rosendorff. 2002. "Why Democracies Cooperate More: Electoral Control and International Trade Agreements." *International Organization* 56 (3): 477–513.
Martin, Lisa. 2013. "Polanyi's Revenge." *Perspectives on Politics* 11 (1): 177–186.
Mearsheimer, John. 1990. "Back to the Future: Instability in Europe after the Cold War." *International Security* 15 (1): 5–56.
Mearsheimer, John. 1994–1995. "The False Promise of International Institutions." *International Security* 19 (3): 5–49.
Mearsheimer, John. 2001. *The Tragedy of Great Power Politics*. W. W. Norton.
Mearsheimer, John. 2021. "The Inevitable Rivalry." *Foreign Affairs* 100 (6): 48–59.
Miller, Christopher. 2016. *The Struggle to Save the Soviet Economy: Mikhail Gorbachev and the Collapse of the USSR*. University of North Carolina Press.
Mueller, John. 2009. "War Has Almost Ceased to Exist: An Assessment." *Political Science Quarterly* 124 (2): 297–321.
Musgrave, Paul. 2019. "International Hegemony Meets Domestic Politics: Why Liberals Can Be Pessimists." *Security Studies* 28 (3): 451–478.
NATO. 2022. "A Short History of NATO." June 3. https://www.nato.int/cps/en/natohq/declassified_139339.htm.
Nye, Joseph. 1990. *Bound to Lead*. Basic Books.
Olson, Mancur. 1982. *The Rise and Decline of Nations*. Yale University Press.
Oren, Ido. 2009. "The Unrealism of Contemporary Realism: The Tension between Realist Theory and Realists' Practice." *Perspectives on Politics* 7 (2): 283–301.
Palik, Júlia, Anna Marie Obermeier, and Siri Aas Rustad. 2022. "Conflict Trends: A Global Overview, 1946–2021." Working Paper. PRIO. https://www.prio.org/publications/13178.
Patel, Dev, Justin Sandefur, and Arvind Subramanian. 2024. "A Requiem for Hyperglobalization." *Foreign Affairs*, June 12. https://www.foreignaffairs.com/china/requiem-hyperglobalization.
Peters, Charles. 1982. "A Neoliberal's Manifesto." *Washington Post*, September 5.
Polanyi, Karl. 1944. *The Great Transformation*. Beacon Press.
Rachman, Gideon. 2022. "The Enemies of Globalization Are Circling." *Financial Times*, August 22.
Reich, Robert. 1991. *The Work of Nations*. Vintage.
Rodrik, Dani. 2011. *The Globalization Paradox*. W. W. Norton.
Romano, Flavio. 2006. "Clinton and Blair: The Economics of the Third Way." *Journal of Economic and Social Policy* 10 (2): Article 5. http://epubs.scu.edu.au/jesp/vol10/iss2/5.
Ruggie, John Gerard. 1982. "International Regimes, Transactions, and Change: Embedded Liberalism in the Postwar Economic Order." *International Organization* 36 (2): 379–415.
Sapiro, Miriam. 1995. "Changing the CSCE into the OSCE: Legal Aspects of a Political Transformation." *American Journal of International Law* 89 (3): 631–637.
Sarotte, Mary Elise. 2021. "Containment beyond the Cold War: How Washington Lost the Post-Soviet Peace." *Foreign Affairs* 100 (6): 22–35.

Shifrinson, Joshua. 2016. "Deal or No Deal? The End of the Cold War and the US Offer to Limit NATO Expansion." *International Security* 40 (4): 7–44.
Summers, Lawrence. 2015. "A Global Wake-Up Call for the U.S.?" *Washington Post*, April 5.
Suri, Jeremi. 2009. "American Grand Strategy from the Cold War's End to 9/11." *Orbis* 53 (4): 611–627.
Themnér, Lotta, and Peter Wallensteen. 2012. "Armed Conflicts, 1946–2011." *Journal of Peace Research* 49 (4): 565–575.
Tooze, Adam. 2018. *Crashed*. Viking.
Trubowitz, Peter, and Brian Burgoon. 2023. *Geopolitics and Democracy: The Western Liberal Order from Foundation to Fracture*. Oxford University Press.
Wallander, Celeste. 2000. "Institutional Assets and Adaptability: NATO after the Cold War." *International Organization* 54 (4): 705–735.
Walter, Stefanie. 2021. "The Backlash against Globalization." *Annual Review of Political Science* 24: 421–442.
Weber, Steven, and Bruce Jentleson. 2010. *The End of Arrogance: America in the Global Competition of Ideas*. Harvard University Press.
Williamson, John. 2004. "A Short History of the Washington Consensus." Working Paper. Peterson Institute for International Economics. September 2004. https://www.piie.com/commentary/speeches-papers/short-history-washington-consensus.
Woodward, Bob. 1993. *The Agenda*. Vintage.
Yergin, Daniel, and Joseph Stanislaw. 1998. *The Commanding Heights*. Simon and Schuster.
Yilmaz, Muzaffer Ercan. 2005. "UN Peacekeeping in the Cold War Era." *International Journal on World Peace* 22 (2): 13–28.
Zellner, Wolfgang. 2005. "Russia and the OSCE: From High Hopes to Disillusionment." *Cambridge Review of International Affairs* 18 (3): 389–402.

3
That Faustian Decade

The Financialization of the American Economy

Jonathan Kirshner

At the dawn of the 1990s in the United States at the national level, the Democratic Party was in disarray, losers of five of the past six presidential elections, mostly by a landslide (and the one win a post-Watergate squeaker). The dismal prospects for the Party and, implicitly, for what it stood for were lamented in rock music and mocked on popular television shows.[1] In the 1988 election many of the party's most prominent figures, rather than running for president, practically fell over themselves racing for the exits, ceding the field to a relatively obscure, uncharismatic northeastern liberal, who was soundly defeated by George H. W. Bush. That pattern seemed poised to repeat in the following cycle; buoyed by his stewardship in the aftermath of Iraq's invasion of Kuwait and then of the Gulf War, Bush's approval ratings touched the intimidatingly high mid-70s in August 1990 and 1991.[2]

It ought not be surprising, then, that in 1992 the Democrats nominated yet another fringe player—a young governor from a very small state—who would drag the party from the left to the center of the political spectrum. This was to some extent a transatlantic phenomenon. As Mark Blyth describes it, "After spending the 1980s trying to defend a social purpose that had already been abandoned by capital, labor and social democratic parties began to mirror the policies of the right." The consequences of this would be transformative. In the United States, an essential foundation of the political strategy of first candidate and then President Bill Clinton (and the "New Democrats" more generally) was a full-on embrace of Wall Street in particular and the financial services sector more generally. The Democratic Party's volte-face regarding the merits of consort with plutocracy was not the singular cause of the catastrophic financialization of the American economy—but it removed the last remaining barrier to that prospect. Rawi Abdelal summarizes this well: "Without the acquiescence of the left, neither the political elites of the right nor the economic elites could have possibly succeeded in their agenda."[3]

In considering the public policy/political economy choices made in the 1990s and the implications of these choices for today, this chapter focuses on the great American financial liberalization project. It reviews the gathering storm—the steady march in the United States of the financial sector toward political ascendance. It then details the broad bipartisan push to free finance and considers the consequences of that transformation. Two stand out. Generally speaking, an economy dominated by its financial sector is an economy disfigured. In particular, uninhibited finance is incompatible with what John Ruggie dubbed the "compromise of embedded liberalism." That disposition—which reflected nothing less than a distinct culture of capitalism—was imprinted with the profound intellectual influence of John Maynard Keynes and his search for a "middle way" between depression-discredited laissez-faire capitalism and the frightening backlash of authoritarian collectivisms that the failure of unfettered capitalism animated. The varied practices of embedded liberalism were associated with the Golden Age of Capitalism experienced in the quarter-century that followed the Second World War. This chapter also details how, as Keynes would have anticipated, finance unbound ushered in an era of yawning economic inequality and the disastrous upheavals to which unfettered finance is inherently and inescapably susceptible. And as he feared, such pathologies would again contribute to a dysfunctional backlash, the manifestations of which are now all too plain to see. In the spirit of this volume, I conclude by considering two key inflection points in the 1990s where different choices could have been made.

To situate this chapter explicitly with regard to the themes laid out by John Ikenberry and Peter Trubowitz in their introductory chapter, in the 1990s the United States sought to transform the international order rather than consolidate the gains associated with the end of the Cold War. It did so due to a confluence of domestic political happenstance, geopolitical calculation, and incentivized ideological folly. In embarking on a grand (and sharp-elbow) project of financial liberalization at home and abroad, American elites anticipated reaping huge financial rewards and calculated that U.S. relative power would be enhanced in a world of globalized finance, a revolutionary initiative buttressed by an erroneous consensus in mainstream macroeconomic theory that reflected a hubris ironically prevalent throughout modern history: that today's financial wizards, better and smarter than the less sophisticated fools of yesteryear, have virtually eliminated the risk of major crisis in the system. On the first point (that the United States, with its massive financial sector, might be relatively empowered in a world of globalized finance), the argument was, in near term, plausible. But the second point was catastrophically wrong and would ultimately undo any of those gains that might have been achieved—a hubristic ambition well-oiled by the fortunes to be made by affiliating with the financial sector. In sum, the United States overreached, and failed miserably. This need not have been, but an alternative pathway, which retained essential financial guardrails at home and recognized the legitimacy of varieties of capitalist practices abroad, was inhibited by an arrogance invited by the virtually unprecedented unipolar moment.

Before the Flood

For the first few decades after the Second World War, finance was a relatively sleepy sector of the American economy, dutifully (if crucially) serving its function as an intermediary that facilitated real economic activity. It was rather sturdily regulated and fairly described as staid in disposition (a reputation most bankers cultivated). The taming of finance was made possible by the Great Depression, which, as Barry Eichengreen explained, was "an implosion so complete" that the demand for fundamental reform, and the introduction of regulation and oversight, overwhelmed the opposition of the decimated financial sector. A broad panoply of new rules, restrictions, and oversight bodies, including the Glass-Steagall Act, contributed to an unprecedented half-century of financial stability in the United States.[4]

Into the 1970s, however, economic changes (such as the growth of international capital markets and the rise of inflation) exposed the limitations to and the obsolescence of some of those rules and of a system that was designed to ensure systemic stability, even at the expense of some private money-making opportunities.[5] Bankers, under pressure (and keen to seek new sources of profit), pushed for reforms, some of which were surely necessary. But the deregulations took on a momentum of their own, and further encouraged by lobbying from the banking sector and the general complacency that long periods of financial stability commonly engender, well-intentioned legislation was seeded with provisions that lifted numerous depression-era prohibitions against a variety of risky financial practices.[6] Banking became exciting again and, predictably and soon enough, tumultuous and havoc-wreaking. In the mid-1980s the savings and loan crisis, which featured the cascading failure of thousands of banks, was contained only by a then-staggering $200 billion government bailout—and marked an end to fifty years of banking stability in the United States.[7]

With the Republican ascendance in 1980, and the appetite of the Reagan administration for freer markets and less regulation, the balance of political power shifted considerably toward those who favored financial deregulation. A formidable barrier stood in the way, however: Paul Volcker, the powerful (and fiercely independent) chairman of the Federal Reserve. Supervision and regulation of the banking sector fell within the Fed's responsibilities, and Volcker's old-school attitudes about financial stability—especially his active, sustained, and unyielding defense of the Glass-Steagall Act—led to repeated clashes with the administration. At one point, a working group headed by Vice President George H. W. Bush proposed outflanking Volcker by shifting regulatory authority from the Federal Reserve to the Justice Department. Volcker won that battle, but, increasingly isolated as "the foremost advocate for the regulation of finance," he lost the larger war. Step by step, the Federal Reserve Board, which tended to defer to Volcker on monetary policy, took measures to erode Glass-Steagall. In 1987 the Board cleared the way for New York banks to expand their operations into securities underwriting. (As the Federal Reserve's official biography observes, Volcker had always sought to protect "the Federal Reserve's regulatory authority and [to restrict] commercial banks' activities that were considered risky" and that "Volcker opposed giving commercial banks the ability to underwrite corporate securities.") A *New York Times* headline was more concise: "Bank Curb Eased in Volcker Defeat." He would leave the Fed within months, at the end of his second term.[8] And in what could easily be imagined as an admonishment from above, two months later the stock market crashed, dropping 22 percent, the largest single-day drop in its history. Always attentive to systemic risk, Volcker attributed the crash to volatility-inducing financial innovations, adding, archly, "I don't think these techniques add much to the sum of human endeavor."[9]

Volcker's replacement as chairman of the Fed was Alan Greenspan, an Ayn Rand acolyte so enthralled with the magic of the free market he thought it (that is, what he called "market stabilizing private regulatory forces") would even prevent, all on its own, financial fraud. Greenspan was baffled by the very notion of regulation and oversight. "Why do we wish to inhibit the pollenating bees of Wall Street?" he mused a few months before the global financial crisis. The polar opposite of his predecessor, Greenspan was very eager to take the reins at the Fed—with one exception: the last thing he wanted to do was serve as the nation's principal regulator of the financial system. Happily, he recalled, "I was in for a pleasant surprise.... [B]eing a regulator was not the burden I had feared." Indeed, in his view, "liberalization in these markets was long overdue," and a decade before Glass-Steagall was officially repealed, the new Fed chair used his authority to loosen the ways in which its strictures would be interpreted.[10]

In setting the stage for the unleashing of finance, the important supporting role of overconfident academics also needs to be acknowledged. The discrediting of "Keynesianism" (a very distinct thing from Keynes, as astute observers such as Raymond Aron observed at the time)[11] led to the triumph of the rational expectations revolution in macroeconomic theory. Even those who would rebrand as "New Keynesians" in the late 1980s embraced this theoretically sophisticated and empirically dubious perspective. (Little matter that the concept is utterly incompatible with the very foundations of Keynes's own understanding of how the economy worked.) In the 1990s macroeconomic theory had become something of a monoculture, an essential attribute of which was rational expectations. From rational expectations flowed the efficient markets hypothesis, which presumed that financial markets were extraordinarily efficient and always knew best. Or as one observer put it, the efficient markets hypothesis "justified, and indeed demanded, financial deregulation."[12] The professors didn't start the fire that torched the safeguards of American finance, but they dumped fuel on it as it burned. "At research seminars, people don't take Keynesian theorizing seriously any more—the audience starts to whisper and giggle to one another," a triumphant, extremely self-assured Robert Lucas crowed in 1980.[13] Decades later Robert Skidelsky would offer this rejoinder: "But these giggling economics students became the architects of the policy that led to the great crash of 2008."[14]

All of these developments rendered even more consequential President Clinton's embrace of Wall Street as he led his party out of the political wilderness. In pursuit of the big prize, in June 1991 the young governor of Arkansas impressed a small group of Wall Street power brokers over a long dinner—most notably Robert Rubin, then co-chairman of Goldman Sachs. As president, Clinton would appoint Rubin to be the first director of his newly created National Economic Council and, subsequently, as secretary of the Treasury. And at the new president's first State of the Union Address, sitting prominently (und unprecedentedly) next to the First Lady, was the chairman of the Federal Reserve Board, Alan Greenspan.[15]

Finance Unbound

With the leadership of the Democratic Party now fully on board (and eagerly joining their Republican colleagues at the open bar of Wall Street largesse) and a gee-whiz libertarian running the Fed, the campaign to liberate finance emerged as the signature public policy mission (and accomplishment) of the decade. The four horsemen of the financial apocalypse were Rubin, in his capacity as secretary of the Treasury; Lawrence Summers, his deputy and successor; Greenspan; and Phil Gramm, chairman of the Senate Banking Committee (whose spouse, previously head of the Commodity Futures Trading Commission, left the government to join the board of directors of Enron and served on its audit committee).[16] Abetted by the thin but shiny veneer of "economic science" (especially its widely held but wildly misguided assumptions about the stability and self-correcting hyperrationality of financial markets) and fueled by the fortune of a massive lobbying effort by the financial sector, the White House, Congress, and the Federal Reserve coordinated the effort that transformed the American economy and dispatched the few dissenters that got in the way.

It was a three-pronged project: deregulate, renounce oversight and supervision, and, as foreign policy, promote financial liberalization overseas. The focus of this chapter is on the first two of these efforts, but the third is not to be casually overlooked or underestimated. (It also, as discussed below, activated a flashing red light that the evangelists of free finance sped through with nary a pause to glance for oncoming traffic.) The U.S. government, often representing the interests of American financial firms eager to crack sheltered foreign markets, pushed this agenda, often very hard, in international institutions and bilateral negotiations. From the American perspective, all good things went together, in this case ideological hubris (personified best by Summers and Greenspan), economic interest, and a general geopolitical consensus that the strategic interests of the United States would be well served in a world characterized by financial globalization. Such motives are intertwined and difficult to disentangle.[17]

Treasury led the global charge. Often, in bilateral negotiations over seemingly unrelated issues (free trade agreements, membership in multinational organizations), Treasury Department officials demanded that other countries abandon prudent measures, such as modest, market-friendly controls of short-term capital inflows. "These areas are all of interest to U.S. financial services community," one Treasury negotiating memo explained. Summers considered opening up the world's financial systems to be in the "strong national interest" of the United States. "Negotiations" were permissible, he said, but the United States was "not prepared to compromise" on market access and had a "rock-solid commitment to the end goal of liberalization." Beginning in the mid-1990s, as one account described, "[w]orking through the IMF or directly with other countries," Summers and Rubin, with the encouragement and support of Greenspan, "pushed tirelessly for . . . free capital flows." This became a source of some controversy during the Asian financial crisis, which the United States plainly attempted to exploit by tying emergency assistance to a similar menu of long-coveted demands. "During the Asian crises, the IMF saw open capital accounts as part of the solution," Alan Blinder recalled, "and it pains me to admit that the U.S. government was a primary pusher of this bad advice."[18]

Bad advice was on offer on the home front as well. The march to repeal the Glass-Steagall Act was afoot, with an eye, in particular, to dismantling the firewalls it had established between commercial and investment banking. Those who understood the dangers of unfettered finance were in the minority, and relatively powerless. The deputy general counsel of the Federal Reserve Bank of New York went public with his concerns, arguing in a prominent op-ed that "the results could be catastrophic" if Glass-Steagall was repealed. He suggested that policy should be decided on the basis of "the public interest," as opposed to "the personal interests of the bankers." He was gone from the New York Fed within weeks, less than a speed bump on the road to its repeal. Such was the tenor of the times that in 1998, Citibank merged with Travelers Group to form CitiGroup *in anticipation* of the subsequent repeal of the laws then on the books that rendered such an operation illegal—a repeal that became official on November 12, 1999, with the passage of the Gramm-Leach-Bliley Act. Greenspan lauded the act as "a milestone of business legislation," from which "we dare not go back."[19]

Feeding the beast of finance involved more than deregulation—it also involved the withdrawal of oversight and supervision. This centered on new and exponentially expanding sectors of the financial economy, which produced massive wealth, fueled the rapid growth of the sector—and were inherent carriers of systemic risk. The interrelated phenomena of routine securitization (the repackaging, blending, and resale of bundles of financial assets such as mortgages) and the astonishing growth of trading in derivatives (any asset whose value "derived" from another asset, from simple futures and options to fantastically complex instruments that enmeshed countless elements of real assets and reinsurance arrangements passed along to an unknowable number of counterparties) forged the financialization of the American economy. These activities were enormously profitable for their issuers and traders and were largely unsupervised by an oversight and regulatory apparatus that was designed long before such products had been invented or even imagined. The growth of these areas reflected, nominally, amounts that were impossible to grasp: trillions upon trillions of dollars, growing endlessly. Greenspan, of course, and those making fortunes on Wall Street as well as those feeding off that largesse, and the insouciant cheerleading champions of efficient markets saw all this as the reflection of a new and revolutionary era of financial sophistication and stability.[20] It was not.

Some voices were raised in concern—and from reputable sources. *The Economist* warned early on that "a derivatives disaster could overwhelm the world's financial system," and the U.S. Government Accountability Office issued a report ominously (and presciently) observing that "the size and concentration of derivatives activity ... could cause any financial disruption to spread faster and be harder to contain." Moreover, the report assessed, "the abrupt failure" of one such market participant "could undermine stability in several markets simultaneously" and lead to "a systemic crisis." The report stressed the "need to revamp and modernize the entire U.S. financial regulatory system."[21] There were also numerous warning signs of potential danger: Orange Country, California, lost a fortune in derivatives trading and was forced to file for bankruptcy, and losses from derivatives trading brought down Barings Bank, the oldest investment bank in Britain. Perhaps most telling of all, at least it ought to have given pause, was the failure of those lauded as geniuses, such as Long-Term Capital Management, whose losses threatened to cascade (the New York Fed helped coordinate a private sector rescue) and, looming, the notorious Enron, then touted as the masters of the new financial economy, soon to be buried underneath an avalanche of financial fraud.[22]

These concerns were brushed off by the friends of finance. Summers, in particular, was especially aggressive, lobbying against the studies from the

Government Accountability Office as they were being written and browbeating subordinates, such as Brooksley Born, head of the Commodity Futures Trading Commission, essentially for doing their jobs. Born repeatedly raised concerns about the risks attendant on unregulated derivatives markets; she resigned in mid-1999. Greenspan, less of a bully, was nevertheless enormously influential. Testifying before Congress, where he routinely held court to rapt bipartisan attention, he insisted there was "no reason to question the underlying stability" of derivatives markets and, setting aside his customary rhetorical opacity, spoke plainly and forcefully: "[R]egulation of derivatives transactions that are privately negotiated [is] unnecessary."[23] In November 1999, Summers and Greenspan were the lead signatories (along with Born's with-the-program successor, and the head of the Securities and Exchange Commission) of a White House study urging that derivatives markets be expressly shielded from any government inhibition. From there the baton was passed to Gramm, who shepherded the Commodity Futures Modernization Act through Congress. The act expressly prevented the regulation of derivatives (including the notorious credit-default swaps that would play a central role in the 2007–2008 financial crisis). As its proponents hoped, passage of the act spurred even faster growth in the already breathtakingly quickly expanding derivatives markets.[24]

The American economy was transformed, now driven by its largest and fastest growing sector. From 1980 to 2002, the share of the financial sector ballooned from 14 percent of gross domestic product to 21 percent—though even this notable metric of growth failed to capture the extent to which financialization had metastasized. The Ford Motor Company, for example, in the early 2000s often made more money from loans to consumers than from actually selling cars. In the middle of that decade, finance accounted for 47 percent of all U.S. corporate profits. Finance was also, increasingly, where the money was. Diverging from trend lines dating back to the 1940s, in which finance looked very much like other parts of the economy, the growth of its profits—and remuneration—galloped ahead of the rest of the private sector. This was true generally but was especially noticeable at the high end, with Wall Street rock stars taking home unfathomable nine-figure bonuses. Such incentives proved irresistible: nearly half of Princeton University's class of 2006 took jobs in the financial services sector; Harvard graduates flocked to Wall Street in droves of similar size.[25] Was this a good thing? If markets always knew best, the very question was impermissible. But old Keynesians (and even anti-Keynesians who had a passing familiarity with economic history), in minority dissent, knew better.

Keynes, Forgotten

The financializaton of the American economy also reflected a great forgetting—not of the postwar practice of what was described as "Keynesianism" but of Keynes's original and repeated admonitions regarding the need to tame the financial sector. Being so well-positioned, unfettered finance played an essential and indispensable role. But Keynes saw it as incompatible with his vision for a thriving liberal, capitalist society, dysfunctional when it became an end rather than a means of economic activity, and inherently (that is, endogenously) prone to crisis. Unfortunately, he was right on all three counts.

In Ruggie's original articulation of the compromise of embedded liberalism, he emphasized the influence of Karl Polanyi, who in his book *The Great Transformation* argued that laissez-faire capitalism was unsustainable and incongruous. And Polanyi certainly did emphasize the notion of embeddedness: "Instead of economy being embedded in social relations, social relations are embedded in the economic system." But Polanyi stood in radical opposition to capitalism, while Keynes, the reformer (and dyed-in-the-wool liberal individualist), set out to save capitalism from itself. And as it emerged, both in theory and practice, embedded liberalism was distinctly and fundamentally a Keynesian conception. His goal—as he developed his "middle way" beginning in the mid-1920s, and especially in *The Treatise on Money* (1930)—was to find a way to embrace and harness the essential engines of capitalism and an expanding international economy, while simultaneously insulating national economies from unmediated, often destructive market forces, so that individual countries might enjoy the autonomy to pursue a variety of domestic social purposes.[26]

Thus although Polanyi's notion of a "double movement" was perhaps inspirational in providing an understanding of the pressures that contributed to the postwar order, ultimately the purpose of embedded liberalism was to permit the practice of the middle way. The control of capital (and the taming of finance more generally) was a necessary prerequisite for this and, not surprisingly, was emphasized by Keynes as he anticipated (and negotiated) that emerging international order. The point is hammered home repeatedly: "Control of capital movements, both inward and outward, should be a permanent feature of the post-war system" and "nothing is more certain than that the movement of capital funds must be regulated." Note, again, that this does not deny the essential role of flows of capital—it simply recognizes (and emphasizes) the difference between productive movements (which support investment) and speculative movements (which do little more than wreak havoc with national economies). The practice of the middle way (or the varieties of domestic practice that the middle way sought to create space for) required insulation from the pressures for macroeconomic conformity imposed by unproductive financial flows. And although it is properly understood that Keynes came away from the Bretton Woods negotiations with much less than he had hoped for, his intellectual influence over the proceedings was enormous: the bargains reached took place within what can be described as a "Keynesian space," informed by his understandings about how economies worked (and failed).[27] Unleashing capital—rooted in changes from the 1970s but notably reflected in the basic policy choices of the 1990s—could not but reinforce pressures against embedded liberalism.

Related to this, but distinctly, is Keynes's conception of the role of the financial sector in a healthy economy more generally. As followers of Keynes have emphasized, repeatedly, although the financial services sector is an essential, crucial, and indispensable element of a mature capitalist society, ultimately its goal is to *facilitate* economic activity—that is, to allocate capital so that it might be put to efficient and productive use. It does not, as an end in itself, offer anything of value. Worse, and distressingly, as Keynes wrote— in 1936—though his words would ring true seventy years later, "[w]hen the capital development of a country becomes a by-product of the activities of a casino, the job is likely to be ill-done."[28] Good Keynesians never shed these instincts. Writing in the 1980s, James Tobin lamented, quite early in the game, the increasing size of the financial sector. He conceded, "[My] views run against current tides—not only the general enthusiasm for deregulation and unfettered competition but also my profession's intellectual admiration for the efficiency of financial markets." Nevertheless, he saw "financial activities remote from the production of goods and services," which "generate high private rewards disproportionate to their social productivity." Robert Solow reached similar conclusions. "The fact is, God created the financial sector to help the real economy, not to help itself," he insisted. "I suspect the financial services sector has grown relatively to the point where it is not even adding value to the real economy. It may be adding compensation to its members but it is not improving the efficiency or productivity of the real economy."[29]

Finally, Keynes thought it was essential to harness finance because, and fundamentally at odds with a "rational expectations" perspective (and in accord with the overwhelming evidence of history), he shared the view that the financial sector was often unstable and a common carrier of systemic risk.[30] As noted previously, one need not follow Keynes to be alert to such concerns. In 1995, Volcker thought it "obvious that if you had a large investment bank aligned with a large [commercial] bank, the possibility of a systemic risk arising is evident." A dozen years later, on the eve of the financial crisis, he again expressed concerns about a financial system that "looks confused and even dangerous, susceptible to excesses and breakdowns." Volcker rejected the notion that "the financial market itself, left free and unfettered by official oversight ... can reliably be self-stabilizing," and he expressed regret at the rejection of an older regulatory disposition, one that was expressly designed "to protect the core of the financial system from the recurrent bouts of speculative excesses and frightful contractions that have marked financial markets from time immemorial."[31]

The proselytizers of financial wizardry, in contrast, at that same moment, on the precipice of epochal ruin, thought they were so smart that the very notion of systemic risk was an anachronism. As Greenspan put it, "[I]ncreasingly complex financial instruments have contributed to the development of a far more flexible, efficient, and hence resilient financial system than the one that existed just a quarter-century ago."[32] For the converts (perhaps well fueled by fat speaking fees), this position was absolute and sacrosanct, and the very hint of a cautious dissent—even from a high priest within the tribe—was seen as apostasy. In 2005, Raghuram G. Rajan (then chief economist at IMF, later governor of the Reserve Bank of India), presented a paper at the Jackson Hole Symposium (an annual gathering of financial titans sponsored by the Federal Reserve Bank of Kansas City). While praising the benefits of recent financial innovations, Rajan nevertheless argued that they also presented new and growing risks to the system as a whole. In the new environment that featured a "myriad of complex claims," a modest disturbance could unexpectedly get out of hand and "may create a greater (albeit still small) probability of a catastrophic meltdown." He suggested a handful of rather modest, market-friendly reforms—and was met with an unrelenting barrage of criticism, in particular by Summers, who opened the ensuing discussion as "someone who finds the basic, slightly Luddite premise of this paper to be largely misguided."[33]

In sum, the shift in attitudes about (and governance of) the financial sector from those associated with the era of embedded liberalism to one characterized by the faiths of rational expectations and the efficient markets hypothesis, produced the three dysfunctional outcomes Keynes would have anticipated: the unleashing of pressures that inhibited varieties of macroeconomic practice; a bloated, byzantine, and self-gratifying financial sector; and one that invited a ruinous financial crisis. Perhaps worse, it would also contribute to the kind of dangerous backlash that Keynes's middle way was designed to prevent. But late in the twentieth century, especially from the perspective of the Cold-War-triumphant, economic colossus, and "hyperpower" that was the United States, the hard and horrifying lessons learned from the upheavals of the 1920s, 1930s, and 1940s were forgotten, or deemed no longer relevant.

The Return of Dickensian Capitalism

Ruggie, in his original articulation of the compromise of embedded liberalism, diverged from many of his colleagues by emphasizing the role of both power and purpose in forging and maintaining the postwar international order. While many situated the implications of the disheartening economic experiences of the 1970s in the context of the relative erosion of American power, he saw, then, more continuity than change. Thus for Ruggie this raised the question "How enduring is embedded liberalism?" His answer: "[The] foremost force for discontinuity at present is . . . the resurgent ethos of liberal capitalism."[34]

Again, with Keynes, this reflects the view that ideas matter. And in the 1990s, new ideas about how the world *should* work—a new culture of capitalism—which had been brewing from the 1980s, triumphed. Out went embedded liberalism; in came "shareholder value," the notion that the sole obligation of firms is to their shareholders, and thus, in turn, the assessment of management skills rested on the ability to deliver increases in the value of the company's stock (almost invariably with a focus on the relatively short run). Anything that might achieve that goal should be embraced, with that singular aspiration in mind. It is thus not surprising to learn that "when a chief executive officer with a business degree ... takes over from a non-business manager, there is a significant decline in wages and the labor share of the firm." The rise of an ethos of shareholder value meshed poorly with a financialized economy, wherein various complex gimmicks could be embraced to produce paper profits; its rise was also coterminous with numerous structural changes that further incentivized a "winner take all" society, with those already well placed and well advantaged in the best position to win.[35]

The new culture of capitalism also, inadvertently, exposed a fundamental fallacy at the heart of the philosophical foundations of the laissez-faire ideology. It turns out that factors of production are not rewarded according to the affectless, irresistible diktats of marginal productivity but rather by the often ruthless and arbitrary exercise of asymmetric economic power, inhibited (or not) by a shared sense of appropriate social practice. Mainstream economic textbooks have it wrong: notably, in the United States a divergence between worker pay and worker productivity emerged in the 1970s and widened ever more broadly through the 2010s. The data tells a sobering story: from 1947 to 1979 productivity and real wages tracked closely together, each growing at a rate of about 2 to 3 percent per year; from 1980 to 2001 productivity grew 86 percent, but real hourly wages grew by 7 percent. In a world ruled by shareholder value, labor does not get what it deserves, and capital seizes all that it can take.[36]

Likely for a variety of reasons—including the great chastening of the Depression, the shared social purpose of the Second World War, the tempering influence of Cold War competition with a rival economic ideology, and the Keynesian consensus—in the embedded liberal era the captains of industry practiced relative self-restraint with regard to their treatment of workers and their own compensation. Anecdotal evidence and descriptive statistics support the contention that norms about executive compensation and attitudes about ostentatious displays of wealth were different in the 1950s than they were in the 1920s—or the 1980s (to say nothing of the decades that followed). In the 1950s, the CEO of a large company earned about 20 times the salary of an average employee; that pay gap widened to approximately 50 times in 1993, reaching multiples of 100 times in 1993, and 278 times in 2018. Once again it is implausible (and unsupported by the evidence) to suggest that this reflects changes in relative productivity—or in essential, irreplaceable services provided to firms by their chief officers.[37]

Classical economists (or new classical economists, or those still clinging to rational expectations theory) assume that firms function on the precarious margins of profitability (lest competitors swoop in to take advantage of above-market returns) and, as a result, simply cannot reward any factor of production (from chief executives to custodians) even slightly more than the marginal value added they bring to the enterprise. In the real world, however, there is money on the table, and raw power, combined with notions of legitimacy, profoundly shape who gets what and why. Twenty-first-century plutocratic (and all too commonly oligopolistic) capitalism is exemplified by companies like Amazon. Jeff Bezos, its executive chairman, is worth well more than $100 billion. In 2020 he added to his collection of homes a thirteen-thousand-square-foot, $165 million mansion in Beverly Hills; at that same moment Amazon warehouse workers earned an average of $15 an hour, tasked with sorting eighteen hundred parcels per hour.[38]

An emphasis on shareholder value, the emergence of a winner-take-all society, and the harrowing, paradigm-subverting divergence between productivity and reward all contributed to the soaring levels of inequality. But the problem—the crisis—is not simply one of inequality; rather it is, and still one more time back with Keynes, about perceptions of fairness, a very different thing. "No man of spirit will consent to remain poor," Keynes held, "if he believes his betters to have gained their goods by lucky gambling." Even the "pre-Keynesian" Keynes stressed this point repeatedly: "The business man is only tolerable so long as his gains can be held to bear some relation to what, roughly and in some sense, his activities have contributed to society." Capitalism cannot be sustained if it is viewed as inherently unfair. And as Abdelal argues, by the second decade of the twenty-first century in the Western world "societies came to feel—correctly—that the distribution of income no longer reflected individual merit."[39]

In assessing the American meritocracy, consider the financial gang of four featured above. As chairman of the Senate Banking Committee, Phil Gramm was showered with campaign contributions and a dizzying array of perks from his benefactors in banking, and in 2002 he left the Senate—but not politics—and joined the financial giant UBS as an investment banker and lobbyist. Larry Summers would go on to draw a $5 million salary for a part-time job at the hedge fund D. E. Shaw and, months before joining the Obama administration, was paid $135,000 by Goldman Sachs for a personal appearance—part of the $2.7 million in speaking fees he was rewarded by Wall Street companies that would subsequently receive government bailout money. (Summers, of course, was an active participant in administration debates about how those firms should be treated during the catastrophe that their reckless behavior had wrought.) Alan Greenspan left the Fed in 2006; the following year he was hired as a special consultant to the Pacific Investment Management Company and signed on to serve as a senior advisor to Deutsche Bank. In 2008, he was retained as an advisor by Paulson & Co., the hedge fund company that made billions betting against the housing market during the financial crisis.[40]

And then there is Robert Rubin. As Clinton's secretary of the Treasury, Rubin oversaw the repeal of the Glass-Steagall Act, which, as noted, made possible the creation of Citigroup, and immediately upon leaving office he joined that outfit, serving on its board of directors as chairman of the executive committee, for which he was paid $125 million over the next decade. Ultimately it was determined that he did not break the law by contacting government officials on Enron's behalf in 2001 (Citi was a major creditor of that not yet disgraced and ruined operation), but in general he proffered some pretty bad business advice. He urged Citigroup to be much more aggressive in taking risks in the new and lucrative financial exotica, and the firm took a deep dive into collateralized debt obligations, issuing them to the tune of billions of dollars in 2003 and then tripling their business within two years. "Mr. Rubin encouraged changes that led Citi to the brink of collapse"—this was a broadly shared assessment—but he "was reportedly critical to securing" its bailout by the federal government.[41]

To understand the state of contemporary American policy, one need look no further than that sentence. The global financial crisis of 2007–2008 and, crucially, its aftermath was a watershed moment. Starting in the 1970s median household incomes in the United States stagnated; in the 1980s a culture of shareholder value capitalism celebrated that change—and averred that people got what the market justly rewarded them. In the 1990s the economy was financialized; in the following decade, the exorbitant bill for the folly of those choices came due. But to whom was the bill presented? The adroit and improvised emergency measures taken at the time were necessary to prevent the financial system from completely melting down. But ultimately those who caused the global financial crisis bore few if any of its costs, whereas those already on the ropes from decades of economic pressure—from international competition, automation, and the elite embrace of Dickensian capitalism—were pummeled by the long, difficult great recession. In the words of Martin Wolf, it was a system in which "well-connected insiders" were "shielded from loss but impose[d] massive costs on everybody else." And drawing from that poisoned well, not surprisingly, led directly to the burn-it-all-down populism and flirtation with know-nothing, nativist personalist authoritarianism, with which contemporary liberalism is now confronted.[42]

After the Gold Rush

The consequences of all this are far-reaching—obviously for the trajectory of American politics but also, profoundly, for the emerging pattern of international relations. Because, to adapt a phrase deployed by Charles Kindleberger in a very different context, due to the domestic dysfunction seeded by those misguided decisions, a quarter of a century later the United States is "just about finished" as a great power. However, to remain focused on the core themes of this volume, rather than speculating about what the future might bring, this concluding section will consider two crucial turning points from the past. Did the 1990s need to unfold as they did? Of course not—we know what happened since, but in those moments, the future was unwritten.[43]

There were arguably two key counterfactual (or counterhistorical) moments when different choices might have led to different outcomes, each in the aftermath of two exogenous shocks: the 1994 midterm elections in the United States and in the wake of the Asian financial crisis of 1997–1998.[44] The former led the Clinton administration to adjust its course and make choices that would accelerate the misguided project of financial liberalization (and the financialization of the American economy); the latter offered an opportunity to reassess the wisdom of that road taken, but rather than pausing or reevaluating, the United States instead stubbornly—and, it should be repeated, with an arrogance borne of hubris—chose to press on the accelerator.

The 1994 elections were little short of a bloodbath for the Democratic Party. The Republicans picked up fifty two-seats—the largest net gain in Congress since 1948—and the Democrats lost control of the House of Representatives for the first time in forty-two years. The Republican Party picked up eight seats in the Senate and claimed the majority there as well. President Clinton, reeling and on the ropes, was described as "frustrated, raging, and depressed" and saw the results, perhaps accurately, as a mortal threat to his future prospects for reelection. He emerged determined to reemphasize his posture as a "New Democrat"—that is, to double down on his strategy of forcing the party toward the center.[45]

Other political and policy pathways could have been chosen, although certainly the loss of Democratic majorities in both chambers of Congress circumscribed the range of the possible. This approach, however, led directly to the ascendance of Rubin, Summers, and Greenspan—a triumvirate breathlessly celebrated on the cover of *Time* magazine as "The Committee to Save the World"—but who in retrospect are of course better seen (in partnership with crucial, co-opted congressional allies) as the principal architects of America's financial ruin.[46] Reshuffling his economic team in the wake of the midterm drubbing, Clinton named Rubin Treasury secretary in January 1995; Summers would become deputy secretary in August. And in early 1996 the president made clear he would appoint Greenspan to a third term as Fed chair, a move that became official in March.

None of this necessarily had to be. In particular, Greenspan's reappointment was not a sure thing—in fact it was almost certainly not the president's original intention—and it was fraught with political controversy. Most observers had anticipated that Alan Blinder, who had been appointed vice-chair of the Fed in June 1994, would be Clinton's choice. But Blinder, a world-class macroeconomist and sober arbiter of sound monetary policy, was nevertheless clearly (and, just as important, perceived to be even more markedly) to the left of the libertarian-Republican Greenspan. As such, Blinder was a casualty of the administration's new disposition (and reduced political circumstances), as was his would-be successor, legendary New York investment banker Felix Rohatyn. With the writing now on the wall, Blinder left his Fed post abruptly, with six months remaining on a two-year term. Rohatyn, Clinton's choice to fill the vacant vice-chair slot, was soon confronted with a public campaign of opposition (and, notably, the behind-the-scenes disfavor of Rubin) and was forced to make a public show of asking the president to withdraw his name as a possible nominee.[47] Under different circumstances, then, the Committee to Save the World could have featured three other faces—and perhaps the world wouldn't have even needed saving. More judicious leadership at Treasury would likely have been more cautious about deregulating the financial sector; Blinder surely would have been more attentive to the dangers of systematic risk and financial fragility than Greenspan, who barely believed that such things existed.

But liberating finance is an invitation to financial crisis, as illustrated by the unanticipated Asian financial crisis, which wreaked havoc on economies then celebrated for their sustained economic growth and lauded for their savvy macroeconomic management. As noted above, the U.S. financial deregulation project had an international component as well: an aggressive push to force other countries to dismantle their capital controls and deregulate their financial sectors. This was dismal advice, rooted more in politics than in economics. (There was no evidence to suggest that this was sound economic policy—if anything, the evidence supported the opposite conclusion—but such measures were seen as advancing American interests.) That such a tumultuous crisis would sweep across this particular region—and with almost every twist and turn a surprise—might have been recognized as a canary-in-the-coal-mine moment and provided an occasion to reassess the grand American vision.

This was certainly a plausible prospect. In fact, a number of leading economists and other observers called for such a reassessment, noting both the absence of empirical support for the ambitious project and the obvious dangers with which it was fraught. One leading voice in this debate, Jagdish Bhagwati, concluded that "the weight of evidence and the force of logic point in the opposite direction, toward restraints on capital flows." A growing if still minority chorus favored the greater caution and stressed the need to "throw some sand into the gears of international finance." More pointedly (if perhaps erroneously), with the eruption and tumult of the Asian financial crisis even some experienced market players reached the conclusion "It's only a bit of an overstatement to say that the free-market I.M.F. Bob Rubin and Larry Summers model is in shambles."[48]

But this was not to be. When you know you're right (even if you're wrong), all evidence, even counterintuitive evidence, is confirming. Rubin insisted that "the turbulence which can occur during a crisis should not cause us to reverse" course. Summers was even more confident, stating, "Recent events in Southeast Asia have only increased our desire to strengthen the world's financial systems—and make them more open." For him the lesson was that the world should "accelerate" rather than "slow the pace of capital account liberalization." And of course Greenspan could not even imagine what an international financial crisis looked like (despite the fact that the Asian crisis fit the trajectory and classic pattern of that phenomena to a T). For the Fed chair, the "root" causes of the crisis could be found in the "poor public policy" of the Asian states themselves. Moreover he asserted, "[O]ne consequence of this Asian crisis is an increasing awareness in the region that market capitalism, as practiced in the West, especially in the United States, is the superior model." This was of course a bizarre and erroneous claim, but one pregnant with enormous consequences for the future of global financial stability.[49]

Rather than reflect on the financial liberalization/capital deregulation project, its architects doubled down, as witnessed in the cases of Korea and Malaysia, two countries whose experiences contradicted the tenets of their model. Even as the crisis grew, no one thought it would reach Korea's shores—yet it did, further evidence that the crisis was not the result of hitherto unseen or unnoticed flaws in its public policy, but instead reflected a rather standard-issue international financial panic. As Martin Feldstein argued, Korea, boasting "an economy to envy," was overtaken by a crisis of "temporary illiquidity," which he distinguished from "fundamental insolvency." Yet under U.S. pressure the country was forced to agree to a set of liberalizing demands that the Americans had long pushed for unsuccessfully: eliminating barriers to foreign direct investment, opening up its markets in insurance and securities dealings, and, of course, however counterintuitive in retrospect, *accelerating* the liberalization of foreign exchange transactions.[50] As if quoting David Bowie, the U.S. mantra about shedding financial inhibitions could be summarized as "Too much is never enough."

The experience of Malaysia offered another lesson about the wisdom of the American way. Unlike most of the countries in the region challenged by the crisis, it eschewed IMF-style orthodoxy in favor of capital controls, combined with a cocktail of other domestic economic measures. Reaction from the West was swift: Greenspan condemned the move and lectured that states introducing such measures would find themselves "mired at a sub-optimal standard of living and slow growth rate." Summers opined that it "would be a catastrophe" if other countries followed suit. Thus although there was good reason to be curious about the lessons that might be drawn from Malaysia's alternative approach, in contrast, as one observer at the time reported, "[i]n Washington, some officials quietly expressed the hope that this experiment would fail so spectacularly that the smoldering ruins of the Malaysian economy would act as a caution to other countries." In fact, the opposite occurred: the controls acted as designed, operating as a circuit breaker in the midst of the panic, and permitted the policies that helped the country avoid the worst of the crisis. Indeed, one year later another account concluded, "Critics were aghast... but now many admit the move succeeded in helping to lift Malaysia out of its worst recession ever."[51]

Many, but not all. The Americans continued, both at home and abroad, to press aggressively for financial deregulation and to embrace the measures and the policies that would, within a decade, directly contribute to the epochal global financial crisis. The United States had other choices it could have made in the 1990s. But like Harry Moseby (Gene Hackman) in Arthur Penn's brilliant 1970s film *Night Moves*, "they didn't see it. They played something else, and they lost. And they regretted it." Or at least they should have.

Notes

1. "Nineteen-eighty, eighty-four, eighty-eight, ninety-two too, too"; "I'm just profoundly frustrated by all this" (R.E.M. 1992). "We can sit here and wait until a Democrat's in the White House... or get this over with" (ABC 1988).
2. See Reinhard 2018.
3. Blyth 2022, 48; Abdelal 2022, 106–107.
4. Eichengreen 2015, 319.
5. Rising prices put pressure on usury laws that restricted the imposition of high interest rates, especially on credit cards (which were becoming much more widespread in their use). In that context, Regulation Q, which as part of the Banking Act of 1933 capped the rates of interest that banks could offer on various forms of deposit accounts (in order to prevent banks from being pressured by competition to take imprudent risks), was rendered unsustainable.
6. The Garn–St. Germain Depository Institutions Act of 1982, which deregulated Savings and Loans Associations. See Sherman 2009, 20, 25; Krippner 2011, 58–59, 79, 81, 100.
7. Grossman 2010, 266, 272, 281; Sherman 2009, 4–6, 7, 8.
8. Cowan 1983; Noble 1984. See Volcker 1985a; see also 1985b. See Federal Reserve System Board of Governors 2020; Nash 1987.
9. Silk 1987.
10. Greenspan 2007, 372, 373–374; see also 370, 489–490.
11. "The ideas derived by postwar governments from *The General Theory* were only vaguely attributable to the author of that book" (Aron [1977] 1996, 193). See also Kirshner 2009.
12. Quiggin 2010, 36 (quote). See Krozner and Shiller (2011, 21, 22, 30) on the efficient markets hypothesis as a cause of deregulation; Davidson 2009, 1, 2.
13. Skidelsky 2018, 202.
14. Skidelsky 2018, 202–203.
15. Cohan 2011, 308–309; Berry 1993. The moment well reflected Mark Blyth's (2022, 49) observation that "the parties that had invented and defended the old bargain abandoned their traditional constituencies and moved to capture richer (older) median voters, changing their policy stances in doing so."
16. Herbert 2002; Lipton 2008.
17. Kirshner 2003, 260–280.
18. Kristof and Sanger 1999; Summers 1997; Klee et al. 1998, 22. See also Blinder 1999, 57.
19. Moscow 1995; Truell 1995; Greenspan 2007, 198–199, 257, 375–376. On Gramm-Leach-Bliley and increased systemic risk, see Akhigbe and Whyte 2004, 435–446.
20. Greenspan 1999.

21. *The Economist* 1992; U.S. Government Accountability Office 1994, 11, 14–15, 39, 124, 126–127.
22. Norris 1994; Spiro and Byrnes 1994; U.S. Government Accountability Office 1994, 7, 8, 12, 15, 31, 32, 85; Lowenstein 2000; MacKenzie 2006, ch. 8; Mallaby 2010, 226. And contrast the Harvard Business School case studies lauding Enron in the 1990s—which, in an act of academic malpractice, have been withdrawn from circulation—with Nanda 2002.
23. Chittum 2009; Sherman 2009, 10–11. For an example of Born's warnings, see Fromson and Skrzycki 1997. See also Financial Crisis Inquiry Commission 2011, 47–48; McClean and Nocera 2010, 98, 100, 104–106, 109; Greenspan 1998d, 3–5.
24. U.S. Department of the Treasury, President's Working Group on Financial Markets 1999. "William J. Rainer, the new chairman of the Commodity Futures Trading Commission, will leave over-the counter-derivatives alone, a policy that the banking industry has been demanding since last year" (Anason 1999).
25. Krippner 2011, 3–4, 28–29; Johnson and Kwak 2010, 5, 60, 115; DeLong and Cohen 2010, 110–111; Stiglitz 2010, 247; Financial Crisis Inquiry Commission 2011, 61–62; Princeton University, *Class of 2006 Survey Report*.
26. Ruggie 1982, 379–415; Polanyi (1944) 1980, 57.
27. Keynes (1941) 1971–1989, 21–33. In Ruggie's (1982, 393) phrasing, there was consensus that "multilateralism would be predicated upon domestic interventionism." On the incompatibility of unfettered finance and the middle way, see Kirshner 1999, 313–337. On Keynes's intellectual influence, see Ikenberry 1992, 289–321.
28. Keynes (1936) 1971–1989, 159.
29. Tobin 1984; Solow 2010.
30. Kindleberger 1978; Reinhart and Rogoff 2009.
31. Silber 2012, 10, 275 (quote); Mehrling 2001, 434–460; Volcker 2008, 101–107.
32. Greenspan 2005 (quote); see also Greenspan 2007, 360, 367, 368, 371, 492.
33. Rajan 2005, 315–316, 318, 332, 336–339, 342, 345–346, 350, 359, 387 (Summers).
34. Ruggie 1982, 413.
35. Stout 2012; Frank and Cook 1995; Foroohar 2016. On managers, see Acemoglu et al. 2022, 1 ("Wage growth has slowed down and the labor share in national income has declined in many advanced economies over the last three decades. We argue that a contributing factor has been changes in wage policies of firms associated with business education of their managers/CEOs" [28]).
36. Fleck et al. 2011, 62; Kochan 2013, 293, 294; Kochan and Riordan 2016, 419–440; Bivens and Mishel 2015.
37. On executive pay and lifestyle, see Blair 1994, 24; Smith and Kuntz 2013; Mishel and Wolfe 2019, 4; Norton-Talor 1955.
38. Jackson 2020; Sainato 2020.
39. Keynes (1919) 1971–1989, 149; Keynes (1923) 1971–1989, 24 (second and third quotes); Abdelal 2022, 116.
40. Lipton and Labaton 2008; McClean and Nocera 2010, 63, 67; Johnson and Kwak 2010, 6, 9, 96, 192; Financial Crisis Inquiry Commission 2011, 55; Zeleny 2009; Gangahar 2008.
41. Oppel 2003; Dash and Creswell 2008; *Wall Street Journal* 2008.
42. Wolf 2014, 352. As Adam Tooze (2018, 566) argues, "The presidential race of 2016 turned out to be more about the financial crisis of 2008 than 2012 had been." See also Kirshner 2016.
43. On this theme, see Kirshner 2022.
44. Arguably, these were endogenous shocks: the former a typical—if exaggerated—countermovement following the presidential election of 1992; the latter made much more likely by the purposeful and dedicated unleashing of uninhibited global capital flows.
45. Jacobson 1996, 203–223; Mitchell 1996.
46. Ramo 1999. The tenor of the story is conveyed by its subhead: "Economist heroes? It sounds silly unless you understand how close we came to economic meltdown last year."
47. Uchitelle 1996; Gerstenzang 1996; Sanger 1996.
48. Bhagwati 1998, 9, 12 (quote); Eichengreen et al. 1995, 162–172; Rodrik 1998, 61; Kirshner 1998; Sanger 1998 (quoting Morgan Stanley's John S. Wadsworth Jr.).
49. Harrison 1997 (Rubin). See also *Asia Pulse* 1997; International Monetary Fund 2003, 18 (Summers); U.S. Department of the Treasury 1998 (Summers); Greenspan 1998a, 1998b. On the crisis more generally, see Abdelal 2007; Chwieroth 2010.

50. Feldstein 1998, 24, 25, 27, 31, 32; Corden 2001, 59–60; Pempel 1999, 236–237.
51. McDermott and Lopez 1998; Abdelal and Alfaro 2002 (Summers quote on 11); Tourres 2003; Greenspan 1998c; Sanger 1998 (smoldering ruins); Duff-Brown 1999 (aghast).

References

ABC. 1988. "Between a Yuck and a Hard Place." *Moonlighting*. December 13.
Abdelal, Rawi. 2007. *Capital Rules: The Construction of Global Finance*. Harvard University Press.
Abdelal, Rawi. 2022. "Of Learning and Forgetting: Centrism, Populism, and the Legitimacy Crisis of Globalization." In *The Downfall of the American Order*, edited by Peter J. Katzenstein and Jonathan Kirshner. Cornell University Press.
Abdelal, Rawi, and Laura Alfaro. 2002. "Malaysia: Capital and Control (TN)." Teaching Note 703-020. Harvard Business School, October. https://www.hbs.edu/faculty/Pages/item.aspx?num=29385.
Acemoglu, Daron, Alex He, and Daniel le Maire. 2022. "Eclipse of Rent Sharing: The Effects of Manager's Business Education on Wages and the Labor Share in the US and Denmark." Working Paper 29874. NBER, March.
Akhigbe, Aigbe, and Ann Marie Whyte. 2004. "The Gramm-Leach-Bliley Act of 1999: Risk Implications for the Financial Services Industry." *Journal of Financial Research* 27 (3): 435–446.
Anason, Dean. 1999. "Futures Commission Head: OTC Oversight Unnecessary." *American Banker*, December 8.
Aron, Raymond. (1977) 1996. *In Defense of Decadent Europe*. Transaction.
Asia Pulse. 1997. "U.S. to Urge Financial Liberalization at WTO Talks." August 13.
Berry, John M. 1993. "The Fed Chief's Unlikely Alliance." *Washington Post*, March 21.
Bhagwati, Jagdish. 1998. "The Capital Myth." *Foreign Affairs* 77 (3): 7–12.
Bivens, Josh, and Lawrence Mishel. 2015. "Understanding and Explaining the Historic Divergence between Productivity and a Typical Worker's Pay: Why It Matters and Why It's Real." Washington, DC: Economic Policy Institute, September 2.
Blair, Margaret M. 1994. "CEO Pay: Why Such a Contentious Issue?" *Brookings Review* 12 (1): 22.
Blinder, Alan. 1999. "Eight Steps to a New Financial Order." *Foreign Affairs* 78 (5): 50–63.
Blyth, Mark. 2022. "The End of Social Purpose? Great Transformations of American Order." In *Downfall of the American Order?*, edited by Peter J. Katzenstein and Jonathan Kirshner. Cornell University Press.
Chittum, Ryan. 2009. "Audit Interview: James L. Bothwell." *Columbia Journalism Review*, July 14.
Chwieroth, Jeffrey. 2010. *Capital Ideas: The IMF and the Rise of Financial Liberalization*. Princeton University Press.
Cohan, William D. 2011. *Money and Power: How Goldman Sachs Came to Rule the World*. Anchor Books.
Corden, W. Max. 2001. "The World Financial Crisis: Are the IMF Prescriptions Right?" In *The Political Economy of International Financial Crisis: Interest Groups, Ideologies, and Institutions*, edited by Shale Horowitz and Uk Heo. Rowman & Littlefield.
Cowan, Edward. 1983. "Bush Group's Proposals on Banking Regulation." *New York Times*, December 24.
Dash, Eric, and Julie Creswell. 2008. "Citigroup Saw No Red Flags Even as It Made Bolder Bets." *New York Times*, November 22.
Davidson, Paul. 2009. *The Keynes Solution: The Path to Global Economic Prosperity*. St. Martin's.

DeLong, J. Bradford, and Stephen Cohen. 2010. *The End of Influence: What Happens When Other Countries Have the Money*. Basic Books.

Duff-Brown, Beth. 1999. "Malaysia Defies Western Orthodoxy with Unorthodox Currency Controls." Associated Press, September 11.

The Economist. 1992. "Taming the Derivatives Beast—The Dangers of Financial Derivatives." May 23.

Eichengreen, Barry. 2015. *Hall of Mirrors: The Great Depression, the Great Recession, and the Uses—and Misuses—of History*. Oxford University Press.

Eichengreen, Barry, James Tobin, and Charles Wyplosz. 1995. "Two Cases for Sand in the Wheels of International Finance." *Economic Journal* 105 (428): 162–172.

Federal Reserve System Board of Governors. 2020. "Federal Reserve History: 'Paul A. Volcker.'" Federal Reserve History. https://www.federalreservehistory.org/people/paul-a-volcker.

Feldstein, Martin. 1998. "Refocusing the IMF." *Foreign Affairs* 77 (2): 1–17.

Financial Crisis Inquiry Commission. 2011. *The Financial Crisis Inquiry Report*. FCIC, January.

Fleck, Susan, John Glaser, and Shawn Sprague. 2011. "The Compensation-Productivity Gap: A Visual Essay." *Monthly Labor Review*, January.

Foroohar, Rana. 2016. *Makers and Takers: The Rise of Finance and the Fall of American Business*. Crown.

Frank, Robert, and Phillip Cook. 1995. *The Winner Take All Society*. Free Press.

Fromson, Brett D., and Cindy Skrzycki. 1997. "CFTC Head Assails Bill Curbing Agency's Powers; Unregulated Markets Called Threat to System." *Washington Post*, February 28.

Gangahar, Anuj. 2008. "Greenspan Joins NY Hedge Fund." *Financial Times*, January 15.

Gerstenzang, James. 1996. "Blinder's Resignation a Sign Greenspan Will Stay." *Los Angeles Times*, January 18.

Greenspan, Alan. 1998a. "The Current Asia Crisis and the Dynamics of International Finance." Testimony before Committee on Banking and Financial Services, U.S. House of Representatives, January 30. https://www.federalreserve.gov/boarddocs/testimony/1998/19980130.htm.

Greenspan, Alan. 1998b. "The Current Asian Crisis and the Financial Resources of the IMF." Testimony before House Agricultural Committee, U.S. House of Representatives, May 21. https://www.federalreserve.gov/boarddocs/testimony/1998/19980521.htm.

Greenspan, Alan. 1998c. "International Economic and Financial Systems." Testimony before Committee on Banking and Financial Services, U.S. House of Representatives, September 16. https://www.federalreserve.gov/boarddocs/testimony/1998/19980916.htm.

Greenspan, Alan. 1998d. "The Regulation of OTC Derivatives." Testimony before Committee on Banking and Financial Services, U.S. House of Representatives, July 24. https://www.federalreserve.gov/boarddocs/testimony/1998/19980724.htm.

Greenspan, Alan. 1999. "Financial Derivatives." Remarks before the Futures Industry Association, Boca Raton, Florida, March 19. https://fcic-static.law.stanford.edu/cdn_media/fcic-docs/1999-03-19%20Greenspan%20Financial%20Derivatives.pdf.

Greenspan, Alan. 2005. "Economic Flexibility." Remarks before the National Italian American Foundation, Washington, D.C., October 12. https://www.federalreserve.gov/boarddocs/speeches/2005/20051012/default.htm.

Greenspan, Alan. 2007. *The Age of Turbulence*. Penguin.

Grossman, Richard S. 2010. *Unsettled Account: The Evolution of Banking in the Industrialized World since 1800*. Princeton University Press.

Harrison, Nathaniel. 1997. "IMF Policymakers Weigh Free Capital Flow in Light of Thai Crisis." Agence France-Presse, September 23.

Herbert, Bob. 2002. "Enron and the Gramms." *New York Times*, January 7.

Ikenberry, G. John. 1992. "A World Economy Restored: Expert Consensus and the Anglo-American Postwar Settlement." *International Organization* 46 (1): 289–321.
International Monetary Fund. 2003. *The IMF and Recent Capital Account Crises: Indonesia, Korea, Brazil*. Washington, DC: IMF.
Jackson, Candice. 2020. "Jeff Bezos Buying $165 Million Estate, a California Record." *New York Times*, February 14.
Jacobson, Gary C. 1996. "The 1994 House Elections in Perspective." *Political Science Quarterly* 111 (2): 203–223.
Johnson, Simon, and James Kwak. 2010. *13 Bankers: The Wall Street Takeover and the Next Financial Meltdown*. Pantheon.
Keynes, John Maynard. (1919) 1971–1989. *The Economic Consequences of the Peace*. In *The Collected Writings of John Maynard Keynes*, vol. 2, edited by Donald Moggridge and Elizabeth Johnson. Macmillan.
Keynes, John Maynard. (1923) 1971–1989. *A Tract on Monetary Reform*. In *The Collected Writings of John Maynard Keynes*, vol. 4, edited by Donald Moggridge and Elizabeth Johnson. Macmillan.
Keynes, John Maynard. (1936) 1971–1989. *The General Theory of Employment, Interest and Money*. In *The Collected Writings of John Maynard Keynes*, vol. 7, edited by Donald Moggridge and Elizabeth Johnson. Macmillan.
Keynes, John Maynard. (1941) 1971–1989. "Post-War Currency Policy." In *The Collected Writings of John Maynard Keynes*, vol. 25, edited by Donald Moggridge and Elizabeth Johnson. Macmillan.
Kindleberger, Charles P. 1978. *Manias, Panics, and Crashes: A History of Financial Crises*. Basic Books.
Kirshner, Jonathan. 1998. "Culprit Is Unregulated Capital." *Los Angeles Times*, September 13.
Kirshner, Jonathan. 1999. "Keynes, Capital Mobility and the Crisis of Embedded Liberalism." *Review of International Political Economy* 6 (3): 313–337.
Kirshner, Jonathan. 2003. "Explaining Choices about Money: Disentangling Power, Ideas and Conflict." In *Monetary Orders: Ambiguous Economics, Ubiquitous Politics*, edited by Jonathan Kirshner. Cornell University Press.
Kirshner, Jonathan. 2009. "Keynes, Legacies and Inquiry." *Theory and Society* 38 (4): 527–541.
Kirshner, Jonathan. 2016. "Trump and the End of Everything." *Boston Review*, June 7.
Kirshner Jonathan. 2022. *An Unwritten Future: Realism and Uncertainty in World Politics*. Princeton University Press.
Klee, Kenneth, and Rich Thomas, with Stefan Theil. 1998. "Defending the One True Faith." *Newsweek*, September 14.
Kochan, Thomas. 2013. "The American Jobs Crisis and the Implications for the Future of Employment Policy." *International Labor Relations Review* 66 (2): 291–314.
Kochan, Thomas, and Christine Riordan. 2016. "Employment Relations and Growing Income Inequality: Causes and Potential Options for Its Reversal." *Journal of Industrial Relations* 58 (3): 419–440.
Krippner, Greta R. 2011. *Capitalizing on Crisis: The Political Origins of the Rise of Finance*. Harvard University Press.
Kristof, Nicholas, and David Sanger. 1999. "How U.S. Wooed Asia to Let the Cash Flow In." *New York Times*, February 16.
Kroszner, Randall S., and Robert J. Shiller. 2011. *Reforming U.S. Financial Markets: Reflections before and beyond Dodd-Frank*. MIT Press.
Lipton, Eric. 2008. "Gramm and the Enron Loophole." *New York Times*, November 14.
Lipton, Eric, and Stephen Labaton. 2008. "Deregulator Looks Back, Unswayed." *New York Times*, November 17.
Lowenstein, Roger. 2000. *When Genius Failed: The Rise and Fall of Long Term Capital Management*. Random House.

MacKenzie, Donald. 2006. *An Engine, Not a Camera: How Financial Models Shape Markets*. MIT Press.
Mallaby, Sebastian. 2010. *More Money Than God: Hedge Funds and the Making of a New Elite*. Penguin.
McClean, Bethany, and Joe Nocera. 2010. *All the Devils Are Here: The Hidden History of the Financial Crisis*. Penguin.
McDermott, Darren, and Leslie Lopez. 1998. "Malaysia Imposes Sweeping Currency Controls—Such Capital Restrictions Win Credence in Wake of Financial Turmoil." *Wall Street Journal*, September 2.
Mehrling, Perry. 2001. "Interview with Paul Volcker." *Macroeconomic Dynamics* 5 (3): 434–460.
Mishel, Lawrence, and Julia Wolfe. 2019. "CEO Compensation Has Grown 940% since 1978." Washington, DC: Economic Policy Institute, August 14.
Mitchell, Alison. 1996. "Stung by Defeats in '94, Clinton Regrouped and Co-Opted G.O.P. Strategies." *New York Times*, November 7.
Moscow, John W. 1995. "Bigger Banks, Bigger Problems." *New York Times* June 28.
Nanda, Ashish. 2002. "Broken Trust: Role of Professionals in the Enron Debacle." Case 903-084. Harvard Business School, December. https://www.hbs.edu/faculty/Pages/item.aspx?num=29479
Nash, Nathaniel. 1987. "Bank Curb Eased in Volcker Defeat." *New York Times*, May 1.
Noble, Kenneth. 1984. "Banking Regulatory Accord Set." *New York Times*, February 1.
Norris, Floyd. 1994. "Orange County Crisis Jolts Bond Market." *New York Times*, December 8.
Norton-Talor, Duncan. 1955. "How Top Executives Live." *Fortune*, July.
Oppel, Richard A., Jr. 2003. "Senate Report Says Rubin Acted Legally in Enron Matter." *New York Times*, January 3.
Pempel, T. J. 1999. "Conclusion." In *The Politics of the Asian Economic Crisis*, edited by T. J. Pempel. Cornell University Press.
Polanyi, Karl. (1944) 1980. *The Great Transformation: The Political and Economic Origins of Our Time*. Beacon.
Quiggin, John. 2010. *Zombie Economics: How Dead Ideas Still Walk among Us*. Princeton University Press.
Rajan, Raghuram G. 2005. "Has Financial Development Made the World Riskier?" Reprinted in *The Greenspan Era: Lessons for the Future: A Symposium Sponsored by the Federal Reserve Bank of Kansas City*, August. https://www.kansascityfed.org/Jackson%20Hole/documents/3326/PDF-Rajan2005.pdf.
Ramo, Joshua Cooper. 1999. "The Three Marketeers." *Time*, February 15.
Reinhart, Carmen, and Kenneth Rogoff. 2009. *This Time It Is Different: Eight Centuries of Financial Folly*. Princeton University Press.
Reinhard, R. J. 2018. "George H. W. Bush Retrospective." Gallup, December 1. https://news.gallup.com/opinion/gallup/234971/george-bush-retrospective.aspx.
R.E.M. 1992. "Ignoreland." *Automatic for the People*. Warner Bros. Records.
Rodrik, Dani. 1998. "Who Needs Capital Account Mobility?" In *Should the IMF Pursue Capital Account Convertibility? Essays in International Finance*, edited by Peter Kenen. Princeton University.
Ruggie, John. 1982. "International Regimes, Transactions, and Change: Embedded Liberalism in the Postwar Economic Order." *International Organization* 36 (2): 379–415.
Sainato, Michael. 2020. "'I'm Not a Robot': Amazon Workers Condemn Unsafe, Grueling Conditions at Warehouse." *The Guardian*, February 5.
Sanger, David E. 1996. "Facing Foes, Rohatyn Ready to Withdraw as Fed Choice." *New York Times*, February 13.
Sanger, David E. 1998. "Gaining Currency: The Invisible Hand's New Strong Arm." *New York Times*, September 13.

Sherman, Matthew. 2009. "A Short History of Financial Deregulation in the United States." Center for Economic and Policy Research, July.
Silber, William L. 2012. *Volcker: The Triumph of Persistence*. Bloomsbury.
Silk, Leonard. 1987. "Volcker on the Crash." *New York Times*, November 8.
Skidelsky, Robert. 2018. *Money and Government: The Past and Future of Economics*. Yale University Press.
Smith, Elliot Blair, and Phil Kuntz. 2013. "CEO Pay 1,795-to-1 Multiple of Wages Skirts U.S. Law." *Bloomberg*, April 30.
Solow, Robert. 2010. "Building a Science of Economics for the Real World." Hearing before Subcommittee on Investigations and Oversight Committee of Science and Technology, U.S. House of Representatives, July 20. https://www.loc.gov/item/2023695163/.
Spiro, Leah Nathans, and Nanette Byrnes. 1994. "Today, Orange County . . ." *Businessweek*, December 12.
Stiglitz, Joseph. 2010. *Freefall: America, Free Markets, and the Sinking of the World Economy*. Norton.
Stout, Lynn. 2012. *The Shareholder Value Myth: How Putting Shareholders First Harms Investors, Corporations, and the Public*. Berrett-Koehler.
Summers, Lawrence. 1997. "Financial Services Negotiations." Lecture. Congressional Economic Leadership Institute Luncheon, August 12.
Tobin, James. 1984. "On the Efficiency of the Financial System." *Lloyds Bank Review* 153 (July): 1–15.
Tooze, Adam. 2018. *Crashed: How a Decade of Financial Crises Changed the World*. Viking.
Tourres, Marie-Aimée. 2003. *The Tragedy That Didn't Happen: Malaysia's Crisis Management and Capital Controls*. Kuala Lumpur: Institute of Strategic and International Studies.
Truell, Peter. 1995. "New York Fed Official Resigns over Article in the Times." *New York Times*, July 21.
Uchitelle, Louis. 1996. "Blinder Plans to Leave Post as Fed's No. 2." *New York Times*, January 17.
U.S. Government Accountability Office. 1994. *Financial Derivatives: Actions Needed to Protect the Financial System*. May. https://www.gao.gov/products/ggd-94-133.
U.S. Department of the Treasury. 1998. "Deputy Secretary Summers, Remarks before the International Monetary Fund." March 9. https://home.treasury.gov/news/press-releases/rr2286.
U.S. Department of the Treasury, President's Working Group on Financial Markets. 1999. "Over-the-Counter Derivatives Markets and the Commodity Exchange Act." November. https://home.treasury.gov/system/files/236/Over-the-Counter-Derivatives-Market-Commodity-Exchange-Act.pdf.
Volcker, Paul A. 1985a. "Statement by Paul A. Volcker." Testimony before House Subcommittee on Banking, Finance and Urban Affairs, U.S. House of Representatives, April 17. https://fraser.stlouisfed.org/title/statements-speeches-paul-a-volcker-451/statement-subcommittee-financial-institutions-supervision-regulation-committee-banking-finance-urban-affairs-house-representatives-8319.
Volcker, Paul A. 1985b. "Statement by Paul A. Volcker." Testimony before House Subcommittee on Banking, Finance and Urban Affairs, U.S. House of Representatives, April 24.
Volcker, Paul A. 2008. "Rethinking the Bright New World of Global Finance." *International Finance* 11 (1): 101–107.
Wall Street Journal. 2008. "No Line Responsibilities: What Robert Rubin Did for His $155 Million." December 3.
Wolf, Martin. 2014. *The Shifts and the Shocks: What We've Learned—and Have Still to Learn—from the Financial Crisis*. Penguin.
Zeleny, Jeff. 2009. "Financial Industry Paid Millions to Obama Aide." *Washington Post*, April 3.

4

When Hegemony Mostly Worked

U.S. Relations with Europe and Japan during the 1990s

Michael Mastanduno

Realist theories of international relations rest on familiar assumptions. States are sovereign but coexist in an anarchical setting in which security and even survival are somewhat uncertain. The accumulation of material power, both military and economic, is therefore prudent. The more power, the better to assure security, territorial integrity, and foreign policy autonomy. At times alliances with other states make tactical sense; alliances, however, tend to be temporary and timebound as states continually recalculate the utility and necessity of alliances based on changing threats and interests.

International relations theorists will continue the long debate over the extent to which these assumptions prove useful in explaining contemporary and historical interstate relations. In retrospect, however, these realist assumptions and the arguments that followed from them proved of limited value when it came to anticipating the international order of the 1990s, especially relations among would-be great powers, after the end of the Cold War.

Prominent realists anticipated a relatively rapid return to multipolarity, the "normal" world of international relations that persisted for three hundred years before collapsing during two world wars into the extraordinary era of superpower bipolarity.[1] With the Cold War over, Kenneth Waltz anticipated the demise of NATO, suggesting its days were not numbered, but its years were. He viewed Japan as "ready to reach the mantle" and take its place as an independent great power.[2] The multipolar world would be more complex, and more conflict-prone, than the relatively stable if often stressful bipolar world. Focusing on Europe, John Mearsheimer foresaw a multipolar structure "substantially more prone to violence" than the four-decade bipolar order.[3] Focusing on Asia, Aaron Friedberg considered the region "ripe for rivalry" for an array of domestic and international reasons,

Michael Mastanduno, *When Hegemony Mostly Worked*. In: *Rethinking the 1990s*. Edited by: G. John Ikenberry and Peter Trubowitz, Oxford University Press. © Oxford University Press (2025).
DOI: 10.1093/9780197813133.003.0004

including the likely U.S. disentanglement from its now anachronistic Cold War commitments.[4] With the collapse of the Soviet Empire and Russia's descent into political and economic instability, many anticipated that the United States, a reunified Germany, and Japan would act as normal great powers, engaging "head to head" in the "cold peace" of economic competition while developing independent and possibly conflicting foreign policy interests and strategies.[5]

The anticipated return of a multipolar system underestimated two possibilities. First, two of the most likely candidates in the anticipated great power contest, Germany and Japan, might choose not to play, for reasons either domestic or cultural, or because they had foreign policy incentives to remain civilian or partial great powers rather than transform into independent, power-maximizing powers. Second, the United States might not be content to default to the role of an ordinary great power in a reconstituted multipolar order. The collapse of its principal rival and its sizable lead in relative capabilities might tempt the United States to act as an extraordinary power.

This second possibility was well-established as an alternative strand of realist theory. In addition to the balance of power, hegemony, based on the dominance of a single state, could serve as a source of stability and order in the emerging international system.[6] Gilpin's realism offered an alternative to that of Waltz.[7] The underlying intuition of hegemonic stability, prominent in the study of international political economy, also applied more broadly to international political and security orders.

Yet, as the Cold War was ending, theorists of hegemony were focused far more on U.S. decline than on America's possible role as architect and champion of a post–Cold War international order. The narrative of U.S. decline emerged during the 1970s and persisted through the 1980s in the context of the collapse of Bretton Woods, the economic recovery of Western Europe and Japan, the OPEC revolution, and the humiliating U.S. retreat from Vietnam along with the domestic turmoil that accompanied it. Gilpin advanced the decline argument most systematically in *War and Change*. His theoretical and historical insights about decreased growth rates, increased consumption, and the corrupting effects of affluence seemed directly applicable to the United States of the late 1980s.[8] Paul Kennedy popularized similar arguments foreshadowing U.S. decline in his famous book published almost precisely as the Cold War ended.[9] One big policy takeaway was that *both* the Soviet Union and the United States, in effect, lost the Cold War. The winners were those civilian economic powerhouses, Germany and Japan, who reaped the benefits of U.S. military protection and outcompeted an America exhausted by defense spending and the related economic burdens of imperial overstretch.

Academic realists, in short, overestimated the likelihood of multipolarity and underestimated the potential for hegemony. Nonetheless, in this instance political actors perceived an opportunity that was less apparent to realist theorists. U.S. policymakers and the foreign policy establishment, surveying the landscape that emerged after the unexpected yet peaceful end of the Cold War, did appreciate hegemony's potential. The normal workings of great power politics might (and did!) reemerge over the longer term, but the shorter and medium term offered, in a "unipolar moment," the opportunity to remake international order.

During the 1990s, U.S. leaders seized the opportunity to pursue hegemony. Their most important foreign policy project—the consolidation and deepening of the Western-centered hegemonic order, which had been forged by successive U.S. administrations during the Cold War—succeeded. In dealing with Europe and Japan during the 1990s, U.S. policymakers got hegemony mostly right. They preserved and strengthened an alliance advantage that, today, is the envy of competing great powers.

Beyond the Western core, however, U.S. policymakers proved too ambitious and overplayed their hand. The extension of the liberal hegemonic project into new regions (e.g., the Middle East during the 2000s) and to potential authoritarian challengers, a defeated Russia and emergent China, eventually failed. Where they came up short was less a function of imperial overstretch (the need to make hard choices in the face of resource constraints) and more a problem of liberal internationalist overreach (the temptation to push hegemony beyond what world politics, domestic politics, and the world economy could bear).[10]

Liberal Hegemony and the Roads Not Taken

"Hegemony" is an overused yet loosely defined term in international relations. Some use it simply as a synonym for preponderant power, while others equate it with leadership or the functional management of political and economic relations. For some (think U.S. liberal internationalists), the term connotes enlightened and benign behavior; for others (think Xi Jinping and

Chinese critics of the West), it is associated with political manipulation or the coercive imposition of one's values on others. Analytically, the key point is that hegemony is simultaneously material and relational.[11] A hegemonic order is hierarchical; one state possesses significantly more material capabilities than do others. But hegemony also involves state relationships and, specifically, some meaningful degree of acceptance and consent by supporting states. Rather than the mere imposition of dominant power, hegemony requires legitimacy, or the acceptance by subordinate powers of the dominant state's position and role. Hegemony encompasses both dominance and consent. Hegemonic orders differ both from empires, which rely more on formal and coercive political relationships, and balance of power systems, which sustain order through the rough equivalence of power among states instead of through hierarchy.

Hegemonic orders are based on tacit political deals between the dominant power and subordinate or supporting powers. Supporting states "buy into" the arrangement to obtain material benefits, such as security protection or economic prosperity based on aid or market access, as well as political or ideational status.[12] Dominant states obtain supporters for their preferred international order. They also get to make the "rules of the game" by advancing norms and institutions that reflect their values and advance their interests. Hegemonic bargains are based more on diffuse reciprocity—each side gets a different and possibly asymmetrical set of benefits that endure over time—than on explicit transactions.

Hegemonic orders are difficult to create and sustain. They require sovereign states, including potentially powerful ones, to subordinate willingly their foreign policies and possibly adapt their domestic political orders to the preferences of a leading state. For its part, the hegemon must both maintain material dominance and exercise sufficient restraint in its foreign policy to reassure others of its benign intent.[13] Not surprisingly, in a world of sovereign states, and especially among potential great powers, the effective combination of subordination and consent on the one hand and domination and restraint on the other is relatively rare.

As Ian Clark observes, although the post-1945 world is commonly referred to as the era of U.S. hegemony, the United States was hegemonic only over a relatively small, albeit important, part of the world.[14] America's two key partners, West Germany and Japan, were situated in Western Europe, the central front of the Cold War, and East Asia, where the actual wars of the Cold War were fought. When the Cold War ended, U.S.

policymakers sought to deepen and broaden liberal hegemony—the pursuit of a consensual, U.S.-led and -centered international order that reflected American values and interests.

Although, with the benefit of hindsight, it might appear as such, the U.S. pursuit of liberal hegemony after the Cold War was neither a political imperative nor a foregone conclusion. In U.S. domestic politics during the first half of the 1990s, there were plausible alternatives to both the "liberal" and the "hegemony" components of liberal hegemony. The alternative to the former was an emphasis on economic nationalism. A popular argument in the United States as the Cold War ended was that U.S. trading partners were free-riding on U.S. defense efforts and violating the rules of free trade to outcompete U.S. firms and take away U.S. jobs. America experienced a severe recession at the beginning of the 1990s, which amplified the political salience of domestic economic issues and focused attention on the seemingly predatory practices of U.S. allies and economic partners.

In the 1992 presidential election, the economic nationalist cause was taken up by a third-party candidate, Ross Perot. Perot campaigned as an outsider and fiscal conservative, railing against free-spending Washington insiders from both mainstream parties. America's enemy was no longer the red flag of communism, he proclaimed, but the red ink of national debt. Perot opposed the North American Free Trade Agreement (NAFTA), infamously claiming that it created a "giant sucking sound" as U.S. manufacturing jobs exited for Mexico. In a preview of the Trump campaign two decades later, Perot was a businessman who embraced the mantle of American populism, claiming to speak for everyday Americans neglected by the U.S. political establishment and exploited by rapacious foreigners.[15] Economic nationalist policies followed naturally from his worldview: America needed to be tougher on its trading partners, skeptical of free trade agreements, and willing to extract burden-sharing commitments from its free-riding allies. Perot proposed that Japan and Germany contribute a combined $100 billion to the U.S. Treasury to defray U.S. defense costs and draw down the U.S. national debt.

Perot captured a noteworthy 19 percent of the popular vote in the 1992 election, despite the disadvantages of being an outsider in a two-party system, running a disorganized and unprofessional campaign, and unexpectedly and temporarily dropping out of the presidential race during the crucial summer months of 1992. Nevertheless, he tapped into a considerable segment of the electorate that, notwithstanding the Cold War victory, was frustrated economically and saw little cause for celebration. Writing in *Foreign Affairs* in 1992, Norman Ornstein characterized U.S. political sentiment as "disgust, disaffection, and disarray" and observed that the end of the Cold War brought not "the thrill of victory, but the agony of victory."[16] Perot's populist appeal (like Trump's in 2016), however limited, suggested potential political space for an alternative to liberal internationalism.

How, then, did international economic liberalism prevail? The winning candidate in 1992, Bill Clinton, similarly focused on domestic economic issues, accusing incumbent President George Bush of presiding over the death of communism abroad and the loss of the American dream at home. Clinton's solution, however, was to redouble support for liberal internationalist policies. "Protectionism," he argued, was a fancy word for giving up. The United States needed to compete internationally and win. His message to U.S. trade partners was that America preferred open competition, but if others insisted on not playing by those rules, the United States would adjust and respond. Clinton also effectively linked liberal trade policy to liberal foreign policy more generally. Support for democratic enlargement, he argued, would serve the U.S. domestic economy by creating more jobs for exporters and would enhance U.S. security since relations among democratic states tended to be peaceful.[17]

Clinton's political framing proved effective because in the early 1990s (as opposed to, say, 2016), the political landscape in the United States on balance still favored economic liberalism. Although pressure was mounting (for example, labor shifted its support to protectionism in the 1970s and 1980s), the principle of free trade and the lessons of the 1930s still commanded a bipartisan consensus within the foreign policy establishment. Politically, support for free trade was not the domestic liability it became for both Democrats and Republicans in subsequent decades. International economic institutions bolstered economic liberalism's appeal; Clinton presided over the transition from the General Agreement on Tariffs and Trade (GATT) to the World Trade Organization (WTO), with a promise to open untapped markets to U.S. exporters and a new dispute settlement mechanism to protect U.S. firms and workers from predatory trade practices abroad. At home, corporate interests in finance, services, and technology championed economic openness, and that powerful coalition threw its political weight behind the Uruguay Round's liberal trade agenda, integrating China into the world economy and promoting the Washington Consensus in support of globalization abroad.

If economic nationalism was the alternative to the liberal part of liberal hegemony, the alternative to the hegemony part was a strategy of restraint. The logic of restraint was articulated in the mid-1990s by scholars seeking to update or "reconfigure" isolationism for a new era in American foreign policy.[18] The key policy idea was military withdrawal, or "the disengagement of America's military forces from the rest of the world."[19] Restraint advocates argued the United States should remain engaged in the world economy and international diplomacy but, in recognition that the Cold War was an extraordinary circumstance, should gradually unwind its forward military positions and resist the temptation to engage in military interventions. Notwithstanding its preponderant power, the United States should abandon its self-appointed roles as regional stabilizer and global policeman.

Although firmly rooted in American history and political tradition, in the early 1990s, on the heels of America's Cold War triumph, it was geopolitically implausible for restraint to emerge full-blown as an alternative grand strategy. It gained little traction in a foreign policy establishment accustomed to a U.S. global role. Restraint did surface within both political parties, as the end of the Cold War removed the existential threat that motivated a broad foreign policy consensus. However, support for restraint was confined to the political periphery. On the Democrat side, it was endorsed by presidential contenders Tom Harkin and Jerry Brown, each of whom promoted a version of "Come home, America" in the 1992 primaries. On the Republican side, candidate Pat Buchanan delivered a wake-up call to the incumbent George H. W. Bush by winning 37 percent of the vote in the New Hampshire Republican primary. Buchanan argued that absent the Cold War the United States did not have vital interests to defend abroad. He called for ending foreign aid, dissolving the U.S-Japan security treaty, removing troops from Europe, and cutting funding to the IMF and World Bank.[20] Trump's campaign themes, twenty-four years later, embraced the "America First" approach of Buchanan, alongside the populism of Perot, in very different domestic and international circumstances.[21]

Although by no means dominant, the idea of restraint, or at least of doing less in foreign policy, surfaced in U.S. public sentiment as well. Public opinion was divided over U.S. intervention in the 1990–1991 Persian Gulf War, as reflected in close votes in the Senate and House in response to President Bush's request for congressional authorization. Notwithstanding the Cold War triumph and America's relative power advantage, the Bush administration appreciated that the specter of Vietnam-like quagmires remained fresh in the public mind and the public's tolerance for an activist foreign policy was limited. In the Persian Gulf crisis, Bush prioritized building the broadest possible international coalition to reassure the public that the United States was not acting as a lone sheriff. He emphasized that U.S. objectives were limited to removing Iraq from Kuwait and did not extend to regime change.[22] Bush's decisive victory, at remarkably low cost in terms of U.S. casualties, was critical in making the case that the United States could play an activist, global role in the post–Cold War world without incurring disproportionate burdens at home.

President Clinton was similarly sensitive to amorphous public concerns about "doing too much" in foreign policy and proved reluctant to commit to military intervention. He waited four years before engaging militarily in Bosnia, pulled out of Somalia at the first sign of trouble, and sidestepped genocide in Rwanda.[23] However, Clinton was far more cautious in undertaking military *intervention* than he was in reestablishing and expanding military *commitments*. As the discussion below will show, his administration reaffirmed and expanded security commitments in Europe and Asia and embraced the hegemonic role of having the United States act as a regional crisis stabilizer. Clinton had sufficient domestic space to pursue hegemony quietly, provided the costs, in terms of lives and resources, were neither high nor immediately apparent domestically.

The strategy of hegemony, prudently applied, won out over the restraint impulse. But in the immediate aftermath of the Cold War, there was one other strategic alternative to hegemony. Given America's formidable relative power advantage, primacy, or the attempt to exploit that advantage, impose U.S. preferences (if necessary, unilaterally) on others, and keep potential great power challengers at bay by weakening their material capabilities was also a grand strategic candidate. The Bush administration's now infamous 1992 defense guidance strategy seemed to imply primacy.[24] It argued that the United States should prevent the emergence of peer competitors and should not allow any other power to combine material capability and hostile intent to pose the type of challenge to American dominance represented by the Soviet Union during the Cold War. That document, leaked to the press in 1992, clearly suggested that the United States had the interest and capacity to repress possible international challengers.

A strategy of primacy, as the George W. Bush administration learned after September 11, 2001, had the potential to be costly domestically and provocative internationally. It could rouse a public more determined to focus on domestic priorities and could trigger a balancing coalition against a unipolar United States. Perhaps not surprisingly, the first Bush and Clinton teams disavowed the primacy logic of the 1992 guidance and promoted multilateralism and U.S. leadership (i.e., the logic of hegemony) as a less costly and more diplomatically palatable alternative. Instead of pushing down would-be great powers, they believed that the way to discourage peer competition was to give all potential great powers, Cold War allies as well as adversaries, a stake in a U.S-led and U.S.-defined international order. Creating a set of supporters, or "responsible stakeholders," meant strengthening them materially in the expectation that they could be enticed to act as junior partners in the American hegemonic project. In the liberal bet of U.S. policymakers, the material gains Russia and China would enjoy from participation in the liberal world economy would be offset by their transformed behavior domestically and by more cooperative foreign policies. For their part, Japan and the new Germany would be locked into "Cold War plus"—their growing economic and military strength, and more activist regional behavior, would be nurtured and managed within the confines of enduring U.S. alliance structures. These Cold War allies were already responsible stakeholders; the United States would encourage them to embrace that role and take on new responsibilities commensurate with their growing hard and soft power.

In short, during the formative decade of the 1990s, U.S. policymakers faced some domestic constraints but were largely unencumbered internationally. Liberal hegemony prevailed over economic nationalism, strategic restraint, or the quest for international primacy.

Hegemonic relationships, however, do not run themselves on autopilot. They need to be cultivated and managed. The U.S. task in Europe and Asia in the 1990s was to keep its Cold War allies embedded and satisfied in an international order while establishing sustained U.S. control over the character of that order. Dominance and consent needed to go hand in hand as the key components of American hegemony.

The next two sections detail America's successful hegemonic effort in relations with Europe and Japan during the first crucial decade after the Cold War. An effective, albeit limited hegemonic order was sustained and now offers the United States the critical alliance advantage it enjoys as it reenters a world of great power competition today. America's success, however, was not unqualified. The setbacks, the costs of which also accumulated over time, had little to do with the expected perils of hegemonic decline. The United States neither faced debilitating resource constraints nor abdicated the leadership responsibilities implied by its side of the hegemonic bargain. The problem instead was overreach. In both international economic and security policy, U.S. hegemony was the victim of its own success. The aggressive promotion of neoliberalism, and its international and domestic consequences, helped to undermine support for U.S. hegemony at home. NATO expansion, a critical part of liberal hegemony, was carried far enough east to alienate Russia and encourage it to be a spoiler rather than a perhaps grudging supporter. If the U.S. hegemonic strategy during the 1990s could be faulted, it would be for doing too much rather than too little.

Maintaining Hegemony in Europe: Anchoring Germany, Managing European Integration, and Expanding NATO

The 1990s were a transformative decade in Europe, witnessing more significant political developments than at any time since the 1940s. Germany reunified. Europe integrated, aspired to a common foreign policy, and, by the end of the decade, had abandoned long-standing domestic currencies for a common one. NATO endured without an existential enemy and expanded eastward. The collapse of Yugoslavia resulted in the first major war on European soil since World War II. In the face of these profound structural and political changes, the United States managed to preserve and renew its postwar hegemonic partnerships. It supported European efforts to integrate economically and politically and develop a more unified foreign policy, while at the same time making certain that the entire European project served U.S. interests and was subordinated to the broader transatlantic hegemonic order. U.S. policymakers promoted the continuation of dominant-subordinate relations, making clear they would not tolerate challenges to their rule-making authority, economic and strategic preferences, or dominant material position. A brief examination of the most salient European developments during the 1990s illustrates the core hegemonic dynamic.

The German Question

German reunification was the most important geopolitical outcome of the post–Cold War settlement. The specific resolution, that of a unified and more powerful Germany playing essentially the same military role in NATO as had West Germany during the Cold War, was neither preordained nor the only possibility. Soviet leaders preferred alternative security arrangements— the dissolution of NATO in favor of a pan-European security institution, a neutral Germany, or even Germany in NATO but with a circumscribed military role.[25] The United States enjoyed the relative power advantage; it was eager to support German unification, but only on its own terms. Anchoring the new Germany in NATO signaled to the collapsing Soviets, and to Germany's uneasy neighbors, east and west, that this new potential great power in the center of Europe would not be independent, but instead would remain embedded within an existing military alliance dominated by the United States. Germany could become, in Beverly Crawford's phrase, an "embedded hegemon" in Europe, its regional hegemony subsumed within the broader U.S. hegemonic order.[26] Given rapid Soviet decline, Soviet leaders were left with little choice than to accept America's preference and work with NATO to manage their long-standing German problem. If, in Lord Ismay's famous phrase, the original purpose of NATO was to keep the Americans in, the Russians out, and the Germans down, to the Bush administration NATO's new purpose was to keep the Americans dominant, bring the Germans up, and keep the Russians engaged yet acquiescent.

The U.S. preference that the new Germany land in the old NATO was not negotiable. U.S. power and West German preferences drove that outcome. But the relational dimension of hegemony, specifically the need to assure that subordinate partners had a stake in outcomes affecting them, suggested that Germany should manage the negotiating process. Bush and Secretary of State James Baker were careful to avoid the appearance of a "new Yalta" in which great powers decided the fates of secondary states not at the table.[27] Instead, as Horst Teltschik, German national security advisor to West German chancellor Helmut Kohl recounted, President Bush conveyed to Kohl and Germany an unexpected offer of "partnership in leadership."[28] Bush and Kohl coordinated closely on the diplomacy of reunification, but Kohl took the lead. President Mikhail Gorbachev of the USSR trusted Kohl, and Kohl convinced him to trust Bush and the Germany-in-NATO solution as well. The deal was sealed in July 1990, not in a superpower summit but in meetings between Kohl and Gorbachev. Bush, in turn, helped convince a skeptical Margaret Thatcher, U.K. prime minister, to trust Kohl and support the unification process. Germany took the financial lead alongside the negotiating lead, putting together the massive aid package that Gorbachev extracted in exchange for his acquiescence.[29]

In a retrospective essay, Baker credited Bush with engineering "the mother of all soft landings" in simultaneously ending the Cold War and unifying Germany.[30] But the soft landing was informed by hard American power and clear purpose. The United States was eager to craft a post–Cold War settlement but had no interest in a twentieth-century version of the Concert of Europe, a set of agreements among independent great powers interacting in a multipolar setting. It sought instead a dominant role with the consent of subordinate yet loyal partners.

Managing European Integration and the Euro

In the late 1940s, U.S. policymakers contemplated the possibility that a recovered and integrated Western Europe might evolve into an independent "third force" in world politics.[31] As the division of Europe hardened, however, so too did the U.S. position on European integration. Western Europe fell on the U.S. side of the Cold War divide. West European integration was welcome if it was subsumed under and contributed to the collective strength of the U.S.-led alliance rather than challenging it, working at cross-purposes to it, or leaving West European states to float independently between the two blocs.

The European integration question reemerged after the Cold War. The Single European Act of 1986 envisioned an integration process deeper than the at-the-border customs union, with expanding membership, that evolved from the Treaty of Rome in 1957. Europe aspired to a stronger supranational identity, a single integrated market, a common currency, a European parliament, and a coordinated foreign and defense policy. German unification accelerated the process since Germany and France, the main engines of deeper integration, each placed a high priority on binding the new Germany more tightly into the collective European project. Simultaneously, the end of the Cold War offered European leaders more geopolitical space and less incentive to rely on the United States. Luxembourg's foreign minister Jacques Poos famously declared in the context of the Bosnian crisis, "[T]he hour of

Europe has dawned."[32] An integrated Europe could, at least potentially, go its own way.

In the face of fluid geopolitics and renewed impetus for integration, the United States stuck with its successful Cold War formula. The Bush and Clinton administrations welcomed deeper European integration provided it took place under the umbrella of U.S. hegemony. The integration process could neither challenge U.S. material dominance nor contradict core U.S. preferences in security and economics. On the security side, U.S. officials encouraged collective European defense efforts on the condition they were building blocks instead of stumbling blocks in terms of the NATO defense effort. Clinton administration defense officials prioritized interoperability, or the capacity of European militaries to work side by side with their more technologically sophisticated alliance partner in NATO intervention scenarios.[33]

Transatlantic economic relations posed a greater challenge. One rationale for Europe's single market was efficiency, to be achieved by eliminating more than one dozen different sets of rules and standards governing production, investment, and trade. A second rationale was neo-mercantilist: the single market could give European countries and firms greater clout in the economic competition with the world's dominant players, the United States and Japan. The single market could evolve into a "Fortress Europe" characterized by state- or region-led industrial policies, protectionist barriers, and the cultivation of European national champions, all designed to tip the massive single market to European rather than North American or East Asian traders and investors.[34] The protectionist threat was well-founded during the early 1990s as the Uruguay Round negotiations of the GATT were mired in stalemate and both Europe and Japan resented the aggressive unilateral trade tactics of the United States.[35]

The response of the Bush and Clinton administrations was consistent with enduring U.S. preferences for a neoliberal world economy characterized by the free flow of trade and investment. U.S. policymakers insisted that Europe's single market must be open, facing outward instead of inward. U.S. trade officials employed multiple tools to prod the single market in their preferred direction. The emergence of NAFTA signaled that the United States also had a neo-mercantilist regional option; if Europe wished to move to a world of competing and possibly preferential economic blocs, the United States could play as well. Alternatively, the two sides could agree that NAFTA and the single European market would be building blocks to the American-style, "behind the border" world economy the United States was simultaneously pushing in the Uruguay Round, with new rules covering services trade, investment, and intellectual property. The successful completion of the Round in 1994, along with the launching of the WTO, reflected those U.S. preferences. Equally important, the United States exercised self-restraint by committing to de-emphasize its coercive and unilateral trade tactics in exchange for European and global adherence to a more enforceable dispute settlement mechanism under the new WTO.

The emergence of the euro implied an additional possible challenge to U.S. hegemony. The postwar dominance of the dollar as an unchallenged global reserve and exchange currency was foundational to U.S. power and hegemonic privilege. U.S. policymakers took full advantage; their willingness to run deficits while foreign central banks accumulated dollar reserves facilitated U.S. power projection abroad and the opportunity to put off difficult trade-offs across consumption, investment, and defense at home. The euro, a currency with the backing of an advanced market economy the size of America's, could challenge the dollar's privileged position in a way that individual national currencies, even the powerful German mark, could not.

The European monetary union project posed a dilemma for the United States. On one hand, it would be politically awkward to promote and support Europe's overall integration project and outward-facing single market yet oppose the common currency that was an integral part of the plan. On the other hand, any viable challenge to dollar dominance would be unwelcome, even if that challenge came from a collection of economic competitors who were also U.S. allies.

The United States was fortunate to have it both ways. It could support the euro with confidence that the new currency would not pose a meaningful challenge to dollar dominance. As Benjamin Cohen argues, strong currencies do not automatically generate political power or foreign policy influence. For the euro to challenge the dollar's privileged role, European authorities would have to exploit the new currency's potential to be a prominent exchange and reserve currency, for example by maximizing its liquidity and encouraging its routine use beyond the eurozone.[36] The euro's role, however, reflected the preferences of Germany, its most powerful member, and the inflation-sensitive German authorities had little interest in running deficits to enhance the euro's appeal as a global currency. Equally important, as a subordinate partner bound to the United States, Germany had little interest in cultivating on Europe's behalf the type of independent and ambitious foreign policy that a powerful global currency could support. In terms of currency competition, the euro turned out to be a supporter rather than a challenger. In Kate McNamara's phrase, the euro served as a "hegemony helper," offering foreign central banks some diversification to the currency of America's partners, while not taking the steps needed to challenge or displace the dollar's privileged global role.[37] In the case of the euro, as in the case of America's European partners more generally, the essential structure of the EU—a coordinated economic powerhouse that never effectively made the leap to become a functioning sovereign state with a potentially independent foreign policy—played to the benefit of U.S. hegemony.

NATO and U.S. Hegemonic Enlargement

Although anchoring the new Germany provided the immediate rationale for maintaining NATO, by itself it was insufficient to justify the long-term necessity of a military alliance that no longer faced its motivating threat. By the early 1990s, the slogan "Out of area or out of business" was popular among NATO observers. NATO did go out of area, in the Bosnian crises of the 1990s and in Afghanistan during the 2000s and beyond. But the out-of-area role was reactive, forcing NATO members to respond (or not) to events around the world for which they often had different interests or perspectives.

Enlargement proved to be a more proactive and unifying mission for NATO. From the perspective of U.S. hegemony, expanding NATO to the east held two advantages. First, it meant broadening the geographic scope of the U.S.-centered order and bringing in new partners on terms preferred by the United States. NATO membership, or entry into the military section of the coveted Western club, was conditional on U.S.-approved developments, including political and economic liberalization, the resolution of border disputes, and civilian control of the military. Second, enlarging NATO offered a stakeholder role to America's existing hegemonic partners in Europe. Current NATO members had a say over which candidate states could join the club and on what terms and time frame. European Union states, which overlapped significantly with NATO states, could run a parallel membership drive, setting conditions for accession to the economic and political section of the Western club. Although it played no formal role in the parallel EU process, the United States supported it since the EU's membership terms reflected and reinforced the values preferred by the United States.

The direct and indirect European expansion of the U.S. hegemonic order was set in motion during the latter half of the 1990s. From the outset, the complication was Russia. Russia could not be part of NATO or the EU, but its leaders would find troubling Western efforts to expand into its former sphere of superpower influence. This would be true for reasons of geopolitics, regardless of whether one believes that the United States pledged not to expand NATO militarily even "one inch" beyond the borders of the former Federal Republic of Germany.[38]

During the 1990s, the United States and its European supporters seemed confident of their ability to finesse the Russia problem. The U.S. plan was for Russia as well to be integrated into the U.S.-centered economic and political order, even if on different terms.[39] It was impractical for Russia to join NATO, but the United States could offer Russia the consolation prize of an ongoing consultative relationship with NATO through the Partnership for Peace. Russia was not an advanced economic power, but the Clinton administration offered it status in the form of membership in the West's economic governance club, the G-7. Western officials dangled before Russia the prospect of prosperity through integration in the liberal world economy, on the condition of Russian economic reform. The logic was that victorious Western governments could provide just enough carrots to enlist Russia's grudging acquiescence in a plan to eliminate the division of Europe on Western terms.

Two developments, arguably foreseeable by U.S. leaders, suggested that the balancing act of engaging Russia while expanding NATO was not viable. First, as the sluggishness of Russia's recovery and the persistence of a relative power gap, in both material and prestige terms, in favor of the United States became apparent, U.S. foreign policy leaders became less interested in reassuring or placating Russia and more in pushing their enlargement agenda forward. As President Clinton famously asserted, NATO expansion was a question of not whether, but when.[40] Russia, in effect, could take it or leave it, with no say in the execution of the U.S. plan. Second, alongside U.S. power, the American style of hegemony made it likely enlargement would take on a life of its own. In the first part of John Ikenberry's well-known phrase, America's liberal hegemonic order was "easy to join," that is, open to any state willing to subordinate itself to U.S. preferences and possess (or, if necessary, cultivate) the proper political and economic credentials.[41] By implication, the enlargement process would always be as much "demand pull" as "supply push." Members with acceptable credentials, or the promise to work on them, pressed their case for admission regardless of, or perhaps because of their geographic proximity to Russia. It became hard to say no to the "nth" candidate, even when it happened to be, like Ukraine or Georgia, perceived by Russia as situated on the other side of a red line.

The NATO expansion of the 1990s was a hegemonic success yet ultimately the victim of that success. It went too far and fueled an inevitable and negative action-reaction dynamic between the United States and Russia. Even if, as Michael Cox argues in this volume, the prospects for genuine U.S.-Russian partnerships were unlikely, Russian leaders perceived NATO's seemingly relentless expansion as provocative and responded in kind by attempting to enforce a sphere of influence, however diminished. Russia's aggressive behavior, in turn, confirmed the necessity and far-sighted wisdom of expansion and created greater urgency for states close to Russia to seek shelter under the NATO umbrella. The United States overreached, pushing its hegemonic aspiration beyond what was geopolitically prudent. Russian weakness abetted U.S. overreach, while Russian behavior helped justify it.

Reasserting Hegemony in East Asia: Suppressing and Anchoring Japan

U.S. hegemony in East Asia during the Cold War was limited and incomplete.[42] The United States secured bilateral, "hub and spoke" partnerships with East Asian allies, most importantly Japan. After the Cold War, U.S. officials tried to create a new subordinate spoke tied to the U.S. hub by integrating an emerging China into the U.S.-led hegemonic order. That ambitious effort ultimately failed. But the United States undertook an equally important parallel effort during the 1990s: to secure Japan's continued cooperation as a loyal yet subordinate economic and security supporter. The maintenance of hegemony required the United States to suppress Japan's economic challenge while not alienating it from the U.S.-led economic order. It also required enabling Japan to expand its security role and footprint in the East Asian region, but under the auspices of the U.S. alliance rather than as an independent great power. The Japan strategy pursued by U.S. policymakers succeeded. The eventual failure of America's China strategy only highlighted the importance of keeping Japan on side.

Suppression and Integration: A Hegemonic Response to Japan's Economic Challenge

The transformation of Japan from brutal adversary to indispensable partner was a remarkable achievement of U.S. Cold War diplomacy. The United States turned Japan, an autocracy that used military force to acquire what it needed economically, into a durable democracy and trading state, a civilian power loyal to and dependent on the United States. By the 1990s, it was clear that the U.S. strategy was perhaps too successful. Japan became an export superpower. Its export-led growth, dependent primarily on the open U.S. market, helped it become the world's second largest national economy. Japan's producers and exporters moved up the value chain, from reliance on inexpensive goods like textiles to industrial goods like autos and machine tools and eventually to advanced technology, mastering semiconductors, computers, and satellites. Japanese economic success, coupled with reliance on the U.S. market, posed a political problem for the United States. Import penetration, symbolized by persistent bilateral trade imbalances, positioned Japan as culpable for the loss of U.S. jobs, leading to "Japan bashing" and public and congressional pressure on successive U.S. administrations to respond. Bilateral trade disputes were endemic from the 1970s through the 1990s.

By the end of the Cold War, the deeper challenge was hegemonic. Assuming it remained a military ally, Japan would not pose a traditional power transition challenge to the United States. But hegemony relied on U.S. economic as well as military dominance, and on the economic side, Japan's challenge was both material and relational. By the late 1980s, Japan was the only state capable of competing with, and in some cases overtaking, the United States in the upper reaches of technologies that had both commercial and military applications. The Soviet Union never posed that type of challenge, European countries were perpetually behind, and China had yet to emerge. U.S. anxiety about Japan's competitive challenge was pervasive at elite and popular levels; public opinion polls during the early 1990s suggested Japan was a greater overall threat to U.S. security than was the Soviet Union.[43] A frustrated U.S. trade official warned that the once dominant United States and Japan were now "trading places."[44]

Japan's success also posed a challenge to U.S. hegemonic status and rule-making authority. To U.S. policymakers, Japan was not beating the United States at its own game but seemed to be playing a different game, and one not in keeping with America's preferred rules of liberal capitalism, where market forces and the calculations of private actors presumably dominated.[45] Instead, Japan engaged in an effective form of state-led capitalism. One-party rule facilitated a consistent long-term strategy, while powerful bureaucrats favored producers rather than consumers, protected the home market, used industrial policy to pick winners, and allocated resources to assure the success of Japanese companies abroad.[46] Even if Japan had little interest in exporting its model along with its products, U.S. officials worried that other countries might emulate the Japanese state-led model in the hope of replicating Japanese success. Rather than engage in a post–Cold War competition among varieties of capitalism, the United States preferred that national economies and global economic rules converged on its own liberal model.

The more consequential risk to U.S. hegemonic authority, even if a somewhat low-probability one, was that a more powerful and successful Japan might rethink its subordinate status. That possibility was raised explicitly by an infamous publication, co-authored by a prominent Japanese nationalist and leading Japanese industrialist, that circulated during the early 1990s almost as an insurgent essay, complete with pirated English translations available in the United States.[47] The theme, captured by the title *The Japan That Can Say No*, was that Japan was now sufficiently strong and confident to abandon its traditional role as a "yes man" taking criticism and orders from a dominant yet declining United States. The book touted the advantages of the Japanese economic model. It depicted the U.S. model, with its emphasis on debt-driven consumption, as flawed and responsible for America's economic decline.

Former deputy minister of international trade and industry Hidehiro Konno, reflecting on the U.S. response to Japan's rise, observed that "when the U.S. thought Japan could be a threat to their status as a hegemon, they squeezed Japan with every means possible."[48] Konno was correct: the United States defended its dominance by attacking on multiple fronts. On the monetary front, in the Plaza Agreement of 1985, the United States used the credible domestic threat of protectionism to undercut Japan's export advantage by forcing a sharp revaluation of the yen.[49] The Japanese economy temporarily soared, but once price effects kicked in, economic growth succumbed to *endaka*, or the challenge of the high yen. When Japanese monetary authorities sought to take advantage of the strong yen to create an Asian Monetary Fund, enshrining the yen as the dominant currency in East Asia, the United States quickly shut it down.[50] On the trade front, U.S. officials exploited the controversial hegemonic privilege of violating rules it expected others to follow. It forced "voluntary" export restraints on Japan and called it out publicly as an unfair trader, bypassing the GATT and threatening sanctions on a tight timeline unless Japan opened its markets to U.S. products. On the investment front, U.S. policymakers pressured Japanese companies to open factories in the United States and employ U.S. labor as a substitute for Japanese exports. (Toyota was both compliant and successful; by 2021 it had become the largest auto producer in the United States.) On the rules front, the United States launched the Structural Impediments Initiative, an ongoing negotiation to undermine the structural features of Japan's state-led capitalism, including industrial policies, close cooperation between government agencies and Japanese firms, and practices (such as working on weekends) that favored producers over consumers.[51]

The U.S. response to Japan's economic challenge was aggressive and coordinated yet always circumscribed by the broader strategic relationship. Japan was America's principal economic competitor but also its most important Asian security partner. U.S. economic negotiators from the Reagan through the Clinton administrations consistently complained that the political and security side of the U.S. government stopped them from applying the full force of U.S. coercive power to beat back the Japanese challenge.[52] Reagan's defense secretary Caspar Weinberger's remark that maintaining night landing rights in Japan was more important to U.S. security than the survival of its machine tool industry was surely an exaggeration, but it did capture the priority U.S. leaders placed on security relations with Japan.[53] The alliance context also implied that while the United States was determined to assure its technological dominance, it was less interested in degrading Japanese economic capabilities than in assuring that those capabilities served broader U.S. foreign policy purposes. Unlike in the current competition with China, the United States had no interest in "decoupling" wholly or partially from Japan. Deep bilateral interdependence was welcomed (hence the demands that Japanese companies move production to the United States and that U.S. producers be allowed to export technology-intensive products like satellites and supercomputers to Japan) as long as Japan was a supporter rather than a challenger.

By the end of the 1990s the Japanese economic challenge had effectively disappeared. That outcome was caused plausibly by some combination of sustained U.S. pressure on Japanese economic practices, the mismanagement of Japan's domestic economy, and the inherent limitations of state-led capitalism, including the difficulty for governments to pick winners at the technological frontier. In any event, the U.S. hegemonic objective—deflect a challenger, but maintain a partner—was achieved. Deputy Minister Konno, reflecting on the bilateral struggles of the 1990s, put it well: "That story is now over. Japan is not a threat anymore; it is a mature economy and status quo power."[54]

Side by Side: Expanding the U.S.-Japanese Security Relationship

The U.S. security challenge in Europe was to manage the end of the Cold War. The East Asian challenge was different: to bring stability to a key geopolitical region where, notwithstanding the collapse of Soviet power, the Cold War had not quite ended. Unlike the division of Germany, that between North and South Korea persisted. The conflict over Taiwan outlived the Cold War. Each of these regional conflicts boiled over as North Korea brandished a nuclear threat in 1994 and China sought to intimidate Taiwan in 1995.

The U.S. response to a region ripe for rivalry was to extend its hegemony rather than step back and rely on a regional balance of power to emerge. The Clinton strategy of deep engagement implied that the United States, including its occupying military forces, would remain in East Asia indefinitely.[55] U.S. officials took on the role of regional stabilizer, acting as first responder to North Korea's nuclear provocations and deploying its navy to enforce deterrence in the China-Taiwan conflict of 1995. The liberal bet, the effort to facilitate China's growth while socializing it into the U.S. hegemonic order, also had its roots in the deep engagement strategy.

Reinvigorating the U.S.-Japanese partnership was a critical component of U.S. strategy. Absent a prominent U.S. regional role, an insecure Japan after the Cold War would have incentives to move in an independent direction. Like Germany, it had served its time in the penalty box of world politics and demonstrated it could be both powerful and responsible. Looking ahead, it could anticipate a nuclear threat from North Korea and a regional power transition with China. In the face of these calculations, America's signal of hegemonic reassurance to Japan was clear: "We are staying, the Cold War alliance endures, and for you to become an independent great power is neither necessary nor desirable."

It was never a partnership of equals, yet after the Cold War it needed to become somewhat more equal. This was for both strategic reasons—Japan possessed sophisticated military capabilities that would come in handy in any regional conflict—and political reasons, since in the absence of a more active Japanese regional role, the alliance might not withstand scrutiny in American domestic politics. The coalition politics of the 1990–1991 Persian Gulf War demonstrated the problem. Japan's sizable financial contribution was castigated in the U.S. press and Congress as "checkbook diplomacy"— the Japanese were donating money while Americans were risking their lives. Alliance proponents on both sides of the Pacific recognized that such a formula would be even harder to defend in the event of a military crisis in Japan's neighborhood.[56]

The obvious hegemonic strategy was for Japan to do more, yet within the confines of U.S. priorities and initiatives. U.S. political and security officials encouraged their Japanese counterparts to step up, and Japanese officials viewed positively the opportunity to be a more effective supporting partner. Japan's long-term goal, constrained by its domestic politics, was to fight "side by side" with the United States, aspiring to the type of special partnership that the United States possessed with the United Kingdom globally and with Germany regionally.[57] Beginning in the 1990s, Japanese leaders took small but meaningful steps in that direction. After September 11, 2001, Japan passed antiterrorist legislation enabling its navy to provide direct support to U.S. forces operating in waters proximate to Afghanistan. Subsequently, the Shinzo Abe government orchestrated a broader interpretation of Japan's Constitution, from allowing national to collective defense, paving the way for Japanese forces to support their U.S. counterparts more actively in the event of an East Asian military conflict. The United States, in turn, reaffirmed its commitment to Japan's territorial defense and clarified that Article V of their bilateral treaty even extended to the defense of the remote Senkaku/Diaoyu islands contested by Japan and China.

America's approach to Japan through the 1990s was a success in terms of hegemony. The United States suppressed Japan's economic challenge while keeping Japan integrated in the U.S.-led liberal economic order, and it facilitated a broader Japanese security role while maintaining Japan as a supporter rather than independent player. However, there are two qualifications to this overall assessment of U.S. effectiveness. On the security side, there was a missed opportunity to create trilateral security cooperation in Northeast Asia. Japan and South Korea are each long-standing allies of the United States, but their relations with each other have long been characterized by hostility and suspicion.[58] During the peak of its power and prestige in the 1990s, the United States might have placed a high priority on turning the hub-and-spoke architecture into an effective security triangle. It had potential leverage in that Japanese officials were consistently eager to cooperate with the United States on security issues as a way to downplay bilateral economic frictions. The United States did not exploit that opportunity during the 1990s; in recent years it has redoubled efforts at trilateral cooperation in the face of the possibility that a vulnerable South Korea might be coaxed away from the U.S. network by the charm offensive of a powerful China.[59]

On the economic side, the problem was overreach. The rapid opening of financial markets in East Asia, in line with the Washington Consensus, helped to trigger the Asian financial crisis of the late 1990s. The U.S. response to that crisis was not to rethink the pace of financial globalization and deregulation but to double down on it. The Asian crisis was a dress rehearsal for the broader and more profound global financial crisis a decade later, which helped to undermine, at home and abroad, support for globalization and the American model of liberal capitalism.

Conclusion

The 1990s offered ideal conditions for the United States to pursue hegemony. The U.S. relative power position was extraordinary, yet it was more admired than feared by other states. Its prestige peaked as it engineered a soft landing to end the Cold War. The ideological appeal of American democracy was widespread, and its economic performance was viewed globally with envy. Rarely does one country in a competitive international environment enjoy such advantages.

Not surprisingly in that context, a familiar critique is that the United States did too little internationally during the 1990s.[60] The Clinton administration was too cautious abroad because it was too deferential to a public weary of international commitments at home. It failed to create a sound financial footing for the UN, liberated from the Cold War standoff, to flourish. Liberal internationalists and neoconservatives disagreed on much but, as became apparent at the beginning of the next decade, shared the sense that U.S.

relative power could accommodate a more activist and purposeful foreign policy.

With the benefit of hindsight, the opposite argument emerges, namely that in several critical ways the United States did too much instead of too little. The expansion of NATO set in motion a process of strategic overreach, with neither sufficient public debate nor geopolitical foresight to anticipate how far was too far. The Russian invasion of Ukraine suggested there was a price to be paid, and not only by Russia. Similarly, the 1990s United States set the stage for overreach in both trade and finance. U.S. policymakers ignored or deflected public discontent over NAFTA and the WTO and pushed neoliberal trade policies to their economically logical yet politically fatal limit.[61] Neoliberalism maximized efficiency but created sufficiently wide disparities between economic winners and losers to undermine support for globalization at home. Abroad, the incessant push for deeper "behind the border" trade liberalization brought the WTO negotiating process to a now three-decade standstill. Financial liberalization, with the U.S. Treasury, IMF, and World Bank coordinating to deliver the same instructions to economies in very different circumstances, also went too far, triggering financial crises and eroding support for America's preferred economic model.

The temptation for overreach is comprehensible in the context of the 1990s. U.S. officials enjoyed preponderant power and believed world politics was moving inevitably in their preferred direction. The first line of the 2002 National Security Strategy captured the sentiment, stating that the great struggles of the twentieth century ended with freedom's decisive triumph and "a *single* sustainable model for national success": America's model.[62] Although U.S. foreign policy officials faced some domestic constraints, they were unfettered by geopolitical, economic, or ideological competitors. Unfettered states do not usually act prudently or with effective foresight. From today's vantage point, it is reasonable to look back to the 1990s and conclude that mistakes were made.

Yet it is important to keep this critical assessment in perspective. Keeping America's partners on side in the geopolitical uncertainty that followed the Cold War was a massive accomplishment, one that seems so obvious in retrospect that it might be tempting to overlook. Hegemony was not the only path for the United States and world politics after the Cold War; the United States consciously chose hegemony and, at least as it pertained to Western Europe and Japan, got it mostly right.

That achievement is even more significant when viewed in the context of today's very different international setting. Hegemony in a competitive international setting is always a long shot, but the liberal bet of trying to coax post–Cold War China and Russia into America's preferred international order was arguably worth taking. For the United States, the fact that power eventually balances power, and that great power competition has returned after an extended historical holiday, might be disappointing but should not be surprising. The most important legacy of the 1990s is that the United States enters that competition with an advantage that its great power challengers must envy: a network of loyal supporting partners who see substantial benefits in the U.S. hegemonic project and have proved willing to stick with it even when the United States itself has been ambivalent about it or, as in the case of Donald Trump's presidency, opening hostile to it.

Notes

1. Waltz 1993; Layne 1993.
2. Waltz 1993, 54–55.
3. Mearsheimer 1990.
4. Friedberg 1993–1994.
5. Thurow 1993; Garten 1992.
6. Gilpin 1981.
7. Wohlforth 2011.
8. Gilpin 1981, ch. 4.
9. Kennedy 1989.
10. Important recent books highlighting U.S. liberal internationalist overreach include Walt 2018; Mearsheimer 2019.
11. Clark 2011; Lake 2009.
12. Under U.S. hegemony, Japan and Germany transformed their identities from international pariahs to "responsible civilian powers." See Katzenstein 2005.
13. Ikenberry 2001.
14. Clark 2011, 123.
15. McGee 2020.
16. Ornstein 1992.
17. Boys 2021.
18. Nordlinger 1995; Gholz et al. 1997.
19. Gholz et al. 1997, 5.
20. Ornstein 1992, 9.
21. Greenfield 2016.
22. Kimmitt 2020.
23. Power 2001.
24. Jervis 2009, 209–210.
25. Sarotte 2021, 33–41; Stent 1999, chs. 4–5.
26. Crawford 2007.
27. Zelikow and Rice 2020, 59–60, 67. The Bush team resisted Henry Kissinger's urging to strike a bargain with the Soviets to avoid potential "explosions" at the Cold War's end.

28. Teltschik 2020, 83.
29. Newnham 1999.
30. Baker 2020.
31. Gaddis 2005, ch. 2.
32. Pond 2002, 55.
33. North Atlantic Treaty Organization 1999.
34. Kallioras 1994.
35. Bhagwati and Patrick 1990.
36. Cohen 2019, 81–85.
37. McNamara 2018.
38. Sarotte 2021, 1.
39. Mastanduno 2019.
40. Goldgeier 1999.
41. Ikenberry 2018.
42. Mastanduno 2003.
43. Oreskes 1990.
44. Prestowitz 1990.
45. McGregor 2017.
46. Johnson 1982.
47. Ishihara 1992. Sony chairman Akio Morita, a co-author of the initial version, subsequently removed his name from the controversial text.
48. Konno quoted in McGregor 2017, 120.
49. Funabashi 1989.
50. Katada 2008.
51. Mastanduno 1992.
52. Prestowitz (1990) offers the most detailed account.
53. McGregor 2017, 99.
54. Konno quoted in McGregor 2017, 120.
55. Nye 1995.
56. Armitage et al. 2000.
57. Ikenberry and Inoguchi 2003.
58. Cha 1999.
59. Cha 2020.
60. Muravchik 1996; Miller 1994.
61. Rodrik 2018.
62. White House 2002, introduction, emphasis added.

References

Armitage, Richard, Joseph Nye, Kurt Campbell, Michael Green, Kent Harrington, Frank Jannuzi, et al. 2000. "The United States and Japan: Advancing toward a Mature Partnership." INSS Special Report, October 11. https://spfusa.org/wp-content/uploads/2015/11/ArmitageNyeReport_2000.pdf.

Baker, James 2020. "Ten Foreign Policy Maxims of a Great President." In *Transforming Our World: President George H. W. Bush and American Foreign Policy*, edited by Andrew Natsios and Andrew Card. Rowman and Littlefield.

Bhagwati, Jagdish, and Hugh Patrick, eds. 1990. *Aggressive Unilateralism: America's 301 Trade Policy and the World Trading System*. University of Michigan Press.

Boys, James. 2021. "Grand Strategy, Grand Rhetoric: The Forgotten Covenant of Election 1992." *Politics* 41 (1): 80–94.

Cha, Victor. 1999. *Alignment Despite Antagonism: The US-Korea-Japan Security Triangle.* Stanford University Press.
Cha, Victor. 2020. "Allied Decoupling in an Era of US-China Strategic Competition." *Chinese Journal of International Politics* 13 (4): 509–536.
Clark, Ian. 2011. *Hegemony in International Society.* Oxford University Press.
Cohen, Benjamin. 2019. *Currency Statecraft: Monetary Rivalry and Geopolitical Ambition.* University of Chicago Press.
Crawford, Beverly. 2007. *Power and German Foreign Policy: Embedded Hegemony in Europe.* Palgrave Macmillan.
Friedberg, Aaron. 1993–1994. "Ripe for Rivalry: Prospects for Peace in a Multipolar Asia." *International Security* 18 (2): 5–33.
Funabashi, Yoichi. 1989. *Managing the Dollar: From the Plaza to the Louvre.* 2nd ed. Peterson Institute for International Economics.
Gaddis, John Lewis. 2005 *Strategies of Containment: A Critical Appraisal of American National Security Policy during the Cold War.* Rev. ed. Oxford University Press.
Garten, Jeffrey. 1992. *A Cold Peace: America, Japan, Germany and the Struggle for Supremacy.* Times Books.
Gilpin, Robert. 1981. *War and Change in World Politics.* Cambridge University Press.
Gholz, Eugene, Daryl Press, and Harvey Sapolsky. 1997. "Come Home, America: The Strategy of Restraint in the Face of Temptation." *International Security* 21 (4): 5–48.
Goldgeier, James. 1999. *Not Whether But When: The US Decision to Enlarge NATO.* Brookings Institution Press.
Greenfield, Jeff. 2016. "Trump Is Pat Buchanan with Better Timing." *Politico Magazine*, September–October. https://www.politico.com/magazine/story/2016/09/donald-trump-pat-buchanan-republican-america-first-nativist-214221/.
Ikenberry, John. 2001. *After Victory: Institutions, Strategic Restraint, and the Rebuilding of Order after Major Wars.* Princeton University Press.
Ikenberry, John. 2018. "Why the Liberal Order Will Survive." *Ethics and International Affairs* 32 (1): 17–29.
Ikenberry, John, and Takashi Inoguchi, eds. 2003. *Reinventing the Alliance: U.S.-Japan Security Partnership in an Era of Change.* Palgrave Macmillan.
Ishihara, Shintaro. 1992. *The Japan That Can Say No.* Simon and Schuster.
Jervis, Robert. 2009. "Unipolarity: A Structural Perspective." *World Politics* 61 (1): 188–213.
Johnson, Chalmers. 1982. *MITI and the Japanese Miracle: The Growth of Industrial Policy, 1925–1975.* Stanford University Press.
Kallioras, Elias. 1994. *Fortress Europe? Realism vs. Neoliberal Institutionalism.* Paschalidis Scientific Publications.
Katada, Saori. 2008. "From Supporter to Challenger? Japan's Currency Leadership in Dollar-Denominated East Asia." *Review of International Political Economy* 15 (3): 399–417.
Katzenstein, Peter. 2005. *A World of Regions: Asia and Europe in the American Imperium.* Cornell University Press.
Kennedy, Paul. 1989. *The Rise and Fall of the Great Powers: Economic Change and Military Conflict from 1500 to 2000.* Vintage.
Kimmitt, Robert. 2020. "'This Will Not Stand': The Liberation of Kuwait." In *Transforming Our World: President George H. W. Bush and American Foreign Policy*, edited by Andrew Natsios and Andrew Card. Rowman and Littlefield.
Lake, David. 2009. *Hierarchy in International Relations.* Cornell University Press.
Layne, Christopher. 1993. "The Unipolar Illusion: Why New Great Powers Will Rise." *International Security* 17 (4): 5–51.
Mastanduno, Michael. 1992. "Framing the Japan Problem: The Bush Administration and the Structural Impediments Initiative." *International Journal* 47 (2): 235–264.

Mastanduno, Michael. 2003. "Incomplete Hegemony: The United States and Security Order in Asia." In *Asian Security Order: Instrumental and Normative Features*, edited by Muthiah Alagappa. Stanford University Press.

Mastanduno, Michael. 2019. "Partner Politics: Russia, China, and the Challenge of Extending U.S. Hegemony after the Cold War." *Security Studies* 28(3): 479–504.

McGee, Suzanne. 2020. "How Billionaire Ross Perot Brought Populism Back to Presidential Politics." *History*, October 6. https://www.history.com/news/ross-perot-populist-1992-election-changed-politics.

McGregor, Richard. 2017. *Asia's Reckoning: China, Japan, and the Fate of U.S. Power in the Pacific Century*. Viking.

McNamara, Kathleen. 2018. "The Euro in Decline? How the Currency Could Spoil the Global Financial System." *Foreign Affairs*, January 12. https://www.foreignaffairs.com/france/euro-decline.

Mearsheimer, John. 1990. "Back to the Future: Instability in Europe after the Cold War." *International Security* 15 (1): 5–56.

Mearsheimer, John. 2019. *The Great Delusion: Liberal Dreams and International Realities*. Yale University Press.

Miller, Linda. 1994. "The Clinton Years: Reinventing Foreign Policy." *International Affairs* 70 (4): 621–634.

Muravchik, Joshua. 1996. "Carrying a Small Stick." *National Review*, September 2.

Newnham, Randall. 1999. "The Price of German Unity: The Role of Economic Aid in German-Soviet Negotiations." *German Studies Review*, October 22 (3): 421–446.

Nordlinger, Eric. 1995. *Isolationism Reconfigured: American Foreign Policy for a New Century*. Princeton University Press.

North Atlantic Treaty Organization. 1999. "Washington Summit." *NATO News*, April 23. https://www.nato.int/cps/en/natohq/news_27286.htm?selectedLocale=en.

Nye, Joseph. 1995. "East Asian Security: The Case for Deep Engagement." *Foreign Affairs* 74 (4): 90–102.

Oreskes, Michael. 1990. "Americans Voicing Anxiety on Japan." *New York Times*, July 10.

Ornstein, Norman. 1992. "Foreign Policy and the 1992 Election." *Foreign Affairs* 71 (3): 1–16.

Pond, Elizabeth. 2002, second edition. *The Rebirth of Europe*. Brookings Institution Press.

Power, Samantha. 2001. "Bystanders to Genocide: Why the United States Let the Rwandan Tragedy Happen." *Atlantic Monthly*, September.

Prestowitz, Clyde. 1990. *Trading Places: How We Are Giving Our Future to Japan and How to Reclaim It*. Basic Books.

Rodrik, Dani. 2018. *Straight Talk on Trade: Ideas for a Sane World Economy*. Princeton University Press.

Sarotte, M. E. 2021. *Not One Inch: America, Russia, and the Making of Post–Cold War Stalemate*. Yale University Press.

Stent, Angela. 1999. *Russia and Germany Reborn: Unification, the Soviet Collapse, and the New Europe*. Princeton University Press.

Teltschik, Horst. 2020. "President George H. W. Bush: A Stroke of Luck for Germany." In *Transforming Our World: President George H. W. Bush and American Foreign Policy*, edited by Andrew Natsios and Andrew Card. Rowman and Littlefield.

Thurow, Lester. 1993. *Head to Head: The Coming Economic Battle among Japan, Europe, and America*. Warner Books.

Walt, Stephen. 2018. *The Hell of Good Intentions: America's Foreign Policy Elite and the Decline of U.S. Primacy*. Farrar, Straus and Giroux.

Waltz, Kenneth. 1993. "The Emerging Structure of International Politics." *International Security* 18 (2): 44–79.

White House. 2002. *The National Security Strategy*. September. https://georgewbush-whitehouse.archives.gov/nsc/nss/2002/.

Wohlforth, William. 2011. "Gilpinian Realism and International Relations." *International Relations* 25 (4): 499–511.
Zelikow, Phillip, and Condoleezza Rice. 2020. "*The End of the Cold War and German Reunification.*" In *Transforming Our World: President George H. W. Bush and American Foreign Policy*, edited by Andrew Natsios and Andrew Card. Rowman and Littlefield.

5
Responsible Sovereignty and Individual Accountability
Liberal Internationalist Aspirations from the 1990s

Jennifer M. Welsh

There is a vast and varied literature that seeks to analyze and explain the end of the Cold War.* It roughly divides into accounts that emphasize systemic factors (the changing distribution of power between the United States and the Soviet Union, as well as other aspects of the latter's external environment),[1] individual factors (the decisions and disposition of Soviet leader Mikhail Gorbachev),[2] and domestic factors (particularly within the societies of the Eastern bloc, where "velvet revolutions" exposed the fragility of communist systems of rule). But existing scholarship also points to the role of transnational social movements across Eastern and Western Europe, inspired by human rights norms buried deep within the 1975 Helsinki Final Act, which pressured governments to implement their legal obligations to the populations living behind the Iron Curtain.[3]

It was the idea of human rights that inspired clandestine meetings of East Germans in churches across the country on Monday evenings in the autumn of 1989, which gradually grew—thanks to the help of West German television and friends on the other side of the wall—into peaceful mass protest. Human rights also animated the political movement New Forum, which demanded dialogue about the right to travel and to participate in free and fair elections. In conversations I had with its members during a trip to Berlin that famous weekend in November, I listened to their dreams of building

---

* An earlier version of the ideas in this paper was presented in the Martin Wight Memorial Lecture at the London School of Economics and Political Science in November 2019. The author also wishes to thank Mary Kaldor, Jonathan Kirshner, and the organizers and participants in the LSE-Princeton "Rethinking the 1990s" project for their comments and suggestions on drafts of the chapter, as well as Bruce Cronin, Dirk Moses, and the participants in the CCNY Human Rights Forum for their helpful feedback.

Jennifer M. Welsh, *Responsible Sovereignty and Individual Accountability*. In: *Rethinking the 1990s*. Edited by: G. John Ikenberry and Peter Trubowitz, Oxford University Press. © Oxford University Press (2025).
DOI: 10.1093/9780197813133.003.0005

a distinct society in the eastern half of Germany—one that would marry the political and civil rights so cherished in the West with commitments to fulfilling the socioeconomic rights articulated in the postwar human rights covenants.

In reflections on the imaginaries that circulated in those dying days of the 1980s and the early years of the 1990s, the idea of human rights—that individuals have a set of inalienable and unconditional rights by virtue of their humanity—and the proposition that states should serve as the vehicle for the expression of those rights vie for a dominant place. As human rights were globalized, their power and reach intensified, shaping the practices of national governments through a combination of transnational advocacy and domestic pressure.[4] They also evolved into what some have referred to as the "doctrine" of *international* human rights: that each person is a subject of global concern and that responsibilities to respect and protect human rights should and can—in principle—extend across political boundaries.[5]

It was also in this decade that individual human rights, as well as minority rights, became prioritized in more concrete ways within international organizations. They were central to the transformation of the old Cold War Conference on Security and Cooperation in Europe (CSCE) into the Organization for Security and Cooperation in Europe, with its new Office for Democratic Institutions and Human Rights and High Commissioner on National Minorities. They were also integral to the launch of a new and more promising era for the United Nations, as articulated in the landmark *Agenda for Peace* in 1992—which recognized that traditional peacekeeping was falling short of delivering peace and prosperity—and as emblemized by the creation of the Office of the High Commissioner for Human Rights in 1993. While both the CSCE and the UN had—at their origins—identified human rights as one of their priorities (in "basket three" of the 1975 Helsinki Final Act and in the preamble to the original UN Charter), it was only in the 1990s that these and other organizations began to view the protection and promotion of human rights as their "core business."

This last development reflected the new realities of an international system in which Western states, particularly the United States, were structurally dominant, enabling their ideas to be operationalized in ways that seemed impossible during the decades of the Cold War. The revolutions in Eastern Europe and the former Soviet Union also gave the doctrine of international human rights significant legitimacy, inspiring already existing human rights movements elsewhere. Indeed, it is important to acknowledge that many of the most powerful human rights "projects" in the 1990s were versions of earlier aspirations, which were now emboldened with greater urgency and momentum. As a result, this decade offered the *possibility* for significant transformation of the prevailing international order, in ways that would prioritize the rights of individuals as well as states.

In the sections that follow, I examine how the 1990s served as fertile ground for two particular expressions of the doctrine of international human rights—both of which informed more assertive forms of liberal internationalism and translated into concrete policy change. The first is the notion of "sovereignty as responsibility": the claim that the meaning of sovereignty has been transformed from the right of absolute state authority over a domestic jurisdiction (and with it, a claim to be free from external interference) to the idea that sovereign rights were conditional upon a state fulfilling its core responsibilities—not only to control its territory but also to protect the fundamental human rights of individuals residing within it. The second is the idea that any individual who commits egregious violations of human rights, regardless of their status or official function, should be held criminally accountable—thereby challenging past practices of impunity or state accountability for the commission of international crimes.[6]

In examining these liberal internationalist expressions of human rights, I also want to ask whether, in hindsight, we should consider them transformational—part of a "revolutionary" phase in international affairs, using the terminology employed by British international relations scholar Martin Wight. When Wight introduced his three traditions of thought on international relations—realism, rationalism, and revolutionism—at the London School of Economics in the 1950s, he always began with revolutionism, given its historical precedence in the form of the medieval *res publica Christiana*. Since the origins of the modern states system, Wight suggested, there were at least three examples of revolutionary efforts to transform the basis of international relations: the religious revolutionists of the sixteenth and seventeenth centuries; the French revolutionists, especially the Jacobins; and the totalitarian revolutionists of the twentieth century. The defining characteristic of revolutionists, according to Wight, is their passionate belief in "the moral unity of the society of states." They not only claim to speak in the name of this unity, he argued, "but also experience an overriding obligation to give effect to it."[7]

Some international relations scholars contend that ideas like sovereignty-as-responsibility marked a new "solidarist moment" in international society, when the consensus on legitimate state behavior by the members of international society had shifted in ways that permitted and encouraged various forms of international scrutiny and—ultimately—intervention.[8] Others adopt a more critical stance, suggesting that liberal renderings of these notions were inherently radical, with the potential to reshape some of the foundations of international order. Philip Cunliffe, for example, refers to liberal states' foreign policies in the 1990s and early 2000s as a case of "inverted revisionism": by recasting international institutions and practices around the extraterritorial enforcement of human rights, it was the core Western states—and not the world's discontented "have-nots"—that were promoting an "ideology of systemic transformation."[9]

As with other revolutionary moments in the history of the modern states system, the vision of the post–Cold War international order promoted by liberal internationalists in the 1990s was based on both prescription and power. It was to be created and preserved not just by a balance of power but by a deeper consensus upon particular political and moral ideas and what Barry Buzan calls "transnational intrusions of political ideology."[10] Even if liberal aspirations in this period did not quite resemble the *civitas maxima* promoted by revolutionary thinkers of the sixteenth and seventeenth centuries, they did suggest—much as Hugo Grotius had done in his writings about the *societas humana* in the early modern period—that the prevailing legal and political order had to more closely approximate the broader *moral* order, rooted in common humanity, that gave recognition to individuals as well as states.

I advance three main arguments that engage with the themes of this volume. The first is about the degree of transformation that unfolded over the 1990s. Sovereignty-as-responsibility and individual criminal accountability, I will suggest, are best conceived as forms of "soft revolutionism." As two expressions of the doctrine of international human rights, they became associated with particular understandings about the possibilities and limits of sovereignty and would inform attempts to recast practices of conflict resolution, intervention, and international justice. At the same time, however, these imaginings were not quite as novel—either in theory or in practice—as some of their liberal proponents suggested; instead, the 1990s were the period in which preexisting ideas moved from existence to consummation.[11] Second, these ideas did not represent the only way that sovereignty and justice could have been understood and practiced following the end of the Cold War. In short, as our editors suggest, other "roads" were possible. While Western states advocated for a particular understanding of sovereignty as responsibility that aimed at enabling more coercive liberal interventionism, an alternative approach could have developed a conception of collective action rooted in emerging Security Council practice and earlier "Third World" understandings of solidarity. Relatedly, the ambitious project of advancing individual criminal accountability through the International Criminal Court (ICC) might have had greater resonance with states of the Global South (particularly in Africa) if it had aimed to work more in partnership with their domestic institutions and approaches to justice. Last, although sovereignty-as-responsibility—as understood and practiced by Western states—at times led to forms of overreach, which would later provoke resistance and backsliding, the pursuit of individual accountability was marked in important ways by underreach. Ultimately, the most powerful exponent of liberal ideas in this decade, the United States, proved to be both reluctant and selective in its commitment to realizing these liberal imaginings in the 1990s, thereby sowing (some of) the seeds for later contestation in the decades that followed.

Responsible Sovereignty

The Origins of an Idea

The central claim underpinning sovereignty-as-responsibility is that in contemporary international relations, sovereignty can and should no longer be conceived as unrivaled control over a delimited territory and the population residing within it—sovereignty-as-authority—but rather as a status and set of rights which are conditional upon certain behaviors and capacities of states. And the most essential task among these, in the words of one of the early proponents of sovereignty-as-responsibility, Francis Deng, is to "preserve life-sustaining standards for its citizens."[12] There were two principal manifestations of this particular reading of sovereignty which appeared in the 1990s: the work of liberal scholars from international law and international relations, and the efforts of policymakers working in the fields of armed conflict, internally displaced persons, and human rights.

To begin, developments in international society over the course of the late 1980s and 1990s led a number of scholars in international relations and international law to contend that the legitimacy of states had come to depend on the fulfillment of certain (liberal) standards, and that the associated rights of sovereignty were now contingent on that fulfillment.[13] This claim affected a wide range of international practices, including the use of force, the membership of various regional and international organizations, and the recognition of new states.

Two examples help illustrate this trend, one from international relations and the other from international law. Drawing on constructivist insights, Samuel Barkin argued that the strengthening of international human rights norms from the early 1970s onward had altered the very "constitution" of sovereignty. With the Cold War's demise, that constitution had been redefined so that a state was "legitimated less by its relationship with a given piece of territory, and more by its ability to ensure the political rights of its citizens." The interventions in Haiti and Bosnia-Herzegovina during the early 1990s, Barkin argued, demonstrated that human rights norms were understood not merely as a constraint on the exercise of (absolute) sovereignty but also as a new element in the nature of sovereignty itself.[14]

There was also a powerful strand of liberal thinking within international law that argued for a reconceptualization of the meaning and place of sovereignty in the post–Cold War era, such that sovereignty would be contingent on the guarantee of basic human rights. In Allen Buchanan's formulation, this move translated into an argument that new entities "ought to be incorporated into the society of states only if they satisfy justice-based criteria,"[15] while for Fernando Teson, the imperative to protect and secure human rights led to a liberal case for humanitarian intervention.[16] Others, such as Ruti Teitel, went a step further, arguing that the impact of the imperative to promote and protect individual rights was the gradual development of a "humanity's law," which was recasting diplomacy and foreign policy. This body of judicial interpretation and state practice—which expanded the content of *opinio juris* and took customary law in more normative directions[17]—cut across the international law of armed conflict, international human rights law, and international criminal law in ways that prioritized the security of persons and peoples rather than the security of states.[18]

Just as sovereignty-as-responsibility had a scholarly home, so too did it find adherents in the world of policy. Beginning in the mid-1990s, with the work of the UN Secretary General's Special Representative on Internally Displaced Persons, Francis Deng, and carrying through the work of the International Commission on Intervention and State Sovereignty (ICISS),[19] which issued its report on the Responsibility to Protect in 2001, an influential set of policy entrepreneurs argued that an absolutist conception of sovereignty had been a key source of international inaction to address a series of human rights crises occurring in international society, including not only the genocides in Rwanda and Srebrenica but also the loss of citizenship rights for internally displaced persons (IDPs).[20] Sovereignty-as-authority, they suggested, had provided a shield behind which humanitarian crises and violations of basic rights unfolded—the result of either weak states or oppressive regimes. While during the Cold War a pragmatic accommodation of political and ideological diversity required a privileging of the state over peoples and individual rights, a series of material and ideational changes in the 1980s and 1990s (it was argued) had called that normative ordering into question.[21] In a 1999 article in *The Economist* titled "Two Conceptions of Sovereignty," former UN secretary general Kofi Annan famously argued, "When we read the Charter today, we are more than ever conscious that its aim is to protect individual human beings, not to protect those who abuse them."[22] Sovereignty was thus increasingly conceived with two faces: an internal dimension, which entails responsibility by sovereign authorities for citizens within their jurisdiction, and an external dimension, which enables and obligates the international community to assist in the fulfillment of sovereign responsibilities.

Unpacking Sovereignty-as-Responsibility

Three aspects of sovereignty-as-responsibility can assist us in assessing its "revolutionary" potential. First, in most of its liberal formulations, a sense of movement or change is conveyed. The so-called Westphalian system of the seventeenth century is described as a phase in which the "sovereign reigned supreme domestically and in its relations with the outside world," and is contrasted with the latter half of the twentieth century and the "steady erosion of the concept of sovereignty" in the face of developments in international human rights.[23] In the words of former director of policy planning in the George W. Bush administration, Richard Haas, there was now an "emerging global consensus that sovereignty is not a blank check. Rather, sovereign status is contingent on the fulfillment by each state of certain fundamental obligations, both to its own citizens and to the international community."[24]

That said, most proponents of responsible sovereignty have never countenanced the transcendence of the nation-state as a key organizing principle for contemporary global politics—hence why it should be considered a form of "soft revolutionism." While sovereignty had often proved inadequate in the protection of individual rights, the prescriptive aim was for sovereignty to be new and improved: it needed to "be put to work and reaffirmed" to meet current challenges "in accordance with accepted standards of human dignity."[25] For Deng, this imperative to reimagine sovereignty was particularly acute for the governments of postcolonial states, many of which had adopted a centralizing logic of Westphalian sovereignty to repress minorities or political opponents in the name of national unity.[26]

Second, there were stronger and weaker versions of sovereignty-as-responsibility in circulation.[27] On the stronger side of the ledger, some moved beyond claiming a normative distinction between liberal and illiberal states to suggest that international law and international organizations should abandon their traditional neutrality toward domestic principles of legitimacy by both privileging those states that adhered to human rights norms and punishing those which systematically transgressed them.[28] For Deng, however, sovereignty-as-responsibility was not ultimately about legitimizing coercive forms of intervention in semi-liberal or illiberal societies. Instead, his understanding of this idea was shaped by his own reflections on his country of origin (the postcolonial state of Sudan) and his participation in the 1980s Brookings Institution project on conflict management in Africa, which focused on the superpowers' potential withdrawal from the African continent—where during the Cold War they had not only been fueling proxy wars but also acting as guardians of stability. Deng's central concern was therefore not with more active forms of Western interventionism but with the prospect of *inaction*. If Africa was marginalized within the international system, he argued, its internal conflicts—a legacy of both the colonial era and earlier superpower rivalry—would create increasingly perilous conditions for populations across the continent as African governments held up the shield of sovereignty and noninterference.[29] In response to this challenge, Deng pinned his hopes on a new generation of African leaders, who could exercise agency and take *collective* responsibility for maintaining stability and responding to humanitarian crises, including by reimagining the notion of sovereignty. This perspective was reflected in the creation of the Kampala Process in the early 1990s (modeled on the Helsinki Process), which promoted the idea of interdependence among states on the African continent and a new partnership with the international community aimed at assisting African states to realize universal standards of human dignity.[30]

The spirit of the Kampala Process shaped Deng's tenure as special representative on IDPs, a population that for him emblemized the limitations of the existing humanitarian and human rights system and pointed to the need to reimagine sovereignty. IDPs, he wrote, had been placed in "the moral vacuum left by the state's failure, deliberate or imposed, to fulfil its normal responsibilities."[31] But by filling the gap, international NGOs had challenged the authority of national governments, provoking them to reassert their sovereignty. Deng believed the solution to this tension was a new configuration of responsibilities that began with the primary responsibility of national governments to protect the rights of their people (an idea that would come to be part of the principle of the "responsibility to protect"), but called on weak or vulnerable states to invite and welcome international assistance to *complement* national efforts and thus enhance national sovereignty.[32] Deng's approach to addressing the plight of IDPs was to move beyond the treatment of their condition as a humanitarian crisis and dig deeper into the causes giving rise to displacement,[33] which more often than not was obscured by "sovereignty talk." His experience in working with states to address displacement challenges led him to believe that sovereignty-as-responsibility would fail if it was pitched solely in negative terms—as states being "punished" by the international community for failing to uphold human rights. The more sustainable path forward was to help states transcend the legacies of colonialism and build capacity to fulfill their responsibilities,[34] thereby avoiding more coercive measures.

The third and final feature of sovereignty-as-responsibility is its contractarian logic. This is clearly evident in Deng's original formulation, when he asserts that to claim that sovereignty is unconditional is to "lose sight of its purpose in the original context of the social contract, taking the means for the end."[35] Though two of the most important early theorists of sovereignty, Hobbes and Bodin, are most often described as absolutist, even their conceptions of sovereignty incorporate diverse forms of restraint and obligation that were *intrinsic* to sovereignty's meaning and aimed at addressing the potential of tyrannical abuses of power. While for these thinkers sovereignty was to imply supremacy—the sovereign as the source of law—it was never conceived as simply the ability to coerce or the capacity to penetrate all aspects of the lives of citizens. In advocating the legally supreme position of the sovereign, these theorists were also concerned about the tyrannical abuse of power. This connection to earlier articulations of sovereignty reinforces the point that sovereignty-as-responsibility is best thought of as soft revolutionism rather than wholly novel or transformational. The assertion that the post–Cold War liberal notion of responsible sovereignty was "new" is based on an ahistorical reading of sovereignty and its meaning—one that takes as a reference point an idealized conception of how sovereignty was allegedly understood, and defended, during the Cold War rather than reaching back to examine sovereignty's longer trajectory.[36]

As Patrick Quinton-Brown has demonstrated through his analysis of the discourse and practice of newly independent states in the developing world, sovereignty in the decades following World War II was not understood as an absolute right which gave states complete license within their borders. Nor was the related principle of nonintervention designed to foreclose any possibility of solidarity or collective action for humanitarian purposes. Instead, the UN General Assembly was the site of competing ideas, in which so-called Third World states promoted their own form of sovereignty-as-responsibility and a particular understanding of nonintervention—one that contracted the scope of a state's domestic jurisdiction and legitimated a series of collective actions to promote what they saw as the most critical human right—the right to self-determination—and to counter lingering racism and colonialism.[37] The key was to ensure that any implementation of shared international responsibilities was consistent with the UN's core principle of sovereign equality.

For the members of ICISS who drew on Deng's ideas, however, the contrarian logic in sovereignty-as-responsibility served another and potentially more revolutionary function: it not only made the rights of sovereignty conditional but also aimed to dissolve the apparent conflict between nonintervention and human rights which was so often asserted in international relations. But it did so without acknowledging or incorporating the Global South's bedrock norm of self-determination. According to the authors of the principle of the responsibility to protect, if the state failed to fulfill its protection role, then it could no longer demand that external actors refrain from taking action within in its sovereign jurisdiction. Where the state is "unable or unwilling to meet its own responsibility ... a secondary responsibility to protect falls on the wider international community."[38] Understood in this way, intervention becomes an ally of sovereignty, and in fact an integral part of restoring it, as long as it is aimed at protecting human rights.

But in order for the contractarian logic to promote this robust form of remedial action, there must be something outside or above that unwilling or unable state to which responsibility can be transferred. In the early formulations of the social contract, sovereign power could not be limited from the outside, since this would imply an authority higher than the sovereign. Though Hobbes accepted that sovereigns had internal obligations, he rejected the idea that they could be externally compelled to comply with those obligations.[39] For some post–Cold War liberals, however, sovereigns existed in a context where an identifiable "international community" could be invoked and called upon as an alternative source to enforce the promotion and protection of human rights.

This notion of an international authority *beyond* the state, that can act in ways that affect the relationship between ruler and ruled, was the more revolutionary claim of 1990s liberal internationalism: it aimed to shift the focus of law and politics from the horizontal distribution of authority between states—encapsulated by the principle of sovereign equality—to a vertical distribution of authority between states and international actors.[40] It also suggested the existence of a coherent and identifiable purpose that is generated not solely from the aggregated "wills" of sovereign states, manifest in their explicit consent to rules and institutions, but also from higher norms and forms of justice, based on consensus. These *jus cogens* or *erga omnes* rules—that are beyond the reach of states[41]—can be used not just to encourage but also to enforce rights-respecting behavior. The implication was that sovereignty not only could be qualified, in cases where these fundamental principles were breached, but could also be suspended or made "defeasible."[42]

Practices of Responsible Sovereignty in the Early Post–Cold War Period

The early post–Cold War period served as a testing ground for some of the core tenets of sovereignty-as-responsibility. As I will show, despite the aspirations of more assertive liberals in the 1990s and early 2000s, their understanding of responsible sovereignty did not take hold or find wide acceptance in international society, thereby limiting the degree to which the "positive" practice of state recognition and the "negative" practice of intervention accorded with a conditional reading of sovereignty.

State Recognition

At first sight, it appeared that the state creation process that accompanied the breakup of Yugoslavia in the early post–Cold War period might follow the liberal reading of responsible sovereignty. In December 1991, European foreign ministers agreed to recognize the independence of former Yugoslav republics, provided they fulfilled certain conditions: commitment to the rule of law, democracy, and human rights; guarantees of ethnic and minority rights; and the acceptance of the inviolability of frontiers.[43] The essence of the European Community's position at that time was an aversion to ethnicity and its allegedly primordial ethos and a championing of modern notions of identity based on multiculturalism and common citizenship. It then fell to the Badinter Commission, an arbitration body composed of five presidents from among the various constitutional courts of Europe, to judge whether the four applicants—Bosnia, Croatia, Macedonia, and Slovenia—met the stated criteria.

Dissension soon arose within the ranks, however, as Germany recognized Croatia and Slovenia even before the Commission rendered its judgment.[44] And although the Badinter Commission concluded that Croatia did not actually meet the conditions, the remaining members of the European Community also recognized these two republics on January 15, 1991. The United States followed suit in April. This episode thus illustrated the significant mismatch between the articulated norms that were meant to guide state creation and the strategic—and some would say chaotic—practices of recognition.

The use of conditionality as a tool of recognition policy, set out most explicitly by the European Community, seemed to invoke the idea of responsible sovereignty. Yet in practice the recognition process was driven by domestic political considerations and great power competition—rather than by the orderly application of rules. As the recognition process morphed into a form of conflict resolution, it generated very uneven results.[45] Indeed, the recognition of Bosnia was less a confirmation of de facto authority and more an attempt to create facts on the ground.[46] Far from being an example of the implementation of sovereignty-as-responsibility, many see the recognition of the states of the Federal Republic of Yugoslavia as a *shirking* of responsibility and a missed opportunity to connect state recognition to principles such as the respect for minority rights. In this case, it was liberal states *themselves* that fell short of implementing their normative aspiration of constituting states on the basis of their capacity to protect human rights—a trend that continued with subsequent instances of state recognition, as in Eritrea and

South Sudan. This suggests that liberal failures in the 1990s may have been less failures of imagination, as suggested elsewhere in this volume, and more the short-term and countervailing interests of powerful Western states which limited their commitment to a "new" post–Cold War order.

Humanitarian Intervention

The notion of responsible sovereignty was also prominent in the debates surrounding the use of force in the 1990s. Yet here too the revolutionary promise of the idea was only partially reflected in state practice. While there was undoubtedly an increased willingness on the part of liberal states to consider the use of force for humanitarian purposes as the Cold War ended—in part as a result of a more functional UN Security Council[47]—the record of state opinion and practice indicates that there was only a modest challenge to preexisting conceptions of sovereignty and rights of nonintervention.

Looking back at the decade of the 1990s, most incidences of the use of force for humanitarian purposes (with the exception of the war in Kosovo) invoked the existing collective security mechanisms of the United Nations and the Security Council's power to redefine what constitutes a threat to international peace and security. The most powerful case from this period, in which the Council authorized force in Somalia *without the consent of the state*, demonstrates states' unease with implementing a more conditional reading of sovereignty. Although the text of Security Council Resolution 794 appeared to dramatically alter the Council's long-standing interpretation of its roles and responsibilities under the Charter to enable so-called humanitarian intervention,[48] the debate among Council members indicates wariness about establishing any new precedent of interference in the domestic affairs of sovereign states on humanitarian grounds. What made the case so "exceptional," diplomats argued, was the *lack* of a responsible government that could act as an interlocutor of the UN for the purposes of consenting to a military action designed to facilitate humanitarian assistance. Even at what many believe to be the high point of liberal internationalism after the Cold War, it was clear that humanitarian intervention was still a controversial practice and that the right of the UN to authorize multilateral action was still ad hoc rather than systematically practiced.[49]

As a result, the post–Cold War period saw very little movement toward legitimizing the unilateral practice of humanitarian intervention,[50] including among most Western liberal states. Generally speaking, since a use of force is a prima facie violation of Article 2(4), any argument for its legality needs to demonstrate either that such a use of force is not contrary to this Charter provision, or that it has become a new principle of customary law. Neither strategy, however, was broadly endorsed or actively pursued, and most international lawyers continued to argue that the use of force by a state or group of states for humanitarian purposes, outside of the Charter framework, did not pass the hurdle of legality.[51] In particular, much of non-Western legal opinion explicitly opposed any interpretation of state practice as contributing to a new right of intervention, as it seemed to suggest that certain types of practice could "count" more than others—that is, the actions of Western states versus the stated opposition from those outside the West.[52]

Similarly, in those instances where force was used unilaterally—in other words, instances of humanitarian intervention that are distinct from actions authorized by the Security Council—there is little evidence of states justifying a new legal right to intervene on humanitarian grounds, even in defense of their own actions.[53] For example, the use of force by the United States to protect so-called safe havens inside Iraq in 1991 was justified not as humanitarian intervention but rather on the basis of a right of self-defense against threats of attack on coalition aircraft patrolling these zones. In the later case of Kosovo, while the United Kingdom asserted that military action was a justified measure to "prevent an overwhelming humanitarian catastrophe,"[54] its position was very much in the minority. U.S. arguments on legality did not espouse any right of humanitarian intervention, and other participating states, such as Germany, denied that the NATO action had a "precedential value" in terms of consolidating such a right.[55] More broadly, the reaction of nonparticipating states did not provide evidence of changing custom; instead, the Ministerial Declaration of the Group of 77 (whose membership exceeded 130 states) explicitly rejected the legality of the use of force in Kosovo.[56]

What therefore emerges from this picture of the 1990s is not a widespread embrace of a unilateral right of humanitarian intervention, based on a new understanding of responsible sovereignty, but rather the continued reluctance of states to accept such a right outside the confines of the UN Charter.[57] There are multiple reasons for this reluctance—among them the unwillingness of third-party states (especially Western liberal ones) to commit material and financial resources to "saving strangers," and a political aversion to becoming embroiled in particular situations of instability that might entail the long-term presence of military forces. In short, the story is less about the imagination of liberal internationalism and more about the unwillingness to exercise political will or to devote resources to advance the universal application of liberal goals. But equally significant is the majority view in international society that broad adherence to the prohibition on the use of force, combined with the collective authorization procedures of the United Nations—however imperfect—are better ways of maintaining international peace and security than the endorsement of a new right to use force on human rights grounds.

Moreover, the United States proved to be a lukewarm and inconsistent supporter of the "new interventionism," given its general concerns about legitimizing a general responsibility to protect populations in peril[58] as well as the early lessons it drew from concrete cases in which it tried to do so. Convinced by his advisors that military action could be short term and risk-free, George H. W. Bush pivoted from his initial reluctance to intervene in Somalia, partly as a response to the pressure from Democratic presidential candidate Bill Clinton but also in light of his own desire to leave a foreign policy legacy.[59] Yet it was the killing of eighteen U.S. soldiers in Mogadishu, under Clinton's watch, that cast a powerful shadow over his administration's response to the unfolding genocide in Rwanda in April 1994 and that prompted the cautious approach to peacekeeping articulated in Presidential Decision Directive 25.[60] PDD-25 set out four specific criteria for any U.S. participation in a multilateral peacekeeping operation: that participation would advance U.S. interests; that risks to American personnel had been weighed and were considered acceptable; that a clear endpoint for U.S. participation had been identified; and that domestic and congressional support existed or could be marshalled.[61]

Although the Clinton administration held no significant structured deliberations about leading or joining a military mission in Rwanda, it is unlikely that the president's advisors would have viewed an intervention to bolster existing UN peacekeepers and stop the genocide as meeting these criteria, given how the conflict was perceived and the relative lack of public pressure for intervention.[62] Indeed, while the conventional wisdom today is that the 1990s gave rise to the mantra "Never again," based on the genocide in Rwanda, U.S. policymakers did not initially draw the lesson that lack of military intervention amounted to an American foreign policy failure. Other interpretations of the international response were not only possible but widely in circulation.[63] It was only later in the decade, when President Clinton issued his famous apology to the Rwandan people at Kigali Airport, that the particular framing of the genocide in Rwanda—as a failure of the United States to engage in military intervention—set in.[64] And even though this framing gave rise to a powerful historical analogy, used by American policymakers in subsequent protection crises such as Darfur (2005–2006) and Libya (2011), the United States, along with its Western allies, remained selective in its willingness to intervene to "save strangers."

Individual Accountability

The Origins of an Idea

There are two key elements underpinning the idea of individual criminal accountability, or what some have referred to as the "nonimpunity norm."[65] The first is the argument that the most severe violations of human rights (such as torture, genocide, and crimes against humanity) cannot be justified as legitimate state acts or part of "ordinary" politics, but must instead be seen as crimes committed by individuals.[66] The second, related claim is that those individuals who commit these crimes can be, and should be, held accountable—regardless of their role or status. These elements, taken together, encapsulate a significant shift from states to individuals as subjects of international criminal law and challenge older, customary protections granting heads of state and government officials immunity from prosecution.[67] They also gesture to wider changes in legal concepts of personality and agency, through which rights and responsibilities extend beyond and are decoupled from the interests of states.[68]

While prior to 1945 the broad consensus in international society upheld the notion of impunity from prosecution for states and state officials, this approach to accountability evolved in the closing period of World War II. Through the UN Declaration on Human Rights and subsequent human rights treaties, a state model of accountability was born, in which the state as a whole was held responsible for human rights violations and was expected to take remedies. But state officials themselves remained immune from scrutiny or accountability,[69] and there was little in the form of redress—beyond "naming and shaming"—if a state failed to provide remedies for victims of human rights violations.

The moves by Allied countries to create the Nuremberg and Tokyo tribunals after the war were more revolutionary, as they were squarely aimed at establishing individual criminal accountability.[70] By charging German and Japanese leaders with the crime of aggressive war, these tribunals overturned the long-standing right of states to wage war as an accepted instrument of national policy[71] and laid the foundations for a new criminal category, crimes against humanity, which encompassed peacetime violations of the rights of civilian populations. At the same time, the Nuremberg and Tokyo trials were products of a specific context: their scope was limited to the actions of the Axis powers, and they operated under the strict control of the Allies, whose military and civilian presence on the ground secured access to witnesses and documents.[72] In this sense, they constituted both the beginning of a trend—which lay dormant for several decades—and the "exception that proved the rule": it was only in cases of complete defeat of an enemy in war that it was possible to hold state officials criminally accountable for egregious human rights violations.[73] Over the next two decades, various initiatives to establish a permanent court to prosecute war crimes and crimes against humanity were met with lukewarm support from the former backers of Nuremberg and Tokyo and were eclipsed by the hardening rivalry of the Cold War.

Early Post–Cold War Practices of Individual Accountability

The end of the Cold War, and specifically the newfound possibilities for consensus within the UN Security Council, provided a more permissive context for renewed efforts to pursue the idea of individual criminal accountability. As major powers on the Council attempted to grapple with the descent of the former Yugoslavia into bloody ethnic conflict, the United States used its disproportionate power and influence to call for a judicial response to the unfolding violence and atrocities.[74] In 1993, the Council drew on its Article 41 powers by voting to establish the International Criminal Tribunal for the Former Yugoslavia (ICTY), and repeated this move only a year and half later following the genocide in Rwanda, with the creation of the ICTR. Western officials explicitly referenced Nuremberg in their deliberations around these new mechanisms of "liberal legalism,"[75] arguing that they would not only "individualize guilt" for war crimes but also—hopefully—deter future episodes of violence.[76] In accordance with this logic, the Security Council resolution authorizing the ICTR proclaimed that the prosecution of persons violating international humanitarian law "would contribute to the restoration and maintenance of the peace."[77] Nevertheless, the supporters of the new criminal tribunals also insisted on the need to transcend Nuremberg's and Tokyo's brand of "victors' justice" and avoid any indictment of a collective group of people[78]—an imperative that was particularly important to the United States.

The ICTY and ICTR were revolutionary moves from a jurisdictional perspective, particularly in expanding the application of individual criminal accountability to cases of internal as well as interstate war. In the case of the ICTY, its reach extended beyond that of the Nuremberg tribunal in that it included instances of persecution committed during the armed conflict, and its jurisdiction began before the conflict's end. It also went significantly further than Nuremberg, by interpreting the reach of crimes against humanity to include systematic attacks not necessarily limited to the civilian populations or even to wartime.[79] The ICTR's statute also entailed an expansion in jurisdictional reach, through its claim that the genocidal violence that occurred within Rwanda's borders was an appropriate matter to place before an *international* tribunal.

Yet the ad hoc tribunals for the former Yugoslavia and Rwanda also demonstrated that liberal aspirations for a new world order after 1989 were a fusion of principles and power: they were created and shaped by the major powers on the UN Security Council, rather than by the international community as a whole, and were "territorially and temporally limited" to the conflicts and atrocities that Council members wanted to prioritize.[80] The first ICTY prosecutor soon bumped up against waning great power interest in the tribunal's work, as reflected in its modest budget, as well as NATO's unwillingness to assist in arresting indicted war criminals. For its part, the Rwandan tribunal experienced a rocky relationship with the government in Kigali, which had in fact voted *against* the Security Council resolution establishing the ICTR. More broadly, critics voiced concern that the tribunals were not meeting the ambitious goals of fostering stability in their respective regions or facilitating reconciliation between former warring communities, thereby undermining their local legitimacy.[81] Security Council members and other key states that backed the development of these judicial tools missed critical opportunities to fully support this effort—both financially and politically—and to embed them in a larger regional and international strategy to manage and resolve conflict.

It is also worth noting, drawing on the work of Kathryn Sikkink, that as radical as the new criminal tribunals appeared to be, they were also mimicking domestic processes. The broader ideal of transitional justice for wrongdoing was operationalized in a particular *liberal* form, through prosecution. As Sikkink explains, the practices of accountability that began to emerge at the end of the Cold War were inspired and facilitated in large part by human rights activists associated with the so-called third wave of democratization, who pressed for prosecutions within their own countries. Once the idea of accountability for individual leaders and state officials began to take hold, its proponents reached for familiar practices from domestic legal systems.[82] While there were significant alternative paths to addressing past human rights violations, such as memorialization and forms of reparation and reconciliation, criminal prosecution stood out in the 1990s as the dominant transitional justice motif for many liberal internationalists. This was in spite of the fact that international criminal law protects only some categories of human rights, by focusing on accountability for violations that result primarily from physical and direct violence, and that the legal form of criminal trial can serve as a barrier to practices of restorative justice by obstructing opportunities for "truth- telling."[83]

As the ICTY and ICTR continued their painstaking work, there was another watershed moment in the development and application of the idea of individual criminal accountability: the October 1998 arrest of General Augusto Pinochet by British police, who were executing a Spanish extradition request designed to enable the former Chilean leader to stand trial in Spain for the egregious violations of human rights committed during his dictatorship. This example illustrated that individual criminal accountability could be operationalized not only through international prosecutions (at an ad hoc tribunal) but also through application of the principle of universal jurisdiction, whereby one state uses its domestic courts to prosecute a (former) state official from another state for the commission of international crimes. Pinochet's arrest sent a powerful signal to leaders that the former norm of head of state immunity was crumbling under their feet, and that their future plans and behavior might need to adjust to that new reality. Looking back at the decade of the 1990s from our vantage point, with striking examples of universal jurisdiction exercised by a variety of states—including the launch of investigations into alleged Russian war crimes in Ukraine in 2022 by states such as Germany, Spain, and Sweden—it is this particular operationalization of the nonimpunity norm that looks the most "revolutionary."

At the same time, these and other efforts to realize justice through the individualization of guilt[84] have been predicated on an understanding of violence that foregrounded a sharp line between victims and perpetrators at a particular point in time rather than the deeper political factors and forms of social and economic exclusion that contributed to both past and present "wrongs."[85] Various scholars have noted that when understood and depicted through a criminal lens, and "in terms of specific individuals having criminal intent," there may be less attention paid to other types of injustice—including distributive injustice—which might have "fuelled or emerged from the conflict."[86] Furthermore, as Bronwyn Leebaw has powerfully argued, the drive to prosecute came to override other moral and political considerations that arise in the context of both transitions from authoritarianism and extreme manifestations of violence such as genocide and crimes against humanity—including complicity in and resistance to past injustice. By depoliticizing atrocity crimes as a "discrete deviation" from the shared norms or standards of a community, masses of victims can be left "in the shadows."[87]

The "Revolution" at Rome

Although the continued creation of ad hoc tribunals for specific "theaters" was one plausible path for international criminal justice, the intensification of atrocity crimes (particularly in the Balkans), combined with "tribunal fatigue" within the UN Security Council,[88] prompted a committed set of international lawyers, national governments, and civil society activists to contemplate the shape of a permanent court for battling impunity. Initially, the idea also enjoyed favor in the U.S. government, which under President Clinton sought to advance international justice and promote the rule of law, even if it harbored concerns about potential prosecution of American military personnel. But it was frustration at the halfhearted and lengthy pursuit of two ICTY-indicted war criminals, Radovan Karadžić and Ratko Mladić, combined with deepening resistance to a proposal that might expose American military personnel to prosecution, that weakened the commitment of the Clinton administration to international criminal justice. As the top American negotiator thus reminds us, the successful negotiation of the Rome Statute was not a foregone conclusion.[89]

Compared with previous efforts at operationalizing the idea of individual accountability for egregious violations of human rights, the ICC is—on first sight—the most revolutionary in terms of scale and scope. Not only is the ICC a permanent (versus ad hoc) court, with universal jurisdiction, but it can also activate investigations of individuals independent of the consent of states. The most ambitious element of the ICC is its claimed ability to assert authority over heads of state and senior government officials—a feature which "strikes to the heart of state sovereignty" and appears to transfer significant aspects of national authority to a supranational institution.[90] From a historical perspective, the ICC's jurisdiction looks particularly radical in that it (theoretically) allows for the pursuit of accountability for senior state officials while they remain in office.

Nevertheless, other core principles underpinning the ICC suggest that this particular expression of international human rights and international justice was also a form of "soft revolutionism" rather than a fundamental transformation. As with the idea of sovereignty-as-responsibility, the ICC's powers are essentially remedial and defined by the principle of complementarity: the Court initiates proceedings only where national authorities are deemed unable or unwilling to act.[91] States therefore retain primary responsibility for the pursuit of accountability through domestic courts and mechanisms—even if their actions are judged against standards enshrined in the Rome Statute.[92] Furthermore, enforcement of the Court's decisions relies on active cooperation from states, which often fulfill the roles of arresting suspects and facilitating access to evidence and witnesses. Last, but certainly not least, states ultimately control the "purse strings," as they finance the Court's operations, and hence can either enable or impede its efforts to pursue individual criminal accountability.

Some of these state-centric elements of the ICC were all but inevitable in an international system rooted in sovereign equality and state consent. In short, it is hard to see how other "roads" were possible. But although the principle of complementarity was an important and valuable feature of the Court, the ICC's particular approach to operationalizing it was not. Nothing in the design of the ICC demanded that it adopt what Phil Clark has called a "distanced" approach to justice, which positioned the Court as *the* objective and impartial actor, and domestic institutions and actors as "infected by political, social and cultural influences."[93] Instead of insisting on adherence to a particular mode of international justice and challenging national approaches that seemed to diverge from that norm, the ICC could have developed a more "relational"[94] understanding of complementarity that—much like Deng's conception of sovereignty-as-responsibility—sought partnership and interdependence with actors in the domestic realm.

Finally, while the ICC was created as an independent legal entity (outside of the UN system), its activities have also been heavily influenced by the Rome Statute's provisions that give the Security Council power to refer cases and to suspend ongoing ICC investigations "in the interests of justice."[95] These constituted concrete policy choices, not inevitable design features of the ICC, which had a critical impact on perceptions of the Court's independence. As David Bosco has argued, the referral power subsequently allowed the Council to "indirectly guide" the ICC away from investigations that its members might consider "inconvenient" or counter to their interests—given that the Court's human and financial resources are scarce. Some major powers have also employed less formal means of control by sending signals to the Court about whether and how to conduct investigations or offering political and material support in some situations but not in others. Hence, although it cannot yet be definitively concluded that powerful states have "captured" the ICC prosecutor, the record of the Court has been described as "cautious and even deferential"[96]—an outcome that might have been different had Security Council members, and other key states, remained committed to building an international criminal court that could consider (and be *perceived* to consider) all potential cases.

Beyond the compromises at Rome that shaped the ICC's operations and created possibilities for selective justice is the shadow cast by U.S. exceptionalism, both during and after the negotiations on the Court's statute. As with other international treaties, such as the Convention on the Law of the Sea, the Rome Statute, in David Scheffer's words, "fell prey to Washington's endless conflicts between sovereignty and global responsibility."[97] A set of stringent demands that included opposition to any independent power by the prosecutor to initiate investigations and a requirement that the consent of the state of nationality of a suspect had to be secured before the ICC could prosecute all but assured that the United States would not accede to the agreed text in July 1998—leaving many to contemplate what additional power the ICC might have enjoyed with full U.S. backing. Even though President Clinton eventually decided to sign the Rome Statute at the end of 2000, on the last possible day, the new administration of George W. Bush would take U.S. exceptionalism in a more strident direction, by signing the American Service Members Protection Act, embarking on efforts to sign immunity agreements with other states,[98] and denying the applicability of the Geneva Conventions in the context of the War on Terror.

The War in Kosovo: A Turning Point for Liberal Aspirations?

As the 1990s came to an end, notions of responsible sovereignty and individual criminal accountability came together during NATO's use of force to respond to ethnic cleansing in Serbia's province of Kosovo. In January 1999, just as Western diplomats were pressuring Belgrade with military action if it failed to end its crackdown on Kosovar Albanians, the prosecutor of the ICTY, Louise Arbour, arrived at Kosovo's border demanding access to investigate alleged atrocities as part of an eventual indictment of Slobodan Milošević. As the bombs started to fall, Arbour intensified her search for the evidence that would ultimately lead to the Serbian leader's arrest and transfer to The Hague as the first sitting head of state to be indicted for war crimes.

But the spring of 1999 also exposed some of the limitations in ways that liberal states were imagining and practicing the ideas of sovereignty-as-responsibility and individual criminal accountability. Most immediately, while Arbour has insisted that her relatively quick pursuit of Milošević was due to the ICTY's change in investigative strategy rather than to the facilitating actions of NATO countries, Western governments undoubtedly "smoothed the way" for the work of the tribunal—thereby giving rise to questions about its independence.[99] Moreover, once the prosecutor (as well as her successor, Carla del Ponte) began to ask uncomfortable questions about NATO's own targeting during the Kosovo War, she was met with either Western silence or indignation that there might be any equivalence in the practices of Serbian and NATO forces. When she realized that NATO would not cooperate with the tribunal, del Ponte recalled, "I understood that I had collided with the edge of the political universe in which the tribunal was allowed to function."[100] This episode thus illustrates the selective commitment to individual criminal accountability. While powerful Western states might be willing to pursue it in particular situations, they would strongly resist any efforts to apply the notion to themselves.

The intervention in Kosovo also generated intense contestation outside of the West, both because it was waged without the authorization of the UN Security Council and thus without broad-based consensus and because it coexisted with other instances of gross and systematic violations of human rights that did not generate a robust response. In April 1999, in a landmark speech in Chicago, U.K. prime minister Tony Blair articulated an ambitious "Doctrine of the International Community," designed to set out a principled approach to reconciling the traditional practice of nonintervention with the need to stop widespread abuses by a government against its own citizens. "We might be tempted to think back to the simplicity of the Cold War," he told his audience. "But now we have to establish a new framework."[101] Yet this more assertive liberal framework did not generate a consistent or robust response to atrocity crimes in the ensuing decades, and thus contributed to growing contestation of the legitimacy of coercive intervention to promote and protect human rights, particularly within the Global South.

Conclusion

Martin Wight saw a central paradox in the successive waves of revolutionist and counterrevolutionist doctrine that have marked the international system since the early modern period: they aimed at uniting and integrating what he called "the family of nations," but in practice they divided it more deeply than it had been before. Was this also the effect of the revolutionary ideas of sovereignty-as-responsibility and individual criminal accountability that emerged after the end of the Cold War? In retrospect, it is clear that the rendering of these ideas by liberal internationalists in the early post–Cold War period did not succeed in revolutionizing the understanding of sovereignty. Not only were these ideas compromised by some of the practices of intervention and state recognition in the post–Cold War period, including by liberal states themselves, but they were increasingly contested by states invoking other powerful normative ideas that arguably have become even more central in our increasingly pluralist world. But the underlying objective of the "soft revolutionism" that inspired liberals in the 1990s—to give individuals, and individual protection, a more central place in international theory and practice—lives on, as do key institutional forms of that revolutionism, such as the ICC, however imperfect their construction.

This brings me to the question of whether liberal internationalists could have taken an alternative path to realizing the doctrine of international human rights. The original creation of ICISS was embedded in a broader 1990s discourse of "human security," which placed the individual, and his or her security, at the center of international affairs and which challenged the traditionally dominant paradigm of state security. This framework was heavily influenced by a related belief, also prominent at this time, that globalization and deep forms of interdependence had made sovereign frontiers less relevant and more porous. Although advocates of responsible sovereignty took pains to stress that human security did not make sovereignty obsolete and that the former would strengthen the latter, their cosmopolitan perspective led them to downplay sovereignty's broader normative status and role in international society.[102] The assertive liberal internationalists of the 1990s therefore gave too little space and attention to the equally powerful ideas of sovereign equality and self-determination when advocating new ways to protect human rights through collective action, or in advocating revision to norms such as nonintervention or state accountability. It is also worth remembering that an approach aimed at punishing those who violate human rights is markedly different from other forms of human rights promotion that might have been given great play, particularly those aimed at supporting political mobilization around issues of social and economic justice.[103]

As responsible sovereignty and individual criminal accountability were practiced in the last decade of the twentieth century, they exposed a fundamental hierarchy of power underpinning the post–Cold War order, in which both the international enforcement of human rights and the pursuit of justice were based either on a seemingly distant and unaccountable "international community" or on the discretion and priorities of Western states. An alternative vision might have adopted a less punitive and more egalitarian and bottom-up perspective—where states fulfill their primary responsibility to protect and pursue accountability for past wrongs but also support one another, as equals, in protecting vulnerable populations and realizing various versions of justice. This was precisely the vision that Deng developed and promoted through his version of responsible sovereignty. It was also part of the vision that inspired newly independent states after 1945 to call for collective action in the name of anticolonialism and international humanitarian duties. Perhaps it constitutes one of the roads not taken in that critical decade of the 1990s.

Notes

1. Deudney and Ikenberry 1991–1992.
2. Brown 1997.
3. Thomas 2001.
4. Risse et al. 1999.

5. Beitz 2009, 1. For the argument that human rights should be enforced, including extraterritorially, see Hafner-Burton 2013.
6. These three models—the individual criminal accountability model, the immunity or impunity model, and the state accountability model—are elaborated in Sikkink 2011, 13–14.
7. Wight and Porter 1991, 8.
8. See, for example, Wheeler 2000.
9. Cunliffe 2020, 41.
10. Buzan 1991, 307.
11. I thank Tolya Levshin for suggesting this wording.
12. Deng et al. 1996, xviii. Deng was the first special representative of the UN secretary general on the rights of internally displaced people in the 1990s, and later served as special advisor, and under-secretary general, on the prevention of genocide.
13. See Simpson 2001. Simpson calls this liberal position "liberal anti-pluralism."
14. Barkin 1998.
15. Buchanan 2004, 260.
16. Teson 2003, 93.
17. Meron 2000.
18. Teitel 2011.
19. International Development Research Centre 2001b.
20. Deng 1993.
21. International Development Research Centre 2001a, 11.
22. Annan 1999, 49–50.
23. Deng et al. 1996, 8.
24. Haas 2003.
25. Deng et al. 1996, xi.
26. Deng 1998, ch. 6.
27. Gerry Simpson (2001) and Jean Cohen (2012) have made similar distinctions between different types of contemporary liberal arguments, depending on the degree to which they are committed to toleration of pluralism at the domestic level.
28. See Hafner-Burton 2013; Teson 2003.
29. For further discussion of this context and how it shaped Deng's approach, see Welsh 2010.
30. *The Kampala Document* 1991. The Kampala Process was spearheaded by the Africa Leaders Forum. For more discussion on the Kampala Process, which was created by the African Leaders Forum, see Deng and Zartman 2002.
31. Deng et al. 1996, xii.
32. Deng et al. 1996, xiii, 28.
33. Cohen and Deng 1998.
34. Deng 1998, 145.
35. Deng et al. 1996, xviii.
36. For similar arguments about the ahistoricism of contemporary liberal views on sovereignty, see Simpson 2001; Glanville 2011.
37. Quinton-Brown 2024, 9. For more on developing countries' understandings of self-determination in the mid-twentieth century, see Getachew 2019.
38. Evans 2009, 42.
39. Instead, if or when the sovereign failed to protect his subjects, Hobbes argued, individuals reverted to the state of nature, where they had a legitimate right to seek their own preservation.
40. Orford 2011, 27.
41. Cohen 2012, 54.
42. Quinton-Brown 2024, 220.
43. European Community (1991) 1993.
44. See, for example, Caplan 2005.
45. Caplan 2005.
46. Rich 1993; Hillgruber 1998.
47. The increased activism of the Council can be assessed quantitatively by comparing the number of resolutions passed from 1946 to 1989 (646 resolutions, or an average of fewer than 15 per year) and from 1990 to 1999 (638 resolutions, or an average of 64 resolutions per year).
48. United Nations Security Council 1992.
49. For more on the Somalia case, see Wheeler 2000, ch. 6.

50. This term refers to a use of force that does not have Security Council authorization; it does not mean that a state is acting alone. States can act collectively, but unilaterally, if they act without the Council's imprimatur. For the purposes of my analysis, I define humanitarian intervention as "the use of force by a state (or group of states acting together) aimed at preventing or ending a humanitarian catastrophe affecting individuals other than its own citizens, without the permission of the state within whose territory force is applied." See International Law Association 2018.
51. See the discussion and review of legal opinions in Lowe and Tzanakopoulos 2012; Rodley 2015, 775–776.
52. See Byers and Chesterman 2003.
53. Chesterman 2021, 5.
54. United Nations 1999.
55. Lowe and Tzanakopoulos 2012, 12.
56. Group of 77, 1999.
57. Lowe and Tzanakopoulos 2012, 12, 17.
58. This reluctance was reflected in the efforts of John Bolton, then U.S. permanent representative to the United Nations, to strike out references to the "shared responsibility to take collective action" during the negotiations in 2005 over the new principle of the responsibility to protect. See Welsh 2012, 109; Bellamy and Luck 2018, 28.
59. Wheeler 2000, 178–182.
60. Power 2002, 329–390 (especially 377).
61. PDD-25 remains classified. The quotation comes from a press briefing on its content. See Lake 1994. I am grateful to Patrick Travers for pointing out this source to me.
62. See Wertheim 2010.
63. One example is the 1999 United Nations *Report of the Independent Inquiry into the Actions of the United Nations during the 1994 Genocide in Rwanda*, whose authors were tasked by Kofi Annan to assess the organization's response. The report allocates blame to a variety of parties for different mistakes. Among these is the UN Assistance Mission for Rwanda (UNAMIR) mission on the ground, which suffered from communication and command issues and failed to fulfill its mandate (United Nations Security Council 1999, 30–31); UN headquarters, which failed in the planning and oversight of the UNAMIR mission, particularly to equip the mission fully (32); and key states within the international community—including the United States—for lack of political will to intervene, their restrictive mandating of UNAMIR, and, in some cases, their active sabotaging of UNAMIR's efforts in Rwanda during the genocide (37).
64. For an analysis of how this particular representation developed over time, see Hergaden 2021.
65. Bower 2019.
66. Sikkink 2011, 13. In a similar way, David Luban (2013, 309) underscores that a core implication of international criminal justice is that those who commit acts such as crimes against humanity or genocide are criminals, as opposed to mere political opponents.
67. Bower 2019, 90.
68. Teitel 2011, 17.
69. Even when individuals brought petitions before the UN Human Rights Committee for violations of the Convention on Civil and Political Rights, these petitions were aimed at a state rather than a specific state official. See Sikkink 2011, 14–15.
70. After World War I, the Treaty of Versailles called publicly to "arraign" the Kaiser for a "supreme offence against international morality," but no legal proceedings ever took place.
71. The Kellogg-Briand Pact of 1928, which also called for the eradication of the right to wage war, was not equipped with enforcement provisions nor explicitly connected to the idea of individual criminal liability. For further discussion of the movement to abolish the right to wage war, see Hathaway and Shapiro 2017.
72. Bosco 2014, 28–29.
73. Sikkink 2011, 5. The limitations of Nuremberg can be seen in its approach to crimes against humanity. While in theory this new crime was meant to apply both in peace and in war, and to cover all civilian populations, in practice the Nuremberg tribunal limited its prosecution of crimes against humanity to instances where allegations could be connected to the conduct of war by the defeated Axis powers. See Teitel 2011, 77.

74. As David Scheffer (2012, 18) argues, this judicial approach was seen as a "softer" and less costly option than full-scale military intervention—a path which would also have encountered disagreement within the Council.
75. Teitel 2011, 81.
76. Bosco 2014, 36.
77. United Nations Security Council 1993.
78. Scheffer 2012, 21.
79. Teitel 2011, 46, 54.
80. Bosco 2014, 37.
81. See the discussion in Teitel 2011, 80–82.
82. Sikkink 2011, 20. This argument about internationalization of the domestic approach is also forwarded by Bass 2000.
83. Nouwen 2024, 214, 206–207.
84. Leebaw 2012, 89. See also Welsh et al. 2023.
85. For a convincing analysis that problematizes victim-perpetrator binaries, see Collins 2008. For a discussion of Collins in the context of atrocity crime prevention, see Welsh 2016.
86. Nouwen 2024, 206. See also Kersten 2016.
87. Leebaw 2012, 56, 188.
88. The term is Scheffer's (2012, 168).
89. Scheffer 2012, 164.
90. Bower 2019, 90.
91. See Article 17 of the Rome Statute.
92. Bower 2019, 91.
93. Clark 2018, 303.
94. Clark 2018, 302. As Clark notes, the ICC's distanced approach has frequently extended to its management of human resources. In key cases relating to Africa, the Court has often used non-African personnel who spent little time in investigation sites, used intermediaries for its investigation, and engaged in minimal outreach with local communities.
95. See Article 16 of the Rome Statute. This power of suspension is on a renewable, one-year basis.
96. Bosco 2014, 21–22.
97. Scheffer 2012, 413.
98. Bosco 2014, 71.
99. Bosco 2014, 64.
100. Cited in Bosco 2014, 66.
101. Blair 1999.
102. I have developed this assessment more fully elsewhere (Welsh 2013).
103. See Nouwen and Werner 2015.

References

Annan, Kofi. 1999. "Two Conceptions of Sovereignty." *The Economist*, September 18.
Barkin, Samuel. 1998. "The Evolution of the Constitution of Sovereignty and the Emergence of Human Rights Norms." *Millennium: Journal of International Studies* 27 (2): 229–252.
Bass, Gary. 2000. *Stay the Hand of Justice: The Politics of War Crimes Tribunals.* Princeton University Press.
Beitz, Charles. 2009. *The Idea of Human Rights.* Oxford University Press.
Bellamy, Alex J., and Edward C. Luck. 2018. *The Responsibility to Protect: From Promise to Practice.* Polity Press.
Blair, Tony. 1999. "The Doctrine of the International Community." Speech to the Economic Club of Chicago, April 24. http://www.britishpoliticalspeech.org/speech-archive.htm?speech=279.
Bosco, David. 2014. *Rough Justice: The International Criminal Court in a World of Power Politics.* Oxford University Press.

Bower, Adam. 2019. "Contesting the International Criminal Court: Bashir, Kenyatta, and the Status of the Nonimpunity Norm in World Politics." *Journal of Global Security Studies* 4 (1): 88–104.
Brown, Archie. 1997. *The Gorbachev Factor*. Oxford University Press.
Buchanan, Allen. 2004. *Justice, Legitimacy, and Self-Determination: Moral Foundations for International Law*. Oxford University Press.
Buzan, Barry. 1991. *People, States and Fear: An Agenda for International Security Studies in the Post–Cold War Era*. Harvester Wheatsheaf.
Byers, Michael, and Simon Chesterman. 2003. "Changing the Rules about Rules? Unilateral Humanitarian Intervention and the Future of International Law." In *Humanitarian Intervention*, edited by J. L. Holzgrefe and Robert O. Keohane. Cambridge University Press.
Caplan, Richard. 2005. *Europe and the Recognition of New States in Yugoslavia*. Cambridge University Press.
Chesterman, Simon. 2021. "Responsibility to Protect and Humanitarian Intervention: From Apology to Utopia and Back Again." In *The Oxford Handbook of the International Law of Global Security*, edited by Robin Geiß and Nils Melzer. Oxford University Press.
Clark, Phil. 2018. *Distant Justice: The Impact of the International Criminal Court on African Politics*. Cambridge University Press.
Cohen, Jean L. 2012. *Globalization and Sovereignty: Rethinking Legality, Legitimacy, and Constitutionalism*. Cambridge University Press.
Cohen, Roberta, and Francis M. Deng. 1998. *Masses in Flight: The Global Crisis of Internal Displacement*. Brookings Institution.
Collins, Randall. 2008. *Violence: A Micro-Sociological Theory*. Princeton University Press.
Cunliffe, Philip. 2020. *Cosmopolitan Dystopia: International Intervention and the Failure of the West*. Manchester University Press.
Deng, Francis M. 1993. *Protecting the Dispossessed: A Challenge for the International Community*. Brookings Institution.
Deng, Francis M. 1998. "African Policy Agenda: A Framework for Global Partnership." In *African Reckoning: A Quest for Good Governance*, edited by Francis M. Deng and Terence Lyons. Brookings Institution.
Deng, Francis M., Sadikiel Kimaro, Terrence Lyons, Donald Rothchild, and I. William Zartman. 1996. *Sovereignty as Responsibility: Conflict Management in Africa*. Brookings Institution.
Deng, Francis M., and I. William Zartman. 2002. *A Strategic Vision for Africa: The Kampala Movement*. Brookings Institution.
Deudney, Daniel, and John Ikenberry. 1991–1992. "The International Sources of Soviet Change." *International Security* 16 (3): 74–118.
European Community. (1991) 1993. "Declaration on the 'Guidelines on the Recognition of New States in Eastern Europe and in the Soviet Union.'" December 16. Reprint, *European Journal of International Law* 4 (1): 7–23.
Evans, Gareth. 2009. *The Responsibility to Protect: Ending Mass Atrocity Crimes Once and For All*. Brookings.
Getachew, Adam. 2019. *Worldmaking after Empire: The Rise and Fall of Self-Determination*. Princeton University Press.
Glanville, Luke. 2011. "The Antecedents of 'Sovereignty as Responsibility.'" *European Journal of International Relations* 17 (2): 233–255.
Group of 77. 1999. "Ministerial Declaration of the Twenty-Third Annual Meeting of the Ministers for Foreign Affairs of the Group of 77." UN Doc. A/54/532, September 24. https://www.g77.org/doc/Decl1999.html.
Haas, Richard. 2003. "Sovereignty: Existing Rights, Evolving Responsibilities." Remarks to the School of Foreign Service and the Mortara Center for International Studies, Georgetown University, January 14. https://2001-2009.state.gov/s/p/rem/2003/16648.htm

Hafner-Burton, Emilie. 2013. *Making Human Rights a Reality*. Princeton University Press.
Hathaway, Oona, and Scott Shapiro. 2017. *The Internationalists: How a Radical Plan to Outlaw War Remade the World*. Simon and Schuster.
Hergaden, Malte F. 2021. "Historical Analogies and Military Intervention: Framing and Representation in Foreign Policy Discourses about Situations of Mass Atrocity." PhD diss., European University Institute.
Hillgruber, Christian. 1998. "The Admission of New States to the International Community." *European Journal of International Law* 9 (3): 491–509.
International Development Research Centre. 2001a. *The Responsibility to Protect: Research, Bibliography, Background*. Ottawa. https://idrc-crdi.ca/en/books/responsibility-protect-report-international-commission-intervention-and-state-sovereignty
International Development Research Centre. 2001b. *The Responsibility to Protect: The Report of the International Commission on Intervention and State Sovereignty*. Ottawa. https://idrc-crdi.ca/en/books/responsibility-protect-report-international-commission-intervention-and-state-sovereignty.
International Law Association. 2018. *Final Report on Aggression and the Use of Force*. https://www.ila-hq.org/images/ILA/DraftReports/DraftReport_UseOfForce.pdf.
The Kampala Document: Towards a Conference on Security, Stability, Development and Cooperation in Africa. 1991. May 19–22. Kampala. https://search.worldcat.org/title/27267039.
Kersten, Mark. 2016. *Justice in Conflict: The Effects of the International Criminal Court's Interventions on Ending Wars and Building Peace*. Oxford University Press.
Lake, Anthony. 1994. "Press Briefing by National Security Advisor Tony Lake and Director for Strategic Plans and Policy General Wesley Clark." May 5. http://www.fas.org/irp/offdocs/pdd25_brief.htm.
Leebaw, Bronwyn. 2012. *Judging State-Sponsored Violence, Imagining Political Change*. Cambridge University Press.
Lowe, Vaughan, and Antonios Tzanakopoulos. 2012. "Humanitarian Intervention." In *The Max Planck Encyclopedia of Public International Law*, edited by Rudiger Wolfrum. Oxford University Press.
Luban, David. 2013. "After the Honeymoon: Reflections on the Current State of International Criminal Justice." *Journal of International Criminal Justice* 1 (3): 505–515.
Meron, Theodore. 2000. "The Humanization of Humanitarian Law." *American Journal of International Law* 94 (2): 239–278.
Nouwen, Sarah. 2024. "Tensions between the Pursuit of Criminal Accountability and Other International Policy Agendas." In *The Individualization of War*, edited by Jennifer M. Welsh, Dapo Akande, and David Rodin. Oxford University Press.
Nouwen, Sarah, and Wouter G. Werner. 2015. "Monopolizing Global Justice: International Criminal Law as Challenge to Human Diversity." *Journal of International Criminal Justice* 13 (1): 157–176.
Orford, Anne. 2011. *International Authority and the Responsibility to Protect*. Cambridge University Press.
Power, Samantha. 2002. *"A Problem from Hell": America and the Age of Genocide*. Basic Books.
Quinton-Brown, Patrick. 2024. *Intervention before Interventionism: A Global Genealogy*. Oxford University Press.
Rich, Roland. 1993. "Recognition of States: The Collapse of Yugoslavia and the Soviet Union." *European Journal of International Law* 4 (1): 36–65.
Risse, Thomas, Stephen C. Ropp, and Kathryn Sikkink. 1999. *The Power of Human Rights: International Norms and Domestic Change*. Cambridge University Press.
Rodley, Nigel. 2015. "Humanitarian Intervention." In *The Oxford Handbook on the Use of Force in International Law*, edited by Marc Weller. Oxford University Press.

Scheffer, David. 2012. *All the Missing Souls: A Personal History of the War Crimes Tribunals.* Princeton University Press.

Sikkink, Kathryn. 2011. *The Justice Cascade.* W. W. Norton.

Simpson, Gerry. 2001. "Two Liberalisms." *European Journal of International Law* 12 (3): 537–571.

Teitel, Ruti. 2011. *Humanity's Law.* Oxford University Press.

Teson, Fernando. 2003. "The Liberal Case for Humanitarian Intervention." In *Humanitarian Intervention: Ethical, Legal, and Political Dilemmas*, edited by J. L. Holzgrefe and Robert O. Keohane. Cambridge University Press.

Thomas, Daniel C. 2001. *The Helsinki Effect: International Norms, Human Rights, and the Demise of Communism.* Princeton University Press.

United Nations. 1999. Document. S/PV.3988, March 24. https://www.securitycouncilreport.org/atf/cf/%7B65BFCF9B-6D27-4E9C-8CD3-CF6E4FF96FF9%7D/kos%20SPV3988.pdf

United Nations Security Council. 1992. UNSC Resolution 794, December 3. https://digitallibrary.un.org/record/154648?ln=en&v=pdf

United Nations Security Council. 1993. UNSC Resolution 827. UN doc. S/RES/955. https://digitallibrary.un.org/record/166567?ln=en&v=pdf

United Nations Security Council. 1999. *United Nations Report of the Independent Inquiry into the Actions of the United Nations during the 1994 Genocide in Rwanda.* https://www.securitycouncilreport.org/atf/cf/%7B65BFCF9B-6D27-4E9C-8CD3-CF6E4FF96FF9%7D/POC%20S19991257.pdf

Welsh, Jennifer M. 2010. "Implementing the 'Responsibility to Protect': Where Expectations Meet Reality." *Ethics and International Affairs* 4 (4): 415–430.

Welsh, Jennifer M. 2012. "Who Should Act? Collective Responsibility and the Responsibility to Protect." In *The Routledge Handbook of the Responsibility to Protect*, edited by W. Andy Knight and Frazer Egerton. Routledge.

Welsh, Jennifer M. 2013. "Norm Contestation and the Responsibility to Protect." *Global Responsibility to Protect* 5 (4): 365–396.

Welsh, Jennifer M. 2016. "'The Narrow but Deep Approach' to Implementing the Responsibility to Protect: Reassessing the Focus on International Crimes." In *Reassessing Atrocity Prevention*, edited by Sheri Rosenberg, Tiberu Galis, and Alex Zucker. Cambridge University Press.

Welsh, Jennifer M., Dapo Akande, and David Rodin. 2023. *The Individualization of War: Rights, Liability and Accountability in Contemporary Armed Conflict.* Oxford University Press.

Wertheim, Stephen. 2010. "A Solution from Hell: The United States and the Rise of Humanitarian Interventionism, 1991–2003." *Journal of Genocide Research* 12: 149–172.

Wheeler, Nicholas. 2000. *Saving Strangers: Humanitarian Intervention in International Society.* Oxford University Press.

Wight, Gabriele, and Brian Porter. 1991. *International Theory: The Three Traditions.* Leicester University Press.

PART II
TAKING STOCK
Western Successes and Failures

6
Populism and the Durability of the Liberal Order in Eastern Europe
EU and NATO Enlargement Reconsidered

Hilary Appel

The reorientation of Eastern Europe and the inclusion of these states as full members in multilateral organizations such as the World Trade Organization, the International Monetary Fund (IMF), the European Union, and NATO are emblematic of the post–Cold War moment in which former communist states embraced—and were embraced by—the West. The 1990s saw the extension of the liberal order, broadening the zone of democracy and free markets. The decision by European and American leaders to expand the membership of key institutions in the 1990s created a critical turning point in the political and economic evolution of East Europe and helped usher in the rejection of the communist past. EU and NATO accession gave momentum to Eastern Europe's democratic and capitalist development, despite the many domestic political challenges associated with this dual transition. By the late 1990s, Eastern Europe's candidate countries seemed to have escaped a quick return to authoritarianism, an outcome feared by theorists who recognized the scope and depth of the transformation needed to avoid this outcome.[1] The prospect of foreign investment, access to markets, the rule of law, and security guarantees incentivized leaders to adopt reforms that prioritized EU and NATO accession.

The aim of this chapter is to examine how Eastern Europe's reorientation toward the West and its accession to leading institutions in the 1990s shaped the liberal trajectory of the region, with a particular focus on Hungary, Poland, the Czech Republic, and Slovakia. Given the subsequent rise of Euroskepticism, illiberalism, and economic nationalism embraced by populist leaders over the past decade, it is useful to explore whether the early and accelerated process of integrating East European states into Western organizations—their most important foreign policy development of the first post–Cold War decade—may have abetted in or detracted from establishing and sustaining a commitment to liberalism. More specifically, this chapter explores whether the illiberal trends over the past decade in Central Europe simply reflect democratic decline as seen across many regions, or whether there was something distinctive about their paths from communism in the 1990s that accounts for their development and trajectory. That is, did the specific ways that EU and NATO accessions were carried out in the 1990s—employing strong if not coercive membership conditionality—contribute to a populist and Euroskeptic backlash after achieving membership? Given recent developments, how does the Russia-Ukraine War fit into this trajectory of liberal development in Eastern Europe? Has Russia's attack on Ukraine inspired a renewed appreciation of the Western liberal order given the intensification of a common security threat, despite recent populist and antidemocratic dynamics that have been surfacing and receding across these countries?

These are the questions that motivate this chapter. While many of the observations would apply to a much larger set of postcommunist countries, this chapter focuses mainly on Poland and Hungary and, to a lesser extent, the Czech Republic and Slovakia. In all four of these Visegrad states, the 1990s were a crucial decade establishing Western-style democracy, capitalism, and the rule of law. The first three had become NATO members in 1999, and Slovakia soon followed in 2004, the same year all four joined the EU as full members. Even earlier, these countries joined the World Trade Organization in 1995 and the Council of Europe in 1990.

Not only were Poland and Hungary at the forefront of joining the West in the immediate aftermath of the Cold War, but they were also at the forefront of violating liberal norms and pushing back on Western institutions. Both countries have seen the rise of populist leaders with authoritarian tendencies who employed anti-EU rhetoric and who were singled out by the European Commission and European Parliament for violating fundamental democratic principles through Article 7 proceedings.[2] Moreover, antidemocratic, populist parties and leaders have also gained prominence and won elections in the Czech Republic and Slovakia in recent times, albeit without triggering Article 7 proceedings.

Defiance of liberal democratic norms and practices was not anticipated in the aftermath of the Cold War. On the contrary, Central Europe provided some of the most promising exemplars of early economic and political liberalization in the 1990s. Even before the reelection of an increasingly populist Robert Fico in September 2023, Slovakia serves as an important case study of the 1990s, since it was the least on track to liberalize and democratize in East-Central Europe but changed course at a critical juncture when its growing illiberal practices were blocking its access to key Western institutions. For all of these reasons, these Central European states provide fertile ground for exploring the 1990s as a critical moment of global realignment. These four cases, especially given recent rising authoritarian tendencies, compel scholars to reexamine whether the rapid and full incorporation of former communist states into multilateral institutions was the right path for cementing and expanding the liberal order in the aftermath of the Cold War.

This chapter argues that the expansion of major multilateral organizations, including the EU and NATO, was instrumental in the fundamental liberal shift in the trajectory of Hungary, Poland, Slovakia, and the Czech Republic. Despite the demands and the speed of membership accession, and despite the substantial loss of domestic policymaking authority in the process, these countries' accession processes on balance contributed significantly and positively to their democratic and capitalist transformations and the embrace of liberal norms.

Despite populist leaders' success in using anti-EU rhetoric and criticism of the EU's imperialist tendencies in Hungary and Poland to gain power, it is important to not lose sight of the fact that joining these organizations allowed all four countries to undertake difficult systemic reforms, in contrast to Belarus, Russia, Serbia, Uzbekistan, Azerbaijan, and other post-Soviet states that have yet to create systems with free markets, the rule of law, good governance, or leadership turnover and accountability. What accession did not achieve is the hoped-for "lock-in effect," binding future leaders to specific liberal norms and practices embraced by the governments in the lead-up to membership.[3]

The structure of this chapter is as follows. First, the chapter briefly reviews the process of Eastern Europe's economic integration into the West and accession into two key multilateral organizations, the EU and NATO, in order to gauge their impact on these countries' political and economic development. It explores the nature of the process, highlighting the relinquishing of policy autonomy during EU accession and the loss of economic control due to dependence on foreign capital. Next, the chapter examines the rise of Euroskepticism and the movement away from liberal norms over the past decade, considering several motivations for these developments and the relative depth of antidemocratic and anti-EU sentiment in society. The chapter concludes with a discussion of how Russia's invasion of Ukraine matters for the attraction of the liberal order in Hungary and Poland, and in Eastern Europe more broadly.

Joining the Western Liberal Order

After the dissolution of the Soviet bloc, Western governments wanted to help East European countries break with their communist past and integrate into core Western liberal institutions. Joining the European Union and NATO became top priorities from the earliest days for most East European leaders and parties, whether hailing from the right or the left side of the political spectrum.[4] They demonstrated a commitment to pursue profound institutional change in order to prepare themselves for NATO and later the EU, a process requiring the transposition of laws and institutions with little room for adaptation to domestic conditions or input from the general public or elite stakeholders. Liberal political reforms featured importantly in the membership criteria for both NATO and the EU, in addition to substantial economic and military reforms. The *political* criteria for membership in both institutions helped to support the emergence of democratic states oriented toward the West, with political systems based on free elections, the rule of law, respect for individual rights, and minority protections.[5]

Gaining membership in these organizations was a goal in and of itself, but it was also a means of attracting foreign capital and fostering economic growth, thereby reorienting these economies toward the West. At this pivotal moment, these states sought to replenish their domestic stocks of capital, worryingly low and broadly obsolete after decades of communism. Aspiring member states sought capital investment to modernize their economies to help them recover from decades of inefficient, stagnant command economies.[6] This need to adopt policies that improved access to capital from private actors and international financial institutions, such as the IMF and the European Bank for Reconstruction and Development, led to the adoption of Washington Consensus policies: free market programs that liberalized trade and capital flows, deregulated prices, stabilized the money supply, and privatized as much state property as quickly as possible. The international financial institutions assessed and ranked countries' performance in instituting market reforms; the IMF offering its "seal of approval" helped countries gain access to capital.[7] In publishing these rankings and indicators, scholars have noted the coercive dimension, with bodies trying to apply normative pressure on governments to adopt certain kinds of policies.[8]

Any alternative path to reform that resisted foreign capital or strayed from IMF neoliberal prescriptions was risky; hence calls for gentler or more gradual approaches to adopting capitalism lost out to more radical approaches.[9] The IMF's lending conditionality and the EU's membership conditionality strongly incentivized East European countries to undertake politically difficult and socially destabilizing economic reforms as quickly as possible.

The shock therapy programs and the full embrace of capitalism in the early 1990s caused significant economic hardship and social dislocation across the region.[10] All of these countries faced severe transitional recessions.[11] Angry citizens resented the erosion of their life savings due to high inflation and feared for their livelihoods, given enterprise closures and labor shedding due to privatization. Inequality increased and poverty became visible in the panorama of everyday life. International policy advisors were wary of the pain of reforms and warned that rising inequality and economic uncertainty would disrupt the political transitions to democracy.[12] Instead of softening the blow, policy advisors recommended that governments undertake economic reforms as deeply and rapidly as possible before an opposition could mobilize and vote the market reformers out of office.[13] Citizens in Poland and elsewhere experiencing the pain of these reforms quipped that the "shock therapy" programs involved a whole lot of "shock" and not much "therapy."

And in the midst of all this pain, a seismic shift was happening: the expansion of the liberal order to postcommunist Eastern Europe. Without question, economic hardship and political resistance to market reform at times delayed the implementation of capitalist reforms, and governments did not complete all the programs promoted by international financial institutions and the EU at the same pace. Implementation of free markets proceeded over an extended period and to varying degrees.[14] That said, the economic regimes based on administrative planning and state ownership were decisively left behind in nearly all of Eastern Europe.[15] The spread of neoliberalism was accompanied by a new commitment to the rule of law, democratic processes, and the political accountability of ruling elites.

Acceding to the European Union

For the EU candidate countries in Eastern Europe, the attainment of full membership not only served as a *recognition* of the successful adoption of competitive markets and liberal values in the region; it also served as an *incentive mechanism* to embrace these values at critical junctures. When political obstacles to liberal reforms emerged, the larger enticement of full membership managed to overpower local opposition. For instance, without EU membership conditionality, Polish leaders may not have found the political will to permit foreign investors, especially from Germany, to gain title to Polish land.[16] In a similar vein, EU pressure and the incentive of membership gave Baltic leaders the political cover needed to grant language and citizenship rights to ethnic Russians living in Latvia and Estonia.[17] It also motivated the last-ditch effort to privatize the steel industry in order to prevent the postponement of the Czech Republic's and Poland's accession until the second round of EU enlargement.[18] Indeed, membership conditionality and the accession process facilitated economic and political liberalization in very significant and precise ways. After all, countless capitalist reforms were highly unpopular and faced concentrated local resistance in the 1990s. Yet the overall foreign policy goal of EU membership remained broadly popular, allowing leaders to assert truthfully that, without adopting certain programs, membership would be delayed, if not derailed entirely.[19] In short, membership conditionality at this critical juncture was real and credible, motivating massive institutional change and quelling dissent in the short term. The impact was so significant that it is hard to conceive of such a speedy and extensive reorientation of the region without this highly structured and monitored process of liberal reform.

The credibility and direct impact of membership conditionality on political liberalization are most acutely seen in the case of Slovakia. In the period following Czechoslovakia's Velvet Divorce and the 1994 reelection of Prime Minister Vladimír Mečiar, Slovakia began to show signs of significant democratic decay. The coalition government failed to respect the autonomy of the presidency, the judiciary, or the central referendum commission and failed to respect the rights of the large Hungarian minority. The Mečiar government also cracked down on parliamentary opposition figures and suppressed media freedoms. Its growing authoritarian tendencies culminated in the critical decision by the European Commission and the European Council to *not* invite Slovakia to begin accession negotiations in 1997 along with its three Visegrad neighbors. Slovakia's democratic shortcomings, identified explicitly and repeatedly by the European Commission in such official documents as *Agenda 2000* and the annual *Regular Reports*, had to be addressed in order for Slovakia to begin the accession negotiation process. The Slovak population understood these political obstacles to accession to Western multilateral bodies and in 1998 voted Mečiar's coalition out of office.[20]

EU leaders had the extraordinary power to influence not just the general direction of reform but the narrow policy choices of governments as well. They had to comply with minute and detailed requirements, with little to no flexibility.[21] During the first wave of EU enlargement, the accession negotiating teams completed their work without approving any exceptions or even transitional periods for nine of the accession chapters, including industrial policy, common foreign and security policy, financial control, and economic and monetary union.[22] Given the complex and diverse political and economic conditions in the ten candidate countries of the 2004 round, the lack of any country-specific arrangements in a large number of chapters in the 2004 round is remarkable. Even in those chapters in which some transitional periods were allowed, like the chapter on tax policy, the exceptions numbered around ten per country and concentrated on rather narrow policy areas (say, excise duties on home spirits), and even then, the approved exceptions were temporary.[23] The accession negotiations—which were "negotiations" only in name, since aspiring members had no negotiating power—highlight the capacity of the EU at this time to promote specific rules, institutions, and practices in East European candidate countries, driving the process of political and economic liberalization. This stands in stark contrast to existing member states that were allowed to negotiate "opt-out clauses" in multiple policy areas.[24]

The extraordinary willingness of governments to cede policymaking authority across so many areas in a condensed time period resulted *only in part* from the expected economic benefits of EU membership. There were important cultural and historical factors abetting Eastern Europe's determination to join the liberal world order through membership in its key institutions. Many Eastern Europeans saw their Cold War alignment with the Soviet Union as the product of external coercion. The achievement of true sovereignty at the end of the Cold War finally gave them the opportunity to return to their place in a democratic Europe. After all, the activists of 1989 had adopted the slogan "Back to Europe!," not "To Europe!"[25]

In addition to a pervasive pro-European identity, a strong fear of the Soviet Union and Russia prevailed, adding further urgency to these countries' reorientation toward the West. Memories of the Warsaw Pact invasion of Hungary in 1956 and Czechoslovakia in 1968, as well as the experience of martial law in Poland in 1981, figured prominently in Central European countries' geopolitical realignment. Resentment at having lost their independence and national sovereignty to the Soviet Union produced a powerful distrust of post-Soviet Russia that lingered long after Eastern European states gained full autonomy. Presidents Václav Havel of the Czech Republic and Lech Wałęsa of Poland believed security from Russian aggression in the long term required firm alliances and full engagement with powerful and prosperous Western countries. Already in May 1992, the presidents of Czechoslovakia, Hungary, and Poland declared their intention of gaining full NATO membership. The United States responded to their requests with the Partnership for Peace Program in 1994, which bought the NATO alliance members some time to study the issue of enlargement. The United States wanted to develop a path to membership that would be acceptable to the existing NATO members, not to mention less damaging to the U.S. relationship with Russia. Slowing down NATO enlargement could be useful to Russian president Boris Yeltsin, who was expected to face strong opposition to this development and a tough reelection bid in 1996.[26] Yeltsin would have a hard time beating Genadii Ziuganov, his communist challenger, given his low popularity, the protracted economic crisis in Russia, and the Chechen War raging at home.

Joining the NATO Alliance

Joining NATO shared some similarities with joining the EU, including the importance of adopting broadly liberal political and economic institutions. For the former Soviet bloc states, NATO's membership criteria became loosely articulated in a 1995 self-study on enlargement. The study determined that the path to membership should incentivize democratic consolidation and market reforms.[27] The study's main documents stated explicitly that new NATO members must have "a functioning democratic political system based on a market economy," "fair treatment of minority populations," "a commitment to the peaceful resolution of conflict," "the ability and willingness to make a military contribution to NATO operations," and a "commitment to democratic civil-military relations and institutional structures."[28] The 1995 study also outlined specific military obligations, like contributions to alliance budgets, targets for defense spending floors,[29] the provision of staff to NATO headquarters and its military structure, and participation in common intelligence-sharing efforts.[30]

Adding new members to NATO required (and still requires) unanimity, as in the EU. All existing NATO members had to agree to invite a country to join NATO, meaning a single member state of any size or security importance could block the accession of an aspiring member. Once again, with an eye to Russia, the study also made explicit that a nonmember could not block enlargement. The study notes presciently, "No country outside the Alliance should be given a veto or *droit de regard* over the process and decisions."[31]

While NATO and the EU imposed political, economic, and human rights conditions on candidate countries, the accession processes for each body differed in several important respects. First, NATO enlargement began much earlier, indeed five years before the EU's first round of enlargement. Second, there was a much smaller NATO bureaucracy tasked with identifying and monitoring candidate countries' progress in fulfilling membership requirements relative to the EU bureaucracy. For both of these reasons, the conditions of NATO membership, while broad in scope, were much looser than those of EU membership. Moreover, under NATO enlargement, there was no single model that aspiring members had to adopt. Beyond requiring civilian control of the military, NATO said little about how member states should organize their militaries and, instead, very rapidly brought Hungary, Poland, and the Czech Republic into the alliance in 1999. As Wade Jacoby explains, "On the basis of vague thresholds in its *Study on Enlargement* . . . it extended invitations to three states in July 1997, and only then conducted a brief set of accession talks (in September and November 1997)."[32] For the Czech Republic, there existed "only a general, four-page National Defense Strategy, hastily approved by the Parliament in March 1997 in order to satisfy NATO requirements."[33] In Hungary, the program to reform civil-military relations as required by NATO was not even formalized in writing prior to accession.[34] In other words, NATO accession did contain membership conditionality, but it was much less coercive and intrusive than EU accession.

The looseness and informality of NATO accession in the 1990s is in contrast with the specificity of EU accession, which gave precise blueprints and contained extensive monitoring of candidate countries' transposition of eighty thousand pages of EU law, the *acquis communautaire*. Even within this less rigid accession process, Slovakia fell behind in meeting the expectations of NATO membership due to the authoritarian, illiberal tendencies of Mečiar's government. His failure to win reelection in 1998 against a broad coalition of anti-Mečiar parties cleared the way for democratizing reforms and ultimately for NATO accession five years after Hungary, Poland, and the Czech Republic acceded. In sum, NATO enlargement, despite being less intrusive than EU enlargement, created incentives for liberalizing reforms and played a crucial role in reorienting Central Europe from East to West, in both security and political dimensions.

Euroskepticism and National Chauvinism

Starting with the process of accession and throughout the course of regional and global integration, Central and East European states became highly reliant upon the West for security, markets, and capital. European integration not only required the loss of policymaking authority, quite intensely during the EU accession period, but it opened these domestic markets to foreign investment and competition from Western imports. In reference to the decline of domestic economic control, Andreas Nölke and Arjan Vliegenthart describe these countries as "dependent market economies" with a high degree of foreign ownership and dependence on the West.[35]

One of the earliest and most prominent Euroskeptic politicians of the region to bemoan his country's growing dependence on foreign capital and loss of control to the European Union was Czech president Václav Klaus. For example, in multiple speeches Klaus warned that the Czech Republic must not allow itself "to dissolve in Europe like a sugar cube in a teacup."[36] In 2004, Klaus refused to endorse a "yes" vote at the time of his country's referendum on EU membership—the only head of state not to do so. Over the course of his career, Klaus repeated and intensified his anti-EU stance,[37] describing Europe as having changed from a "historically evolved bundle of sovereign and independent countries to the very authoritative and centralistic empire called European Union."[38] In the 1990s, Klaus seemed to be an outlier, but in retrospect the Czech leader was instead a harbinger of Euroskepticism in the region. His anti-EU rhetoric and his fierce criticisms of supranational governance became common and were adopted by several Czech populist successors, most notably President Miloš Zeman and Prime Minister Andrej Babiš.

Klaus's counterparts in Hungary, Poland, and elsewhere have also seemed to take a page from his playbook recently, using anti-EU rhetoric built upon the same theme of the EU as an empire that fails to respect the sovereignty of its member states. Hungarian prime minister Viktor Orbán stated in March 2011, "We did not let Vienna dictate us in 1848, we did not let Moscow dictate us in 1956, and we won't let Brussels or others dictate us now."[39] In 2012 and 2013, respectively, Orbán professed, "We are not prepared to allow foreigners to govern us" and "We will not be told by bankers and foreign bureaucrats how to live our lives."[40] More recently, Orbán stated, "Brussels today is ruled by those who want to replace an alliance of free nations with a European empire: A European empire led not by elected leaders of nations, but by Brussels bureaucrats ... an elite separated from its national roots; an alliance with multinational power groups; a coalition with financial speculators."[41]

Orbán's nationalist, xenophobic language attracted global attention and condemnation when Hungary, like many European states, became a transit country for North African and Middle Eastern refugees. Orbán employed anti-immigrant, anti-Muslim, xenophobic rhetoric and refused to follow EU rules on the processing and treatment of refugees during the 2015 European migrant surge. Despite EU obligations, Orbán asserted Hungary's sovereign right to remain ethnically Hungarian and Christian and to resist becoming a country of immigrants. He was able to use the migrant crisis in Europe to mobilize his supporters around his broadly illiberal agenda, intensifying the populist movement in Hungary.

Beyond his position on migration, Orbán's nationalism also translated into the economic realm. In the aftermath of Europe's financial and debt crises, Orbán could feed off popular frustration with the state of the economy, the skyrocketing cost of foreign mortgages, and Hungary's need for an IMF bailout. Instead of recognizing the assistance of the European Central Bank, the European Commission, and the IMF in helping Hungary avoid default, Orbán blamed outside financial actors for the state of the economy.[42] His animus toward foreign ownership of Hungarian banks led to his pledge to return Hungarian-majority ownership to the banking sector, asserting there were too many foreign banks in the country. He honored this promise quickly by imposing a new confiscatory banking tax,[43] which helped the

Hungarians assume majority national (albeit nonstate) ownership of the banking sector.[44]

Like Orbán, leaders in Poland employed populist and nationalist rhetoric based upon a sensitivity toward yielding authority to an external power.[45] The head of the Freedom and Justice Party, Jarosław Kaczyński, adopted language that emphasized resentment toward the loss of policy sovereignty and the EU's efforts to shape Poland's domestic affairs. For example, Kaczyński stated in 2015, "We will let no one in the EU indicate what path we should take."[46] He criticized the EU for using budgetary funds to "obtain a mighty regulatory power over Poland."[47] At an anti-EU "summit" in December 2021,[48] he signed a joint declaration along with Orbán (and others, including France's Marine Le Pen and Italy's Matteo Salvini) proclaiming their commitment to "protecting the sovereignty" of EU member states. The Polish leader further added that the EU was seeking a "cultural revolution" aimed at "destroying the current social structures" and building a "superstate" through the EU's "efforts to centralize policy-making."[49] According to an analysis by Robert Csehi and Edit Zgut, both Orbán and Kaczyński often drew on classic populist tropes in their appeals to the electorate, characterizing the EU as "led by a corrupt elite against the will of the people."[50]

Illiberal Practices in Hungary and Poland

The Euroskeptic rhetoric of Poland's and Hungary's most influential leaders has been accompanied by autocratic, illiberal practices, prompting the EU to seek penalties for the two countries' governing parties, Poland's Law and Justice Party and Hungary's Fidesz. As noted above, the European Commission in the case of Poland and the European Parliament in the case of Hungary initiated Article 7 proceedings following several illiberal, antidemocratic developments. In Hungary, Fidesz used its supermajority in Parliament to restructure the country's electoral rules to the party's advantage, adjusting the proportional representation procedures and using gerrymandering to favor it. In addition, Parliament passed a new constitution that weakened the judicial branch and pushed out Constitutional Court justices who disagreed with Orbán or his agenda. The Fidesz government has also repressed academic institutions and nongovernmental organizations, including criminalizing the activity of prominent human rights organizations.[51] In addition, Orbán has managed to assume massive control over Hungary's media and to exert influence over information flows to his advantage.[52]

Poland's illiberal practices also became more salient and extreme over time as well. The Law and Justice Party advanced illiberal and populist programs, undermining the rule of law by weakening Poland's judicial branch. New laws neutered Poland's highest court (the Constitutional Tribunal), diminished the independence of the public prosecutor's office (*prokuratura*) by merging it with the government-controlled Ministry of Justice, and engaged in the deliberate intimidation of independent-minded judges. Moreover, the country's electoral laws were changed such that the electoral commissioners (the actors who ensure against electoral fraud) were no longer independent but were subordinate to the Ministry of the Interior (and by extension the party in power).[53] Likewise, the Law and Justice government undermined the country's previously free media by harassing journalists and issuing fines against private media outlets for their coverage of sensitive issues (for example, fining TVN24). Unable to punish Poland and Hungary using Article 7 given bureaucratic limitations of the procedure, the EU opted to fine Poland for its violations of European norms beginning in October 2021. From October 2021 to January 2022, the EU actively sought ways to pressure Poland to meet its obligations and pay its fines, including blocking Poland's access to EU COVID-19 relief funds.

What became clear through these efforts was that the EU's power to promote liberalism during the accession negotiations of the 1990s did not extend into the postaccession period. Indeed, the progress made in embracing new liberal institutions during this key period, while deeply transformative, did not fully shield these countries from the appeal of populist, antiliberal leaders. As in Western Europe and the United States in roughly the same time period, new leaders with antidemocratic tendencies found ways to appeal to voting publics and rise to prominence.

An Exogenous Shock: Russia's Invasion of Ukraine

For EU officials, the worsening antidemocratic dynamics in Hungary and Poland and, to a lesser extent, in the Czech Republic, took a backseat after Russia fully invaded Ukraine on February 24, 2022. Western leaders turned their attention to the more immediate security threat and prioritized unity in the EU and the NATO alliance. Relative to Hungary, Poland's support for a unified economic and political response to Russian aggression was easy to secure. Poland's Law and Justice Party had always been anti-Russian, and successive Polish governments over many decades have favored policies that other members of the EU and NATO shied away from in order to avoid antagonizing Russia. The leader of the Law and Justice Party, Jarosław Kaczyński, was previously a dissident and an active supporter of the Solidarity movement, and his behavior and statements have consistently been anti-Russian since the breakup of the Soviet Union. In addition, his party was known to promote the narrative that Russia played a direct role in a plane crash that killed his brother, the late president Lech Kaczyński, along with other top Polish leaders on board. For all of these reasons, Poland's support for a strong and unified European response to Russian aggression was abundantly forthcoming. Poland has stood out as a strong supporter of NATO enlargement for years and since February 2022 has provided substantial assistance to Ukraine's military effort and has absorbed over 1.5 million refugees.[54] Hence, due to the war, the issue of growing authoritarianism and the outstanding fines related to violations of judicial independence have retreated from the forefront in EU-Polish relations; in June 2022 the EU announced it would release Poland's COVID-19 relief funds in recognition of its support for Ukraine, although delays in the release of EU funds continued. For example, Brussels suspended the release of a new round of Cohesion Funds for regional aid due to Warsaw's failure to comply with EU requirements on judicial reforms.[55] Poland's new legislation creating a commission to investigate Russian influence in Polish politics, which was widely interpreted as a ploy to disqualify opposition candidates from running in elections, jeopardized Poland's access to EU funds yet again.[56] However, with the defeat of Law and Justice in October 2023 and the return of a pro-EU government, Poland's EU relationship improved.

By contrast, Hungary's government has remained one of the most illiberal and pro-Russian governments in Europe for nearly a decade. Hungary became a much less reliable partner for NATO and the EU prior to and during the war in Ukraine, not only due to Orbán's authoritarian and populist tendencies but also due to his rapprochement with President Vladimir Putin and several new Russian-Hungarian areas of cooperation. More specifically, Fidesz courted major investments from Russian firms in the sectors of energy, transportation, finance, engineering, and pharmaceuticals, including the import of Russian COVID vaccines in 2021 without the approval of

EU regulators. Hungary has also opted out of voluntary agreements among EU states to reduce imports of Russian oil.[57]

In the past, Orbán presented himself as strongly anti-Russia, especially in the aftermath of the Cold War, famously calling for the expulsion of Russians from Hungary at the start of his career.[58] Therefore, his close relationship with President Putin and the country's economic cooperation with Russia represent a departure from his earlier position. More striking, Orbán's positive relations with Putin are accompanied with an explicit appreciation for Russia's illiberal political and economic model. Orbán shocked many when, in a major policy speech in 2014, he stated that Hungary was building "an illiberal state, a non-liberal state."[59] He elaborated, "When I mention the European Union, I am not doing this because I think it is impossible to build an illiberal nation state within the EU. I think this is possible. Our EU membership does not rule out this option.... A trending topic in thinking is understanding systems that are not Western, not liberal, not liberal democracies, maybe not even democracies, and yet making nations successful. Today, the stars of international analyses are Singapore, China, India, Turkey, [and] Russia."[60]

Orbán's pro-Russian and pro-authoritarian rhetoric (not to mention his efforts to play the EU and Russia off each other) briefly halted after Russia invaded Ukraine in February 2022. For a short period, Orbán was more restrained in his support for Russia and more cooperative with the West, agreeing to support EU sanctions against Russia and even calling Ukrainian president Volodymyr Zelensky to offer his support in the early days of the war. However, Orbán's message reverted shortly thereafter. Not only did his support for Ukraine become muted; he made clear that a positive bilateral relationship with Russia was the key to Hungary's own physical and energy security, having just visited Russia earlier in February 2022 to negotiate favorable access to cheap Russian gas.[61] This message of "peace and low energy prices" helped secure Orbán's reelection on April 3, 2022, and emboldened him to return to his previously positive line toward Russia.[62]

As a result, Hungary's contribution to a unified Western response to Russia's war in Ukraine as well as Hungary's place in the liberal world order are faltering. Hungary has proclaimed that it would remain neutral and therefore forbid the transit of weapons through Hungarian territory.[63] It also would not support an embargo of Russian oil, intended to prevent the flow of funds needed for Russia to wage war. Only briefly, then, did the vision of Russian tanks rolling across borders and Russian missiles lobbed at Ukrainian civilian areas help the Hungarian leadership appreciate the *benefits* of being part of the transnational alliance and a unified liberal order.

The election of Prime Minister Robert Fico from the Smer Party in Slovakia in October 2023 once again raised concerns that Hungary could tap a new partner in avoiding EU efforts to sanction the government, now that Orbán could no longer rely on Poland with the 2023 defeat of the Freedom and Justice Party. During the campaign, Fico employed strongly Euroskeptic rhetoric and expressed sympathy for Hungary's position vis-à-vis Russia and the EU. However, the antidemocratic stance of Fico's campaign has not provided Orbán with the partner he had hoped for, even before the assassination attempt against Fico in May 2024, incapacitating him for an extended period. Instead, Orbán may have to wait for new elections in the Czech Republic or another EU state to shield his country from European pressure and penalties.

The Durability of the Liberal Order in Eastern Europe

Recent developments in Hungary, Poland, the Czech Republic, and Slovakia do not paint a clear picture of what the war in Ukraine means for the resilience of the liberal order. While some scholars speculated initially that the exogenous shock of the war in Ukraine would help reinvigorate the West and underscore the value of liberalism and transatlanticism,[64] Orbán and Fico's postinvasion electoral successes are not encouraging signs. They suggest that economic nationalism and populist appeals are still effective electoral strategies, despite the brutal and shocking images from the Russia-Ukraine War. Citizens who feel resentful or left behind in Eastern Europe's turn to the West, and who dislike their country's de facto lower status within EU and NATO structures, may very well continue to support populist, illiberal parties and leaders who, in turn, pull their countries away from multilateral organizations and weaken democratic norms at home. At some point populists may seek to inflame anti-refugee sentiments, as the war in Ukraine drags on. Despite the defeat of the Freedom and Justice Party in Poland, there are many indications that some groups, such as farmers and truckers, are losing patience with pro-Ukrainian policies that undermine their livelihood. The economic costs and the disruption caused by both the war and Europe's coordinated response hit the poor disproportionately, making these voters more susceptible to authoritarian and Euroskeptic appeals in subsequent election cycles.

Despite this distinct possibility, one encouraging fact, that may well be in part a product of the accession dynamics of the 1990s, is that the depth of antiliberal sentiment in these countries, according to public opinion polls, does not run deep—at least relative to other European countries. Not only did Hungarian, Polish, Slovak, and Czech voters support the national referenda to join the EU in overwhelming majorities (92 percent in Slovakia, 77 percent in the Czech Republic, 84 percent in Hungary, and 77 percent in Poland), but these populations continue to register very high support for the EU and NATO in opinion surveys. Importantly, popular support for the EU did decline in 2012 and 2013 in Poland, the Czech Republic, and Hungary during the depths of the European debt and financial crises,[65] but in the middle of the decade popular support for the EU began to recover. In the final Eurobarometer survey just prior to the Ukraine War, public opinion surveys showed very high EU support, and Hungarians and Poles offered some of the most pro-EU opinions in Europe.[66] After Russia's invasion of Ukraine, support remained high: in Hungary, 61 percent of respondents say the EU promotes peace, 69 percent say it promotes democracy, and 66 percent say it promotes prosperity, according to an April–June 2022 Pew Research poll; in Poland, 92 percent of respondents say the EU promotes peace, 84 percent say it promotes democracy, and 83 percent say it promotes prosperity according to a March–May 2022 Pew Research poll.[67] The polling data show that before and after the Ukrainian War, Hungarians and Poles are not more Euroskeptic than the average EU citizen, and if anything, they are more positive.[68] Furthermore, in Eastern Europe there is no "Leave" campaign à la Brexit. If anything, the recognition of the value of multilateralism and the momentum for enlargement of NATO have grown throughout Europe,[69] with Finland and Sweden becoming full members.[70]

In sum, East European citizens for now have shown no interest in pulling away from multilateral organizations and seem to identify strongly with Europe and the West. Despite their leaders' behavior, liberal democratic norms embraced in the 1990s by the populace endure, even in the face of the challenges related to the economy and migration in the 2010s.[71] Indeed, the EU remains surprisingly popular among the Hungarian and Polish people. As Ivan Krastev writes, "Eastern Europeans are among the most pro-EU publics on the continent, yet they vote for some of the most Eurosceptical governments. These governments, in turn, use Brussels as a rhetorical punching bag while benefiting from its financial largess."[72]

Conclusion

Returning to the main focus of this volume—the impact of the 1990s on the spread and endurance of the liberal order—there does not seem to be any evidence that the West's overarching policy toward Eastern Europe, as well as the specific way in which the EU and NATO incorporated East European member states, are responsible for Euroskepticism or illiberal dynamics in the region. In the period leading up to and following enlargement, there was a strong consensus among the vast majority of politicians and citizens favoring accession. The populations still favor membership in Western organizations, and Euroskepticism is on average higher in the rest of the EU than it is in Eastern Europe. Thus the relationship between democratic decay and Euroskepticism seems at most tenuously related to the exercise of EU membership conditionality in the 1990s. Additionally, a rhetorical backlash against NATO or NATO accession among new members has never materialized. Instead, the 1990s were a crucial decade for the spread of the liberal order and a reflection of an ambitious and visionary policy of inclusion of former communist states. It is hard to imagine what these countries would look like without access to Western markets, capital, institutions, and security guarantees, but Ukraine, Moldova, Serbia, and Georgia may give some indication of what unrealized aspirations of joining these multilateral organization can mean for a country's democratic development and territorial integrity.

This chapter argues instead that the explanation for the rise (and sometimes the decline) of populist leaders and parties lies elsewhere. Not only did populism and Euroskepticism emerge later, mainly during the 2010s, but they seem more related to the financial crisis and discrediting of the Social Democrats in Hungary. In Poland, the weakening of centrist mainstream parties, especially the center-left, also allowed for the ascent of populist politicians. Moreover, the repeated electoral successes of populist parties—Hungary's Fidesz, Poland's Freedom and Justice Party, Slovakia's Smer, and the Czech Republic's Ano Party—can be traced to many factors, including the manipulation of electoral laws and gerrymandering (in Hungary certainly), the weakening of the institutions of accountability, and failure of the mainstream parties to respond to popular concerns.[73]

Beyond domestic factors, it is important to note that the flourishing of populism in East Central Europe did not occur in a vacuum, as populism and antidemocratic dynamics are on the rise globally. It is quite likely that populist politicians in Eastern Europe saw their counterparts abroad violate liberal principles and stray from democratic principles in the late 2010s and pay no price: no regional or global isolation, no loss of investors, and no meaningful repudiation within NATO, the Council of Europe, the EU, the World Trade Organization, or elsewhere. They realized that with just a bit of coordination punishment in the EU can be difficult: most EU penalties require unanimity, which are easily avoided when two countries work together. Autocrats acting with impunity over the past decade have likely had a demonstration effect, creating a permissive environment with few deterrents—unlike the 1990s, when the populism of Mečiar and even Klaus was kept in check. The zeitgeist of the 2010s and 2020s, when populism and autocracy are mainly ignored, differs importantly from that of the 1990s, when liberal norms were ascendant and autocratic behavior precluded meaningful opportunities.[74]

Granted, EU and NATO enlargement could have been managed better. For example, in retrospect, the urgency to finalize EU membership by 2004 for the ten first-round countries and the rigidity with which the process was carried out seem unjustified now. The invasive scrutiny, extensive monitoring, and coercive membership conditions made many elites and citizens wary of the loss of autonomy, especially so soon after gaining true sovereignty from the Soviet Union. And yet the EU's popular appeal was highest precisely when these countries were under the strictest constraints related to membership conditionality. For this reason, the rise of populist politicians with antidemocratic tendencies seems to have little to do with the nature of EU and NATO enlargement during the 1990s. Rather, a theory of East European populism would likely need to begin with the study of Europe's financial crises, migration spikes, and, most important, the collapse of centrist parties in the 2010s.[75] The decade of the 1990s, by contrast, was a key moment for the spread of liberalism in the region and the popular embrace of democratic norms.

In sum, EU accession in the 1990s and beyond could have shown greater care and concern for the citizens in these countries, in terms of both their material suffering and their identities as self-ruling agents within new democratic regimes. By the same token, NATO enlargement might have been pursued in ways to appear less threatening to Russia, which has assumed a more aggressive, revanchist stance in the current order. That said, on balance, the full incorporation of Hungary, Poland, Slovakia, the Czech Republic, and other countries into these multilateral organizations brought energy and momentum to the liberal transformation of these polities and societies. The prospect of a future in Europe and the West dampened the appeal of demagoguery and nationalism of the sort that erupted in the Balkans. In this regard, the credible membership prospects in multilateral trade and security institutions may have helped keep the peace after the Velvet Divorce in Czechoslovakia and diminished the attraction of revanchism in Hungary and Poland related to lost territory after the first and second world wars.

Without membership conditionality and their full incorporation into democratic and capitalist institutions, they might have looked closer to authoritarian states further to the east that had no credible hope of membership. Accession to these organizations contributed to their democratic consolidation and subsequent economic growth. The rise of populism, nativism, and the efforts to concentrate power and weaken independent institutions, like the judiciary in Poland and Hungary, should not be attributed to their experiences with accession and the West's policies of inclusion in the 1990s. That decade was a time of liberal institution building. While not all of these institutions, practices, and norms achieved the "lock-in effects" that some scholars predicted or hoped for, the expansion of multilateralism and the full membership of thirteen former communist countries in peak organizations launched a new liberal trajectory for East European states that is being tested in the current era.

Notes

1. Przeworski 1991; Sachs 1994.
2. In October 2021, the EU began fining Poland 1 million euros per day for its violations of judicial independence. Prior to that, the European Union had initiated Article 7 proceedings for Poland in December 2017 and for Hungary in September 2018 in response to serious and repeated breaches of European values and democratic norms in these countries.
3. Moravcsik 2000; Sedelmeier 2012.
4. Grzymala-Busse and Innes 2003.
5. Sasse 2008; Schimmelfennig and Sedelmeier 2004, 2020.
6. Appel and Orenstein 2018.
7. Appel and Orenstein 2018.
8. Cooley and Snyder 2015; Schueth 2011.

9. Appel and Orenstein 2016.
10. Ghodsee and Orenstein 2021.
11. According to data from the European Bank for Reconstruction and Development (2000, 4, cited in Appel and Orenstein 2018, 26), during the first three years of transition (1990–1992) Hungary's GDP contracted 17.6 percent, Poland's GDP contracted 15.6 percent, and Czechoslovakia's GDP contracted 15.4 percent. As severe as these were, Bulgaria and Romania suffered even worse GDP contractions, at 25.6 and 25 percent, respectively, during the same period.
12. Comisso 1990; Dahrendorf 1990; Przeworski 1991.
13. Sachs 1994; Balcerowicz 1994.
14. Rutland 2013; Ban 2016; Appel and Orenstein 2018.
15. Bandelj 2008.
16. Appel 2011.
17. Kelley 2006; Hughes 2005.
18. Sznajder Lee 2016. Neither the Czech Republic nor Poland could close the chapter on competition policy in the accession negotiations since they had not succeeded in privatizing the steel industry. At the eleventh hour these governments had to choose between selling their steel mills to Rotterdam-based LNM Group in an uncompetitive bid or postponing EU membership. For more detail, see Sznajder Lee 2016.
19. Grzymala-Busse and Innes 2003.
20. As Schimmelfennig et al. (2003, 506) sum up, "EU conditionality had an effect on the parliamentary elections of 1998 in which the Mečiar government was defeated. Indeed, public opinion data suggest that a majority of Slovak citizens was aware of, and preoccupied by, the deterioration of their country's standing in Europe and its exclusion from EU enlargement." Also see Bútora and Bútorová 1999; Haughton 2001.
21. Jacoby 1999; Vachudova 2005.
22. All candidate countries had to commit to work toward fulfilling the Maastricht criteria for monetary union, which required reaching certain targets for inflation, interest rates, debt to GDP ratios, and more. Despite these stated commitments, many new members have yet to meet the criteria by choice, while others have failed to reach these targets despite a preference for adopting the euro.
23. Appel 2011.
24. Vachudova 2005.
25. Lázár 2015; Klaus 2004; Appel 2004.
26. Jacoby 2004, 121.
27. Epstein 2008.
28. NATO 1995.
29. Jacoby (2004, 138–139) outlines how countries in the first round worked to reach defense spending floors in the years following membership.
30. Appel and Taw 2020.
31. NATO 1995.
32. Jacoby 2004, 122–123.
33. Szayna 1999, 134, quoted in Jacoby 2004, 151.
34. Jacoby 2004, 151.
35. Nölke and Vliegenthart 2009.
36. Milos and Macková 2015.
37. In a systematic study of Vaclav Klaus's speeches while in office from 1995 to 2013, Milos Gregor and Alena Macková (2015) find that in 62 percent of cases, "the attitude expressed in the speeches towards the EU was negative"; Klaus referred positively to the EU in only 3 percent of his speeches and neutrally in 8 percent of his speeches.
38. Klaus 2021.
39. Csehi and Zgut 2020, 59.
40. Csehi and Zgut 2020, 59.
41. Orbán 2018, quoted in Csehi and Zgut 2020, 59.
42. Orbán scapegoated foreign-owned banks, writing in 2010, "It is a system built to overpower while pretending to compete.... The state must step up against such situations." He also repeatedly criticized the IMF and pushed back on its terms as funds flowed in—similar to his position on the EU. See discussion in Dunai 2022; and Orban's 2014 speeches, Orbán 2014a, Orbán 2014b.

43. Johnson and Barnes 2015.
44. Dunai 2022; Johnson and Barnes 2025.
45. Bonikowski et al., 2019, 78.
46. Csehi and Zgut 2020, 23.
47. Csehi and Zgut 2020, 61.
48. Referred to as the "Warsaw Summit of Conservative Leaders of Europe," participants at this meeting issued a declaration criticizing "the disturbing idea of creating a Europe governed by a self-appointed elite" and opposing the "arbitrary application of EU law," in reference to the EU's assessment of Poland's and Hungary's abuse of the rule of law. See Rettman 2021.
49. Kurasinska 2021.
50. Csehi and Zgut 2020, 63.
51. For more on the ban, see Amnesty International 2018.
52. Zerofsky 2019; Appel 2021.
53. Sadurski 2019.
54. Minder et al. 2023.
55. Minder and Fleming 2022; Miller et al. 2023.
56. Sierakowski 2023.
57. Landler 2022.
58. Sierakowski 2018.
59. Orbán 2014a.
60. Orbán 2014a.
61. Krekó 2022; *Hungary Today* 2022; Scheppele 2022.
62. Krekó 2022.
63. Scheppele 2022.
64. Way 2022; Gans-Morse and Kelly 2022.
65. Pew Research Center 2013.
66. For example, the 2019 Pew Research Center surveys show substantial support for the EU—with 67 and 62 percent of Polish and Hungarian respondents, respectively, agreeing that their "country's membership in the EU has been a good thing," which is above the EU median of 59 percent.
67. Clancy 2022.
68. For more on 2022 comparative data on positive assessments of the EU which contextualizes Hungary and Poland across other countries, see Pew Research Center data from a 2022 survey at Faggan and Gubbala 2022. Briefly, the number of respondents with a favorable view of the EU is high in Poland (89 percent), Hungary (69), Germany (78), France (66) Greece (50), and the United Kingdom (68) (Gubbala 2023).
69. Appel and Taw 2020.
70. Following the invasion of Ukraine, unity among NATO, the EU, and their partners is at the highest level in decades. Italy, Germany, and other EU states previously displayed great caution toward Russia, treading extremely carefully around the issue of EU and NATO enlargement, given their energy dependence (Appel and Taw 2020). Now they are fully participating in the sanctions regime and are more open to further enlargement. European energy dependency on Russia is down, with greater reliance on supplies from Norway, the United States, and Qatar (Reed and Eddy 2023).
71. Popular support for democracy remains strong in opinion polls. According to Pew Research Center surveys, the percentage of respondents who say "democracy is preferable to any other form of government" is high in Poland and Hungary relative to other countries in the region (Pew Research Center 2015–2016); according to YouGov surveys, anti-immigrant sentiment in Eastern Europe is lower than in France, Germany and the United Kingdom. See YouGov 2016, "Authoritarian Populism Study."
72. Krastev 2018, 52.
73. Grzymala-Busse 2019.
74. Shin 1994; Doorenspleet 2000; Huntington 1991.
75. Zaun and Servent 2023; Santana et al. 2020; Grzymala-Busse 2019.

References

Amnesty International. 2018. "Hungary: Draconian Anti-NGO Law Will Be Resisted Every Step of the Way." June 20. https://www.amnesty.org/en/latest/news/2018/06/hungary-draconian-anti-ngo-law-will-be-resisted-every-step-of-the-way/.

Appel, Hilary. 2004. *A New Capitalist Order: Privatization and Ideology in Russia and Eastern Europe.* University of Pittsburgh Press.

Appel, Hilary. 2011. *Tax Politics in Eastern Europe: Globalization, Regional Integration and the Democratic Compromise.* University of Michigan Press.

Appel, Hilary, and Mitchell A. Orenstein. 2016. "Why Did Neoliberalism Triumph and Endure in the Post-Communist World?" *Comparative Politics* 48 (3): 313–331.

Appel, Hilary, and Mitchell A. Orenstein. 2018. *From Triumph to Crisis: Neoliberal Economic Reform in Post-Communist Countries.* Cambridge University Press.

Appel, Hilary, and Jennifer Taw. 2020. "Has Russia's Anti-NATO Agenda Succeeded?" *Problems of Post-Communism,* 68 (6): 468–476. doi: 10.1080/10758216.2020.1844024.

Baczynska, Gabriela. 2022. "Poland Gets Formal EU Demand to Pay Fines over Judicial Regime." Reuters, January 20. https://www.reuters.com/world/europe/poland-gets-formal-eu-demand-pay-fines-over-judicial-regime-2022-01-20/.

Ban, Cornel. 2016. *Ruling Ideas: How Global Economic Paradigms Go Local.* Oxford University Press.

Balcerowicz, Leszek. 1994. "Understanding Postcommunist Transitions." *Journal of Democracy* 5 (4): 75–89.

Bandelj, Nina. 2008. *From Communists to Foreign Capitalists: The Social Foundations of Foreign Direct Investment in Postsocialist Europe.* Princeton University Press.

Bojar, Abel, Zoé Gáspár, and Dániel Róna. 2022. "Can They Ever Win? The Past and Future Prospects for an Opposition Victory." *Review of Democracy,* April 30. https://revdem.ceu.edu/2022/04/30/prospects-for-an-opposition-victory-in-hungarys competitive-authoritarian-regime/?fbclid=IwAR16yV_LAv-FZWC1uA5_-oZg46VOF_cxi YC_z113DNsAp1veep_1p-xaX18.

Bonikowski, B., D. Halikiopoulou, E. Kaufmann, and M. Rooduijn. 2019. "Populism and Nationalism in a Comparative Perspective: A Scholarly Exchange." *Nations and Nationalism* 25 (1): 58–81.

Brack, Nathalie, and Nicholas Startin. 2015. "Introduction: Euroscepticism, from the Margins to the Mainstream." *International Political Science Review* 36 (3): 239–249.

Brubaker, Rogers. 2017. "Between Nationalism and Civilizationism: The European Populist Moment in Comparative Perspective." *Ethnic and Racial Studies* 40 (8): 1191–1226. doi:10.1080/01419870.2017.1294700.

Bútora, Martin, and Zora Bútorová. 1999. "Eastern Europe a Decade Later: Slovakia's Democratic Awakening." *Journal of Democracy* 10 (1): 80–95.

Clancy, Laura. 2022. "Despite Recent Political Clashes, Most People in Poland and Hungary See the EU Favorably." Pew Research Center. https://www.pewresearch.org/short-reads/2022/10/18/despite-recent-political-clashes-most-people-in-poland-and-hungary-see-the-eu-favorably/.

Comisso, Ellen. 1990. "Property Rights, Liberalism, and the Transition from 'Actually Existing' Socialism." *East European Politics & Societies* 5 (1): 162–188.

Cooley, Alexander, and Jack Snyder, eds. 2015. *Ranking the World: Grading States as a Tool of Global Governance.* Cambridge: University of Cambridge Press.

Cooper, Helene. 2023. "U.S. Defense Secretary Urges Swift NATO Membership for Sweden." *New York Times,* April 19.

Csehi, Robert, and Edit Zgut. 2020. "We Won't Let Brussels Dictate Us: Eurosceptic Populism in Hungary and Poland." *European Politics and Society* 22 (1): 53–68.

Dahrendorf, Ralf. 1990. *Reflections on the Revolution in Europe.* Transaction.

Doorenspleet, Renske. 2000. "Reassessing the Three Waves of Democratization." *World Politics* 52 (3): 384–406. http://www.jstor.org/stable/25054118.

Dunai, Marton. 2022. "The Bank of Victor Orbán." *Financial Times*, May 29. https://www.ft.com/content/f9ba0f39-429d-4d9d-bd2e-fb78b363dfe4.

European Bank for Reconstruction and Development. 2000. *Transition Report 2000: Employment, Skills, and Transition*. European Bank for Reconstruction and Development.

Epstein, Rachel A. 2008. *In Pursuit of Liberalism: International Institutions in Postcommunist Europe*. Johns Hopkins University Press.

Erlanger, Steven, and Andrew Higgins. 2023. "Finland on the Cusp of Joining NATO, but Maybe Not Sweden." *New York Times*, March 1.

Fagan, Moira, and Sneha Gubbala. 2022. "Positive Views of European Union Reach New Highs in Many Countries," Pew Research Center, October 13. https://www.pewresearch.org/short-reads/2022/10/13/positive-views-of-european-union-reach-new-highs-in-many-countries/.

Gans-Morse, Jordan, and Ian Kelly. 2022. "Ukraine Is on the Front Line of Defending Western Democracy." *Chicago Tribune*, March 30.

Ghodsee, Kristen, and Mitchell Orenstein. 2021. *Taking Stock of Shock: Social Consequences of the 1989 Revolutions*. Oxford University.

Gregor, Milos, and Alena Macková. 2015. "Euroscepticism the Czech Way: An Analysis of Václav Klaus' Speeches." *European Journal of Communications* 30 (1): 404–417.

Grzymala-Busse, Anna. 2019. "How Populists Rule: The Consequences of Democratic Governance." *Polity* 51 (4): 707–717. https://doi.org/10.1086/705570.

Grzymala-Busse, Anna, and Abby Innes. 2003. "Great Expectations: The EU and Domestic Political Competition in East Central Europe." *East European Politics and Societies* 17 (1): 64–73.

Gubbala, Sneha. 2023. "People Broadly View the EU Favorably, Both in Member States and Elsewhere." Pew Research Center. October 24. https://www.pewresearch.org/short-reads/2022/10/13/positive-views-of-european-union-reach-new-highs-in-many-countries/.

Hanley, Sean. 2004. "From Neo-Liberalism to National Interests: Ideology, Strategy and Party Development in Euroscepticism of the Czech Right." *East European Politics and Societies* 18 (3): 513–548.

Hanley, Sean. 2007. "A Nation of Sceptics? The Czech EU Accession Referendum on 13–14 June 2003." *West European Politics* 27 (4): 691–715.

Haughton, Timothy. 2001. "HZDS: The Ideology, Organisation and Support Base of Slovakia's Most Successful Party." *Europe-Asia Studies* 53 (5): 745–769.

Hughes, James. 2005. "'Exit' in Deeply Divided Societies: Regimes of Discrimination in Estonia and Latvia and the Potential for Russophone Migration." *Journal of Common Market Studies* 43 (4): 739–762.

Hungary Today. 2022. "PM Orban: With Russian Gas, Utility Bills Can Be Kept Low." February 2.

Huntington, Samuel. 1991. *The Third Wave: Democratization in the Late Twentieth Century*. University of Oklahoma Press.

Jacoby, Wade. 1999. "Priest and Penitent: The European Union as a Force in the Domestic Politics of Eastern Europe." *East European Constitutional Review* 8 (1): 62–67.

Jacoby, Wade. 2004. *The Enlargement of the European Union and NATO: Ordering from the Menu in Central Europe*. Cambridge University Press.

Johnson, Juliet, and Andrew S. Barnes. 2015. "Financial Nationalism after the Crisis: The Hungarian Experience." *Review of International Political Economy* 22 (3): 535–569.

Johnson, Juliet, and Andrew S. Barnes. 2025. "Contemporary Financial Nationalism in Theory and Practice." *Nationalities Papers* 53 (2): 260–278. doi:10.1017/nps.2024.46.

Kaniok, Petr and Ví Hlousek. 2014. "Shaping of Czech Debate on the Euro: Position of Václav Klaus in 1999-2002 Period." *Romanian Journal of European Affairs* 14 (2): 42–62.

Kelley, Judith. 2006. *Ethnic Politics in Europe: The Power of Norms and Incentives.* Princeton University Press.
Klaus, Václav. 2004. "Speech for the Commonwealth Club of California and World Affairs Council of Northern California, San Francisco." November 8. https://www.klaus.cz/clanky/567.
Klaus, Václav. 2021. "The Progressively Growing Self-Destruction of the West and Its Acceleration by the Covid Epidemic." May 8. https://www.klaus.cz/clanky/4752.
Kopstein, Jeffrey, and David. A. Reilly. 2000. "Geographic Diffusion and the Transformation of the Postcommunist World." *World Politics* 53 (1): 1–37.
Krastev, Ivan. 2018. "Eastern Europe's Illiberal Revolution." *Foreign Affairs* 97 (3): 49–56.
Krekó, Péter. 2022. "Viktor Orbán Is the West's Pro-Putin Outlier." *Foreign Policy*, March 3.
Kurasinska, Lidia. 2021. "Poland's Law and Justice Signs Joint Declaration with Euroskeptic Parties." *Forbes*, July 2.
Landler, Mark. 2022. "The Ukraine War's Economic Toll Is Testing the West's Unity Against Russia." *New York Times*, May 11.
Lázár, Nóra. 2015. "Euroscepticism in Hungary and Poland: A Comparative Analysis of Jobbik and the Law and Justice Parties." *Politeja* 33: 215–233. doi:10.12797/Politeja.12.2015.33.11.
Miller, Christopher, Raphael Minder, and Barbara Erling. 2023. "Polish Government Faces Backlash over Pro-Russian Activities Inquiry." *Financial Times*, June 1.
Minder, Raphael, Barbara Erling, and Sam Fleming. 2023. "Poland Pledges More Fighter Jets to Europe." *Financial Times*, April 5.
Minder, Raphael, and Sam Fleming. 2022. "Poland Takes Steps toward Unlocking EU Recovery Funds." *Financial Times*, October 10.
Moravcsik, Andrew. 2000. "The Origins of Human Rights Regimes: Democratic Delegation in Postwar Europe." *International Organization* 54 (2): 217–252.
NATO. 1995. "Study on NATO Enlargement." September 3. Accessed April 30, 2022. https://www.nato.int/cps/en/natohq/official_texts_24733.htm.
Nölke, Andreas, and Arjan Vliegenthart. 2009. "Enlarging the Varieties of Capitalism: The Emergence of Dependent Market Economies in East Central Europe." *World Politics* 61 (4): 670–702.
Orbán, Viktor. 2014a. "Viktor Orbán's Speech at Băile Tuşnad (Tusnádfürdő) of 26 July 2014." *Hungarian Spectrum*, July 31. Accessed April 2, 2022. https://hungarianspectrum.org/2014/07/31/viktor-orbans-speech-at-the-xxv-balvanyos-free-summer-university-and-youth-camp-july-26-2014-baile-tusnad-tusnadfurdo/.
Orbán, Viktor. 2014b. "Viktor Orbán's Speech at the Friends of Hungary Conference." January 27. Accessed September 26, 2022. https://2010-2014.kormany.hu/en/prime-minister-s-office/the-prime-ministers-speeches/prime-minister-viktor-orban-s-speech-at-the-friends-of-hungary-conference.
Orbán, Viktor. 2018. "Viktor Orbán's Speech on the 62nd Anniversary." October 23. Accessed May 12, 2025. https://abouthungary.hu/prime-minister/prime-minister-viktor-orbans-speech-on-the-62nd-anniversary.
Pew Research Center. 2013. "The New Sick Man of Europe." May 13. Accessed May 10, 2023. https://www.pewresearch.org/global/2013/05/13/the-new-sick-man-of-europe-the-european-union/.
Pew Research Center. 2015–2016. Survey. June–July. https://www.pewresearch.org/global/2015/06/02/faith-in-european-project-reviving/.
Pew Research Center. 2019. Global Attitudes Survey. Spring. Accessed May 10, 2022. https://www.pewresearch.org/global/wp-content/uploads/sites/2/2019/10/Pew-Research-Center-Value-of-Europe-report-FINAL-UPDATED.pdf.
Przeworski, Adam. 1991. *Democracy and the Market: Political and Economic Reforms in Eastern Europe and Latin America.* Cambridge University Press.

Reed, Stanley, and Melissa Eddy. 2023. "Europe Has Weathered an Energy Crisis, for Now." *New York Times*, February 24.
Rettman, Andrew. 2021. "Kaczyński and Le Pen Make Friends at Anti-EU Summit." *EUObserver.com*, December 6.
Rutland, Peter. 2013. "Neoliberalism and the Russian Transition." *Review of International Political Economy* 20 (2): 332–362.
Sachs, Jeffrey. 1994. *Poland's Jump to the Market Economy*. MIT Press.
Sadurski, Wojciech. 2019. *Poland's Constitutional Breakdown*. Oxford University Press.
Santana, Andrés, Piotr Zagórski, and José Rama. 2020. "At Odds with Europe: Explaining Populist Radical Right Voting in Central and Eastern Europe." *East European Politics* 36 (2): 288–309. doi:10.1080/21599165.2020.1737523.
Sasse, Gwendolyn. 2008. "The Politics of EU Conditionality: The Norm of Minority Protection during and beyond EU Accession." *Journal of European Public Policy* 15 (6): 842–860. https://doi.org/10.1080/13501760802196580.
Scheppele, Kim Lane. 2022. "In Hungary, Orban Wins Again—Because He Has Rigged the System." *Washington Post*, April 6.
Schimmelfennig, Frank, Stefan Engert, and Heiko Knobel. 2003. "Costs, Commitment and Compliance: The Impact of EU Democratic Conditionality on Latvia, Slovakia and Turkey." *Journal of Common Market Studies* 41 (3): 495–518.
Schimmelfennig, Frank, and Ulrich Sedelmeier. 2004. "Governance by Conditionality: EU Rule Transfer to the Candidate Countries of Central and Eastern Europe." *Journal of European Public Policy* 11 (4): 661–679. https://doi.org/10.1080/1350176042000248089.
Schimmelfennig, Frank, and Ulrich Sedelmeier. 2020. "The Europeanization of Eastern Europe: The External Incentives Model Revisited." *Journal of European Public Policy* 27 (6): 814–833. https://doi.org/10.1080/13501763.2019.1617333.
Schueth, Sam. 2011. "Assembling International Competitiveness: The Republic of Georgia, USAID, and the Doing Business Project." *Economic Geography* 87 (1): 51–77.
Sedelmeier, Ulrich. 2012. "Is Europeanisation through Conditionality Sustainable? Lock-In of Institutional Change after EU Accession." *West European Politics* 35 (1): 20–38. doi:10.1080/01402382.2012.631311.
Shin, Doh Chul. 1994. "On the Third Wave of Democratization: A Synthesis and Evaluation of Recent Theory." *World Politics* 47 (1): 135–170. doi:https://doi.org/10.2307/2950681.
Sierakowski, Sławomir. 2018. "How to Break Up Europe's Axis of Illiberalism." *Foreign Policy*, January 8.
Sierakowski, Sławomir. 2023. "Poland's Electoral Inquisition." *Project Syndicate*, May 31. https://www.project-syndicate.org/commentary/poland-pis-russia-influence-commission-by-slawomir-sierakowski-2023-05.
Szayna, Thomas. 1999. "A Small Contributor or a Free Rider." In *America's New Allies: Poland, Hungary, and the Czech Republic in NATO*, edited by Andrew Michta. University of Washington Press.
Sznajder Lee, Aleksandra. 2016. *From Behemoths to Subsidiaries: The Rise of Transnational Capitalism in East Central Europe's Heavy Industry*. University of Michigan Press.
Vachudova, Milada Anna. 2005. *Europe Undivided: Democracy, Leverage, and Integration after Communism*. Oxford University Press.
Vachudova, Milada Anna. 2008. "The European Union: The Causal Behemoth of Transnational Influence on Postcommunist Politics." In *Transnational Actors in Central and East European Transitions*, edited by Mitchell A. Orenstein, Stephen Bloom, and Nicole Lindstrom. University of Pittsburgh Press.
Way, Lucan. 2022. "The Rebirth of the Liberal World Order?" *Journal of Democracy* 33 (2): 5–17.
YouGov. 2016. "Authoritarian Populism Study." October. https://yougov.co.uk/politics/articles/17145-many-europeans-say-immigration-has-meant-they-dont.

Zaun, Natascha, and Ripoll Servent. 2023. "Perpetuating Crisis as a Supply Strategy: The Role of (Nativist) Populist Governments in EU Policymaking on Refugee Distribution." *Journal of Common Market Studies* 61 (3): 653–672. https://doi.org/10.1111/jcms.13416.

Zerofsky, Elisabeth. 2019. "Viktor Orbán's Far-Right Vision for Europe." *New Yorker*, January 14.

7
Who Lost Russia?
The 1990s Revisited

Michael Cox

Long before Vladimir Putin launched his brutal war against Ukraine, the liberal international order was already facing a number of major challenges. Indeed, among several academics the emerging consensus seemed to be that whatever its earlier achievements might have been in terms of increasing world trade, promoting democracy, and settling long-standing regional disputes, the liberal order was, as even its chief theorist was prepared to concede, confronted by a series of problems.[1] Whether one looked for the deeper cause of the malaise in the project itself, America's less than liberal response to 9/11, the great economic crash of 2008, the populist backlash against globalization, or the rise and further rise of China did not really matter much. To all intents and purposes the promise of creating a liberal order following the fall of communism had in the eyes of some writers—if not all liberals themselves—turned out to be a false one.[2]

Nor, we were told, should this have come as a surprise. In fact, the whole project, according to critics, was constructed around the twin myth that either the international system could escape the logic of great power competition or Western policymakers could turn illiberal polities into what came to be defined as "responsible stakeholders." Consequently the whole strategy was doomed to fail.[3] Even the tragedy in Ukraine could in large part be laid at liberalism's door. There were no doubt many reasons why Putin attacked Ukraine. But according to Steve Walt at least, the "special military operation," as Putin preferred to call it, was less the outcome of his own imperial ambitions or even his KGB outlook—standard explanations in the West—and more the result of the United States and its European allies succumbing to "hubris and wishful thinking" flowing from a "flawed theory of world politics" known as "liberal idealism."[4] John Mearsheimer made the same point with perhaps even greater force. Ukraine did not happen because

Michael Cox, *Who Lost Russia?*. In: *Rethinking the 1990s*. Edited by: G. John Ikenberry and Peter Trubowitz, Oxford University Press. © Oxford University Press (2025). DOI: 10.1093/9780197813133.003.0007

Putin wanted to re-create the USSR or claim that there was a special relationship between Ukraine and Russia.[5] Rather it occurred, he insisted, because of the West's "liberal delusion" that it could enlarge NATO, expand the EU, and promote democracy without this causing Putin to react.[6]

Even if we are not persuaded by Walt's and Mearsheimer's controversial and contested view that the West and Western liberalism were largely to blame for Putin's invasion of Ukraine, there is little doubt that liberalism as a wider project had for years been facing a testing time.[7] There is little doubt either that developments in Russia contributed in significant ways to this loss of confidence.[8] Indeed, as we shall go on to show, Western liberalism and the West more generally had already acquired a less than positive reputation in Russia even by the end of the 1990s. But then, a whole series of events from Putin's assault on democracy in Russia itself accompanied by a number of interventions in its "near abroad" and increasingly vitriolic attacks on NATO and the West fairly quickly dashed any hope that Russia could be turned into a contributing member of the liberal international community.[9] Russia may have remained keen to develop its economic links with Western businesses, attract foreign capital, and sell its not inconsiderable stores of energy to Western markets. Even as late as 2012 it was allowed entry into the World Trade Organization while still remaining a member of the G-7 (until it was expelled in 2014). Yet these were small rays of economic sunshine in an otherwise darkening political sky.[10]

The central question then becomes Was there ever a serious chance of Russia becoming a stable liberal polity or accepting a rules-based order organized on Western principals? Some at the time thought it would be possible, including of course a number of Europeans, not to mention Presidents Bill Clinton and George W. Bush. Others remained far more skeptical. Russia was always going to be a lost cause, they argued.[11] Its long authoritarian past stretching right back through the Soviet era to the nineteenth century made anything other than an illiberal outcome most unlikely. As one rather catchy headline suggested some time after relations with the West had moved beyond the point of no return, "the problem" was not so much Putin as "Russia" itself.[12] Turning postcommunist Russia into a liberal polity may have been a noble goal. But this failed "to acknowledge the weight of history."[13]

Ironically, Putin today would probably agree with this view. In fact, over the past few years he has almost waxed lyrical about the profound differences that have always divided Mother Russia from the liberal West.[14] But more modern events have also helped shape his outlook.[15]

Whether or not his instrumentalized reading of the 1990s bears very much relationship with the "facts" matters less than its power to persuade Russians that the years before he took over were a period of unequaled disaster. Of course, Western leaders might now claim that their intentions toward Russia were benign. Germany might even point to how much money it "loaned" Russia, as indeed does the International Monetary Fund. But this makes no difference in Putin's telling of the story.[16] Carefully skating over the somewhat embarrassing fact that during this period he became very wealthy himself, Putin remains adamant: the liberal West in general—but the Americans in particular—had nothing but malign intentions toward Russia. Assuming that it was now master of the universe and could effectively do what it liked to whomever it liked (including Russia), the United States acted as if the world was its plaything. Many may now look back on the 1990s as a period of missed opportunities. Putin, in contrast, has come to view "the entire post–Cold War era" as "a period of Russia's humiliation at the hands of a hostile and jeering West" whose expert advice only led to economic decline and whose only reward for Russia's good international behavior was to enlarge NATO.[17]

Rather than try to hold Putin's claims up to the evidence and judge whether he is right or wrong—a somewhat pointless undertaking—what I have tried to do in what follows is to look at the evolution of Russia in the 1990s and the relationship between what those in Washington in particular thought they were trying to do and what was actually happening on the ground. As I show, these were extraordinarily unstable times over which hardly any actor—Russian or American—appeared to have much control. It is easy now for critics to claim that if only different policies had been pursued, Russia may have become a liberal polity with a "normal" market economy. Mikhail Gorbachev believed until his death that Russia could have been "saved" for the West if only more economic support from abroad had been forthcoming.[18] However, the evidence supporting this claim is less than convincing. Western policymakers are certainly not above criticism, and sometimes what they did—most obviously pushing ahead with NATO enlargement and supporting the most "shocking" of economic shock therapies—did little to boost the cause of liberalism within Russia itself. It would, however, be going too far to claim that Russia was, as Putin now claims, betrayed by the West or the United States. There is little doubt that the changes which took place in Russia during these years were traumatic. This, though, had less to do with some Western attempt to destroy Russia and more with the multiple problems confronting a country as it tried to replace its command economy with something vaguely resembling "free market capitalism" while trying to deal with the fallout from the breakup of a once united multiethnic state over which it had ruled for so many years.[19] It is often said that when empires implode the results are rarely benign. In the case of Russia they turned out to be toxic.

To explore these various questions, I begin first by looking briefly at the early efforts by Washington to manage the transition from the end of the Cold War in 1989 through to the quite unexpected fall of the USSR two years later. As I argue, U.S. policymakers might have been more than happy to bag all the concessions that Gorbachev seemed prepared to make at the time. On the other hand, even those who had always been skeptical about what was taking place in the USSR under Gorbachev did not wish to see its old rival humiliated. The White House may have always been skeptical about giving extensive financial aid to the Soviet Union. As Secretary of State James Baker observed in late 1989, "you cannot build a market economy by throwing money at a disintegrating command economy."[20] But this did not mean that the United States wanted to see the USSR, let alone Gorbachev, driven into the ground.

I then deal in much more detail with the crucial Clinton years and why, on the one hand, Clinton engaged with Russia with such enthusiasm, but why, on the other, that engagement realized so little except perhaps a not unimportant agreement to prevent nuclear proliferation, not to mention a number of important arms control agreements. Clinton, as we know, took more than a passing interest in Russia; indeed, as his memoirs show, he developed a close personal relationship with Boris Yeltsin (according to some of his advisors, too close).[21] But no amount of meetings between "Bill and Boris" could change the critical situation facing Russia as it moved beyond communism.[22]

Finally, I analyze the emergence of Putin and how his coming to power affected Washington's understanding of what was happening in Russia and whether it brought to an end any hope that it was still possible to engage Moscow in serious dialog. As the record indicates, the first few months and years did not in and of themselves point inexorably toward a complete breakdown in relations with the West. Indeed, at first there was some relief in all Western capitals (including Washington) that Putin would now stabilize the situation following the chaotic Yeltsin years. Yet, as I suggest, the chances of a leader like Putin accepting a place for Russia within a Western-led order were slim to say the least. Of course, much would have to happen before relations soured completely. But his own insecurities at home, the challenges he faced in his own near abroad, combined with a desire to make Russia "great again"—not to mention a series of actions taken by the West itself—meant that the relationship, never stable at the best of times, was more likely to implode than improve, less likely to lead to trust than to enmity.

Gorbachev, Bush, and Soviet Collapse

> All around Gorbachev had unleashed irreversible processes of "disintegration" which had earlier been covered up by the arms race, the fear of war, myths about the international communist movement, the socialist community, the world wide revolutionary process, and proletarian internationalism. (Diary entry, May 1989, Anatoly Chernyaev, Gorbachev's senior foreign policy advisor)[23]

When Gorbachev became leader of the Communist Party of the Soviet Union in 1985 the USSR was still a functioning superpower, albeit one with an inefficient economy, a series of apparently insoluble foreign policy problems, and an "empire" of sorts which, as many experts in Moscow had by the early 1980s conceded, was increasingly becoming an economic burden. Six years later, when he was removed from power following a failed coup by "conservatives" and a successful one by his arch-liberal rival Yeltsin, Russia's control over Eastern Europe had evaporated, Germany was fast uniting, the USSR was on the edge of collapse, and the economy was in free fall. Gorbachev may in the process have won many friends in the West for having brought the Cold War to an end. But as one of the more critical studies on his life and times has shown, if success or failure is measured by how a leader manages the affairs of state and builds a base of solid support at home for his policies, then by any measure Gorbachev was a failure.[24] Moreover, his failure had longer-term consequences for the whole reform project. As one of the more skeptical members of the U.S. foreign policy team noted at the time, because Gorbachev had "screwed it up"—a not isolated view by insiders at the time—it was going to be "all the harder for some subsequent leaders, more determined and skilful" than he, "to get his countrymen ever to support reform again."[25]

Nor for all his efforts did Gorbachev receive much in the way of reward for pushing forward with his program of change. Ronald Reagan may have courted him assiduously once he had been urged to do so by Margaret Thatcher. However, his successor team in the White House, which included such cold warriors as Dick Cheney and Robert Gates, were never more than lukewarm about perestroika. Many inside the Beltway even seemed to regard Gorbachev as a dedicated communist whose goal was to divide NATO before returning to the ideological offensive. And even when Washington did begin to engage seriously when it was impossible not to do otherwise, there remained quite a few within the administration who either thought Gorbachev would be ousted by hardliners—thus why invest any political capital in backing him—or simply did not believe his various proposals of reform could ever succeed in turning the economy around.[26]

Naturally enough, the collapse of Soviet power in Eastern Europe, accompanied by the coming down of the Berlin Wall, changed everything. The apparently impossible had happened, and all that policymakers like President Bush and Secretary of State Baker could then do was try to catch up with a fast-changing landscape which they had neither planned for nor expected. Indeed, until it happened, the view in most Western capitals was that the Soviet Union would remain where it was in Europe and Germany—in part because the bloc acted as a buffer zone between itself and NATO, and in part because Moscow's whole security posture since the end of the Second World War had been premised on Germany remaining divided. Retreat might also have had one other unfortunate consequence: it might have encouraged calls for change in the USSR itself. Nor were policymakers wrong to be worried. In fact, within a year of the end of the Cold War in Europe and Germany "the economic and political troubles of the Soviet Union" itself had become so acute that it didn't even look as if Gorbachev himself would survive. The West might have had much to thank him for. After all, none of the "dramatic changes in Soviet foreign policy" could have happened without his leadership. But there was now a chance that he would not be around for very much longer. And so it turned out to be.[27]

The actual collapse of the USSR—the greatest "geopolitical tragedy" of the twentieth century, according to Putin—is a dramatic story that has been told so many times by now that it is difficult to say anything new or original about it. U.S. intelligence was certainly well aware of the crisis facing the Soviet Union.[28] Nationalist agitation accompanied by an almost complete collapse of the economy between 1989 and 1991 certainly did not point to a bright future. Surprisingly few policymakers, however, thought the system would disintegrate and do so as quickly as it did without hardly a shot being fired in its defense. Indeed, if what happened in 1989 came as a surprise, then what occurred in late 1991 was an even greater shock.[29] Whether or not this constituted yet another failure of intelligence has been the cause of much speculation.[30] Even so, there were few at the highest level who predicted the other superpower would dissolve itself, and perhaps even fewer that dissolution would come from the center rather than the periphery.[31]

Moreover, though some in Washington were delighted when the USSR fell apart, many more were worried that its collapse would throw up all sorts of dangers to which there would be no easy answer.[32] As the last American ambassador to the USSR noted at the time, even if the divorce occurred relatively peacefully, there was no knowing what would happen next either to all those "loose nukes" located around the former Soviet Union or indeed to an economy already in sharp decline. The departure of Gorbachev and the ascent of Yeltsin might have opened up a political space that would allow Russia to go further than it had ever been able to before with implementing more radical economic reform. But where this might lead was by no means clear—least of all to the incoming Clinton administration.[33]

Clinton Engages Russia

> The collapse of Communist society left Yeltsin vulnerable in the Kremlin and a proud beggar among the great nations. (Bill Clinton, 1993)[34]

When Clinton entered the White House in early 1993, he identified two critical foreign policy problems: Bosnia and Russia. Bosnia, as it turned out, would prove to be a major regional headache. Russia, on the other hand, was a much bigger challenge. Its long imperial past, its historical role as an outsider power in the twentieth century, its pivotal position within the UN system, and of course its several thousand nuclear warheads spread across four independent states within the old USSR meant that this was a country that would have to be handled with the greatest of care. The stakes could not have been higher. Certainly, if the United States with its allies' help could facilitate the transition to a more Western-style political economy—as was beginning to happen in Central and Eastern Europe—then the future for both Russia and the world looked reasonably bright. If, however, reform in Russia failed, the West would face a very insecure future with the strong possibility, according to Secretary of State Warren Christopher, of "a renewed nuclear threat, higher defence budgets, spreading instability, the loss of new markets and a devastating setback for the worldwide democratic movement." For all these reasons, and many more besides, "this circumstance deserve[d] the attention of each and every American."[35]

Defining a strategy and talking in grandiloquent terms of building what his key advisor on Russian affairs, Strobe Talbott, liked to term a new "strategic partnership with Russian reform" was of course the easy part.[36] The more difficult challenge was what to do in a country like Russia where the obstacles still standing in the way of a Western-style democracy were immense.[37] Ever the optimist Clinton had every confidence he could make a difference. Nevertheless, he had no illusions whatsoever about the task that lay before him. "Up to his ears in alligators," as Clinton liked to describe Yeltsin's position, the road ahead looked anything but smooth. As Clinton put it in his typically folksy way, "Yeltsin had a hard row to hoe."[38]

But so too did Clinton as he navigated a course between endorsing a controversial Russian leader whose behavior was not always predictable and encouraging democracy in a country where opposition to change was gathering force. Indeed, even by the beginning of 1994 it was already looking as if Clinton's idea of an alliance with a reforming Russia was in trouble. Exploiting his own popularity, Yeltsin managed to negotiate his way through the first of his many crises in April 1993 when he won his referendum in which voters were asked to back him and support his government's socioeconomic policies and early elections for both the presidency and parliament. He then navigated the even greater crisis in October of the same year, but only after having bombed and then closed down the Russian parliament.[39] The third crisis, however, proved far more difficult to resolve, not merely because the elections in December 1993 revealed strong opposition to economic change, but more significantly because those hostile to reform now had a mandate. As was clear at the time, this was not just a minor bump on the road leading to a "market democracy" oriented toward the West, but a major setback.[40]

Perhaps one indicator of the seriousness with which the Clinton administration viewed the situation in Russia was its halfhearted public attempts to play down the significance of the December elections and the "rise" of Vladimir Zhirinovsky and the vote for the Russian Communist Party. The official line at first tried to make light of the antireform vote, more or less dismissing it as a "protest" against short-term problems that would evaporate once things improved. This exercise in damage limitation could not hide the administration's concern, however. According to one source, the White

House was "startled and shaken" by the outcome. Vice President Al Gore, it is reliably reported, was "dazed and speechless" when the results came in. So confused was he in fact that he and others attempted to place at least some of the blame on Western economic policies. In Talbott's famous or (infamous) phrase, there had been too much imposed "shock" and not enough "therapy" in Russia. Hence it was necessary, or so he implied, both to slow down the reforms and to take account of their negative social consequences.[41]

Once the dust had settled, the White House set about picking its way through the debris. Some modifications would clearly have to be made to the original strategy. However, both Talbott and Clinton were determined to soldier on. The administration was not about to abandon Russia. Nor, as I have suggested elsewhere was it going to move Russia from being "the most highly favoured of nations beyond the old iron curtain to being only in the second rank".[42] Clinton himself made this perfectly clear on his visit to Russia in early January 1994. Indeed, during the trip he went out of his way to reassure Russians of America's continuing support and friendship. He also played to Russian amour propre by talking (somewhat overenthusiastically) of the nation's "greatness" and U.S. recognition of its special place in world affairs. Urged on by former president Richard Nixon to stand by Yeltsin, and having no obvious alternative candidate to support, Clinton was clear: Yeltsin for the moment was the only game in town. Moreover, gains were being made. In December 1994, for example, the START I Treaty entered into force. Then, in the same month, the United States and the United Kingdom together succeeded in transferring Soviet treaty obligations to reduce or eliminate nuclear weapons from all the post-Soviet successor states—including Ukraine—which, under the terms of the famous "Budapest Memorandum," agreed to transfer the weapons to Russia, though doing so only on the specific understanding (later breached) that Russia would forever recognize their territorial integrity.[43]

None of this, however, changed the situation on the ground. As Talbott made clear in an important statement to the House Committee on Foreign Affairs, Russia was passing through its own "time of troubles." More reason therefore to stay the course. In fact, precisely because there was what he called a "titanic struggle" going on in Russia, in which the United States had a "huge stake," it was more important than ever to remain engaged. Moreover, according to Talbott, the situation was more "mixed" than the pessimists claimed. The democratic process was up and running. Over one quarter of the labor force was now employed in the private sector. In the near abroad there had been progress, although there were some problems still left to resolve. On the security front, too, things were getting better, with Ukraine having just decided to transfer all its nuclear weapons to Russia, and the United States and Russia having agreed to "detarget" each other. It was not all doom and gloom, therefore.

Naturally, Talbott accepted that things could still go badly wrong. The "next two and a half years—between now and the elections scheduled for mid-1996—would be critical." But Russia had not yet passed beyond the point of no return. There was still everything to play for. What the United States should not do, he warned, was base its policy today on "worst-case assumptions about what tomorrow may bring." This would not only be foolish but could lead the United Sates to "fall into the trap of the self-fulfilling prophecy." America had to remain patient and steady, therefore, and continue to work for the integration of Russia rather than begin planning for its containment. The advantages of doing so were self-evident, for "a Russia integrated rather than contained," Talbott argued, would "mean fewer tax dollars spent on defence; a reduced threat from weapons of mass destruction; new markets for US products; and a powerful, reliable partner for diplomacy as well as commerce in the twenty-first century." There was still a world to be won.[44]

Clinton under Pressure

> The Clinton Administration has pursued an accommodationist and misguided policy toward Moscow. (Republican Party Platform, August 12, 1996)[45]

If one result of the December "wake-up call" was to cause initial confusion followed by a resolute White House defense of its original strategy, the other was to open a floodgate in the United States itself out of which poured a tide of criticism. A good deal of this, clearly, had as much to do with Republican frustrations and right-wing dislike of the Clintons as it did with the administration's policy on Russia. Yet it would be wrong to conclude that all Clinton's critics were motivated only by political animus. There were genuine questions that needed an answer, first, about how to deal with a Russia in which communists and nationalists were now in a majority in the new parliament; second, about a Russia that was showing an alarming tendency to reassert its prerogatives in the near abroad; and finally, a Russia in which the reformist Yeltsin seemed able to hold on to power only by stealing the rhetorical clothes of his antireformist enemies. To many, indeed, it looked as if Clinton's "love affair" with Yeltsin and his fear of "losing Russia" were now standing in the way of a more balanced American approach to post-Soviet problems.[46]

In good Cold War fashion the debate over Russia reached a critical point following the disclosure that a senior CIA official had been working for Moscow for several years, apparently with deadly consequences. As one of Clinton's more vocal opponents noted in late February 1994, "Americans really did not need a major spy scandal to tell them that the honeymoon with Russia was over. But the arrest of the CIA's Aldrich Ames makes the point with some finality".[47] With this discovery (coinciding as it did with a particularly tough statement by Yeltsin on Russian foreign policy) the attacks against Clinton intensified. The Republicans' chief spokesperson on foreign affairs, Richard Lugar, declared that the United States had "to get over the idea" that it was involved in a "partnership" with Moscow. "This is a tough rivalry," he insisted.[48] Much the same point was made at Talbott's confirmation hearings for the post of deputy secretary of state in February 1994. Here the Republicans launched a bitter attack on what one senator called a policy that endangered "our national interests." The Republicans also used the occasion to criticize Clinton's foreign policy more generally. "If Ambassador Talbott is confirmed by the Senate," argued Senator Alfonse D'Amato, "another wrong signal will be sent: that the people who carry out our foreign policy offer nothing but inexperience and naiveté."[49]

The case against Clinton was certainly a powerful one, which led some of his more articulate critics—Zbigniew Brzezinski being the most prominent—to some fairly radical conclusions. Brzezinski was no passive observer of the foreign policy scene, and since the collapse of the USSR had been indulging in what one observer called "a bit of freelance foreign policy",[50] the primary goal of which was to cultivate links with the non-Russian states of the former Soviet Union, to which he thought "the American government should have been paying more attention." Believing that Talbott's "romantic fascination with Russia" (Russophilia, even) was getting in the way of clear strategic thinking, Brzezinski called for a number of changes to U.S. policy. Most important, he argued that the countries of Eastern and Central Europe should be invited to join NATO sooner rather than later. This was critical. Furthermore, in his view, the United States should set as its main objective "the consolidation of geopolitical pluralism" within the space once occupied by the old Soviet Union. Only in this way could countries like Ukraine be assured and America achieve a more balanced relationship with the new Europe as a whole. Indeed, according to Brzezinski, the creation of a belt of independent states around Russia, closely allied to the West, would not only serve America's interest but would help Russia as well, for only when its periphery was secured and Moscow no longer tempted to play a spoiling role there, could it become both stable and democratic itself.[51]

The net result of all this pressure was to bring about a certain adjustment in U.S. policy. This first took the form of a change in tone. Hitherto, the Clinton team had talked quite boldly and optimistically about an alliance with Russia and Russian reform. Now this line was modified to include recognition that, on certain international issues at least, there were bound to be serious divergences between the two countries. As Defense Secretary William Perry pointed out in March 1994, "even with the best outcome imaginable in Russia, the new Russia" would have different interests from America's. Nor should the United States be particularly concerned about this, for as Perry pointed out (picking his countries carefully), "even with allies like France and Japan, we have rivalry and competition alongside our partnership," and so it will be with Russia.[52]

The second tilt in policy was in the U.S. attitude toward the other new republics. Clinton had always been aware that there were other actors in the post-Soviet space. But sensitive to the charge that the administration had tilted too far toward Moscow and Yeltsin, Washington now began to make a much greater effort in building stronger relations with countries other than Russia. This pleased not only a number of countries in the former USSR but Brzezinski too, who saw this as exactly the sort of initiative the Clinton administration should have taken much earlier. Whether the White House saw it this way is much less clear, but there was no mistaking the shift in policy. This expressed itself in many ways—both symbolic and practical. Thus, during a scheduled visit by the new Ukrainian president to Washington in March 1994 (the first ever undertaken), Clinton reaffirmed "American support" for Ukrainian independence. Four months later Clinton met with the three leaders of the Baltic republics. Other meetings were held during the course of the year. At the same time, the United States issued a series of warnings to Moscow that good relations between Russia and the United States assumed—indeed, presupposed—better relations with its neighbors.[53]

Third, these various moves were accompanied by perhaps the biggest shift of all in U.S. policy: toward NATO and NATO expansion. Accepting now that there could be no halfway house for the countries of Central and Eastern Europe, the Clinton administration decided during the course of 1994 that it was time to extend the privileges of full NATO membership to Poland, the Czech Republic, and Hungary. Having initially been persuaded by Talbott back in 1992 that this was not the way to go after the events in Russia, the White House felt it had no alternative but to do so. Though in part a move designed to assuage critics both at home and abroad—and to find a new mission for NATO in a post-Soviet world—clearly underlying the move was a growing recognition that Russia's future looked decidedly problematic. Once spoken of as only a theoretical possibility, by late 1994 the likelihood of the reform process in Russia either going into reverse or of nationalists opposed to the West gaining the upper hand no longer seemed an outside possibility. According to defenders of the policy, there were sound reasons for the United States to hedge its bets and secure peace in Europe by guarding against a resurgent Russia in the future. Russian policymakers, including, significantly, Yeltsin, were less than thrilled with all this. As he pointed out to Clinton, enlarging a military organization associated in Russian minds with the Cold War did not make his job any easier at home. Significantly too, he even asked Clinton to guarantee that NATO would not go any further in order to assuage the hardliners back in Moscow. Equally significant, Clinton declined the request. The seeds of a future clash over European security had already been planted.[54]

Russia in Crisis

Look back at Weimar and start to worry about Russia. (Niall Ferguson)[55]

While the United States took what it regarded as sensible measures to guard against any future eventuality, it still did not accept that the situation in Russia was hopeless. As Talbott reminded the Senate in early 1994, though the United States would be acting cautiously, it had no intention of planning for the worse. Possibly encouraged by somewhat loose talk in the West about Russia's "economic success story," there was as yet no reason to assume the reform process had hit a wall.[56] Even so, storm clouds were gathering. Thus in December 1994 Yeltsin formally came out against NATO expansion.

In the same month, Moscow launched its ill-fated invasion of Chechnya. In early 1995, Russia then sold two light-water nuclear reactors to Iran. And in the race for the Russian presidency in June of the following year, Yeltsin only just managed to win and then only by some fairly nefarious means! Even Clinton was beginning to take stock. As he remarked a little while later, Yeltsin was fast becoming a "shadow" of his former self, his health undermined by bouts of heavy drinking and his grasp on affairs becoming ever more tenuous.[57]

Worse was yet to come, especially on the economic front. Indeed, nearly all of the main indicators pointed to further economic decline and possible political instability too.[58] One rather obvious sign of the times was Yeltsin's somewhat startling decision in March 1998 to sack his entire government—"good theatre but poor politics," opined one Western source.[59] Another was a stark warning then delivered by the new Russian prime minister Sergei Kiriyenko, who claimed Russia was now living on what he called the "never-never." He did not mince his words. Russia's foreign debt, he noted, stood at about $140 billion, workers were not getting paid, and capital continued to leave the country at a far more rapid rate than it was coming in. Meanwhile, living standards for all but the wealthy few continued to decline. Russia, he warned, was staring into the abyss. Extremely dangerous days lay ahead.[60]

How dangerous became only too clear when in August Russia's financial system effectively collapsed, in the process wiping out ruble savings overnight. Furthermore, coming when it did (in the midst of a wider global financial crisis), the very real fear was that meltdown in Russia could easily spark a worldwide recession. As the *Wall Street Journal* pointed out, although the international weight of the Russian economy was small, accounting for just over 1 percent of the world's GDP, any move to default on its large foreign debt could easily precipitate similar actions elsewhere. Equally, if Russia took steps to prevent foreigners from getting their money out, then other "at risk" countries might be tempted to do the same. As the newspaper speculated, "already Malaysia has imposed rigid controls" and there was a genuine worry that if Russia did the same, then others would follow suit.[61]

The impact of these momentous events precipitated yet another "great debate" within the United States. One guru of doom was Martin Malia, the American historian who had earlier predicted the failure of perestroika. "The only certainty in Russia's present crisis," he argued, "is that it marks the end of an era—the Yeltsin years." In his view, it also marked the "end of a theory," the one advanced by Francis Fukuyama in the late 1980s, which suggested "that market democracy had triumphed as a universal ideal."[62] George Friedman was even more pessimistic. Indeed, whereas Malia had simply noted the *passing* of the liberal Western model in Russia, Friedman predicted its *replacement* by a new form of Stalinism combining economic and geopolitical "anti-Westernism." And there was nothing the West could do about it. "The new Stalinism [could] not be stopped," he asserted. This left the United States with only one option: to abandon a strategy that assumed that reform was possible and adopt a new policy which assumed it was not.[63]

Confronted with the crisis, U.S. officials charged with Russian policy clearly had an uphill task, made all the more difficult by yet another change of government in Russia itself. Certainly, the new Russian prime minister, the talented and able Yevgeni Primakov—described by one analyst as "a former KGB agent, a friend of dictators in Iraq and Serbia, and an enemy of the West"[64]—was not someone likely to reassure policymakers in the West. A later description of him by one noted Western leftist as "a bold critic of the oligarchs and their neoliberal capitalism, and a staunch defender of Russian national interests after the pro-western foreign policy of the early post-Soviet years" was as good a description of Primakov as any. Even so, for those in the West looking forward to a new Russia that was both capitalist and pro-Western, this was hardly the news they had been waiting for![65] Furthermore, while Primakov himself talked reassuringly about his commitment to the international community and his opposition to strident nationalism, his selection of economic advisors seemed to point back to the pre-Yeltsin years rather than forward to the market. As one seasoned observer noted, his choice "sent strong signals that his approach will be a throwback to another era when economists tried to introduce some free market ideas within a Soviet system." The return of this cast of Soviet characters, according to the American journalist Celestine Bohlen, was "eerie, even alarming."[66]

American disquiet at the direction now being taken by Russia was expressed most forcefully by Madeleine Albright, since 1997 the American secretary of state. In her first comprehensive review of U.S.-Russian relations since Primakov was confirmed as prime minister, Albright was in no mood to pour oil on Russia's troubled waters. Washington, she declared, was "deeply concerned" about the direction in which Russia now seemed to be moving. Of particular concern was the apparent shift in economic policy. While praising Primakov as what she called a foreign policy pragmatist, she was highly critical of the new government's economic proposals, which included, among other things, plans to print new money, index wages, impose price and capital controls, and restore state management of "parts of the economy." This was not the way to go. Indeed, she made it abundantly clear that Washington's "initial reaction to some of the directions" was not "positive" at all. Moreover, if Moscow continued along this particular road, it would raise a major question mark about the future of the U.S.-Russian relationship. Though the United States was keen to maintain the partnership and "help Russians help themselves," if the new leadership in Moscow took the country down the path of statism rather than free enterprise, America's ability to support Russia in any way would "go from being very, very difficult to being absolutely impossible."[67]

Significantly, the view that Russia had by now reached a crossroad was stated with equal force by Talbott—the original architect of American policy. Talbott did his best to defend his original creation. The partnership, he argued, had been a useful one and in a short space of time had done much to draw Russia out of its traditional isolation. Russia, moreover, was now playing an increasingly responsible role in a number of major international institutions, such as the G-8, the Council of Europe, and the United Nations. As he observed, Russia had "gone from being a spoiler to a joiner." But there was no hiding the fact that the reform process in Russia had reached an impasse to such an extent, he argued, that Western terms like "reform" and "the market" had gone from "being part of the vocabulary of triumph and hope, to being, in the ears of many Russians, almost four-letter words."[68] Furthermore, though Russia had gone a long way to "joining the European mainstream," according to Talbott, there was a very real danger that it could take the wrong turn in the future. This would depend on many factors, but the most critical in his view was Russian economic policy. If the country decided to persist with painful but unpopular reform, then it had a chance of rejoining the international community. If, on the other hand, it began to assert its own economic identity and distance itself from the West, the most likely result would be "heightened tensions over security and diplomatic issues." Russia had changed a good deal since the collapse of the USSR in 1991. But if it formally and finally abandoned Western-style economic reform, then there was a very real chance that the film of history could run backward.[69]

Enter Putin?

> While life was not good under the Soviet Union, for the majority things became much worse once it was gone. In Russia people felt they had been cheated twice, by Gorbachev in the recent past and now by Yeltsin. (Vladislav Zubok)[70]

The election of Vladimir Putin seemed to confirm many of America's worst fears about the unfolding situation in Russia. A former member of the KGB who had friends in some very dubious places hardly looked like democracy's chosen emissary in postcommunist Russia. Even so, policymakers in Washington, and indeed policymakers in other Western capitals, at first appeared to give Putin the benefit of the doubt. His smooth accession to power with Yeltsin's warm words of endorsement ringing in his ears, as well as his early promises that there would be no great change in Russia's relations with the West, did something to reassure officials. Albright noted in December 1999 that the United States had been especially pleased "by the way in which the transition" had taken place. Washington had been equally reassured by promises made by Putin that there would be "no shift in terms" of Russian "foreign policy." This was also confirmed in conversations with Foreign Minister Igor Ivanov, with whom she had secured "agreement on a whole host of issues." There were differences of course, especially over the Balkans, where the two found themselves supporting opposing sides to the conflict there. But these need not prevent Russia and the United States from being able to continue to work "together around the world." The future remained open.[71]

The implication that Putin was a man with whom the United States could do business was expressed with equal force by the influential U.S. ambassador to NATO, Alexander Vershbow. In the context of a sweeping speech in the first month of the twenty-first century, Vershbow provided a sober but balanced assessment of the state of U.S.-Russian relations. There was, it was true, much to be concerned about. The rule of law had not been established; Russia did not yet have "an effective judicial system"; and there had been a worrying growth of Russian chauvinism. But it was essential to maintain a sense of balance. Putin obviously presented a challenge. On the other hand, statements made by him since he assumed power were reassuring. His commitment to the market—something he had talked about at some length in his important "Millennium Document"—his willingness to abide by the constitutional process, and his stated desire to remain engaged with the West while encouraging further trade and investment had all been most welcome. There was no reason to be downhearted; therefore "a return to the competitive relationship of the Cold War" was not on the cards.[72]

The view expressed by Vershbow, "that there were too many areas of common interest for Russia and NATO not to work together," was also endorsed by the director of the CIA in a statement to the Senate Foreign Relations Committee two months later. Careful not to engage in idle speculation about Russia's future over the long term—though he did predict that "Acting President Putin" would win the March 26, 2000 election—Director George Tenet pointed to what he saw as some positive signs. The most obvious, perhaps, was Putin's "voiced support for finalizing the START II agreement and moving toward further arm cuts in START III—though the Russians, he added, would "want US reaffirmation of the 1972 ABM Treaty in return for Start endorsements." Putin and "many Russian officials" had also expressed "a desire to integrate more deeply Russia into the world economy." Finally, "with regard to its nuclear weapons, Moscow" appeared "to be maintaining adequate security and control." This did not mean there were no areas for U.S. concern. As Tenet pointed out, there were several issues that would test U.S.-Russian relations in the coming months and years. But on "some issues" he argued "things" could still move in "a more positive direction".[73]

U.S. efforts to put what many saw (and some criticized) as an unnecessarily positive gloss on the turn of events in Russia, did not mean that policymakers were insensitive to the problems that lay ahead. Indeed, for every upbeat statement made by officials there were equally significant downbeat evaluations made as well.

The first cause of concern was the sheer ruthlessness which Putin displayed in Chechnya between 1999 and 2000. Clinton himself had warned his Republican critics a few years back that the Chechens were not exactly liberals fighting for the cause of democracy. But Russia's demolition of Grozny went beyond anything ever witnessed before. Taking firm action against known jihadists was one thing; reducing its capital to rubble so that it resembled Stalingrad more than a modern city was something else altogether. Equally worrying for the future was that Putin's popularity soared as a result. Nor was there anything Washington could do to stop the slaughter. As Vershbow rather wearily admitted, "[S]ad to say, it is hard to be optimistic that Russia will heed our calls for an end to an indiscriminate use of force."[74]

If the brutal war in Chechnya hung like the sword of Damocles over U.S.-Russian relations, so too did the figure of Putin himself. Efficient and young though he undoubtedly was—perhaps even a welcome change to the by now bumbling Yeltsin—he was nonetheless a long-serving member of the security services who surrounded himself with advisors drawn from a similar background, key figures like Sergei Ivanov (head of the Security Council), Nikolai Patrushev (head of the Federal Security Service, or FSB), and Viktor Cherkesov (the FSB's first deputy director). This "KGB-ization" of Russian politics at the highest level raised at least two critical questions.

The first concerned the future of Russian democracy and whether Putin could he trusted to protect basic human rights. There were severe doubts about this, expressed not only by Americans but even more significantly by civil rights campaigners in Russia itself, who feared that Putin's elevation represented a new stage in Russian history, or what Yelena Bonner (Andrei Sakharov's widow) characterized as "modernized Stalinism".[75] Others were equally wary of Putin's ready manipulation of enemy images as a way of consolidating his position at home. Thus while his initial pronouncements to Western visitors sounded reassuring, when he spoke to Russian audiences he sent out quite different signals. It did not go unnoticed in Washington that in December 1999 he declared in the immediate aftermath of the collapse of the USSR, "[W]e fell prey to an illusion that we have no enemies." Nor was it especially reassuring to hear the future president of Russia refer regularly to some of his political competitors at home not as legitimate opponents but as traitors to the country.[76]

A third American worry was more precisely economic. Having confidently predicted in the early 1990s that a regimen of privatization and market reforms would in due course transform Russia, nearly ten years on U.S. officials were sounding decidedly less confident. Even the most upbeat of Americans could not ignore the fact that the form of "crony capitalism" that had emerged in Russia, with its huge concentrations of economic power in a few hands, did not correspond to their preferred model of a competitive, open market economy. Moreover, though an economic meltdown had been avoided after the great financial crash of 1998 (partly because of a rise in the price of oil and partly because of an improvement in the trade balance caused by devaluation and a sharp downturn in Western imports), the situation for the majority of Russians remained grim. The U.S. response to this was not to deny the statistical evidence but to argue, somewhat unconvincingly, that it would take many more years than originally anticipated to reform the Russian economic system. As Under Secretary of State Thomas Pickering noted in a keynote speech a few days before Putin's election, the long view was needed when assessing Russia's economic future.[77]

Then there was the open wound called NATO and NATO expansion. Naturally enough, American policymakers hoped (against hope perhaps) that they might be able to convince the Russians that NATO and Russia might become security "partners" rather than "protagonists." Indeed, at one stage Putin himself even seemed to be open to the idea of Russia joining NATO and of NATO playing a constructive role in European security.[78] NATO moreover did a fair bit to make this possible and set out an eight-point plan of action to facilitate cooperation. This included, among other things, discussing respective military strategies, working together "to prevent further proliferation," cooperative efforts in "the area of theatre missile defence against rogue states," and sorting out "ways to improve the capacity of their military forces to operate together in peace support operations." But Western policymakers were not naïve and were only too aware that Putin's own nationalist inclinations and well-known objections to NATO expansion in the past meant that relations between the organization and Russia were likely to remain frosty at best, downright hostile at worst.

A final American worry concerned Putin's oft-repeated assertion that his ultimate objective was to rebuild Russian power after nearly a decade of neglect. Talbott addressed this issue in some detail in a speech delivered at Oxford University in 2000. According to Talbott, there was one consistent theme in Putin's speeches and writings: "a desire to see Russia regain its strength, its sense of national pride and purpose." Talbott conceded that this was not an illegitimate objective; on the contrary, it was "not only understandable" but "indispensable" if Russia was going to prosper. There were two dangers, however. One was that Putin might decide to rebuild Russia's strength at the expense of his immediate neighbors in the former USSR (a prescient warning given what later came to pass); the other was that he could easily come to define Russian security in zero-sum terms. This would not only fail to bring Russia the security it craved; according to Talbott, it was bound to generate a hostile reaction in an already suspicious West as well. Putin thus had to choose between two concepts of security: today's or yesterday's—and how he chose could easily determine U.S.-Russian relations in the new millennium.[79]

Conclusion

Putin's emergence in the front rank of Russian politics at the turn of the twenty-first century thus posed several difficult questions for American and Western policymakers, to which they readily admitted there was no easy answer. In many ways the only thing that could be done in the near term, it was reasoned, was to "wait and see." Albright noted in 2000, "[T]here's little to be gained by trying to make final judgment at this point—because we don't really know the answer, because we're going to have to deal with what Putin does, not with what he thinks." And what he did was more likely to be determined—as always—by events which one could not predict and over which one had little control. Which raises the critical question Was the relationship now doomed to failure?

According to most contemporary analysts writing in the shadow of what has happened over the past few years, the answer is a very clear yes. There were, it is now argued, few reasons ever to be optimistic. After all, Russia by 2000 was led by a former (or perhaps current) member of an organization not known for its benign view of the West. Many ordinary Russians meanwhile had not only not experienced any real improvement in their lives since 1991 but the opposite. For years Russians had been forced to listen to Western advisors telling them about how Russia could become a "normal" country. Yet in the process of becoming "normal" like the West, life expectancy had fallen, crime had surged, and former Soviet assets had been taken over by an oligarchic elite. To make matters even worse, Russia had moved from being a respected and feared member of the international club to becoming a global "has-been." Putin understood this only too well. One could not turn the clock back completely. That was clear. On the other hand, he was quite prepared to tap into that yearning for order and predictability as a way of building up a base of support at home. Having suffered years of misery under reformers overly influenced by Western notions of freedom, many Russians were now all too ready to listen to Putin's unambiguously clear message that, at long last, Russia was back.

Of course this did not mean that, at least for a while, Russia could not get along with the West or the United States. Terrorism provided at least one cause around which both the West and Moscow could unite; another was pure economic self-interest. Indeed, it is worth noting that during his first ten years in the Kremlin, as oil prices soared and the Russian economy began to recover its equilibrium, economic relations between the West and

Russia went from strength to strength. Even its oligarchs started to invest in the West, buying up the occasional football team, sending their children to Western schools, and hiding their money overseas using Western-created shell companies as cover.[80]

There was no material reason therefore why some form of "live and let live" policy of accommodation could not have continued. Yet as time passed the forces pulling in another direction proved to be too powerful, and one event after another, from the U.S. war in Iraq, NATO's intervention in Libya, Washington's support for democratic reform in Russia's "backyard," and, most problematically, America's willingness to keep the door of NATO open to all comers—including Ukraine—finally convinced Moscow that there was little point seeking a constructive and cooperative relationship with the United States and the West. No doubt emboldened by his new relationship with Xi Jinping's China, and inclined anyway by his own reading of Russian history and experiences in the 1990s to beware of the West, it was but a short step for Putin to declare liberalism to be the problem and America and the West the enemy. It was no less of a step on behalf of policymakers in the West to conclude that Russia would always pose a threat to the kind of order it was seeking to defend and uphold around the world. Certainly, long before Putin attacked Ukraine in 2022, the relationship had gone beyond the point of no return. At what point and for what reason Russia was "lost" has been the subject of intense debate ever since it became clear that something resembling a new cold war was beginning to take shape. But those seriously interested in understanding what finally came to pass would be well advised to return to the 1990s, a period of hope and high expectation, when Western policymakers who sought one outcome ended up confronting a Russia totally at odds with what they had hoped for.

Notes

1. Ikenberry 2018.
2. Porter 2020.
3. Mearsheimer 2019.
4. Walt 2022.
5. Putin 2022.
6. Mearsheimer 2014.
7. Sorensen 2011.
8. Lucas 2008.
9. Gessen 2012.
10. Belton 2020.
11. Szamuely 1974.

12. Graham 2017.
13. Graham 2002.
14. Drost 2022.
15. Malinova 2021.
16. Kim 2021.
17. Radchenko 2020.
18. Till 2011.
19. Kotkin 2001.
20. Negroponte 2016.
21. Clinton 2004.
22. Marsden 2005.
23. Chernyaev 2000, 226.
24. Zubok 2021.
25. Beschloss and Talbott 1994.
26. Cox and Hurst 2002.
27. Oberdorfer 1998.
28. U.S. Government Accountability Office 1991.
29. Arbel and Edelist 2001.
30. Trachtenberg 2018.
31. Beschloss and Talbott 1994.
32. Talbott 2017.
33. Matlock 1995.
34. Quoted in Branch (2009, 48).
35. U.S. Department of State Dispatch 1993a.
36. U.S. Department of State Dispatch 1993b.
37. White 1998.
38. Quotes from Clinton (2004, 503, 504) and Branch (2009, 49).
39. Sokolov and Kirilenko 2013.
40. Sakwa 1995.
41. *The Economist* 1993.
42. Cox 2022, 40–54.
43. U.S. Department of State, Office of the Historian n.d.
44. Talbott 1994.
45. The American Presidency Project n.d.
46. Krauthammer 1994.
47. Cox 2022, 45.
48. Cox 2022, 45.
49. Dewar 1994.
50. Brzezinski 1994, 67–82.
51. Brzezinski 1994.
52. Gordon 1994.
53. See The White House (n.d.) on Clinton's defense of his policies toward the non-Russian republics.
54. On Clinton's discussions with Yeltsin on NATO enlargement, see Clinton 2004, 654–655, 750.
55. Ferguson 2005.
56. Aslund 1994.
57. Branch 2009, 483.
58. *The Economist* 1997.
59. Lloyd 1998.
60. Meek 1998.
61. *Wall Street Journal Europe* 1998.
62. Malia 1998.
63. Friedman 1998.
64. Safire 1998.
65. Steele 2015.
66. Bohlen 1998.
67. Erlanger 1998.
68. Talbott 2003.

69. Talbott 1998.
70. Quote from Zubok 2021, 435.
71. Secretary of State Madeleine K. Albright Press Conference 1999.
72. For Alexander Vershbow's subsequent reflections on "what went wrong" in the U.S.-Russia relationship, see Vershbow and Fried 2020.
73. Tenet 1999.
74. McFaul 2003.
75. See 'Vladimir Putin's Honeymoon', CBS News, March 20, 2000.
76. *Moscow Times* 2020.
77. Pickering 2000.
78. Robertson 2002.
79. Perlez 2000.
80. Mitchell 2022.

References

The American Presidency Project. n.d. "Republican Party Platform of 1996." August 12, 1996. https://www.presidency.ucsb.edu/documents/republican-party-platform-1996.

Arbel, David, and Ran Edelist. 2001. *Western Intelligence and the Collapse of the Soviet Union 1980-1990*. Frank Cass.

Aslund, Anders. 1994. "Russia's Success Story." *Foreign Affairs* 73 (5): 58-71.

Belton, Catherine. 2020. *Putin's People: How the KGB Took Back Russia and Then Took on the West*. William Collins.

Beschloss, Michael R., and Strobe Talbott. 1994. *At the Highest Level: The Inside Story of the End of the Cold War*. Little Brown.

Bohlen, Celestine. 1998. "Gorbachev's Economists Back at the Helm." *International Herald Tribune*, September 16.

Branch, Taylor. 2009. *The Clinton Tapes: Wrestling History with the President*. Simon & Schuster.

Brzezinski, Zbigniew. 1994. "The Premature Partnership." *Foreign Affairs* 73 (2): 67-82.

Chernyaev, Anatoly. 2000. *My Six Years with Gorbachev*. Pennsylvania State University Press.

Clinton, Bill. 2004. *My Life*.Hutchinson.

Cox, Michael. 2022. "Failed Crusade ? The United States and Post-Communist Russia" in *Agonies of Empire*, Bristol University Press, pp. 40-54.

Cox, Michael, and Steven Hurst. 2002. "'His Finest Hour': George Bush and the Diplomacy of German Unification." *Diplomacy and Statecraft* 13 (4): 123-150.

Dewar, Helen. 1994. "Senate Backs Talbott for State Department." *Washington Post*, February 21.

Drost, Niels. 2022. "How Vladimir Putin Uses the History of the Russian Empire." *Clingendael Magazine*, March 1.

The Economist. 1993. "Reforming Russia's Economy." December 11.

The Economist. 1997. "Russia's Reforms in Trouble." November 22.

Erlanger, Steven. 1998. "Economy Shift in Russia Worries US, Albright Says." *New York Times*, October 3.

Ferguson, Niall. 2005. "Look Back at Weimar and Start to Worry about Russia." *The Telegraph*, January 1.

Friedman, George. 1998. "Russian Economic Failure Invites a New Stalinism." *International Herald Tribune*, September 11.

Gessen, Masha. 2012. *The Man without a Face: The Unlikely Rise of Vladimir Putin*. Riverhead Books.

Gordon, Michael R. 1994. "Perry Says Caution Is Vital to Russian Partnership." *New York Times*, March 15.

Graham, Thomas. 2017. "The Problem Is Not Russia, It's Putin." *Politico*, August 12.
Graham, Thomas E., Jr. 2002. *Russia's Decline and Uncertain Recovery*. Carnegie Endowment for Peace.
Ikenberry, G. John. 2018. "The End of the Liberal International Order?" *International Affairs* 94 (1): 7–23.
Kim, Lucian. 2021. "Putin's War on History." *Russia File*, March 21.
Kotkin, Steven. 2001. *Avoiding Armageddon: The Soviet Collapse 1970–2000*. Oxford University Press.
Krauthammer, Charles. 1994. "Honeymoon Over, the Two Powers Must Go Their Own Way." *International Herald Tribune*, February 26–27.
Lloyd, John. 1998. "Yeltsin Leaps into the Abyss." *The Times* (London), March 24.
Lucas, Edward. 2008. *The New Cold War: Putin's Russia and the Threat to the West*. Palgrave Macmillan.
Malia, Martin. 1998. "In Russia, the Liberal Western Model Has Failed." *International Herald Tribune*, September 5–6.
Malinova, Olga. 2021. "Framing the Collective Memory of the 1990s as a Legitimation Tool for Putin's Regime." *Problems of Post-Communism* 68 (5): 429–441.
Marsden, Lee. 2005. *Lessons from Russia: Clinton and US Democracy Promotion*. Aldershot.
Matlock, Jack. 1995. *Autopsy of an Empire: The American Ambassador's Account of the Collapse of the Soviet Union*. Random House.
McFaul, Michael. 2003. "US Foreign Policy and Chechnya." March. https://fsi-live.s3.us-west-1.amazonaws.com/s3fs-public/US_Foreign_Policy_and_Chechnya.pdf.
Mearsheimer, John. 2014. "Why the Ukraine Crisis Is the West's Fault: The Liberal Delusions That Provoked Putin." *Foreign Affairs* 93(5): 77–89.
Mearsheimer, John. 2019. "Bound to Fail: The Rise and Fall of the Liberal International Order." *International Security* 43 (4): 7–50.
Meek, James. 1998. "Russia Stares into the Abyss." *The Guardian*, April 2.
Mitchell, Taylor S. 2022. "The West May Have Fueled the Russian Oligarchy They Now Seek to Punish." *Business Insider*, April 7.
Moscow Times. 2020. "Putin Lashes Out at National Traitors with Pro-Western Views." March 18.
Negroponte, Diana Villiers. 2016. "The Hesitant US Rescue of the Soviet Economy." *Wilson Quarterly*, Fall. https://www.wilsonquarterly.com/quarterly/the-lasting-legacy-of-the-cold-war/the-hesitant-us-rescue-of-the-soviet-economy
Oberdorfer, Dan. 1998. *From the Cold War to a New Era: The United States and the Soviet Union, 1983–1991*. Johns Hopkins University Press.
Perlez, Jane. 2000. "US Official Dims His View of Russia's Future." *New York Times on the Web*, January 23.
Pickering, Thomas R. 2000. "Russia at a Decision Point." U.S. Department of State Archive, March 21. https://1997-2001.state.gov/policy_remarks/2000/000321_pickering_russia.html.
Porter, Patrick. 2020. *The False Promise of Liberal Order: Nostalgia, Delusion and the Rise of Trump*. Polity.
Putin, Vladimir. 2022. "On the Historic Unity of Russians and Ukrainians." Kremlin, July 21. http://en.kremlin.ru/events/president/news/66181.
Radchenko, Sergey. 2020. "'Nothing but Humiliation for Russia': Moscow and NATO's Eastern Enlargement, 1993–1995." *Journal of Strategic Studies* 43 (6–7): 769–815.
Robertson, George. 2002. "A New Russian Revolution: Partnership with NATO." NATO On-line Library, January 23.
Safire, William. 1998. "Primakov Is No Short-Termer." *International Herald Tribune*, September 18.

Sakwa, Richard. 1995. "The Russian Elections of December 1993." *Europe-Asia Studies* 47 (2): 195–227.
Secretary of State Madeleine K. Albright Press Conference. 1999. U.S. Department of State Archive. July 26. https://1997-2001.state.gov/www/statements/1999/990726b.html.
Sokolov, Mikhail, and Anastasia Kirilenko. 2013. "20 Years Ago Russia Had Its Biggest Political Crisis since the October Revolution." *The Atlantic*, October 3.
Sorensen, George. 2011. *A Liberal World Order in Crisis: Choosing between Imposition and Restraint*. Cornell University Press.
Steele, Jonathan. 2015. "Yevgeny Primakov: Obituary." *The Guardian*, June 28.
Szamuely, Tibor. 1974. *The Russian Tradition*. Secker & Warburg.
Talbott, Strobe. 1994. "America Must Remain Engaged with Russian Reform." U.S. Department of State Dispatch, January 31.
Talbott, Strobe. 1998. "Dealing with Russia in a Time of Troubles." *The Economist*, November 21.
Talbott, Strobe. 2003. *The Russia Hand: A Memoir of Presidential Diplomacy*. Random House.
Talbott, Strobe. 2017. "The Man Who Lost an Empire." Brookings, December 7.
Tenet, George J. 1999. "Remarks of Director of Central Intelligence George J. Tenet at the Greater Nashua Chamber of Commerce Annual Dinner." June 28.
Till, Brian. 2011. "Mikhail Gorbachev: The West Could Have Saved the Russian Economy." *The Atlantic*, June. https://www.theatlantic.com/international/archive/2011/06/mikhail-gorbachev-the-west-could-have-saved-the-russian-economy/240466/.
Trachtenberg, Marc. 2018. "Economic Performance during the Cold War: A Failure of Intelligence?" *Texas National Security Review* 1 (2): 76–101.
U.S. Department of State Dispatch. 1993a. "Securing US Interests While Supporting Russian Reform." March 29.
U.S. Department of State Dispatch. 1993b. "A Strategic Alliance with Russian Reform." April 12.
U.S. Department of State, Office of the Historian. n.d. "Bill Clinton, Boris Yeltsin and U.S.-Russia Relations." https://history.state.gov/milestones/1993-2000/clinton-yeltsin.
U.S. Government Accountability Office. 1991. "Soviet Economy: Assessment of How Well the CIA Has Estimated the Size of the Economy." September 30.
Vershbow, Alexander, and Daniel Fried. 2020. "How the West Should Deal with Russia." Atlantic Council, November 23. https://www.atlanticcouncil.org/event/how-the-west-should-deal-with-russia/
Wall Street Journal Europe. 1998. "Domino Effect: How a Little Market Like Russia Set Off a Global Chain Reaction." September 22.
Walt, Steve. 2022. "Liberal Illusions Caused the Ukraine Crisis." *Belfer Center for Science and International Affairs*, January 19, Harvard University.
White, Stephen. 1998. "Rethinking the Transition: 1991 and Beyond." In *Rethinking the Soviet Collapse: Sovietology, the Death of Communism and the New Russia*, edited by Michael Cox. Pinter.
The White House. n.d. "Promoting Democracy and Sovereignty in the New Independent States." https://clintonwhitehouse5.archives.gov/WH/EOP/NSC/html/nsc-13.html.
Zubok, Vladislav. 2021. *Collapse and Fall of the Soviet Union*. Yale University Press.

8

Reconsidering Engagement with China

Authoritarian Power and International Order

Miles Kahler

In an era of partisan polarization in U.S. politics, growing antagonism toward China has become a rare point of consensus among the political class and many international affairs experts.* The policies of the first Trump administration—from initiating a tariff war with China, to labeling the relationship as one of "strategic competition," to blaming China publicly for the corona virus pandemic—appeared to signal that "the era of engagement with China has come to an unceremonious close."[1] In a recent article, engagement was described as a "dirty word" in U.S. policy circles; China experts declined the label of "engagers" in favor of "responsible managers" or "responsible co-existers."[2] The Biden administration has not signaled a significant departure from this more skeptical and confrontational line, and China's stance during the Russian invasion of Ukraine has only diminished its standing in the eyes of U.S. politicians and public.

The deterioration of the U.S.-China relationship, reaching its lowest point since normalization of diplomatic relations in 1979, has profound implications for the existing international order and its future architecture. Inevitably, Washington's reassessment of its relations with China has also led to a reevaluation of the foundations of those relations in the immediate post–Cold War decade of the 1990s. Both scholars and policymakers ask, "What went wrong?," and some look to that origin story for the current malaise. John Mearsheimer, one of the most vocal of these critics of engagement, for example, echoes the Trump administration's rhetoric, contending

---

* The author thanks Alan Alexandroff, Michael Doyle, Stephan Haggard, Harry Harding, John Ikenberry, Robert Ross, James Shinn, Susan Shirk, Helen Thompson, Joseph Torigian, Peter Trubowitz, and participants in the June 2022 LSE conference, the October 2023 Princeton conference, and the WZB Berlin Social Science Center Global Governance Colloquium for their comments on an earlier draft of this chapter. The author also acknowledges and thanks Frieder Dengler and Kaitlyn Hill for their research assistance.

Miles Kahler, *Reconsidering Engagement with China*. In: *Rethinking the 1990s*. Edited by: G. John Ikenberry and Peter Trubowitz, Oxford University Press. © Oxford University Press (2025).
DOI: 10.1093/9780197813133.003.0008

that U.S. policymakers were "beguiled by misguided theories about liberalism's inevitable triumph" and a misplaced belief that China would "become a peace-loving democracy and a responsible stakeholder in a US-led international order."[3] Others have taken issue with this reading of policy decisions in the 1990s and the choice of engagement then and in subsequent decades.[4]

A reconsideration of the relationship between China and the United States as the U.S.-led, post–Cold War order took shape permits an evaluation of the choices made at that time and whether they have shaped current discontents. U.S. policy toward China during the 1990s has been amply documented; the Chinese perspective can be charted indirectly, utilizing informed Chinese commentators and U.S. China experts.[5] As David Lampton has explained, U.S.-China relations in the 1990s were bookended by two turning points: violent repression of pro-democracy demonstrations in Tiananmen Square and other Chinese cities in 1989 and passage of permanent normal trade relations (PNTR) legislation by the U.S. Congress in 2000, opening the way for China's accession to the World Trade Organization (WTO). The decade was punctuated by a third turning point: the Taiwan Strait crisis of 1995–1996.[6] As James Steinberg notes, the U.S. response to Tiananmen and China's accession to the WTO with U.S. support are also among the alleged mistakes that are cited by critics of the policy of engagement.[7]

Engagement emerged as the dominant descriptor of U.S. policy in the decade divided by these three defining episodes, examined in the following sections. Tiananmen confirmed that China would be a major and awkward exception to the third wave of democratization that had swept away most communist regimes. The second episode, the Taiwan crisis in 1995–1996, threatened a military confrontation between the United States and China, but U.S. policy did not shift from engagement to containment. Although China looms very large in debates over the global order today, during the turmoil of the early 1990s—the breakup of the Soviet Union and Yugoslavia, the battle over the North American Free Trade Agreement (NAFTA) in Congress, the aftermath of the first Iraq War—China often failed to reach the top of the U.S. foreign policy or global agenda.[8] As the unipolar moment began, any military threat posed by China appeared to lie in the future, even to the most pessimistic observers. At the end of the decade, the third episode—approval of PNTR by the U.S. Congress—signaled the rise of an economic relationship that would ultimately reshape engagement. Each of these episodes contributed to the variegated pattern of policy that was labeled "engagement," a capacious term that encompassed different meanings and different expectations, none of them naïvely optimistic.

Finally, political responses to the success of economic engagement, responses that led to a redefinition and, ultimately, a rejection of engagement in the twenty-first century, are outlined in a final section. As conflict deepens between the United States and China, the record of U.S. policy in building a post–Cold War order that aimed to include China provides a guide for policy toward other countries that have stood, in greater or lesser degree, outside of or in opposition to that order. Engagement also sheds light on similar strategies that have relied on growing economic interdependence to produce political and foreign policy change.

Tiananmen, Human Rights, and the New Politics of U.S. Foreign Policy

The 1989 repression of the pro-democracy movement in China occurred at a moment of uncertainty and flux in the global order: the Soviet Union's East European empire was fracturing, although the fall of the Berlin Wall was months away. The Soviet Union itself would survive for two more years. The George H. W. Bush administration, which had been in office for only a few months, inherited a policy toward China that was largely determined by the national security bureaucracy and the White House and was directed toward a clear, common goal: countering the Soviet threat during the Cold War.

Tiananmen overturned that embedded consensus and, most important, the policy process on which it rested. The need for China as a strategic partner was called into question, questioning that would only intensify as the Soviet bloc and the Soviet Union disintegrated. At the same time, the politics of China policy, which witnessed an activist Congress (controlled by the opposition Democrats) and the mobilization of interest groups to influence congressional action, undermined the ability of the executive branch to dominate relations with China.[9] Because of Tiananmen and congressional activism, a powerful normative element was introduced into the political discourse. Human rights became part of U.S. negotiations with China, although the issue's position on the agenda would rise and fall. In addition, Tiananmen produced a collapse in favorable public views of China, which transitioned rapidly from "leading communist reformer to political atavism."[10] Public opinion would never fully recover its earlier positive view of China; only the most recent precipitous decline in U.S. public attitudes during the Trump administration would match the post-Tiananmen reaction.[11] The debate over an appropriate response to Tiananmen raised a central question for the relations of the United States and its allies, as authoritarianism stabilized in China: the ability of international pressure to produce domestic political change in China and whether such change was necessary for China's integration into the emerging liberal international order.

Following Tiananmen, sanctions were imposed by the United States and the G-7, including an end to military sales and suspension of military exchanges as well as bilateral and multilateral development assistance to China. The reaction in Europe was stronger but hardly more long-lasting than the response of Asian governments, an early indication that U.S. policy would be constrained by the actions of its allies. Apart from Japan and Taiwan, no Asian government condemned the June 4 repression, and even Japan resumed development assistance after one year.[12] High-level U.S. negotiations with China were halted after a sharp, negative domestic reaction to the visit by National Security Advisor Brent Scowcroft to Beijing in December 1989. No national security advisor would visit again until 1996.

As recently released documents confirm, President Bush was deeply invested in maintaining the U.S.-China relationship, whether because of a far-sighted awareness of China's importance to global order in a post–Cold War world or a misguided clinging to Cold War verities of China's strategic importance.[13] However, the bipartisan political consensus that had underpinned China policy since the Nixon administration now shattered, as leading Democrats took issue with the Bush administration's China policy. The battle between the administration and Congress over sanctions "produced an embittered Congress that was fracturing along party lines with respect to China policy."[14] Domestic political conflict during the Bush administration ensured that the U.S. stance toward China would reappear during presidential campaigns as a perennially useful club for the opposition party to use in attacking the incumbent administration.[15] The Bush administration responded, as future administrations would, with a revision of the strategic defense of China policy made during the Cold War: China might no longer be necessary in the global contest with the USSR, but its support was essential in dealing with challenges such as environmental degradation and the proliferation of missiles and weapons of mass destruction.[16]

The most significant political conflict over relations with China during the Bush and first Bill Clinton administrations revolved around the terms of reengagement with China, after Tiananmen, specifically efforts to link expanding economic relations to human rights observance. Linkage took concrete form in the attachment of conditions to China's most favored nation (MFN) trade status. During the Bush administration, myriad interests had attempted to influence Congress in setting the conditions for MFN extension, reflecting the new and more complex politics of China policy.[17] Winston Lord, assistant secretary of state in the Clinton administration, and President Clinton, who had criticized Bush administration China policy as too conciliatory, argued for combining continued MFN status with "moderate and realistic conditions" regarding progress in the observation of human rights in China.[18]

Initially, Clinton extended China's MFN status, with further extension beyond July 1994 subject to conditions: "significant progress in improving [China's] human rights record."[19] In July 1993, Lord prepared a memorandum for the president that outlined and advocated, for the first time, a policy of "comprehensive engagement," in which these conditions could be embedded.[20] Lord was disenchanted with the "overly soft approach" of the Bush administration and believed that the United States could "have engagement of a hard-headed nature," a clear sign that proponents of engagement, from the start, did not eschew conditions or sanctions.[21] Lampton noted, "[E]ven fervent 'engagers' recognize the need for force and credibility and the need to employ unilateral sanctions in the economic and proliferation realms on occasion."[22]

Nevertheless, the success of conditioning economic engagement on human rights observance was a failure in the short run. Lord and others argued that China's own successful economic development would ultimately depend on a free society in "the age of information."[23] China's leadership, having stabilized its rule after Tiananmen, clearly disagreed. The negative example of Mikhail Gorbachev was prominent in the party's "lessons learned": the Chinese senior leadership believed that only reinforcing party control would allow them to avoid the fate of the Soviet Union.[24] Discussions within the leadership, described in the Tiananmen Papers, attributed the 1989 demonstrations to a small band of radicals, egged on by the United States, Europe, and its old Nationalist enemies on Taiwan.[25] In the years after the crisis, the Chinese Communist Party leadership continued to rely on these lessons, viewing its regime as under siege from international forces encouraging "bourgeois liberalization" or "peaceful evolution" and threatened by division within the party.[26] Paradoxically, language used by some U.S. supporters of engagement, predicting eventual political change in China as a result of economic and cultural ties, only increased the fears of China's party elite.[27]

As a result, U.S. representations regarding human rights in China, especially public pressure, were regarded by the Chinese government as unwanted and illegitimate intervention in its internal affairs. During the Clinton administration, linkage within the new framework of engagement obtained only a few minor concessions on human rights from China, perhaps the most significant—since it fit its emerging strategy—was agreement to work with the United States in legal and judicial cooperation.[28] Broader political liberalization, if it were to occur, was only a long-run goal.

These initial efforts to link economic exchange with progress on human rights ended with Clinton's announcement in May 1994 that renewal of MFN would be based on the "broader strategic interests" of the United States rather than China's human rights record. As his critics pointed out, Clinton was echoing justifications used by predecessor Republican administrations. Clinton also pointed the way to an argument for engagement based on long-term structural change in China: "Will we do more to advance the cause of human rights if China is isolated or if our nations are engaged in a growing web of political and economic cooperation and contacts?"[29]

This turn in policy was confirmed in May 1996 in an address by Secretary of State Warren Christopher, who argued that high-level exchanges with Chinese leaders were necessary and that "economic and security progress should not be held hostage to human rights differences."[30] For those who applauded the end of linkage, the consolidation of engagement without direct linkage to human rights criteria signified that "paradoxically, human rights are most effectively promoted by putting other issues first."[31] For those who labored to construct the earlier, tenuous linkage, such as Lord, "disarray" in the United States undercut its significant bargaining advantages with China: "vociferous" business opposition to any conditions on MFN status, a position backed by the economic agencies in the U.S. government (Treasury, Commerce, and U.S. trade representative). Given this public divide, Lord believed that the Chinese government saw little likelihood that it would lose MFN status, undermining the United States in its negotiations on human rights.[32]

The opposition identified by Lord marked political battle lines that would characterize conflict over engagement and its terms for the rest of the 1990s and into the next century. Human rights NGOs and labor representatives, finding a voice among Democrats in Congress, as well as religious conservatives mobilized by Chinese violations of religious freedom, would continue to press for conditions linked to domestic policy change in China.

Experts on China, aware of the Communist Party's resistance to such change, and many Washington think tanks were more skeptical. For example, a "large majority" of the Committee on U.S.-China Policy, a high-level, nongovernmental panel that reported early in the Clinton administration, supported no further withdrawal or conditioning of MFN coupled with "vigorous and quiet dialogue" on human rights at the senior level.[33] Most important was the growing influence of U.S. international business, better organized and more vocal than they had been immediately after Tiananmen, advocating against any policy that would endanger their rapidly growing opportunities in China.[34] As Lord noted, they found strong support in the economic agencies of the U.S. government.[35] Rather than viewing China as a military threat, the Pentagon argued for reestablishing military contacts with China, in part to encourage Chinese support in dealing with the North Korean nuclear program.[36]

At this time, only a few on the fringes of public debate argued for U.S. pressure aimed at regime change or democratization in China.[37] Even those who argued for linkage to promote human rights endorsed a gradualist view of political change. Although pressure for economic engagement from U.S. business was an increasingly powerful barrier to linkage, the use of economic sanctions was constrained by three additional considerations. First, sanctions could impose collateral damage on Hong Kong, which faced a difficult transition from British to Chinese rule in 1997, and Taiwan, which was, in contrast to China, rapidly democratizing in the 1990s. Second, allies, equally motivated by the economic promise of China, were less likely to support linkage and would therefore enjoy a competitive advantage in trade and investment with China. A final, equally important constraint was the need for Chinese cooperation in building a global and regional security order that was in flux at the end of the Cold War.

Taiwan, U.S. Allies, and Global Security: China as Threat and Partner

Taiwan had served as a point of conflict between the United States and China since the foundation of the People's Republic in 1949. After normalization, support for Taiwan within the U.S. Congress and the Republican Party ensured that friction would continue, particularly over arms transfers. Over the course the 1990s, Taiwan became another anomaly in the post–Cold War world, a mirror image of the much larger anomaly of an authoritarian China. China would not give up its historical claims to Taiwan, nor would the PRC forgo the possible use of force if Taiwan declared independence. The old conflict between two regimes that claimed to govern all of China was superseded during the 1990s by a conflict between a rapidly democratizing Taiwan that was developing an identity separate from the mainland on the one hand, and, on the other, an entrenched authoritarian regime in Beijing that aimed to prevent that identity from producing separatism. From the U.S. point of view, managing the China-Taiwan relationship was further complicated by growing economic interdependence between China and Taiwan (constraining the use of economic sanctions) and widening political support for Taiwan across the political spectrum in Washington. Although U.S. business opposed linkage that endangered their economic interests in China, supporting Taiwan meshed with their extensive connections to that economy.[38] The old "Taiwan lobby" had found a home with the conservatives of the Republican Party; now Taiwan enjoyed bipartisan support in Congress. Taiwan was also an astute Washington lobbyist, ranked by Lord as "second place, just behind Israel and just ahead of Greece."[39]

The 1995–1996 Taiwan Strait confrontation between China and the United States was "a low point in US-China relations during the first Clinton term."[40] The crisis was precipitated by democratization on Taiwan, particularly the concern in an insecure Chinese leadership that Taiwanese president Lee Teng-hui and the Democratic Progressive Party were aiming for independence. Congressional pressure induced the Clinton administration to permit Lee to make a "private" visit to his alma mater, Cornell University, which only increased anxiety in Beijing. An initial round of Chinese missile tests near Taiwan in July 1995 was followed by an announcement of additional tests and live-fire exercises, closer to Taiwan, in March 1996. This militarized demonstration clearly aimed for intimidation during the Taiwanese presidential election. In response, several U.S. naval vessels transited the Taiwan Strait in July and December 1995, and, after the 1996 Chinese actions, the United States dispatched two aircraft carrier battle groups to the vicinity of Taiwan. Despite heated rhetoric from the Chinese media and the U.S. Congress, the two militaries did not come to blows. Lord believed the risk of a Chinese attack on Taiwan to be low; however, the use of force at a lower level was possible. Most important was a risk of miscalculation on either side.[41]

The Taiwan crisis, coupled with China's rapid economic growth and its military modernization, raised the issue of its evolving orientation toward the United States and the possible military threat that it might pose in the future. By the end of the decade, even though China was not a peer military competitor, Thomas Christensen argued that China could "pose major problems for American security interests, and especially for Taiwan, without the slightest pretense of catching up with the United States by an overall measure of national military power or technology."[42] The overwhelming global military advantage of the United States in the 1990s was also offset by questions about its willingness to remain committed to Asia-Pacific security after the Cold War. The 1992 presidential campaign witnessed two "America First" candidates, Patrick Buchanan and Ross Perot. Although our image of the United States during these years is one of a self-confident great power bent on creating a new world order, it appeared at the start of the Clinton administration that domestic problems might absorb the United States and reduce its activism abroad.[43]

The Clinton administration's decision to maintain and reinforce its bilateral alliance system in Asia, especially its alliances with Japan and South Korea, indicated that engagement would be accompanied by hedging against future Chinese behavior. Despite the growing investment and trade by these two allies with China, the Chinese response to these steps, like Russian complaints over NATO enlargement, was to label them a renewal of containment and view them through the lens of its claims of sovereignty over Taiwan.[44] Although the United States did seek to engage China in new regional organizations, such as the ASEAN Regional Forum and Asia-Pacific Economic Cooperation, as well as the Track 1.5 Northeast Asian Cooperation Dialogue, those initiatives did not match NATO's outreach to Russia. Given China's suspicion of most regional organizations at this time, it is unlikely that a more formal institution would have succeeded. Since the United States had only recently set aside its own resistance to regional organizations that might compete with transpacific bilateral alliances, advancing a multilateral regional security architecture was not a U.S. priority.

U.S. allies in Asia and Europe continued to present an obstacle for American policymakers intent on conditional engagement: as China's economy opened and its expansion continued, its neighbors in East Asia, like U.S. business, became supporters of de facto unconditional engagement. If the United States chose to use economic leverage to achieve Chinese policy change, it was unlikely to find support from Japan, South Korea, or, by the end of the decade, Taiwan. Lord described allied response to efforts at linkage: "Our friends would hold our coats when we raised some of these tough issues with the Chinese ... and then take the trade contracts."[45] Although the G-7 imposed economic sanctions and an embargo on arms sales following Tiananmen, allied pressure for the resumption of normal economic relations quickly appeared. The G-7 summit in July 1990 agreed to the resumption of World Bank lending to China, a particular benefit to Japan, and one that gave Japan an opening for returning to business as usual.[46] However, Japan's proximity to China introduced more tension in their relations relative to European economies. By the end of the decade, Taiwan and competing claims in the East China Sea, as well as the strengthening of the U.S. alliance, had produced rising distrust that would sharpen during the Koizumi Junichiro government (2001–2006).[47] Nevertheless, Japan in the 1990s declined to use the term "engagement" for its China policy, since it viewed its economic influence as directed at Chinese external and commercial policy, not Chinese domestic politics. Also, as China's economy grew, Japan's economic leverage, in the form of large flows of overseas development assistance, declined.[48]

European policies toward China during the 1990s were even less complicated than those of the Asian allies of the United States: they were driven almost entirely by economic interest. Just as Japan's desire to resume normal economic ties with China had promoted a resumption of World Bank lending, German chancellor Helmut Kohl's "business first" visit to Beijing in 1993 added international competitive pressure to the lobbying of domestic business when the Clinton administration decided to abandon linkage of economic exchange and human rights.[49] Earlier, the European Council and Parliament had resumed institutional exchanges with China (October 1990) and, in January 1992, "the full range of assistance and collaborative programs."[50] China's importance for European exports and investment expanded rapidly over the decade.[51] As a result, the Chinese leadership was not only able to play European and Japanese interests against U.S. efforts at linkage, but China also set up competition among European countries for economic benefits.[52] Although Britain's concerns over the transition of Hong Kong from colonial to Chinese rule and France's sales of military aircraft to Taiwan produced temporary stumbles on the road to growing economic ties, by the end of the decade European governments, like the Asian allies of the United States, were drawn by the magnet of rapid Chinese opening and economic growth. And, as François Godemont writes, during this "honeymoon" period "Europeans, often armed with very little knowledge of the working of the Chinese party-state bureaucracy, generally believed that with China, business followed diplomacy."[53] Beginning in 1998, the EU declined to submit a resolution on China to the UN Human Rights Commission, and European governments were also able to discover ways to circumvent the G-7 arms embargo, in place since Tiananmen.[54]

China found a final source of leverage in the security interests of the United States, based on its permanent membership on the UN Security Council and in the U.S. aim to have China join global security regimes, especially those directed at nuclear nonproliferation. The Bush administration had found Chinese cooperation necessary after the Iraqi invasion of Kuwait in August 1990. As the UN Security Council became increasingly active in peacekeeping and conflict resolution during the 1990s, Chinese acquiescence (abstention) or support on the Council was essential. China's embrace of the United Nations set it apart from past revisionist states, such as Japan and Germany in the 1930s. Its ability to withhold UN approval for American-sponsored interventions led China to elevate the United Nations as a core element in its foreign policy and to collaborate with Russia in opposition to U.S. interventions that lacked a UN mandate.[55]

The United Nations was not the only international organization that attracted Chinese membership after the Cold War. In stark contrast to its record before 1980, China sought membership in global institutions. By the 1990s, despite its level of economic development, its participation in international institutions had reached the level of major industrialized and developing countries, although it remained in what Alastair Johnston called a period of "noviceness."[56] In some cases, China ratified international agreements, such as the Convention on Biological Diversity, that the United States declined.[57] Particularly striking was its increasing participation in global security treaties and institutions, given the sensitivity of those issues and the military predominance of the United States.[58] For example, in contrast to the Maoist position of vehement opposition to the Nuclear Nonproliferation Treaty and its regulatory regime, China became a signatory of the treaty in 1992.

In U.S. policy and politics, the issue of China's compliance with its nonproliferation obligations became another test of the policy of engagement. The possible imposition of sanctions for China's violation of a 1992 commitment to abide by the Missile Technology Control Regime arose early in the Clinton administration. The dispute over export of missiles to Pakistan was ultimately resolved after a complex negotiation that saw the United States lift sanctions first, followed by China's restatement of its earlier commitment not to export the missiles. China's support of Pakistan and its nuclear program became an issue again in 1996 because of a shipment of ring magnets, a dual-use product that could be used in gas centrifuges. Once again, in the face of intense congressional pressure and demands from nonproliferation advocates, the Clinton administration threatened sanctions, as required by legislation (Nuclear Nonproliferation Prevention Act, 1994). Careful negotiation seemed to produce results: China agreed to issue a statement that it would not cooperate with unsafeguarded nuclear programs if the United States withheld sanctions for the ring magnets shipment.[59]

These episodes illustrate several aspects of China's participation in the emerging global order of the 1990s. First, although the United States had discovered that economic sanctions failed to produce compliance with its human rights conditions, in other instances linkage did appear to produce changes in Chinese foreign policy behavior. Second, it was clear to both the Clinton administration and the Chinese government that nonproliferation of weapons of mass destruction had become a high-priority international and U.S. agenda item after the Cold War. Third, China claimed—and U.S. experts agreed to accept—that the ring magnets dispute resulted from shortcomings in China's export control regime for dual-use products. Following the resolution, China agreed to consultations with the United States on a "workable export control administration."[60] Finally, and most important, China had accepted most of the important global security regimes during the 1990s. Although the United States responded to congressional and domestic political pressure, its demands were typically directed to Chinese compliance with multilateral obligations that China had freely accepted. Since China had signed but not ratified the International Covenant on Civil and Political Rights, accepting U.S. demands on human rights could more easily be portrayed as a bilateral imposition rather than compliance with its international obligations.

In the background of U.S. bargaining with China, however, was the declining credibility of U.S. economic sanctions, given the growing significance of trade and investment with China in the calculus of U.S. business and its Asian and European allies. Even Taiwan, threatened by China, was increasingly tied to the mainland economy. This new balance of domestic and international politics would become apparent in the debate over China's accession to the WTO.

The Heart of the Matter: China in the World Economy and WTO Accession

By the early 1990s, the transformation of China's economy, and especially its orientation to the global economy, offered both a promise of beneficial economic exchange with the United States and other economies as well as the threat of disruptive adjustment. Its economic rise was identified as unique: a communist country that had embraced extensive economic reform and opening, a low-income developing economy that was already a significant participant in international trade and finance, and a country that ran a persistent trade surplus with the United States.[61]

During the George H. W. Bush administration, trade and investment had been advanced as "essential tools to keep China open to the outside world and encourage responsible behavior in areas like human rights and arms proliferation."[62] By the late 1990s, a looming test of engagement arose in negotiations over China's accession to the WTO, created in 1995. U.S. support for China's WTO accession remains one of the most controversial elements in past American engagement with China. The 2017 U.S. trade representative report during the Trump administration argued that the United States should not have supported China's accession "on terms that have proven ineffective in securing China's embrace of an open, market-oriented trade regime."[63] In addition to the terms of China's accession, a subject of Chinese negotiations with all WTO members, accession would involve U.S. acceptance of PNTR with China, removing the annual review of MFN that awarded leverage to skeptics of engagement inside and outside the U.S. Congress.

Despite the booming U.S. economy and China's high levels of economic growth, powerful political interests in both countries were suspicious of growing economic interdependence and the uneven costs that it imposed on sectors of their economies. As China grew in importance as a trading power, the United States and other industrialized economies expected greater commitments to openness, bound by international rules. China, however, in the absence of Deng Xiaoping's political weight in favor of economic reform, faced a less secure leader in Jiang Zemin and a large state-owned enterprise sector that was not internationally competitive. "New Left" and nationalist intellectuals opposed to economic reform found a galvanizing issue in WTO entry.[64] The Asian financial crisis, which began in July 1996, made the Chinese leadership aware of the vulnerability produced by economic opening, especially the risks to its unreformed financial sector. By late 1999, despite these obstacles, the Chinese leadership, particularly Premier Zhu Rongji and advocates of economic reform, had come to see WTO membership as an essential instrument to eliminate bottlenecks that prevented further economic advance and to attract additional foreign investment.

Rapidly growing Chinese exports could be attributed in large part to the transfer of labor-intensive manufacturing to China, first from Hong Kong and Taiwan, and then from other Asian countries. Nevertheless, the bilateral trade deficit had become a political issue in the United States by the start of the 1990s. At the same time, Congress began to award China's trade practices a prominent place on its agenda, supported by a 1991 Treasury report that China was deliberately increasing its trade surplus through "generalized and pervasive administrative controls over external trade."[65] Later in the decade, protection of U.S. intellectual property in China became an issue of concern for the U.S. trade representative, when a 1995 agreement appeared to be quickly violated. In this instance, as had been the case with nonproliferation, the threat of sanctions in the background of engagement seemed to work. Robert Suettinger explained, "Engagement—with clearly defined goals, intensive and respectful negotiations and discussions with a broad array of Chinese officials, obvious benefits for both sides, and the threat of sanctions as a last resort—proved workable and politically successful," easing the way for congressional approval of China's MFN status.[66] Despite these partial successes, both the Chinese trade surplus with the United States and its failure to protect American intellectual property remained points of contention in their economic relations.

The Clinton administration campaign for congressional approval of PNTR for China was "the central lasting element of the Clinton-Gore legacy regarding China."[67] Supporters of engagement uniformly argued that "a stable, prosperous China integrated into the world community was preferable to a weak, divided, and fearful China."[68] Although the United States did not attempt to link WTO accession to changes in China's observation of human rights, Chinese domestic politics did figure in the U.S. decision, specifically a concern that failure to accept accession and award PNTR would undermine those favoring economic reform in China.

Domestic politics in the United States had aligned in favor of engagement, as demonstrated in the critical House of Representatives vote on May 24, 2000. PNTR was approved by a "surprisingly wide margin," wider than the vote for NAFTA earlier in the decade.[69] The vote demonstrated that China policy was not divided along clear partisan lines, despite often bitter relations between Clinton and the Republican House majority. Three out of four Republicans voted in favor; two out of three Democrats voted against. The major business lobbies waged their "largest ever campaign for a single legislative issue," which swayed a Republican Party still closely allied with business. Republicans were also influenced by the support for China's accession by Taiwan's new president, Chen Shui-bian, a marker of the rapidly growing trade and investment by Taiwan in the mainland. In opposition were labor unions as well as religious, human rights, and environmental groups, mobilized by both principle and material interest—fear that China's entry would become a second NAFTA, encouraging companies to offshore manufacturing employment.[70]

Although business support for engagement has faded over the past decade, these political battle lines over China's entry into the global economy would persist into the next century. Despite claims that the United States should have opposed PNTR and China's entry into the WTO, China's growing importance as a trade and investment partner during the 1990s rendered alternatives unrealistic or unattractive.[71] Domestic politics, the stance of major allies, and the need for Chinese support on other global issues reinforced the Clinton administration's decision to support PNTR and China's accession to the WTO.

Defining Engagement: China and Global Order at the Turn of the Century

By the end of the 1990s, it appeared to many observers that engagement's supporters were "well-entrenched . . . both in the U.S. and in Europe and Asia," and that engagement would "remain the core of U.S. policy toward China."[72] A new contingent of doubters had arisen in foreign policy and military networks, however, challenging engagement, not on the economic and human rights grounds that were prominent in the battle over WTO accession but over China's likely long-term challenge to American primacy as its economy and military capabilities expanded. The emerging "Blue Team" contested what they perceived as the dominance of China specialists over U.S. China policy: "The Sinologists have practiced 100 variations on the theme of 'you don't understand China.' In some cases, they are right, but in most cases it doesn't matter."[73] This network of conservatives raised the option of containment as an alternative to engagement, an option that would resurface repeatedly when relations between China and the United States deteriorated. Their skepticism would be reinforced in the Republican Party by anticommunist neoconservatives and the religious right.[74] By the time of the George W. Bush administration, strategic competition had emerged as an alternative to engagement, although the rhetoric of that administration continued to endorse a "constructive, cooperative, and candid relationship" with China.[75]

Before considering containment and other alternatives to engagement, engagement and its assumptions must be defined, a task that was as difficult at the end of the 1990s as it is today. As Steinberg asserts, the term "engagement" is "too amorphous and procedural to capture the essence of the policy": "At its core, America's China policy was based on the belief that a stable, prosperous China would serve the interests of the United States, while a weak and insecure China was at least as likely to pose risks for the United States and its allies."[76] Although the party-state regime appeared to have stabilized since Tiananmen, the political stability and spectacular economic growth that China has experienced since 2000 were not guaranteed in the 1990s. Few predicted a regime collapse like those in other communist countries, but concerns about the downside risk of Chinese disintegration and its international impact were more widespread.[77]

Analysts at the turn of the century noted variants within the mix of polices labeled "engagement," variants that made different assumptions about Chinese behavior and the integration of China into the global order. One variant relied on growing economic interdependence and negotiation of (presumably modest) differences over time, without the threat or imposition of sanctions.[78] Few policymakers adopted this benign view of China's future, which was more widespread among international business. Although President Clinton, whose administration endorsed engagement, is often portrayed as espousing a misguided, optimistic view of its effects on China, a careful examination of his statements reveals a much more qualified and realistic assessment.[79] An extension, appeasement, which would seek to avoid militarized confrontation and accommodate future Chinese hegemony in East Asia, had no political support in the United States.[80]

Within the engagement camp, distinctions were made among instruments (bilateral negotiation, involving China in multilateral conventions and institutions, and building society-to-society relationships as part of an "entanglement" strategy).[81] More significant were the addition of sanctions ("conditioning" or "conditional engagement"), maintaining alliances and a U.S. military presence in Asia ("hedging"), and even aiming for the "transformation" of the Chinese political system.[82] The United States and other industrialized countries deployed a mix of these policies throughout the late 1990s and into the new century. Even conditional engagement proponents might divide on whether the "conditions" were set by the United States or consisted of "basic rules for international conduct" that were "reasonably congruent with current behavior and international undertakings," an interpretation that pointed toward more multilateral engagement.[83] Proponents often noted that engagement would add to American bargaining leverage in its negotiations with China, an assumption of continuing asymmetry in the U.S.-China relationship.[84] In practice, engagement was not simply about constraining and entangling China or changing Chinese preferences. Hedging—maintaining military options in the Asia-Pacific—remained part of U.S. policy toward China; in Chinese eyes, hedging could easily appear as a variant of containment.

Most controversial—and providing ammunition for the critics of engagement—was its relationship to China's political evolution and democratization. Contemporary accounts of engagement often portray its proponents in the 1990s as naïfs who assumed that greater economic integration and rapid economic development would inevitably lead China to a liberal democratic future. Arguments made at the time were more nuanced and contained both short-term and long-term assumptions. In the immediate future, engagement was believed to strengthen those in favor of *economic* reform in the Chinese leadership, an argument that was powerful during the WTO accession debate. Premier Zhu and his allies took considerable political risks in the face of Clinton administration hesitation regarding WTO accession; at that moment in time, engagement and continuing economic reform in China seemed to reinforce one another.

In the longer run, as Johnston argues, engagement proponents did not argue for straight-line or inevitable progress toward democratization in China. Instead, their arguments centered on the changes in Chinese society that were likely to result from further economic liberalization and integration in the international economy: greater pluralization, increased space for civil society organizations and the private sector, and growing demands for government accountability.[85] Those who engaged directly in sectors central to political liberalization, such as the legal system, were often pessimistic regarding the prospects for "sustained development of meaningful legal institutions."[86] Further, proponents of engagement did not agree on the effects of democratization on China's international orientation. Some claimed that "even a pluralist, quasi-democratic China ... would pose an enormous problem."[87] Others, echoing nascent democratic peace research, suggested that a less revisionist China might require a "more fundamental solution: the liberal democratization of China."[88] Overall, engagement aimed at the political transformation of China only in an indirect way over the long run with uncertain prospects for success. Even those who questioned the positive effects of economic interdependence and the likelihood of democratization argued that conditional engagement was an "attractive, strategically prudent alternative."[89]

Supporters of all variants of engagement agreed on their opposition to containment. Although it had relatively little political support at the end of the 1990s, its proponents projected Chinese economic growth and military capabilities into the future and aimed to "thwart China's rise to full great power status."[90] Through the lens of engagement, the implicit and explicit assumptions of containment were not credible: the ability or desirability of an American policy aimed at curbing China's economic success and the willingness of allies—even more attached to the economic benefits of engagement—to support containment.[91] Although containment focused on China's growing capabilities and not its aims or preferences, it was predicted by skeptics to have political consequences: economic isolation would lead to "a wave of nationalism, increased political control of the population, and greater military influence over foreign policy."[92]

The Chinese view of engagement was ably summarized at the end of the decade by Jin Canrong, a leading "America watcher" in China. China definitely preferred engagement to containment, but it was not satisfied, since engagement "puts China in a subordinate position," even though it was the "best situation China [could] enjoy under current international circumstances."[93] American analysts accepted that the post-Tiananmen perspective of the Chinese leadership was suspicious of engagement, viewing its ultimate goals as political transformation through "peaceful evolution" and, in the meantime, imposing constraints on China's freedom of maneuver.[94] These Chinese perspectives shed additional light on engagement, highlighting that its successes in the 1990s may have been owed to the asymmetry in economic and military power between the United States and its allies on the one hand and China on the other.[95] In evaluating engagement as a means of building a post–Cold War global order with Chinese support, however, concentrating on the contrast between a convergence in capabilities without a convergence in aims may be too simplistic. A more complete assessment must compare engagement with the alternatives as well as examine both subsequent decades and contemporary debates.

Mistakes Were Made? Engagement with China and the Liberal International Order

At the end of the 1990s, Lampton described three plausible futures for U.S.-China relations: a *"broadly cooperative* relationship," a return to Cold War–style conflict, or a *"mixed* relationship in which cooperation coexists with significant competition and friction." He regarded the first option, a cooperative partnership based on trust, was unlikely with "an authoritarian government with a nationalist populace." He regarded the "mixed relationship" as both "feasible and essential."[96]

Although relations between the United States and China are not the only determinants of the future of a somewhat tattered liberal international order, they are central. Since the mixed relationship that engagement had produced by 2000 has now veered toward the "broadly conflictual relationship" that Lampton and others had hoped to avoid, evaluating engagement, as it was pursued in the 1990s, may provide a partial explanation for the current rupture and perhaps an avenue for its repair. Such an assessment may also shed light on other policies built on economic interdependence, such as Germany's policies of *Ostpolitik* and *Wandel durch Handel* (change through trade), which have been under intense scrutiny since China's repression of Hong Kong's pro-democracy movement and Russia's invasion of Ukraine.[97]

As Steinberg, Johnston, and others have argued, plausible counterfactuals do not support a radically different approach to the rapidly globalizing China of the 1990s. Containment seems as unattractive in retrospect as it did to most China experts and the political class at the time. Compared to the China of Mao—hostile to nearly every aspect of the international order, a revolutionary power supporting violent insurgencies in neighboring states and presiding over an impoverished population—postreform China was a welcome addition to the post–Cold War global order.

Apart from attempting to thwart China's economic development—and preventing massive poverty reduction, one of its major achievements—it is far from clear what containment in the 1990s would have meant. Preventing regional hegemony was hardly a central concern; in a neighborhood of well-armed, prosperous states, even the China of today would have difficulty establishing such dominance.

Perhaps a different mix of policies within engagement might have produced better results. One could replay engagement with a more "dovish" approach toward China, working to design a new security architecture for the Asia-Pacific region that would include China. The reliance of the United States and its allies on the existing bilateral alliance structure as a hedge against future Chinese behavior presented a significant barrier, however, and the ASEAN Regional Forum, a minimalist institution, was the sole security initiative that ventured in the direction of regional multilateralism. Without a substantial increase in trust between China and the United States and its allies, which was unlikely given China's authoritarianism, lack of transparency, and territorial claims, any more robust initiative of this kind would have risked undermining the credibility of existing alliances, which were also directed against other threats, such as North Korea.

As an alternative, engagement could have been more "hawkish" by imposing more sanctions for noncompliance with global norms and rules. During the 1990s, as described earlier, sanctions did appear to shift Chinese policy toward compliance under specific circumstances. As China's economy opened and grew, however, economies aligned with the United States, as well as Taiwan and Hong Kong, were likely to suffer substantial collateral damage from economic sanctions, and few allies appeared willing to support a comprehensive program of linkage. As China's economy and its trading power grew, the bargaining asymmetry between the United States and China that existed in the 1990s declined. Equally important were the difficult tasks of defining rules or norms that required China's compliance and ensuring compliance by the United States.

Although engagement as constructed in the 1990s continues to compare favorably to its counterfactual alternatives, its evolution and implementation reveal both flaws and unforeseen consequences. Domestic politics and policy choices produced and continue to produce many of these shortcomings. Both Steinberg and Wang Jisi, a leading Chinese scholar of international relations, have rejected the inevitability of conflict as a result of China's rising economic and military power, the so-called Thucydides trap. Instead, they look to domestic dynamics, "internal political changes in the two countries [that] have interacted with one another."[98] Two domestic developments and one international consideration distorted and undermined engagement as promoted in the 1990s.

Redefining Engagement

First, because of the power of the business lobby in the United States, Europe, and Japan, engagement was increasingly defined as the unconditional promotion of economic exchange with China.[99] The Bush administration's pro-globalization bias in economic policy shaped the effects of China's WTO accession on the U.S. economy and politics. In her careful reexamination of the aftermath of China's entry, Jennifer Hillman documents the tools that were available to curb the disruption produced by imports from China: very few were deployed.[100] In dealing with China's broader lapses from WTO norms, the "big, bold, coalition-based case" at the WTO recommended by Hillman was not developed either.[101] In response to contemporary critics of China's accession, Philip Levy argues that "the commitments China made in 2001 do not cover all of the behaviors that are now of concern," such as restrictions on foreign investment, suppression of labor rights, and subsidies that favor Chinese firms. The failure of the WTO (and its most powerful members, including the United States) to negotiate those new rules is a principal source of current trade conflict, not China's membership in the WTO.[102]

Political Backlash

The accelerating integration of China into the global economy was not self-reinforcing; instead, it produced backlash in both China and the United States. Engagement "worked" in China, but the political response was not a deepening of Chinese economic reform and political pluralization. Under the leadership team of Hu Jintao and Wen Jiaobo, China continued its high-speed growth and attracted growing volumes of investment from U.S. and European multinationals. The very limited effects of the global financial crisis on China only reinforced stasis in its economic policy, however, and undermined incentives for China to use the WTO's Doha Round of trade negotiations to reinforce domestic reforms.

It is important to underscore that political backlash resulted in part *because* engagement had produced the intended result of greater political pluralization and intellectual questioning in China, under continued party control.[103] As Susan Shirk describes, the first years of the Hu-Wen leadership produced tentative moves toward intraparty democracy and "a high point of media and internet freedom in China that hasn't been equaled since."[104] Intellectual questioning, however, could take the form of attacks on liberal economic reform and its advocates. Confident predictions in the West that the internet would produce greater space for liberal intellectuals and their programs were correct, but the internet also "helped sustain voices advocating increased state dominance of the economy" and intensified ideological control.[105]

Rapid economic growth that followed China's opening to the world economy renewed fears of "peaceful evolution" and the emergence of a Chinese Gorbachev among the party oligarchy that led China. Instead of a cycle of reform inducing further reform–the hope of proponents of engagement– China's economic model and the Communist Party itself appeared to be in a crisis produced by factional divides and rampant corruption.[106] A failure to understand these internal and unintended consequences of engagement meant that the United States was unprepared when Xi Jinping reasserted party and state power over the economy and ideological control over civil society. Xi's new turn only deepened the official Chinese position that Western liberal values "were an existential threat to the party and its principles."[107]

In the United States and other industrialized countries, political backlash with economic roots also appeared. The Barack Obama administration responded to the success of economic engagement and China's economic advance by reengaging with the Asia-Pacific region in its military pivot and in the economic initiative of the Trans-Pacific Partnership. However, neither the Bush nor the Obama administration recognized and addressed the "China shock" produced by surging Chinese manufactured imports. As a result, sectors and locales in the United States and Europe endured economic decline from which recovery was difficult and political backlash, especially the rise of populist, antiglobalization movements, was profound.[108]

China as a Rising Power

China's integration into the international economy, owed in part to policies of engagement, also produced a more influential global power, one whose cooperation was required by the United States for a growing number of twenty-first century issues. The growing demand for Chinese participation and cooperation, which had already appeared in the early 1990s, deepened in the new century. The emergence of a new common threat on 9/11—transnational terrorism—produced a return to engagement with China following the George W. Bush administration's initial hawkish orientation. Collaboration with or acquiescence by China was required as the war in Afghanistan brought U.S. forces into central Asia. The threat of nuclear proliferation by North Korea also reinforced the role of Chinese diplomacy. The Iraq War deepened the U.S. shift in attention to the Middle East and away from the Asia-Pacific; China as strategic competitor was redefined as a necessary collaborator in the Bush administration's new security priorities.

The Bush administration's turn to unilateralism and its willingness to intervene in Iraq without UN Security Council approval also weakened U.S. ability to build a common negotiating position with other governments vis-à-vis China, as well as undermining American complaints about Chinese failure to become a "responsible stakeholder." A contemporary evaluation of U.S. and Chinese compliance with global norms across issue areas found that neither country was especially solicitous of international commitments.[109] The global financial crisis (more precisely, Atlantic financial crisis) that began in 2008 further undermined the U.S. model of economic governance and reinforced Chinese perceptions of a United States in decline.

After Engagement: The United States, China, and Future World Order

Engagement, at least in its economic dimension, has produced a more powerful China in which economic reform has faltered and political liberalization failed to appear, as well as a United States needing China's cooperation but lacking a political basis for promotion of deepening integration across the Pacific. Backlash in domestic politics has produced Xi and Trump—and deepening U.S.-China conflict across policy domains.

Even before the election of Trump in 2016, the engagement policy consensus had frayed.[110] The Biden administration and U.S. policy circles retreated from engagement, especially its unconditional variant. The Biden administration's 2022 National Security Strategy emphasized competition with China, with a nod toward a desire to "coexist peacefully" and a willingness to "engage constructively" on global priorities—the only mention of engagement in the document.[111]

Two broad options are now part of the U.S. political discourse and increasingly that of its allies. Reflection on the history of the 1990s calls both into question. A return to conditional engagement under a different brand would face two obstacles, revealed in the record of the 1990s. Consistent leadership and a coherent strategy across administrations were difficult to construct as China policy became the target of competing political interests. The broad consensus that produced PNTR in 2000 has collapsed and is unlikely to be rebuilt. Long-standing critics of engagement, such as labor unions and human rights organizations, have been joined by many leaders in both political parties; international business, long the most influential constituency for engagement, has voiced increasing skepticism regarding China's commitment to opening and reform. The growing economic symmetry between the United States and China also means that conditionality is less likely to succeed, as the Trump trade war has demonstrated. As China's embrace of the private sector and international markets have been called into question under Xi, the negotiation of rules that could encompass both China's new reality and the demands of its economic partners is daunting. Hillman contends that "the WTO should not and cannot serve as the only forum for working out America's concerns with the rise of China."[112] New negotiating forums in trade and other issue areas, alternatives that are inclusive, effective, and politically acceptable, will be difficult to construct. Finally, even with success, a contradiction lies at the heart of such a renewed economic bargain: greater compliance by China with U.S. economic demands could produce better Chinese economic performance and a more competitive and militarily powerful China.

The second option, economic decoupling—whether using a scalpel or an ax—combined with neo-containment seems no more attractive than it did at the close of the 1990s. The likely domestic effects on China would be a sharpening of nationalist appeals and further consolidation of state control of the Chinese economy, precisely the consequences that engagement had hoped to avoid. Despite growing concern among U.S. allies over China's mercantilism and foreign policy assertiveness, they are unlikely to follow the United States down a road of economic separation and isolation.

Before retreating from much-maligned engagement, however, its effects on Chinese foreign policy, rather than China's domestic politics, should not be underestimated. A final counterfactual—the likely external behavior of a China not so enmeshed in economic ties to the rest of the world—does not suggest a country more amenable to international norms or more restrained in its actions. For example, consider the care with which China has avoided sanctions in its support for Russia during the invasion of Ukraine. Despite its recent threatening behavior toward Taiwan, the costly economic and political consequences of military conflict across the Taiwan Strait have only been enhanced by dense economic ties within the Asia-Pacific region. What the 1990s demonstrated clearly, however, was the unwillingness of the Chinese Communist Party-state to accept any conditions that would weaken its hold on power. Its survival and the economic success of China under communist rule called into question a narrative of the 1990s as a decade of uniform transformation toward economic liberalization and democratization. Like other Leninist regimes that came to power without the assistance of Soviet bayonets—Vietnam, Cuba, and North Korea—China has demonstrated resilience under pressure and resistance to political liberalization. Political engineering from the outside, whether through the benign processes of engagement, the imposition of sanctions, or costly military intervention, have either failed, produced unintended consequences, or had positive effects only in the long run.

Such uncertainty regarding the efficacy of past engagement on political change should not, however, prevent the promotion of society-to-society engagement. The obstacles imposed in recent years by the COVID-19 pandemic have underscored the tremendous costs to information flows and personal connections that a collapse of engagement would entail. Such nongovernmental ties have played—and will continue to play—an important role in stabilizing U.S.-China relations.[113] The turn away from engagement risks exaggerating the monolithic quality of Chinese society and politics as well as extinguishing one of the avenues for producing change in the longer run. Different coalitions within the party-state have produced different outcomes over time: economic and political opening in the 1980s; reassertion of both economic liberalization and political authoritarianism in the 1990s; relaxation of social and media control in the 2000s before the current return to political repression and state control of the economy under Xi. Overestimation of U.S. ability to shape China's political future should not be replaced by a hardened consensus on the impossibility of change.

Since engagement has not produced political liberalization, much less democratization, will this defiantly illiberal, authoritarian state remain a supporter of—and be accepted by other supporters of—an international order, however frayed, that is defined by liberal norms and principles? At best, the Chinese leadership will pick and choose which parts of the global multilateral order it will accept and support, which it will ignore, and which it will seek to revise.[114] This conundrum was apparent at the end of the 1990s, when two scholars asked, "How should we evaluate a state that clearly adheres to some dominant global normative discourses while rejecting others?"[115] Barring unlikely political change in China, the rest of the world will need to contend with a major economic and military power that, for purely pragmatic reasons, pursues à la carte support of the existing order. Given recent political evolution in the United States, that may prove to be the choice of other great powers as well, producing an ever more fragmented global order rather than the seamless liberal architecture that seemed within reach three decades ago.

Notes

1. Campbell and Sullivan 2019, 96.
2. Hille 2022.
3. Mearsheimer 2021. Others disappointed by China's trajectory have urged an end to "hopeful thinking" that has guided U.S. policy (Campbell and Ratner 2018, 70).
4. For example, Ikenberry et al. 2022; Johnston 2019; Steinberg 2019–2020.
5. Lampton's (2001) history provides an excellent overview, written immediately after the decade's end. Other accounts include Mann 2000, Sutter 2010, ch. 5; Suettinger 2003.
6. Lampton 2001.
7. Steinberg 2019-2020, 121.
8. In President Bill Clinton's initial briefings by the CIA, China did not rank as one of the most prominent foreign policy problems that he was likely to confront (Mann 2000, 275).
9. For a contemporary assessment of the importance of interest groups in China policy, see Bush 1995, 149. For an account that links domestic politics to U.S.-China bargaining in this period, see Ross 2000–2001.
10. Lampton 2001, 31.
11. On post-Tiananmen public opinion, see Gallup, n.d. On the most recent decline, see Galston 2021.
12. Lampton and Wilhelm 1995, 18–19.
13. Shambaugh et al. 2019.
14. Shambaugh et al. 2019, 25.
15. In the 1992 presidential campaign, every candidate opposing President George H. W. Bush was critical of his China policy (Mann 2000, 261).
16. Mann 2000, 228.

17. Mann 2000, 233.
18. Winston Lord in Tucker 2001, 458–459.
19. Clinton's 1993 statement on MFN status for China is reproduced in Kennedy 2003, 135–138.
20. As Lampton (2001, 132–133), suggests, engagement had been used earlier and applied more broadly by President Bush ("To the world, too, we offer new engagement.").
21. Lord in Tucker 2001, 452–453.
22. Lampton 2001, 136.
23. Lord in Tucker 2001, 454.
24. Blanchette 2019, 38.
25. The papers, summarized by Andrew Nathan (2001), are controversial, since their authenticity cannot be conclusively verified against original or archival documents.
26. Nathan 2019, 82. See the more recent, detailed analysis by Jiang Shigong (2020, 17), a Chinese academic who is close to the Chinese leadership.
27. Mann 2000, 236.
28. Lampton 2001, 139.
29. Clinton's press conference (May 26, 1994) is reproduced in Kennedy 2003, 143–145.
30. Cited in Kennedy 2003, 138.
31. Kennedy 2003, 154.
32. Lord in Tucker 2001, 460–461, 467.
33. Lampton and Wilhelm 1995, 9.
34. Mann 2000, 308–309.
35. Lampton 2001, 43.
36. Mann 2000, 288.
37. For example, see Charles Krauthammer in Kennedy 2003, 165–167.
38. Mann 2000, 318.
39. Lord in Tucker (2001, 478); endorsed by Lampton (2001, 102): only Israel has been more successful as a lobbyist. James Sasser, former senator and U.S. ambassador to China, labeled China "the worst lobbyist" in Washington during the 1990s: the PRC had one registered lobbying firm; Taiwan had fourteen (Lampton 2001, 295).
40. Lord in Tucker 2001, 483.
41. For a detailed account of the crisis, see Suettinger 2003, 200–263; Ross 2000.
42. Christensen 2001, 7.
43. Contributors to the U.S.-China Policy Committee provided a list of domestic priorities that closely resemble contemporary agenda items. Merritt and Blundell cited "the problems of the inner cities, the impact of drugs, doubts about the nation's education system, decay of infrastructure ... health care" as part of a "perceived national malaise." Casimir Yost remarked that "the power of our example is less credible than it has been in the past," and the United States was likely to be "more inward looking" in the future (Lampton and Wilhelm 1995, 195, 212, 217).
44. For example, the response to the 1996 U.S.-Japan Joint Declaration (Suettinger 2003, 268).
45. Lord in Tucker 2003, 470.
46. Mann 2000, 240–241.
47. On China-Japan relations during this period, see Bush 2009.
48. Drifte 2003, 170.
49. Mann 2000, 293. Chinese premier Li Peng declared before Kohl arrived, "Chancellor Kohl is sure to fly back with full suitcases." (Tempest 1993).
50. Balducci 2011, 113–114.
51. At the time of negotiations for China's accession to the WTO, China had become the EU's third largest trading partner outside Europe; by 2000 "the EU was, for the first time, the largest net foreign direct investor in China" (Balducci 2011, 104–105).
52. "Their inability to co-ordinate more closely their respective foreign policy toward China ... renders European countries an easy catch—easy to read, easy to manipulate and difficult to take seriously in the long run" (Sandschneider 2002, 44).
53. Godemont 2020, 254.
54. Godemont 2020, 254.
55. Lampton 2001, 228–229.
56. Johnston 2008, 33–34.

57. The United States is the only member of the United Nations that has not ratified this Convention.
58. Johnston 2008, 36, table 1.1.
59. For a complete account of these episodes, see Suettinger 2003, 171–174, 266–271.
60. Suettinger 2003, 269–270.
61. Lardy 1994, 4.
62. Garrison 2005, 117.
63. U.S. Trade Representative 2017, 2
64. Blanchette 2019, 63–65.
65. Kaufman 1995, 163.
66. Suettinger 2003, 275.
67. Osius 2001.
68. Osius 2001, 126.
69. This account is based on Schmitt and Kahn 2000.
70. Schmitt and Kahn 2000.
71. Levy 2018.
72. Byman and Cliff 1999, 446.
73. Philip D. Zelikow, quoted in Campbell 2000.
74. Mann 2000, 352.
75. Harding 2023, 74–76.
76. Steinberg 2019–2020, 128.
77. On the collapse prediction, see Goldstone 1995; for alternative trajectories, see Shinn 1996, 5–6.
78. Harding (2023, 68–74) defines the "engagement paradigm" in this way.
79. Thomas 2019.
80. Ross 1999, 185.
81. Ross 1999, 188–189.
82. Byman and Cliff 1999, 425.
83. Shinn 1996, 8.
84. Johnston and Ross 1999, 286.
85. Johnston 2019, 104.
86. Lubman 2000, 23. Also see Tucker (2001, 497): "political change will come slowly."
87. Shinn 1996.
88. Johnston and Ross 1999, 298.
89. Byman and Cliff 1999, 446.
90. Ross 1999, 185.
91. Ross 1999, 185.
92. Byman and Cliff 1999, 440–441.
93. Jin 2001, 134.
94. Lampton 2001, 363; Byman and Cliff 1999, 440.
95. Steinberg 2019–2020, 131.
96. Lampton 2001, 358, 360.
97. See, for example, Wintour 2022.
98. Steinberg 2019–2020, 132; Wang 2022.
99. Jiang Shigong (2020, 13), a critic of the consequences of engagement for China, labels the years between 1993 and 2009 "the golden years of relative political détente and close economic cooperation between China and the United States."
100. Hillman 2023, 417. A participant in the negotiations for China's accession to the WTO confirmed that negotiators counted on continuing economic reform in China and were also unprepared for the meteoric Chinese growth of the 2000s. As a result, the United States and the EU did not pursue actions against China in the WTO immediately, restraint that was not revisited as China's reforms stagnated.
101. Hillman 2023, 421.
102. Levy 2018.
103. I owe this insight to Joseph Torigian.
104. Shirk 2022, 26, 92.
105. Blanchette 2019, 67.
106. Shirk 2022, 95, 110.

107. Economy 2018.
108. Autor 2018; Autor et al. 2013a, 2013b, 2020, 2021; Colantone and Stanig 2018; Kennedy and Mazzocco 2022.
109. Foot and Walter 2011.
110. Harding (2015) outlines the state of the China policy debate at the end of the Obama administration.
111. White House 2022.
112. Hillman 2023, 426.
113. On the role of such exchange, see Kennedy and Wang 2023a, 2023b.
114. Kastner et al. 2019; Weiss and Wallace 2021.
115. Johnston and Ross 1999, 296.

References

Autor, David H. 2018. "Trade and Labor Markets: Lessons from China's Rise." *IZA World of Labor.* (February): 431. doi: 10.15185/izawol.431.

Autor, David H., David Dorn, and Gordon H. Hanson. 2013a. "The China Syndrome: Local Labor Market Effects of Import Competition in the United States." *American Economic Review* 103 (6): 2121–2168.

Autor, David H., David Dorn, and Gordon H. Hanson. 2013b. "The Geography of Trade and Technology Shocks in the United States." *American Economic Review: Papers & Proceedings* 103 (3): 220–225.

Autor, David H., David Dorn, and Gordon H. Hanson. 2021. "On the Persistence of the China Shock." Discussion Paper No. 14804. Bonn: Institute of Labor Economics.

Autor, David H., David Dorn, Gordon H. Hanson, and Kaveh Majlesi. 2020. "Importing Political Polarization? The Electoral Consequences of Rising Trade Exposure." *American Economic Review* 110 (10): 3139–3183.

Balducci, Giuseppe. 2011. "The Role of the European Union in China's Accession to the WTO." *Il Politico* 76 (2): 101–121.

Blanchette, Jude. 2019. *China's New Red Guards: The Return of Radicalism and the Rebirth of Mao Zedong.* Oxford University Press.

Bush, Richard C. 1995. "Domestic Political Considerations That Shape U.S. Policy toward China, Hong Kong, and Taiwan." In *United States and China Relations at a Crossroads*, edited by David M. Lampton and Alfred D. Wilhelm Jr. University Press of America.

Bush, Richard C. 2009. "China-Japan Tensions, 1995–2006: Why They Happened, What to Do." Policy Paper 16. Washington, DC: Brookings Institution.

Byman, Daniel, Roger Cliff, with Phillip Saunders. 1999. "US Policy Options toward an Emerging China," *Pacific Review* 12 (3): 421–451.

Campbell, Kurt M. 2000. "China Watchers Fighting a Turf War of Their Own." *New York Times*, May 20.

Campbell, Kurt M., and Ely Ratner. 2018. "The China Reckoning: How Beijing Defied American Expectations." *Foreign Affairs* 97 (2): 60–70.

Campbell, Kurt M., and Jake Sullivan. 2019. "Competition without Catastrophe: How America Can Both Challenge and Coexist with China." *Foreign Affairs* 98 (5): 96–110.

Christensen, Thomas J. 2001. "Posing Problems without Catching Up." *International Security* 25 (4): 5–40.

Colantone, Italo, and Piero Stanig. 2018. "Global Competition and Brexit." *American Political Science Review* 112 (2): 201–218.

Drifte, Reinhard. 2003. *Japan's Security Relations with China since 1989.* RoutledgeCurzon.

Economy, Elizabeth. 2018. *The Third Revolution: Xi Jinping and the New Chinese State.* Oxford University Press.

Foot, Rosemary, and Andrew Walter. 2011. *China, the United States, and Global Order*. Cambridge University Press.
Gallup. n.d. "China." Accessed April 26, 2022. https://news.gallup.com/poll/1627/china.aspx.
Galston, William A. 2021. "A Momentous Shift in US Public Attitudes toward China." Brookings Institution, March 22. https://www.brookings.edu/blog/order-from-chaos/2021/03/22/a-momentous-shift-in-us-public-attitudes-toward-china/.
Garrison, Jean A. 2005. *Making China Policy: From Nixon to G. W. Bush*. Lynne Rienner.
Godemont, François. 2020. "China's Relations with Europe." In *China and the World*, edited by David Shambaugh. Oxford University Press.
Goldstone, Jack A. 1995. "The Coming Chinese Collapse." *Foreign Policy* 99 (Summer): 35–53.
Harding, Harry. 2015. "Has U.S. China Policy Failed?" *Washington Quarterly* 38 (3): 95–122.
Harding, Harry. 2023. "The United States and China: From Partners to Competitors in America's Eyes." In *Cold Rivals: The New Era of US-China Strategic Competition*, edited by Evan S. Medeiros. Georgetown University Press.
Hille, Kathrin. 2022. "The Cost of China's Information Vacuum." *Financial Times*, September 27.
Hillman, Jennifer. 2023. "China's Entry into the WTO: A Mistake by the United States?" In *China and the WTO: 20 Years On*, edited by Henry Gao, Damien Raess, and Ka Zeng. Cambridge University Press.
Ikenberry, G. John, Andrew J. Nathan, Susan Thornton, Sun Zhe, and John J. Mearsheimer. 2022. "A Rival of America's Making? The Debate over Washington's China Strategy." *Foreign Affairs* 101 (2): 172–188.
Jiang, Shigong. 2020. "The Critical Decade." Introduction and translation by David Ownby. Reading the China Dream. https://www.readingthechinadream.com/jiang-shigong-ten-crucial-years.html.
Jin, Canrong. 2001. "A Response to Ted Osius: Policy Legacy and Political Context in U.S. Relations with China." *Asian Affairs* 28 (3): 134–137.
Johnston, Alastair Iain. 2008. *Social States: China in International Institutions, 1980–2000*. Princeton University Press.
Johnston, Alastair Iain. 2019. "The Failures of the 'Failure of Engagement' with China." *Washington Quarterly* 42 (2): 99–114. doi:10.1080/0163660X.2019.1626688.
Johnston, Alastair Iain, and Robert S. Ross. 1999. "Conclusion." In *Engaging China: The Management of an Emerging Power*, edited by Alastair I. Johnston and Robert S. Ross. Routledge.
Kastner, Scott L., Margaret M. Pearson, and Chad Rector. 2019. *China's Strategic Multilateralism: Investing in Global Governance*. Cambridge University Press.
Kaufman, Richard F. 1995. "U.S.-China Economic Relations and Prospects for the 1990s." In *United States and China Relations at a Crossroads*, edited by David M. Lampton and Alfred D. Wilhelm Jr. University Press of America.
Kennedy, Scott, ed. 2003. *China Cross Talk: The American Debate over China Policy since Normalization*. Rowman & Littlefield.
Kennedy, Scott, and Ilaria Mazzocco. 2022. "The China Shock: Reevaluating the Debate." Big Data China, Center for Strategic and International Studies, October 14. https://bigdatachina.csis.org/the-china-shock-reevaluating-the-debate/.
Kennedy, Scott, and Wang Jisi. 2023a. "America and China Need to Talk: A Lack of Dialogue, Visits, and Exchanges Is Raising the Risk of Conflict." *Foreign Affairs*, April 6. https://www.foreignaffairs.com/china/america-and-china-dialogue-need-lack-risk-conflict.
Kennedy, Scott, and Wang Jisi. 2023b. *Breaking the Ice: The Role of Scholarly Exchange in Stabilizing U.S.-China Relations*. Center for Strategic and International Studies.
Lampton, David M. 2001. *Same Bed, Different Dreams: Managing U.S.-China Relations, 1989–2000*. University of California Press.

Lampton, David M., and Alfred D. Wilhelm Jr., eds. 1995. *United States and China Relations at a Crossroads*. University Press of America.

Lardy, Nicholas R. 1994. *China in the World Economy*. Institute for International Economics.

Levy, Philip. 2018. "Was Letting China into the WTO a Mistake?" *Foreign Affairs*, April 2. https://www.foreignaffairs.com/articles/china/2018-04-02/was-letting-china-wto-mistake.

Lubman, Stanley B. 2000. "Sino-American Relations and China's Struggle for the Rule of Law." In *China and Hong Kong in Legal Transition*, edited by Joseph W. Dellapenna and Patrick M. Norton. American Bar Association.

Mann, James. 2000. *About Face: A History of America's Curious Relationship with China, from Nixon to Clinton*. Vintage Books.

Mearsheimer, John J. 2021. "The Inevitable Rivalry: America, China, and the Tragedy of Great-Power Politics." *Foreign Affairs* 100 (6): 48–58.

Nathan, Andrew. 2001. "The Tiananmen Papers." *Foreign Affairs* 80 (1): 2–48.

Nathan, Andrew. 2019. "The New Tiananmen Papers: Inside the Secret Meeting That Changed China." *Foreign Affairs* 98 (4): 80–91.

Osius, Ted. 2001. "Legacy of the Clinton-Gore Administration's China Policy." *Asian Affairs* 28 (3): 125–134. doi:10.1080/00927670109601490.

Ross, Robert S. 1999. "Engagement in US China Policy." In *Engaging China: The Management of an Emerging Power*, edited by Alastair I. Johnston and Robert S. Ross. Routledge.

Ross, Robert S. 2000. "The 1995–96 Taiwan Strait Confrontation: Coercion, Credibility, and the Use of Force." *International Security* 25 (2): 87–123.

Ross, Robert S. 2000–2001. "The Diplomacy of Tiananmen: Two-Level Bargaining and Great-Power Cooperation." *Security Studies* 10 (1): 139–178.

Sandschneider, Eberhard. 2002. "China's Diplomatic Relations with the States of Europe." *China Quarterly* 169: 33–44.

Schmitt, Eric, and Joseph Kahn. 2000. "The China Trade Vote: A Clinton Triumph; House, in 237–197 Vote, Approves Normal Trade Rights for China." *New York Times*, May 25.

Shambaugh, David, Evan Medeiros, Susan Thornton, James Mann, James Green, Orville Schell, et al. 2019. "The Other Tiananmen Papers: A ChinaFile Conversation." July 8. https://www.chinafile.com/conversation/other-tiananmen-papers.

Shinn, James. 1996. *Weaving the Net: Conditional Engagement with China*. Council on Foreign Relations.

Shirk, Susan. 2022. *Overreach: How China Derailed Its Peaceful Rise*. New York: Oxford University Press.

Steinberg, James B. 2019–2020. "What Went Wrong? U.S.-China Relations from Tiananmen to Trump." *Texas National Security Review* 3 (1): 119–133.

Suettinger, Robert L. 2003. *Beyond Tiananmen: The Politics of U.S.-China Relations, 1989–2000*. Brookings Institution Press.

Sutter, Robert G. 2010. *U.S.-Chinese Relations: Perilous Past, Pragmatic Present*. Rowman & Littlefield.

Tempest, Rone. 1993. "Kohl Seeks China Contracts with No Tie to Rights Issue." *Los Angeles Times*, November 16.

Thomas, Neil. 2019. "Matters of Record: Relitigating Engagement with China." Macropolo, September 3. https://macropolo.org/analysis/china-us-engagement-policy/.

Tucker, Nancy Bernkopf. 2001. *China Confidential: American Diplomats and Sino-American Relations, 1945–1996*. Columbia University Press.

U.S. Trade Representative. 2017. "2016 Report to Congress on China's WTO Compliance." https://ustr.gov/sites/default/files/2016-China-Report-to-Congress.pdf.

Wang, Jisi. 2022. "How, and Why, China-U.S. Relations Have Worsened Since 2021?" Eighth Annual Nancy Bernkopf Tucker Memorial Lecture. Wilson Center, April 22. https://www.wilsoncenter.org/event/eighth-annual-nancy-bernkopf-tucker-memorial-lecture.

Weiss, Jessica Chen, and Jeremy L. Wallace. 2021. "Domestic Politics, China's Rise, and the Future of the Liberal International Order." *International Organization* 75 (2): 635–664.

White House. 2022. National Security Strategy. https://www.whitehouse.gov/wp-content/uploads/2022/10/Biden-Harris-Administrations-National-Security-Strategy-10.2022.pdf.

Wintour, Patrick. 2022. "'We Were All Wrong': How Germany Got Hooked on Russian Energy." *The Guardian*, June 2.

9
The Return of/to Europe and the New Politics of Globalism

Harold James

This chapter examines the origins, in the aftermath of the collapse of communism in 1989–1991, of a radically new view of politics and what the state could do: the new logic emphasized how international openness produced limitations on state action. There were two drivers that stood in mutual tension, even though at the time the extent of their inherent conflict was not realized: on the one hand, the mobility of factors of production and the growing importance of international business provided a pragmatic argument about the limitations on policy in a purely national frame; on the other hand, a heightened awareness of global ethical and moral norms made for a new universal perspective. Both stood in another tension too, with an older version of a political focus on the nation-state that also seemed to be revived in the aftermath of the collapse of the large supranational project of communist internationalism.

The result of the temporary confluence of practical and intellectual rethinking curtailed room for maneuver in a domestic political setting. In its extreme form, it presented politics as having no alternatives (the TINA philosophy: There Is No Alternative). That approach ruled out thinking in terms of policy options or counterfactuals (taking a different policy course). As a consequence, if we want to imagine alternative developments, they will appear rather radical: radical options for ways not followed. This chapter suggests five:

1. If the Soviet Union and its satellite empire in Central and Eastern Europe had not collapsed, Western politicians would have gone on with their old politics.
2. If there had been a quicker backlash against the new politics, akin to that which emerged in the aftermath of the 2008 great financial crisis,

the prosperity that was generally brought by the TINA would also have ended earlier.
3. If that politics of backlash had emerged more quickly, it would have led to an earlier adoption of some version of national communism or national social democracy, akin to the versions actually practiced in Europe in the 2010s by Fidesz in Hungary or Law and Justice in Poland or advocated by Marine Le Pen in France and Matteo Salvini in Italy, perhaps also a foreign policy alignment with a Russia under some version of Putinism.
4. If there had been no move to a European Monetary Union, one of the key cements that held in place the logic of TINA would have been removed, and the politics of backlash would have begun earlier.
5. Finally, in the new environment generated by the backlash, the politics of morality and ethics launched in the 1990s (and which was labeled by its enemies as "wokeness") would have crumbled earlier and been replaced by aggressive doctrines of realpolitik, in which groups put forward their own interests as the national interest.

The TINA approach was particularly influential in Europe, where it drove a debate about the obsolescence of the nation-state and of the Westphalian notion of sovereignty, and a concern with thinking of government and governance on multiple levels ("subsidiarity') and government as the business of accomplishing quite specific tasks (providing public goods) but not (or engaging less in) redistribution. That outcome in the 1990s and 2000s appeared attractive, perhaps less because its ethical prescriptions were generally shared and more because for the moment it delivered the goods: growth combined with stability and prosperity.

But the dynamic established at that time produced an increasing disillusionment with Europe and with globalization. In the middle of the nineteenth century, as modern globalization was starting, the romantic poet Joseph von Eichendorff in an amusing way melded the concept of "world pain" (*Weltschmerz*) that tears people apart with disillusion with Europe in his poem "Ein Auswanderer" (1857):

> "Europe, you false creature!
> We agonize about culture,
> put a locomotive at the front,
> and then someone puts another one at the back,

one pushes forward, the other backward,
and so the whole culture gets stuck.
Another tells me,
'We'd like to know,
if they are tired of Europe
and torn apart by world pain.'"

Europa, du falsche Kreatur!
Man quält sich ab mit der Kultur,
Spannt vorn die Lokomotive an,
Gleich hängen sie hinten eine andre dran,
Die eine schiebt vorwärts, die andere retour,
So bleibt man stecken mit der ganzen Kultur
Ein andrer mich erstaunt besieht:
"Mir möchten gerne wissen,
Ob sie vielleicht europamüd
Vom Weltschmerz so zerrisen?"

The Globalization Paradigm

The new politics of the late twentieth century was shaped by a new vocabulary. The 1990s was driven economically by a process—globalization—and politically and intellectually by a debate over the concept of globalization. The narrative was intertwined with the interpretation of the end of the Cold War. In the course of the narrative struggles, politically parties and movements flipped, as did individuals. The term *Wendehals* (turncoat; it is also the name of a bird, the Eurasian rufus-breasted wryneck) became popular in Germany as a way of describing former communist officials and ideologues who embraced the free market. And some went the other way: the Hayekian free marketeer John Gray in 1990 turned himself into an analyst and critic of the "false dawn" of neoliberalism.[1]

"Globalization" as a concept first swept the world in the 1990s and reached its initial high point of popularity in 2000 and 2001, amid worldwide protests against globalization. Everywhere the term became a focus of mobilization, but especially in France, which mobilized its revolutionary traditions to remake itself as a center of the contestation of globalization. In 2001, for instance, *Le Monde* contained more than thirty-five hundred references to

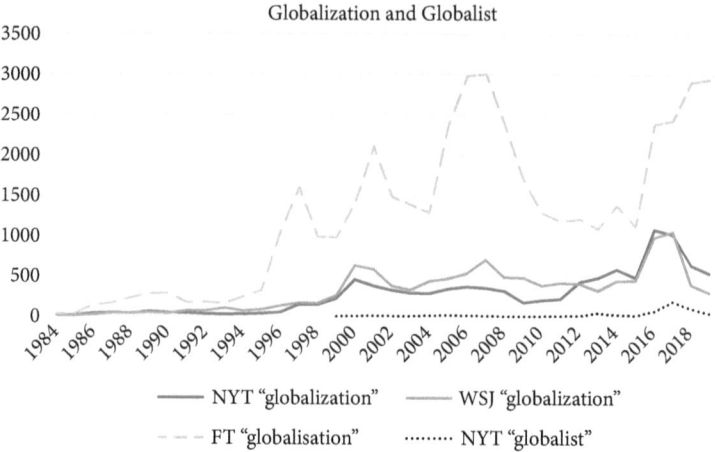

Figure 9.1 Use of the terms "globalization" and "globalist" in major English-language newspapers.

mondialisation, the French equivalent of "globalization." But then the figure steadily fell—more than 80 percent by 2006. Since the outbreak of the financial crisis in 2007, the word's usage in major global newspapers such as the *New York Times* and the *Financial Times* has fallen still further, and it seemed to go further out of fashion during the global financial crisis, until it encountered a revival of use in 2016 (see Figure 9.1). Globalization was conceptually on its way out, but then came back into widespread use, buoyed by a new sense of urgency and a new critical discourse in the aftermath of the Brexit referendum and the Trump election, which appeared to herald a new antiglobalization mood.

Globalization is inherently linked and associated with the ideas that ideologies have become redundant and that the nation-state and the ideology of nationalism have reached particular limits. In the wake of 1989, there was a widespread sense that utopian ideologies, antimodern politics, and ideological cleavages had contributed to the European disasters of the mid-century. In the 1960s, an influential book by Daniel Bell announced "the end of ideology," in essence prematurely but correctly.[2] One way of popularizing this message was to claim that the "isms" had become, or were becoming, "wasms."

Another version of the story is increasingly popular as an anti-neoliberal consensus emerged in the wake of the global financial crisis of 2008 and intensified in the 2010s to the point that institutions such as the International Monetary Fund (IMF), often held to be a central representative of the neoliberal policy framework, began to reject neoliberalism. In this version of the story of the 1990s the dangerous and destructive move to the new globalization paradigm followed from the removal of the socialist alternative that had tamed capitalism and led to the establishment of a social democratic alternative. As Gary Gerstle puts it, "Another consequence of communism's fall may be less obvious but is of equal importance: It removed what remained in America of the imperative for class compromise. A compromise between capital and labor had been foundational to the New Deal order."[3] The fall of the Soviet Union thus opened the way for the victory of a newly galvanized and aggressive capitalism. Fritz Bartel argued that one of the newly discovered strengths of democracy was that it made coercion easier, and he quotes Mikhail Gorbachev to the effect that it was democracy that "provides the strongest grip on power." Another Soviet reformer, Alexander Yakovlev, claimed simply that "democracy is discipline."[4]

> *Counterfactual 1*: If the Soviet Union and its satellite empire in Central and Eastern Europe had not collapsed, Western politicians would have gone on with their old politics and would have been less inclined to opt for fiscal discipline or to rely more on the market to generate growth.

The new defining ideas of the end of the twentieth century in Europe were more concrete than the fast-fading "isms": civil society, governance, and subsidiarity. "Civil society" was a term taken from Hegel and Marx (*bürgerliche Gesellschaft*) to refer to a sphere of social organization and institution-building that was not centrally directed or political or dependent on law. Hegel believed that it was incomplete without the state. Marx used the term in the same sense, as an incomplete social world. Oppositionists in Central Europe before 1989 used the demand for "civil society" as a way of demanding freedom to organize voluntary associations. At the same time, in advanced industrial societies the demand for more civil society was founded on the idea that modern life had become increasingly atomized. After the end of communism, the term "civil society" became widely used as a way of describing a network of pressure and advocacy groups (Amnesty International, Greenpeace, Oxfam, Médecins sans Frontières, to list only a few of the most influential and productive) that had quite strong political aims. Such organizations became much more powerful in the course of the last years of the century.

"Governance" is a clearer term and became widely used in the 1990s as a way of expressing the demand for an end to the politics of corruption. Good governance required rules about the conduct of political and business life, many of which were quite specific (such as the application of auditing principles). The controversial aspect related to who should bear the responsibility for improving governance: would it come as a result of the initiative of civil society, or did it need to be imposed as part of the conditionality applied by international or supranational institutions such as the European Union or the International Monetary Fund?

Finally, the doctrine of subsidiarity came from Catholic social theory and had been used in 1931 by Pius XI to explain the organization of the Church hierarchy. The principle was that decisions should be made at the lowest administrative level possible and be consistent with general principles of good governance. For the European Union, subsidiarity meant trying to dispel the idea of a centralized dictatorship in the Brussels administration. Powers and decisions—such as on standards and trade descriptions—should be left to national authorities as far as was consistent with the internal market. Further down, subsidiarity meant that federal states such as Germany would leave powers with their component states and should promote a greater move to regionalism. In this way, it is at the center of the erosion of the powers of the nation-state—toward the center in some areas, and toward regions in other. Since the nation-state was the area in which most twentieth-century "isms" were played out, this too is part of the movement away from ideology.

In the great upheavals of 1989, at the western end of the Eurasian land mass, two major ideas stood out: a return of the formerly communist countries to "Europe" and a return to "civil society." The development had an international, global impact. Both concepts turned out to be quite problematical when applied in practice. They were interdependent, in that European values were supposed to be about tolerance, reconciliation, civility, and, more particularly, the rule of law, the restoration of property rights, and representative government. But were these concepts European, "Western," or universal? Between 1914 and 1956 Europe and its values had been anything but civilized. In December 1989 at the superpower summit at sea off the coast of Malta, which definitively ended the Cold War, when U.S. secretary of state James Baker talked about Germany and "western values," the general secretary of the Communist Party of the Soviet Union asked why democracy and the market were "western" and whether they were not values which "belonged to the whole of humanity"?[5] For a moment, actually for two decades, the world cheered.

> *Counterfactual 2*: If there had been a sharp and quick economic setback, the new quest for a reformulated vision of society would have appeared quickly as unjust or as unsustainable.

A process of normalization, and a pushback against politics as the twentieth century understood it, may be considered as a return of practical issues. Francis Fukuyama's famous 1989 essay complained, "The worldwide ideological struggle that called forth daring, courage, imagination, and idealism, will be replaced by economic calculation, the endless solving of technical problems, environmental concerns, and the death of this satisfaction of sophisticated consumer demands. In the post-historical period there will be neither art nor philosophy, just the perpetual caretaking of the museum of human history."[6] Within a few years, Bill Clinton earned widespread ridicule when, after the failure of big reform projects, he made car seatbelts a pressing issue. (It led to 1997's Executive Order 13043.) The management of the economy and financial stability was reduced to a consumer protection issue. There were thus new practical issues, driven by demographic issues and the evolution of business practice. What was left of politics was reconceptualized as morality.

Civil society was a beautiful goal, and it was hard to attain in the East. But it was also pretty difficult in the West. Yet despite all the difficulties of the so-called transformation process in the formerly communist countries, the former East and the West converged at a surprisingly quick pace: the problems they had in the 1990s, and the answers they sought, were quite similar. They were fundamentally the inevitable and inescapable problems of states and peoples faced by the challenges of a globalizing world.

Post–Cold War normality was not easy. The difficulties of normalization were perhaps most evident in the largest member country of the European Community (European Union after 1992): Germany. Many German politicians, particularly those in government, liked to think that the process of unification and the diplomacy of the Two Plus Four process had ended the abnormal situation of postwar Germany. They longed to be normal. In fact, in domestic political terms, the inclusion of the former East made the country—as the only elected minister-president of the GDR, Lothar de Maizière, predicted in 1990—more Eastern (i.e., socialist or suspicious of the market economy) and more Protestant (in a largely secularized sense, i.e., moral).[7] The population remained frightened of potential disturbances to the status quo, profoundly worried by war, and skeptical of foreign military action. In international politics, some of the institutional legacies of the war remained, in particular the absence of a former empire, the absence of nuclear weapons, and the absence of a permanent seat on the UN Security Council. There was for Germany a much reduced international leverage. Consequently, Germany repeatedly emphasized that it sought normalization only in a European setting and through multilateral organizations and institutions. That in fact was the European way of the 1990s.

Nation-states do not obviously represent the best institutional form for dealing with new problems and issues, which are sometimes better tackled on a supranational or international level, by new institutions and codes, and sometimes better handled by local or regional political processes. For most of Europe, the most important and powerful of the international institutions was the European Community and European Union. Even apart from its influence on its own members, its presence and the ideas that it embodied provided a powerful attraction for many ex-communist countries and an incentive to stay the course of democratic and market-oriented reform—at least until they actually got into the club. For less developed or geographically more remote ex-communist countries, in southeast Europe and in the Soviet Union, a more important role was played by global international institutions, in particular the Bretton Woods twins, the IMF and the World Bank. But their part in the reform process often polarized the domestic debate much more than did the European-level institutions. Both European and global multilateralism were responses to the challenges of a process that was taking place on a global rather than merely a continental level. That process created new divisions, as an elite seemed to benefit from the new chances presented by mobility, whereas a substantial part of the population felt left behind or marginalized.

For many former communist states, there was a deep disconnect: the collapse of the Soviet Union was interpreted as the defeat of an imperial project, and in its place was reborn an old idea of the nation-state as the best form of political society that would renew civil society. The most perspicacious contemporary analysis was provided by a French (Georgian-born) political scientist, Hélène Carrère d'Encausse. In 1978, she wrote the brilliantly prophetic work *L'empire éclaté: La révolte des nations en U.R.S.S.* Her immediate response to the collapse of the Soviet Union, *Victorieuse Russie*, set out a vision in which the communist elites had been preparing a religiously based transition to national assertion even before 1990–1991.[8] Some later analyses focus on nostalgia as the main psychological mechanism for comprehending communist collapse.[9] The reassertion of a principle of national interest would be in the longer run the great challenge to the settlement of the 1990s: it arose above all because the new world of international business—the *biznezmen* of the former planned economies where Boris Yeltsin sounded the note of "Let's enrich ourselves"—became a target of envy or contempt or disdain.

> *Counterfactual 3*: If the politics of backlash had emerged more quickly, it would have led to an earlier adoption of some version of national communism or national social democracy, akin to the versions actually practiced in Europe in the 2010s by Fidesz in Hungary or Law and Justice in Poland or advocated by Marine Le Pen in France and Matteo Salvini in Italy, perhaps also a foreign policy alignment with a Russia under some version of Putinism.

Normalized Politics

In commenting on the Czech "Velvet Revolution," Timothy Garton Ash said, "Take a more or less representative sample of politically aware persons. Stir under pressure for two days. And what do you get? The same fundamental Western, European model: parliamentary democracy, the rule of law, market economy. And if you made the same experiment in Warsaw or Budapest I wager you would get the same basic result. This is no Third Way. It is not 'socialism with a human face.' It is the idea of 'normality' that seems to be sweeping triumphantly across the world."[10]

That liberal idea of normality might have been deceptive. Quite soon, a bout of post-totalitarian hangovers hit the reform countries. They began to look abnormal again and to think of themselves once more as special cases. But the perception of abnormality was actually more deceptive than the normality, for the problems that gripped postcommunist societies were actually those common to all post–Cold War (some might term this "postmodern") societies.

During the era of the Cold War, European politics had been relatively stable for several reasons:

- The external ideological constraints of the Cold War.
- The security blanket created by nuclear weapons on both sides of the Iron Curtain.
- A party political dynamic (in the West) in which a left and a right played against each other in a battle to redistribute more (the left) or less (the right), in a framework set by Keynesian macroeconomic demand management. In this framework, each side needed to moderate its position and appeal to the political middle in order to secure election victories. If the left appeared radically redistributionist, it would deter middle-income voters; so would the right if it resisted any form of redistribution or the many aspects of the welfare state that had a largely middle-class clientele.

The domestic political game in European countries also changed, in that the extent of embeddedness in an international economy, in which factors of production were highly mobile, limited the possibilities for direct redistribution. In addition, with state shares in GNP lying between 40 and 50 percent in almost all European countries, the scope for further expansion of the share controlled by the state was minimal. The old political game thus no longer made any sense. Social democratic parties still aimed at the political middle, but now had to de-emphasize the promise of income or wealth redistribution. There was thus more convergence and consensus about the idea of the market economy than at any previous time in the twentieth century. A joint paper by German chancellor Gerhard Schröder and British prime minister Tony Blair (and in practice worked out by Bodo Hombach and Peter Mandelson) in 1999, "The Way Forward for Europe's Social Democrats," set out the new politics of what they called a "new middle." It was strongly market oriented: "The weaknesses of markets have been overstated and their strengths underestimated." It pleaded for an economic deregulation and liberalization that had to a great extent already taken place in the United Kingdom, but not in Germany: "Product, capital, and labour markets must all be flexible." And it admitted that the old left/right dichotomy no longer made much sense: "Most people have long since abandoned the world view represented by the dogmas of left and right. Social democrats must be able to speak to those people."[11]

Indeed they did. In the British general election of 1997, 36 percent of the professional and managerial classes voted Labour (in 1992 the share had been 16 percent), and 36 percent voted Conservative (59 percent in 1992).[12]

One response to this was the emergence or strengthening of radical parties on the political extremes who collected protest votes against the "system." Both right and left protested against internationalization and globalization and its bureaucratized institutions, the IMF and the EU. There were some powerful voices on the right who tried to raise national issues and national myths as a challenge to globalization and who attracted cross-national attention (and usually disapprobation): Jean-Marie Le Pen, Jörg Haider, Christoph Blocher, the German "Republican" movement, the Northern League in Italy. The left rejectionists found it hard to mobilize behind charisma and tended to form fractious and fissiparous parties. A provisional high point of both tendencies (the right search for rejectionist charisma and the left descent into rejectionist cantankerousness) came in the French presidential elections of 2002, where it was fostered by the system of two-round voting, with a final run-off election. In the first round, the two leading candidates who thus went into the final ballot were the incumbent president, Jacques Chirac (82.1 percent of the second-round vote), and Jean-Marie Le Pen (17.9 percent). The left was divided among a large number of candidates who thought that the mainstream left presidential candidate, the incumbent prime minister Lionel Jospin, had made too many concessions to the system.

These trends—the convergence of the center and the radicalization of the extremes—affected the formerly communist countries, too. In the majority of countries, former communist parties quickly adapted to become centrist social democratic reformists, who accepted and embraced the idea of private property. Some of the old nomenklatura elite did extremely well out of the privatization of state enterprises and supported policies that would allow continuing social benefits and economic profits. In Poland, after an initial burst of "shock therapy reform," the former communist party, the SLD, returned to power from 1995 to 1997 and then again after 2001. In Hungary, the left similarly returned in 1994 to 1998 and after 2002. In both cases, the left governments kept strictly to market-oriented, economically liberal programs. All the responsible parties wanted to join the EU as quickly as possible and saw it as a guarantee of political decency.

Meanwhile the disaffected and the poor moved to extreme parties—in some cases, notably in Russia, to old-style communist movements which thrived on whatever nostalgia for a communist past existed. They also turned to right-wing, nationalistic, xenophobic, and anti-European parties.

Instead of concentrating on the battle for redistribution, which had been the political theme of the world after the depression and after the Second World War, societies in the East and the West looked for new political issues. This was in part because many people became convinced of the hopelessness of conventional politics, which seemed to offer no real choice. It was also because conventional politics were straightforwardly about redistribution, whereas the redistributionist aspects of the new politics became quite carefully concealed. When capital flows undermined the capacity and the efficacy of national redistributionist politics, old-style politicians looked quite helpless.

In the 1980s, as cross-border economic integration ("globalization") increased, the room for political choice had been reduced, and politicians themselves wished to reduce it. Margaret Thatcher followed Geoffrey Howe in responding to the Conservatives' unusual and unpopular 1981 budget with the phrase "There Is No Alternative." The analysis became a hallmark of critics of globalization: "Globalization is a myth suitable for a world without illusions, but it is also one that robs us of our hope . . . for it is held that Western social democracy and socialism of the Soviet bloc are both finished. One can only call the political impact of 'globalization' the pathology of diminished expectations."[13]

European politicians replied more often to the same problem by looking for a nonnational, nonpolitical solution from the European process of integration. It had been the genius of Jacques Delors, as France's economy and budget minister in 1983, to see this way out of the impasse of French domestic politics. As president of the EC Commission (after 1985), he was well placed to realize the political potential in "Europe" as a way of restricting domestic politics.

The clearest example of this came in the 1990s, with the Treaty of Maastricht, concluded on December 11, 1991, which amended the Treaty of Rome to create the European Union and severely limited national monetary and fiscal policies. Maastricht firmly endorsed the principle of "subsidiarity," that decisions should be made at the most local level feasible. There was to be a common European citizenship, so that EU citizens could vote in local and EU elections in other member countries where they resided. The Treaty created the Council of the Regions and a blueprint for the elaboration of a common foreign and security policy. In practice, this was the least satisfactory part of European integration in the 1990s, as countries continued to view foreign policy priorities largely in national terms.

The most obvious and controversial innovation of Maastricht was the timetable it established for a move to European Monetary Union. At the latest, the new currency (which was eventually named the "euro") was to be introduced in 1999. This timetable was actually realized, and a new money as an accounting unit was established at that time, superseding national currencies in twelve member countries of the EU. The introduction of the new currency in physical form took place three years later, on January 1, 2002.

> *Counterfactual 4*: If there had been no move to the European Monetary Union, one of the key cements that held in place the logic of TINA would have been removed, and the politics of backlash would have begun earlier.

At the same time as the members of the European Community moved to monetary union, they also rejected a logical move that might have accompanied a single currency and which would have offered a powerful and convincing response to the collapse of communism and the geopolitical upheaval of 1989–1991. There was an urgent security question that threatened European stability until the discussions in the mid-1990s about a pathway to NATO expansion. (The Czech Republic, Poland, and Hungary joined in 1999.) A dramatically bold European response to the uncertainty might have been a political union, which would necessarily have been a military union. There had notoriously been plans for a European defense community that were rejected by the French National Assembly in 1954. The Maastricht Treaty of course introduced the concept of European citizenship (Article 9), as well as a common foreign and security policy and cooperation in the fields of justice and home affairs. But the union was incomplete, national citizenship remained, and the classic tests of civic value (Are you prepared to die for your country?) were not administered. The defense ministries of the European countries and, more important, the influential military industrial lobbyists in the major states of France, Germany, and the United Kingdom rejected any possibility of a military union, continuing to rely on NATO. Thus, when there was a need for a grand European gesture after 1989, there could be no plan for a common European army, but there was already a well-worked-out roadmap for monetary union.

Those plans existed not because of any geopolitical tension but because the problem they set out to deal with—the issue of current account imbalances in Europe as well as globally—had been on the agenda for decades, not years.

The security dimensions of European politics were widely discussed in the run-up to Maastricht and formed a key part of the perceived tension between agreements on the European Monetary Union and on a European political union. France in particular was pressing for a stronger role of the defense organization of the Western European Union, that is, the European members of NATO. That was seen by the United Kingdom as unrealistic, or as Prime Minister John Major's private secretary put it, a move that would "detach" Germany from NATO.[14] At the same time, Greece was also strongly opposed to a strengthening of the Western European Union unless there were a guarantee of all European borders, and the Greek prime minister Konstantinos Mitsotakis told the Dutch presidency of the Maastricht Intergovernmental Conference that Greece would veto the arrangement.[15] As it happened, on December 8, just a few days before the Maastricht conference met, the issue of security appeared to become much less acute as the three largest units in the Soviet Union concluded an agreement in Viskuli, near Belovezh in Belarus, to end the Union Treaty of 1922 that had created the Soviet Union; with that, the Soviet implosion seemed complete, and any security threat less than urgent. Thus attention focused on the monetary side, and the Maastricht process was lopsided.

At the time of the negotiations, the Maastricht Treaty was frequently viewed as the product of a political compromise: a German concession to a French demand for a greater institutionalized influence on monetary policy in Europe, which under the European Monetary System had fundamentally been set by the German Bundesbank in Frankfurt, in return for French agreement to German political unification. Germany insisted throughout the unification process that it wanted to overcome its national trauma only in the context of greater European integration. But the basis of monetary union had already been laid in the later 1980s, before anyone thought of the German question, and it corresponded to doubts about the long-term sustainability of a simple fixed exchange rate regime (that would be vulnerable to speculative attacks).

In large part Maastricht was a response to a simple and immediate question: How could national governments be restrained from fiscal irresponsibility, from creating debt that the European Central Bank would be obliged to monetize? The Maastricht Treaty laid down the criteria for a stability pact, according to which public-sector deficits were limited to 3 percent of GNP, and public-sector debt to 60 percent of GNP. A non-bailout clause restricted the ability of the new European Central Bank to monetize the budget deficits of member countries. Inflation and interest rates had to move into line before the monetary union for countries to qualify to participate, and exchange rates were not to move by more than the normal 2 percent margins that existed in the European Monetary System. The convergence criteria then became the underlying basis for the operation of a currency union after 1999 (with new banknotes and coins circulating after 2001).

In practice, public controversy about Maastricht and its budgetary implications soon rocked European politics, but also the financial system organized around the European Monetary System. Denmark narrowly voted in a referendum not to participate in the European Monetary Union; a similar referendum in France looked uncertain; and at the same time, Germany set high interest rates because of the surge of demand created in the wake of political unification. In September 1992, speculative attacks forced Italy, Spain, and the United Kingdom out of the narrow exchange rate bands of the European Monetary System. The United Kingdom left the system altogether, while Italy and Spain worked with new parities and larger bands of fluctuation. France was subject to a similar speculative attack in 1993, but withstood it because of large German intervention in support of the French franc on the foreign currency markets.

The new vulnerabilities of a globalized world were demonstrated spectacularly in the early 1990s. The currency crises rocked the British government and produced a nervous paralysis. The currency fluctuations also provoked fears of a trade backlash against the market opening provided by the Single European Act, since the Italian and Spanish devaluations made the products of those countries (in particular agricultural products, but also important industrial goods such as automobiles) cheaper in the other EU members. In France in particular, the idea was raised of an import tariff to compensate for the competitive effects of devaluations; such a move would clearly have completely destroyed the process of trade liberalization which constituted the raison d'être of the European process since 1958. At the same time, a surge in immigration followed the end of the Cold War and the dismantling of boundaries against movement; this too produced populist backlashes.

The external limitations imposed by the Stability Pact were used most conspicuously in Italy as the basis of a stabilization program and were endorsed with great enthusiasm by center-left governments in the mid-1990s. The result was to bring down Italian inflation and interest rates spectacularly. (And the interest rate reduction produced fiscal savings.) For Italy, the EU's most important role lay in the way in which it created objective and unmovable constraints on policymaking. This role appealed not just to member countries but also to the many former communist countries that wanted to join and applied for membership. In this way the Pact did a great deal to create stability. It also affected formerly communist countries that wanted to join the EU and started to accept its stability criteria in advance of membership. At the Copenhagen summit in 2002 the EU governments agreed to the accession of Cyprus, the Czech Republic, Estonia, Latvia, Lithuania, Hungary, Malta, Poland, Slovakia, and Slovenia in 2004 and of Bulgaria and Romania in 2007. It also agreed to hold membership talks with Turkey in December 2004, but there was little progress and many Europeans increasingly feared the inclusion of a large Islamic country in the EU.

But the externally induced stability came at a price. One of the main methods that the EU used was to create an impression of complete necessity. A veteran EU politician, Prime Minister Jean-Claude Juncker of Luxembourg, put the point very neatly: "We decide on something, leave it lying around and wait and see what happens. If no one kicks up a fuss, because most people don't know what has been decided, we continue step by step until there is no turning back."[16] This obvious strategy clearly poses a challenge to political activity as conventionally understood as a process of debating and reaching informed decisions. If politics is no longer about choices, what is it about? In 1991 Nigel Lawson explained, "I think it was Pierre Mendès-France who said that to govern was to choose. To appear to be unable to choose is to appear to be unable to govern."[17] The technocratic approach produced a discussion of the "democratic deficit" at the heart of modern European politics and a demand for a more political instance to control the European dynamic and to offer real choices. By 2002, the president of the European Commission, Romano Prodi, could publicly state that he considered the Stability Pact to be "stupid." The euro would be at the center of debates about the European order after the 2008 global financial crisis.

The New Politics: Morality and Foreign Policy

The case about morality and politics was raised in a most acute way by the experience of one region in the aftermath of the collapse of communism: that of former Yugoslavia, where new or newly revived aggressive nationalisms brought violence and conflict to what elsewhere had been an amazingly peaceful rev. If Poland had been the country around which a wide-ranging international debate about society and politics centered during the 1980s, that role was taken in the 1990s by the successor states of Yugoslavia. Yugoslavia created a moral challenge for Europe. It revived a discussion about human rights in international politics that had been raised already in the 1970s, notably by U.S. president Jimmy Carter, and which had played a major role in the establishment of the Helsinki Conference for Cooperation and Security in Europe. Through much of the 1980s, however, this discussion had been obscured by the focus on military and economic competition in the confrontation of the superpowers. Then, at the end of the Cold War, there no longer seemed to be constraints on effective international action, as the Soviet Union in November 1990 endorsed UN Security Resolution 678, which set a firm deadline for Iraqi withdrawal from Kuwait. The blockage of the Cold War now appeared to have come to an end.

In 1992–1993, as the major powers began to agonize about the consequences of their inaction in the wars and struggles produced by the disintegration of Yugoslavia, human rights groups suggested the creation of a war crimes tribunal on the Nuremberg model. During the 1992 presidential campaign, Clinton attacked President George H. W. Bush for being soft on tyrants, and called for "steps to bring [the perpetrators] to justice for these crimes against humanity."[18] Eventually, in 1993 the UN Security Council passed a resolution which established the International Tribunal for the Prosecution of Persons Responsible for Serious Violations of International Humanitarian Law Committed in the Territory of Former Yugoslavia since 1991.

In 1995, Croatia began to win the long-drawn-out war with Serbia, and very large numbers of Serb refugees from Croatia fled into Bosnia, looking for new homes. By August, the Serbs had been driven out of the Krajina. In Bosnia the level of violence increased dramatically. In July, the Serb armies in Bosnia began an offensive against Srebrenica, which was protected by a small force of Dutch soldiers. Some of the Dutch peacekeepers were taken hostage by the Serbs, but the Dutch developed an increasingly disdainful attitude to the Muslim population of Srebrenica, whose security was their responsibility. Victims who have been systematically attacked and humiliated can begin to look unappealing and even no longer fully human—their clothes are in tatters, they smell, they complain—and the Dutch soldiers seem to have treated the Srebrenica Muslims with increasing contempt. Their Serb oppressors, on the contrary, had smart uniforms, were often courteous with foreigners, and might sit down to a friendly drink. The commander of the Dutch forces admired greatly the dash and charm of the brutal Serb military commander, General Ratko Mladić, and thought the Muslim population to be difficult, whining, and idle. He still referred to Mladić as a "good guy" in a press conference after the fall of Srebrenica. The pro-Serbian attitude of the Dutch forces ("Dutchbat" in the lingo of the UN operations) was strengthened when Bosnian soldiers killed a Dutchman retreating from Srebrenica. Between seventy-five hundred and eight thousand Muslims were massacred when Srebrenica fell, atrocities which were in part witnessed (and even filmed) by Dutch soldiers but against which the Dutch took no action.

The mechanism by which people are marginalized, made to appear inhuman, and then persecuted and killed, resembled closely that of the genocide of the Second World War. The Dutch saw how Muslim men were separated from women and children and mishandled. The fallout from the scandal of how UN peacekeepers could watch genocide, and the official Dutch inquiry into it, eventually—seven years later—produced the resignation of the Dutch government.

The massacre of Srebrenica and the continuous and deliberate strategy of "ethnic cleansing" raised issues about the defense of human rights that had not been seriously debated since the Second World War. The Europeans had talked about talks, while postponing any action, for much too long. After Srebrenica, many influential European politicians believed that their soldiers had been bystanders to a new holocaust.

To justify their inaction, both Yugoslav and world leaders at first used and abused history in outrageous ways. Slobodan Milošević, the president of Serbia, repeatedly told his interlocutors that the history of the Second World War showed that the Croats were Nazis. President François Mitterrand of France at one point told a German reporter that history showed that the Serbs could not have concentration camps. The most common line of analysis was that everyone was at fault and that the problem had arisen from "ancient hatreds," a position which no serious historian ever endorsed or could endorse. Even if it were true that some hatreds continue over long periods of time, any serious analysis would have to explain the mechanisms by which such behavior was transmitted to new generations, which is not at all self-evident or self-explanatory. President Clinton in early 1994 spoke about how Bosnia-Herzegovina "basically degenerated back to the conflict which had been there for hundreds of years. And you can—there is no perfect solution for life's problems, you know. But in this case, the truth is, people there keep killing each other."[19] John Major told the British House of Commons in 1993, "The biggest single element behind what has happened in Bosnia is the collapse of the Soviet Union and of the discipline that that exerted over the ancient hatreds in the old Yugoslavia. Once that discipline had disappeared, those ancient hatreds reappeared."[20] Some of the most powerful books on the Bosnian crisis start off with an examination of the astonishing popularity of such facile so-called historical analyses. Noel Malcolm correctly pointed out that there had been no Soviet discipline since the expulsion of Yugoslavia from the Cominform in 1948.

Only in August 1995 did NATO forces begin a significant aerial bombardment of the Serbian forces in Bosnia. It was a relatively small-scale operation: 3,515 air sorties were flown, the equivalent of one day's fighting in the Gulf War. The Croatian forces attacked the key Serbian defensive point in the Krajina, Knin, and another wave of 150,000 Serb refugees fled to Bosnia. Through all of this fighting, Milošević in Belgrade had always disclaimed any responsibility or control over the "irregular" Serb forces that were in fact being financed from Belgrade.

In May 1996, Duško Tadić, a relatively low-ranking soldier accused of mistreating and killing Muslim inmates of the Bosnian Serb concentration camps at Omarska and Keraterm, became the first war criminal to appear before the UN Tribunal in the Hague. The first indictments looked relatively unpromising, the equivalent of the border guards who had been tried in Germany for shootings at the Berlin Wall. During the Dayton negotiations, the Western powers were worried that the arrest of leading Bosnian Serbs—Mladić, Radovan Karadžić, who would be the first president of Republika Srpska—would threaten the negotiation of peace. After that, NATO troops and their commanders worried about the casualties that might follow from attempts to arrest war criminals. The existence of the Tribunal, nevertheless, gave a signal that an international standard of justice might be applied to those guilty of war crimes.

In 1996–1997, morality became explicitly a major element in making policy with regard to former Yugoslav territories. This was in large part the result of changes in administration: in the second Clinton presidential term, Madeleine Albright became the new secretary of state and maintained the determined stance on human rights she had shown as U.S. ambassador to the UN. Albright, the daughter of a Czech refugee from the Nazis and Soviets, liked to use historical analogies in the plea for a more active foreign policy, explaining that her "mindset is Munich." She explained that "the violence is an affront to universal standards of human rights we are pledged to uphold." In 1994, she had stated, "We believe that establishing the truth about what happened in Bosnia is essential to—not an obstacle to—national reconciliation."[21]

The new Labour government in Britain after 1997, with Blair as prime minister and Robin Cook as foreign secretary, took a very similar line and claimed to be staking out a new morality in foreign policy. (It also, for the same reason, took a leading role in the debate over the "Nazi gold" issue, the question of whether Swiss banks and the Swiss government had benefited from wartime trading with Germany.) Blair explained in a newspaper interview that he believed in a natural-law order of the world, and that he felt the more common utilitarian stance of politicians was dangerous. "There used to be an idea that you just looked after your national interest, and of course it's true that you have to look after your national interest. I also think that there is a moral dimension to it."[22] The moral dimension became a critical part of the German acceptance, for the first time in the country's postwar history, of a duty of military intervention. It was defended by politicians who came out of the student protest movement of the 1960s, including Chancellor Schröder and his foreign minister Joschka Fischer, as being part of the responsibility created by the legacy and burden of the German past. In 1998 and 1999, NATO soldiers began to make arrests of suspected war criminals, and most of Mladić's immediate subordinates were seized and sent to The Hague. In 1999 Milošević himself was indicted.

In the 1990s conflicts elsewhere in the world also directly raised human rights issues: in the Middle East, in the long struggle of East Timor for independence from Indonesia, and above all in the genocidal civil war in Rwanda (where the United Nations also demonstrated a remarkable passivity). Unlike these conflicts, the Yugoslav drama was very close to some of the world's richest industrial countries. Throughout the Yugoslav wars, trains in the Vienna South Station with Cyrillic lettering took passengers to the

Serb capital, Belgrade. Many West Europeans knew coastal Yugoslavia from vacations. Many Yugoslavs worked in Germany, and elsewhere in the EU, as "guest workers." Most obviously, refugees from the conflict areas fled into the EU and Switzerland. The human dimensions of the tragedy were thus brought home in a direct way, while Europe's elites went on with "business as usual" in the face of mass murder. The governments did not act until they were pushed by the United States, and it took a long time to make the link between morality and foreign policy.

Counterfactual 5: If there had been a backlash against TINA, the politics of morality and ethics launched in the 1990s (and which was labeled by its enemies as "wokeness") would have crumbled earlier and been replaced by aggressive doctrines of realpolitik, in which groups put forward their own interests as the national interest.

Tensions and Contradictions

The new concern with global morality and the pressures created by economic and business globalization do not necessarily fit easily with each other. The system was held together by a global combination of economic growth with stable prices, so that the malaise of the 1970s disappeared. The world might appear in the new circumstances as NICE, in the acronym popularized in the 2000s by the governor of the Bank of England, Mervyn King: Non-Inflationary Continuing Expansion. The British government celebrated Cool Britannia.

In retrospect, the NICE world doesn't seem completely nice. In particular, it appears as if globalization was undermining human rights in critical areas. At the same time as German businesses were devoting resources to investigating their moral failures during the Nazi period and repeating mantras about learning responsibility from facing up to the past, they built up new engagements in what appeared to be exciting and lucrative areas of the globe. German banks and German energy and engineering companies poured money into developing Russia's natural resource economy. German automobile companies that had examined the use of slave labor in the 1930s and 1940s started to produce in China. In 2013, Volkswagen opened a cooperation project with the Chinese state-owned company SAIC in Xinjiang province, using Uighur slave labor. If any rationale was given for the wisdom of investment in corrupt and possibly criminal activities, the standard reply was a version of the globalization lesson that was thought to have led to 1989: that commercial engagement would make for a gradual permeation of liberal values throughout the world. After all, German companies had engaged heavily in trade with the Soviet Union and, from the 1970s, in the construction of a gas pipeline. That had brought the Soviet Union to a realization of the importance of long-term reliability and of keeping to the terms of contracts. The economic rapprochement was conceived of as a strategy of "change through trade" (*Wandel durch Handel*). It is not at all clear that this strategy was misconceived in the 1990s; it was only with the 2007–2008 global financial crisis, which brought a temporary shudder to the globalization process, that Russia and then China (after 2012 under Xi Jinping) turned to more aggressive and confrontational policies and stepped up violations of human rights. But the business logic had created a momentum which carried business leaders with it even when the intellectual and political circumstances had changed.

It is possible to use income data, but that data suffers from considerable measurement problems in the case of pre-1989 planned economies. Taking demographic data is a rough and ready way of circumventing some of those measurement issues, and there the result is a dramatic convergence occurring in the 1990s, with substantial improvements in both Eastern and Western Europe. By the end of the twentieth century, Western and Central Europeans lived substantially longer. Life expectancy at birth for French males, which had been 63.7 years in 1950, rose by over a decade by the end of the century (74.6 in 1998). The corresponding female rates are 69.4 and 82.6. In the United Kingdom, the male rate rose from 66.2 to 74.8 years, and the female from 71.1 to 80.1. Age-specific mortality, which in many ways gives a better indication of the experience of the adult population (since the more widely cited life expectancy figures are highly sensitive to changes in infant mortality), shows the same development: Europeans lived longer, and adult mortality dropped.

This success story needs some relativizing in regard to Central and Eastern Europe. In communist Central Europe, adult female and particularly male mortality had risen from the 1960s; it fell again with the transformation process, quite dramatically in the case of the most successful conversions to the market economy (Hungary, Poland, Slovenia). Even in the case of less rapid adjustments to capitalism, as in Romania, the rise in mortality of the communist era stopped, and by the mid-1990s showed some signs of a slight improvement. On the other hand, further east, in the former Soviet Union, where the transformation was less immediately successful and was associated with big income falls, mortality rates initially rose. Traditional causes of death, such as cancers, cardiovascular disease, and violence, were now also accompanied by rises in drug- and AIDS-related mortality. But even here, the rate of the rise in mortality slowed down in comparison with the communist era, and the often politicized attempt to blame increases in death rates on the transition to capitalism was misleading, given the longer-term demographic perspective.

There was always a tension in the globalization discourse. Many people and politicians argued that freedom was good because it produced greater prosperity and well-being. The outcome of the 1990s seemed to justify that position. When the belief in prosperity faltered, the room was opened to reimaging a re-creation of the Soviet universe, with Putinism providing an ideological core for an alternative to TINA. That new, radically nostalgic worldview was embraced with destructive passion by the Alternative für Deutschland, which started characteristically as an anti-euro, anti–European Monetary Union party, whose themes were echoed in Italy by Salvini and the Liga Nord, by Marine Le Pen and the Rassemblement national (previously Front national) in France, and above all by Nigel Farage, a Putin apologist who singlehandedly organized the political mobilization that forced a Conservative U.K. government to hold a referendum on membership in the European Union. The summary of all our five counterfactuals is thus quite simple: **If the Soviet Union had not collapsed, there would not have been either the invention of a new politics of openness or the assertion of the need to revive some version of Sovietism as a counterweight to what seemed objectionable in modern existence.**

The East European dissidents of the 1980s had wanted to make a quite different, and intellectually more powerful, case for freedom—not that it was materially beneficial, though it might be, but that it allowed the realization of a fuller and better-lived life. Amartya Sen interpreted freedom as the realization of human capacity. In this line of argument, the material outcomes were irrelevant, but it was the material outcomes that figured prominently in the discourse of politicians' promises on globalization.

The replacement of politics by morality was, as the Oxford philosopher Isaiah Berlin pointed out in a remarkable essay titled "European Unity and Its Vicissitudes" in 1959, a historical return. He saw a reversion to a Europe that was universal in that it rejected the celebration of the particular and the different in late eighteenth-century romanticism. Before that era, the world was "a single, intelligible whole. It consisted of certain stable ingredients, material and spiritual; if they were not stable they were not real." After the catastrophes of the mid-twentieth century, which could not as easily be overcome politically or psychologically as they were materially (in the age of the Marshall Plan), there was a need for a new vision: "[T]here is a return to the ancient notion of natural law, but for some of us, in empiricist dress—no longer necessarily based on theological or metaphysical foundations."[23] But the empiricist dress looked rather like the "materialist bias" lambasted by Fukuyama. Globalization or multilateralism thus rested either on very deep and profound foundations that had become increasingly shallow in the late twentieth century or on a superficial sense of material interest. The gap between these two visions produced disillusion, eloquently described for the European case by Tony Judt.[24]

By the end of the twentieth century, a historical reversal of institutional and political forms set in, in the manner predicted by Berlin. The end of the twentieth century brought an unraveling of the threads that had constituted what older analysts had once believed to be a one-way process of modernization in the form of the building of a strong state: 1989 immediately and obviously undid 1917 and the legacy of the Bolshevik Revolution, but the business of undoing historically formed ideas and institutions did not stop there. Already in 1928, Leon Trotsky, deported by Stalin to Alma Ata, had noted that "the film of revolution is running backwards."[25] In the 1990s, Europe went back before 1789, that is, before the era of ideological politics. By 2003, in the aftermath of the Iraq War, the world appeared to be going back before 1648, when the Peace of Westphalia that ended the Thirty Years' War effectively introduced the concept of an international order based on a community of sovereign states. Fissiparous pressures dismantled the political institutions of the nation-state that most Europeans for most of the twentieth century had assumed to be eternally durable, even when they generated problems and disasters.

In terms of basic expectations about life—sickness and health, old age, welfare—Europe looked more certain and stable at the end of the twentieth century than at the beginning. But when people thought about a broader world, their impressions were different and much less secure. Politics no longer assured control of economic, social, or cultural forces. Part of the problem stemmed from the sense of a need for natural law as a guide to conduct, but without any of the theological and metaphysical foundations on which it had previously been based. A part of the confusion at the beginning of the twenty-first century came from the impression that time no longer ran unambiguously forward.

In the 1980s, Gorbachev referred very frequently to "our common European house" that included both East and West. It would end the division of Europe, the competition of systems, the security threat, and the Cold War of the superpowers. Gorbachev indeed frequently used the idea of Europe to suggest that the bipolar world dominated by the superpowers was at an end. But many commentators in both East and West remarked in the 1980s on how vague the details of the "common European house" were in reality. In his speech to the Council of Europe on July 6, 1989, Gorbachev admitted to uncertainty about "the architecture of our common house, or how it should be built and even how it should be furnished."[26] President George H. W. Bush jibed that if it were really a common European house, people should be free to wander from one room to another.

One decade after the collapse of communism, it was clear that there was a substantial amount of convergence: in the democratic form of politics, in the rise of new political issues, in the redundancy of right and left as previously understood, but also in a commitment to economic reform, the acceptance of the market and the principle of private property, and improvement in mortality rates. But the uncertainty about the architecture in Europe, and indeed on a global scale, remained just as real as when Gorbachev was using the rhetoric of Europe and old European values in the politics of the fading Cold War. The European Union and NATO had embarked on a transformatory expansion. French and Germans saw their remarkable act of national reconciliation in the 1950s as being extended to the whole continent (under their leadership). Americans unsympathetic to the European Union talked about a "new Europe," driven by the more recent members, the United Kingdom, the Mediterranean, and above all the Central European states, replacing the "old Europe" centered around France and Germany. And the jibe about many Europeans not being able to move around the rooms of the common European house still applied. Globalization was a promise that inevitably didn't quite deliver. And, perhaps inevitably, it paved the way for a radicalized backlash.

Notes

1. Gray 1998. I record my deep gratitude to John. I knew him in the 1980s, when he courageously participated in innovative and transformative underground lectures in Poland and Czechoslovakia, and I met my wife in February 1991 when he lectured in Princeton.
2. Bell 1960.
3. Gerstle 2022, 146.
4. Bartel 2022, 186.
5. Gorbachev 1993, 128–129.
6. Fukuyama 1989, 18.
7. Bullard 1990.
8. Carrère d'Encausse 1978, 1990, 1992.
9. Von Eschen 2022.
10. Garton Ash 1990, 105.
11. Blair and Schröder 1999.
12. Williams 1998, 183.
13. Hirst and Thompson 1996, 6.
14. Stephen Wall memo for Prime Minister, November 13, 1991, U.K. National Archive (TNA), PREM 19/3317, fol. 160.
15. Cable from British embassy in Athens, November 22, 1991, TNA PREM 19/3317.
16. *Economist* 2004, 55.
17. Lawson 1992, 1005.
18. Bass 2000, 214.
19. Cohen 1998, 244.
20. Malcolm 1994, xx.
21. Auerswald and Auerswald 2000, 104; Bass 2000, 262–263.
22. Interview with Anne Applebaum, *Sunday Telegraph,* March 19, 2001, https://www.telegraph.co.uk/news/uknews/4722273/I-am-still-normal.html
23. Berlin 1990, 175, 204.
24. Judt 1996.
25. Deutscher 1959, 460.
26. Speech by Mikhail Gorbachev to the Council of Europe in Strasbourg, "Europe as a Common Home," July 6, 1989, https://digitalarchive.wilsoncenter.org/document/speech-mikhail-gorbachev-council-europe-strasbourg-europe-common-home?__cf_chl_tk=_HABr8Tu2zfatI2096mns_TODllKP15M0mFY6SYgIgs-1745974912-1.0.1.1-NEa6HiVdyUzkDeM7P7rGDrC.Tw84Ox1RxpeOQroMgIA

References

Auerswald, Philip E., and David P. Auerswald. 2000. *The Kosovo Conflict: A Diplomatic History through Documents*. Kluwer.

Bartel, Fritz. 2022. *The Triumph of Broken Promises: The End of the Cold War and the Rise of Neoliberalism*. Harvard University Press.

Bass, Gary Jonathan. 2000. *Stay the Hand of Vengeance: The Politics of War Crimes Tribunals*. Princeton University Press.

Bell, Daniel. 1960. *The End of Ideology: On the Exhaustion of Political Ideas in the Fifties*. Free Press.

Berlin, Isaiah. 1990. "European Unity and Its Vicissitudes." In *The Crooked Timber of Humanity: Chapters in the History of Ideas*. John Murray.

Blair, Tony, and Gerhard Schröder. 1999. "The Way Forward for Europe's Social Democrats." https://library.fes.de/pdf-files/bueros/suedafrika/02828.pdf.

Bullard, Julian. 1990. "Time to Feed the Country's Western Roots." *Financial Times*, October 29.

Carrère d'Encausse, Hélène. 1978. *L'empire éclaté: La révolte des nations en U.R.S.S.* Flammarion.
Carrère d'Encausse, Hélène. 1990. *La Gloire des nations.* Fayard.
Carrère d'Encausse, Hélène. 1992. *Victorieuse Russie.* Fayard.
Cohen, Roger. 1998. *Hearts Grown Brutal: Sagas of Sarajevo.* Random House.
Deutscher, Isaac. 1959. *The Prophet Unarmed: Trotsky 1921–1929.* Oxford University Press.
Economist. 2004. "No Love Lost." September 25.
Fukuyama, Francis. 1989. "The End of History?" *National Interest*, no. 16.
Garton Ash, Timothy. 1990. *The Magic Lantern: The Revolution of '89 Witnessed in Warsaw, Budapest, Berlin, and Prague.* Random House.
Gerstle, Gary. 2022. *The Rise and Fall of the Neoliberal Order: America and the World in the Free Market Era.* Oxford University Press.
Gorbachev, Mikhail. 1993. *Gipfelgespräche: Geheime Protokolle aus meiner Amtszeit.* Rowohlt.
Gray, John. 1998. *False Dawn: The Delusions of Global Capitalism.* Granta Books.
Hirst, Paul, and Graham Thompson. 1996. *Globalization in Question.* Polity Press.
Judt, Tony. 1996. *A Grand Illusion? An Essay on Europe.* Hill and Wang.
Lawson, Nigel. 1992. *The View from No. 11: Memoirs of a Tory Radical.* Bantam.
Malcolm, Noel. 1994. *Bosnia: A Short History* Macmillan.
von Eschen, Penny M. 2022. *Paradoxes of Nostalgia: Cold War Triumphalism and Global Disorder since 1989.* Duke University Press.
Williams, Hywel. 1998. *Guilty Men: Conservative Decline and Fall.* Aurum Press.

PART III
FALSE DAWN
Western Overreach or Underreach?

10
Ever Deeper and Wider?
The Globalization of the Liberal International Order and the End of the Cold War

Tanja A. Börzel

The evolution of the liberal international order (LIO) is often described as a linear process which started with its establishment after World War II. The story goes like this. The LIO was anchored in Western democracies and dominated by the United States and its liberal allies.[1] At the same time, the LIO's universal principles were at least selectively endorsed by the communist East, notably the Soviet Union and the People's Republic of China. The end of the Cold War ultimately globalized the LIO as liberalism became the dominant script for organizing world politics.[2]

The chapter argues that this teleological account ignores the inherent tension within the LIO between deepening its liberal content and widening its membership.[3] Parts of the LIO have been global in scope, open to any sovereign state. Other parts offer universal membership but only to states that adhere to liberal principles. This variable geometry suggests a trade-off between the deepening and widening of the LIO as long as a significant number of states around the globe do not follow a liberal script for organizing their societies.[4] In this sense, the end of the Cold War brought the United States and its liberal allies to a critical juncture at which they chose to extend the liberal content of international institutions and strengthen their political authority. While meant to anchor the ensuing widening of the LIO by states endorsing economic and political liberalism, parts of the LIO became more liberal, which made it, however, less global. The wave of contestations by rising and declining autocracies, on the one hand, and authoritarian populism within Western democracies, on the other, have curbed the reach of the LIO. Putin's war of aggression against Ukraine has dealt another blow to the post–Cold War LIO on the way to its decline. Alternatively, the LIO could face its next transformation toward a global but less liberal, or a more liberal but less global, variety.

The chapter investigates the relationship between the deepening and widening of the LIO in historical perspective. It starts by developing a framework that allows us to conceptualize and analyze the tension between the universalism of the liberal principles inscribed in the post–World War II LIO and the exclusion or denigration of those who do not adhere to these principles. The second part of the chapter traces the relationship between the widening of the LIO's membership and the deepening of its liberal purpose, demonstrating that the end of the Cold War brought a deepening but ultimately no global widening of the LIO. The third part explains this outcome in terms of the strategies pursued by states contesting the LIO. The demise of the Soviet Union left the United States and its European allies with the power to push for reforms aimed at deepening the LIO to anchor its widening. With liberalism being the only game in town, they saw no need to look for an alternative. Russia, in contrast, had gone from pushing back the deepening of the LIO to withdrawing, before it engaged in outright dissidence. China is still sitting on the fence, particularly after Putin's war of aggression against Ukraine. The chapter concludes by discussing the implications of its findings for the future of the LIO.

The Deepening and Widening of the Liberal International Order

Deepening versus Widening?

The international relations literature used to suggest that the deepening and widening of the LIO went hand in hand, even in times of contestation and crisis. Hegemonic stability theory sees the LIO as the product of the dominance of the United States as the liberal hegemon. Despite its hegemonic decline since the 1970s, the United States has remained the world's leading economic and military power.[5] Rationalist institutionalism focuses on the effectiveness of international institutions in managing the relations between interdependent states serving their national interests. Rule-based cooperation in multilateral institutions has facilitated the opening of markets, the establishment of collective security systems, and the protection of human rights. They mitigate the effects of international anarchy and provide benefits to both rising and established powers.[6] Sociological institutionalist approaches emphasize the embedding and socialization of newly independent states as well as rising powers into the (liberal) norms and principles espoused by established powers and enshrined in the LIO.[7]

Research on the European Union shows that the relationship between deepening and widening is not necessarily a positive one. Widening may require deepening to maintain the effectiveness of international institutions, particularly if membership becomes more diverse with regard to domestic political and economic institutions and the level of socioeconomic development. Growing diversity is likely to result in a trade-off between deepening and widening. The more members with diverse preferences an institution has, the more difficult it becomes to reach agreement on policies and institutional reforms.[8]

To conceptualize the relationship between deepening and widening, the chapter draws on the work of Börzel and Zürn on the contestation of the LIO.[9] They explain the wave of contestations the LIO has faced since the early 2000s as a result of the deepened liberal authority of international institutions in the early 1990s. International authority concentrates decision-making power in the hands of executives of powerful states, backed up by technocrats. On the one hand, these executives utilize international institutions to affect the policies of less powerful states. Like cases are often not treated alike. On the other hand, the exercise of international authority can overrule decisions of elected governments. The postnational liberalism of the post–Cold War LIO pushes states to respect human rights, the rule of law, and democratic principles, placing universal liberal ideas over popular sovereignty. The promotion and protection of liberal norms by international institutions increase the propensity, particularly for authoritarian populists inside and outside liberal societies, to contest the intrusiveness of the postnational LIO.

These arguments imply a trade-off between deepening and widening. The deepening of the LIO has triggered contestations by states which reject the universalism of liberal principles. International relations scholars see the emergence of a "multiplex world order," which is "politically and culturally diverse but economically and institutionally interlinked" and in which the liberal script will no longer be dominant for organizing world politics but will coexist with alternative ideas and institutions.[10] Whether this means a less deepened and more widened or more deepened and less widened LIO, however, remains an open question. This chapter argues that the globalization of the LIO crucially depends on the strategy states choose to contest the liberal intrusiveness of the LIO.

Contesting the Liberal International Order

Conceptualizing the relationship between the deepening and widening of the LIO requires an understanding of globalization that includes the acceptance of liberalism as the dominant script for organizing world politics. This is not only a question of membership in liberal international institutions. Beyond the commitment to liberal principles, states also have to adhere to them. Nonliberal states are critical cases, particularly when they have the power to contest the validity or application of liberal norms.

The strategy of contestants is determined by a combination of two factors: (1) their position toward liberal authority and (2) their relative position in the contested institution. The first factor is about actor *preferences* regarding liberalism.[11] While some contestations are directed against the specific exercise of liberal authority (rejection of the exercise of authority), others defy the mere existence of liberal authority (rejection of authority). In the case of the post–Cold War LIO, this distinction refers to the question of whether an international authority in place is rejected as such or whether its practices (decisions and decision-making) are challenged. The second factor refers to the degree to which an actor has the *power* to shape the decisions of an institution that holds liberal authority. Institutional influence consists of a formal layer that refers to its material capabilities and the institutional rules an actor can draw on to affect decisions. This also involves an informal layer, which describes the extent to which the actor is part of background talks prior to decisions or is stigmatized as a troublemaker that needs to be regulated, as opposed to an order-maker that regulates others.

The combination of preference and power leads to four different strategies. *Pushback* describes a strategy to reduce liberal authority from the inside. For years, Russian president Vladimir Putin has been contesting the liberal intrusiveness of the European peace and security order in the Organization for Security and Cooperation in Europe (OSCE) or the Council of Europe, seeking a return to a more Westphalian order based on equal sovereignty of states, their territorial integrity, and noninterference in domestic affairs. Actors that are dissatisfied with the way authority is exercised but accept liberal authority in general should opt for *reform*, if they can make their demands for change heard within the institution. Examples are LGBTQI+ rights which many liberal states have introduced. In contrast, outsiders that see little chance to change how liberal authority is exercised are likely to opt for *withdrawal*. This can take the form of "counter-institutionalization," that is, the creation of new liberal authorities, without necessarily leaving the existing ones. Countries with limited power, such as Greece, opted for another form of withdrawal by simply disregarding EU rules of asylum that it deemed too costly. Finally, *dissidence* refers to the strategy that aims at the destruction rather than the reduction of liberal institutions because actors reject any liberal authority but lack the power to defy it. Putin's war in Ukraine is a violent form of dissidence.

The relationship between deepening and widening depends on which strategy contestants choose. In principle, nonliberal states should have a preference to constrain the liberal purpose of the LIO. Those who have the power push back, seeking to return to a thinner variety of the LIO that is compatible with the survival of authoritarian rule. Those without sufficient power will openly and violently defy liberal international institutions. If rising powers that reject liberal authority join forces in pushing back, we are likely to see less deepening but more widening, that is, a more global but much thinner LIO that prioritizes national sovereignty over individual human rights. If nonliberal states fail to "make the world safe for autocracy"[12] and establish an alternative international order that competes with the LIO, there will be less widening but possibly a further deepening, depending on whether liberal states agree on reforming liberal international institutions strengthening their liberal authority.

The next section traces empirically how the LIO has deepened and widened since the end of World War II, focusing on the end of the Cold War as a critical juncture for "world order making."[13] It employs the typology of contestations to account for why the United States and its Western allies managed to deepen the LIO, making it more liberal but ultimately less global.

The Globalization of the Liberal International Order

Mapping the Liberal International Order: Content, Authority, and Membership

The LIO as it became dominant after World War II is often described as consisting of different parts:[14]

- *Economic liberalism*, meaning an open, rule-based, and free economic order with regard to trade, investments, and capital flows as promoted

by the World Trade Organization, the International Monetary Fund, and the World Bank.
- *Political liberalism*, embodying core liberal values of freedom and human rights as reflected in the United Nations Charter and various international and regional human rights regimes.
- *Liberal internationalism*, encapsulating a commitment to the peaceful resolution of conflicts, principled multilateralism, and the willingness to solve global governance problems cooperatively.

The three components capture the depths of the LIO. Economic and political liberalism denote the liberal content of international institutions. International institutions tend to focus on either trade (economic liberalism) or human rights (political liberalism).[15] Liberal internationalism refers to the authority of political institutions constraining the national sovereignty of their member states. The authority of international institutions is a function of their autonomy from states in making decisions, on the one hand, and the extent to which their decisions, procedures, and rules are binding for states, limiting their discretion regarding a number of policy functions, on the other.[16]

The stronger the liberal content and the authority of international institutions, the more intrusive they are,[17] and the deeper the LIO becomes.

Figure 10.1 traces the evolution of the depths of the LIO, focusing on the liberal content and the authority of thirty-four major international organizations (covered by the International Authority Database).[18] We see two steep rises in the liberal intrusiveness of the LIO—one after 1945, resulting from the creation of new international organizations, and the other after 1990, driven by the strengthening of existing international organizations.

The global reach of the (deepening) LIO depends on the width of its membership. The number of states joining liberal international institutions has continually increased. Figure 10.2 depicts the aggregate number of states that are members in the thirty-four international organizations included in Figure 10.1 in a given year. Membership has grown by seven times over the past seven decades. Even when controlling for the overall number of states (dotted line), international organization membership has widened. Again, we see two major rises, both due to a concentration of states becoming independent: after decolonization in the 1960s and after the demise of the Soviet Union in 1991.[19]

EVER DEEPER AND WIDER? 263

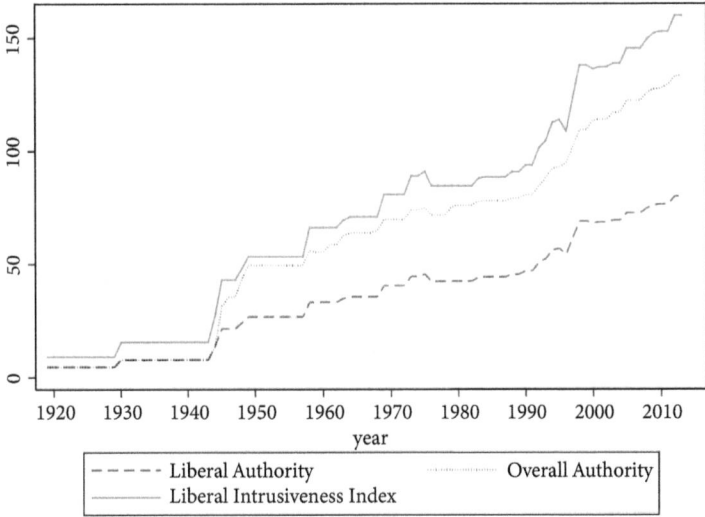

Figure 10.1 The deepening of the LIO.
Source: Börzel and Zürn 2021.

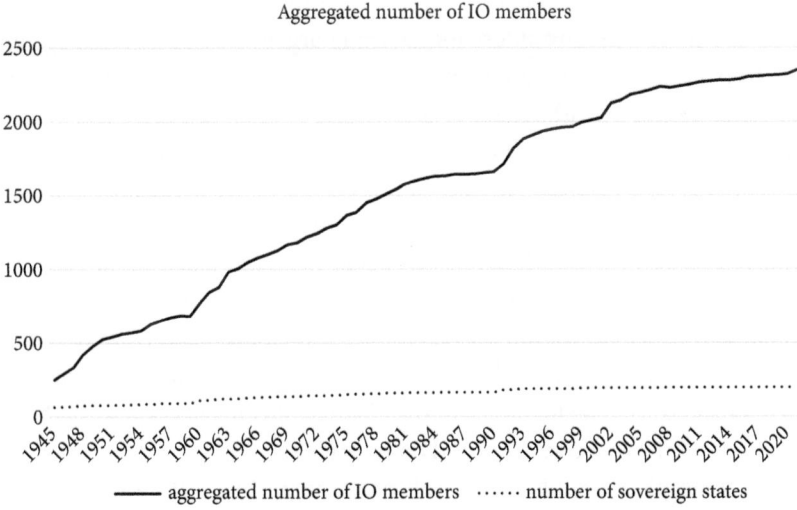

Figure 10.2 The widening of the LIO. (LIO stands for "liberal international order.")
Source: Author's compilation, with data from the Correlates of War Project 2017. Cf. Pevehouse et al. 2007.

The data suggest that the LIO has become both deeper and wider over time, particularly after the end of the Cold War. Yet a closer analysis reveals that the post-1990 transformation from liberal multilateralism to postnational liberalism made the LIO deeper but ultimately less wide or global.

The Liberal Multilateralism of the Postwar Liberal International Order

The first period of growth of the postwar LIO was driven by the founding of new international organizations. They constituted the core of liberal multinationalism, which characterized the LIO during the Cold War.

Economic liberalism was built into the Bretton Woods institutions. The World Bank, the International Monetary Fund, and the General Agreement on Tariffs and Trade (GATT) were to promote free trade and the free flow of capital. At the same time, their authority was constricted, and states retained the freedom to regulate their economies to reduce unemployment. This "embedded liberalism"[20] was regionally limited to the Western world of capitalist economies. The General Agreement on Tariffs and Trade started with only seventeen members in 1947, even though the attempt at the creation of a more intrusive international trade organization had failed in the U.S. Senate. The limited authority of the General Agreement on Tariffs and Trade, for example, with regard to the settling of trade disputes, might have facilitated the widening of its membership in the 1960s, when most of the postcolonial states joined. This also applies to the World Bank and the International Monetary Fund. Loan conditionality introduced in the 1980s was linked to economic (neo)liberalism, including trade and capital account liberalization, fiscal austerity, and public sector reform.[21] The liberal conditionality of the Organization for Economic Cooperation and Development, in contrast, has been much deeper, which explains its continually narrowing membership.[22] States wishing to join have been required to be both functioning market economies and democracies.

The centerpiece of political liberalism in the postwar LIO was the international human rights regime. Its multiple instruments have provided for a comprehensive protection of basic human rights, such as freedom from torture and racial discrimination. The various human rights treaties, however, have lacked enforcement power. Each state is party to at least one of the eighteen major international human rights treaties. The more intrusive their provisions are, however, for example, with regard to optional protocols, the fewer state parties have ratified them.

The United Nations is the only truly global international institution. Charged with the maintenance of international peace and security, the United Nations is open to universal membership, the only requirement being that states are internationally recognized. The principles of sovereign equality and peaceful resolution of conflicts have been recognized by liberal and nonliberal states alike. At the same time, these principles—together with the veto power of the permanent members of the United Nations Security Council—have constrained the intrusiveness of UN institutions.

The widening of the postwar LIO in the early 1960s was driven by decolonialization. Most postcolonial states joined the United Nations and its specialized agencies, including the World Health Organization and the Food and Agriculture Organization, as well as the Bretton-Woods institutions. The LIO became more global, which was facilitated by its limited depth. Membership in its core institutions required a commitment to rule-based multilateralism, basic human rights, and free trade rather than democracy, the rule of law, and a free market economy. At the same time, the LIO was still deep enough to exclude the Soviet Union, China, and other socialist countries, which were principally opposed to economic and political liberalism. Thus the post–World War II international system was constituted by two partially overlapping orders: the Westphalian order, with its core principles of sovereign equality and territorial integrity of states, and the LIO, built around economic and political liberalism. The United Nations was at the intersection between the two orders.[23] As the United Nations is a global institution, LIO membership was not confined to Western liberal states only. Nonliberal states had bought in parts of the LIO, for example, the General Agreement on Tariffs and Trade or the United Nations Anti-Torture Convention. Liberal states, most notably the United States, had opted out of international liberal conventions, such as the International Convention of Economic, Social and Cultural Rights. At the same time, international institutions with greater liberal intrusiveness were mostly formed by Western liberal democracies at the regional level, such the Organization for Economic Cooperation and Development, the Council of Europe with its European Convention on Human Rights, the European Community, or the North Atlantic Treaty Organization (NATO).

The End of the Cold War as a Critical Juncture

The evolution of the LIO during the Cold War suggests that its widening was facilitated by its limited deepening. Only some parts of the LIO have been truly global, while others made membership conditional on adherence to liberal principles. This variable geometry suggests a trade-off between the deepening and widening of the LIO. In this sense, the end of the Cold War became a critical juncture for the globalization of the Western-dominated LIO. The demise of the Soviet Union made liberalism the dominant script for organizing politics at the domestic and the international level. It also left the United States as the only superpower, with no nonliberal state being capable of pushing back its world-ordering initiatives. The admission of new countries would have provided an opportunity to respond to long-standing demands of the Global South[24] and rising non-Western powers,[25] but also of antiglobalization movements in the Global North, to make liberal institutions more inclusive and less intrusive. With regard to liberal internationalism, non-Western countries could have been given a stronger voice, for example, in the United Nations Security Council, the World Bank, or the International Monetary Fund. Economic liberalism could have been made more equitable, such as through a reform of the Bretton Woods institutions, which would have taken up key themes of the New International Economic Order,[26] revoking the neoliberal parts of the Washington Consensus. Political liberalism, finally, could have become more inclusive by strengthening social and economic rights.[27]

Such reforms of the postwar LIO would have required a more procedural interpretation of liberalism as suggested, for example, by the late Ernst B. Haas, who understood liberalism as "a certain procedure for the making of collective decisions, not with a distinct moral substance." Decision-making procedures provide for the representation of a plurality of interests and ideologies and protect minorities against majority decisions. But they do not commit to "a single substance formula of justice, rights, or expectations."[28] The liberal multilateralism of the postwar LIO entailed such a procedural understanding of liberalism. The Conference (later Organization) for Security and Co-operation in Europe (CSCE) is a case in point. It used to encompass the regional security institutions with the widest coverage in terms of both participants and geographical reach. Established by the Helsinki Final Act of 1975, the CSCE provided a framework of cooperation and confidence-building, which reduced military tensions between East and

West and improved respect for human rights in the East. The CSCE did so by getting liberal and socialist states to agree on fundamental principles to avoid and deal with conflict between them, including the nonuse of force and peaceful settlement of disputes, sovereign equality, territorial integrity, and noninterference in internal affairs, as well as disallowing the strengthening of one state's security by infringing upon the security of others.[29] These principles—all of which Putin had already violated in 2014, when he invaded and then annexed Crimea—are enshrined in the United Nations Charter. They are to protect the sovereign equality and territorial integrity of states and the right to choose the script they want to follow.

The postwar LIO underwent substantial reform. Yet instead of building on a more procedural multilateral liberalism that facilitated at least partial globalization during the Cold War, the end of the Cold War saw a deepening of parts of the LIO toward a more substantive, postnational liberalism.

The Postnational Liberalism of the Post–Cold War Liberal International Order

Liberal constraints on national sovereignty are the defining difference between the liberal multilateralism of the post-1945 LIO and the postnational liberalism of the post-1989 LIO. Not only did the authority of existing international institutions become strengthened; their content became more liberal as international institutions were tasked to protect and promote individual economic as well as political and civil rights with a stronger emphasis on the rule of law, democracy, and the free movement of people. Liberal internationalism continued to stipulate the cooperation of states by international institutions exercising authority regulated by international law; this authority, however, was increasingly infused with political liberalism being grounded in human rights as constitutional rights (particularly political and civil rights). The extended principles of political liberalism have been instantiated and protected by specific institutional arrangements that emerged mainly in the 1990s and early 2000s.[30] They consisted of conditionally sovereign states, which gained legitimacy by enforcing and guaranteeing liberal rights, rules, and decisions. National sovereignty was further curbed by economic liberalism. Open markets and supranational bodies maintaining the rules for an international economic order pushed states toward further liberalization. The world economy took another neoliberal turn in the 1990s, especially when it expanded to promote the free flow of capital.[31]

The European Union exemplifies this deepening of the LIO. The completion of the European single market supplemented the free movement of goods with liberalizing services, labor, and capital, the internal market's "four freedoms."[32] With the introduction of the euro as the single currency, member states granted the European Union full authority over monetary policy, which has severely curbed their sovereignty to embed economic liberalism in welfare state policies.[33] In the realm of internal security, the European Union acquired far-reaching decision-making powers, including migration and asylum.[34] States wishing to become a member of the European Union were not only obliged to adopt the entire body of EU law before joining; they also had to demonstrate that their institutions were able to uphold the free market, democracy, the rule of law, and human rights (the "Copenhagen criteria" of 1993).

The European Union's deepening has been followed by other regional organizations. The Council of Europe and the European Convention on Human Rights extended their liberal reach. The transformation of the CSCE into the OSCE in 1995 had been preceded by the Paris Charter of 1990 committing the state parties to democracy, human rights, and the rule of law as the fundamental values governing the future practice of their relations. Regional organizations outside Europe started to adopt and monitor compliance with liberal norms. The Organization of American States and the American Convention on Human Rights became more authoritative in the Americas. The African Union, the African Charter on Human and Peoples' Rights, and subregional organizations, such as the Economic Community of West African States, responded to rights violations and worked to support democratic governance in Africa. The Economic Community of West African States and the African Union even acquired the right to militarily intervene in their member states to enforce democratic norms. These delegations of authority combined with broader and more detailed prescriptions regarding human rights, democracy, and the rule of law, together with new mechanisms to promote and protect them. Regional organizations around the world followed a "global script" of regional postnational liberalism.[35] Although countries in Asia did not adopt a human rights treaty or a regional body to monitor and enforce protections, they responded to the broader normative context. The Association of Southeast Asian Nations, for example, formed an Intergovernmental Commission on Human Rights that, in turn, adopted a Human Rights Declaration.

Why Postnational Liberalism?

Why did Western states choose to use the end of the Cold War to make the LIO more intrusive rather than admitting new states first, allowing them to have a say on institutional reforms later? The short answer is: the states who had the preference to deepen the LIO had the power to do it. A fundamental change in the material and ideational distribution of power offered the United States and its Western allies the opportunity to transform the postwar LIO into a new form of postnational liberalism to anchor the adherence of formerly socialist and authoritarian states to liberal principles, at both the domestic and the international level.

Socialism as the only real alternative to liberalism, after fascism had been defeated in 1945, was discredited by the collapse of the Soviet Union. The rise of China had only started and seemed to be driven by a cautious opening toward economic liberalism. With liberalism left as the only game in town, the transatlantic partners saw no need to look for alternative world-ordering models.[36] They worked together in conveying liberal norms through reforming multilateral institutions, such as the United Nations and its specialized agencies, as well as the International Monetary Fund, the World Bank, and the World Trade Organization.[37] They also cooperated through new transatlantic initiatives developed during the 1990s under the first Bush and the Clinton administrations, such as the New Transatlantic Agenda to promote peace, democracy, and economic integration.[38]

The Western choice for deepening the LIO appears theoretically overdetermined. Realists argue that the end of the Cold War left the United States as the only superpower, using international institutions to expand its liberal hegemony.[39] Rational institutionalists explain the deepening of liberal multilateralism as the best way to promote security, peace, and prosperity, locking in the liberal transition of former socialist states and integrating them into existing alliances.[40] In a similar vein, sociological institutionalists emphasize the role of strong international institutions in socializing postsocialist states into liberal norms.[41]

The different theoretical approaches suggest a positive relationship between deepening and widening. By making the LIO more liberally intrusive, liberal states secure the admission of new members. This seemed all the more plausible as many states endorsed liberalism, with its promise to provide peace, prosperity, and freedom. The end of the Cold War saw a third wave of democratization,[42] which got anchored in the LIO.[43] The demise of the Soviet Union as the major antiliberal power in 1991 caused a major boost in membership in liberal international institutions.

At the same time, the deepening of the LIO had two major implications for its further evolution. First, the scope of its widening turned out to be regional rather than global. Twenty-three postsocialist states, including fourteen former Soviet republics, joined liberal international institutions. Only five of them are not considered to be part of "wider Europe."[44] Two-thirds became members of the European Union to lock in their democratization[45] or successfully applied for a membership perspective (including the Western Balkans and, recently, Ukraine, Moldova, and Georgia). The European postsocialist countries account for 62 percent of the increase in the membership of the thirty-four international organizations included in Figure 10.1. Moreover, their membership is concentrated in four European and transatlantic organizations: the Council of Europe, the European Union, the OSCE, and NATO. The number of members in the Council of Europe more than doubled, from twenty-two in 1989 to forty-seven in 2007. And EU membership tripled, from nine to twenty-seven during the same period. The increase is less dramatic for the OSCE, since Central and Eastern European states had been founding members. NATO enlargement lagged a few years behind; while it had still sixteen members in 1998, it rapidly grew to twenty-eight by 2009. So the widening of the LIO pertains to its Western-dominated parts.

Second, the deepening of the LIO triggered a wave of contestations, not only from outside the West but also from within.[46] The postnational liberalism of the post–Cold War LIO has been less accommodating of states with diverse cultural, political, and economic backgrounds than the liberal multilateralism of the postwar LIO. The surge of Islamic fundamentalism, revisionism in Russia, the rise of China, and antiglobalization movements, as well as the proliferation of authoritarian populism in Europe and the United States, emerged as new (or renewed) challenges for liberal societies. These contestations also target the way liberal societies have chosen to organize their relations at the international level. They express and mobilize civilizational, religious, and ethnonationalist claims and have converged in the critique of a universal understanding of individual rights backed by strong international institutions, which interfere with the sovereignty of states in organizing their societies and economies. Borders are emphasized again, and the free movement of capital, goods, services, and people is increasingly challenged. In addition, diverse lifestyles (gender relations, multiculturalism, LGBTQI+) are dismissed as "unhealthy." All this is accompanied by a growing rejection of political authority beyond the nation-state, fueled by criticism of the use of double standards, for example, regarding military interventions, and the (continued) institutionalization of state inequality in the United Nations Security Council, the World Bank, or the International Monetary Fund.[47] The legitimacy of liberal international institutions protecting and promoting economic freedom, security, human rights, democracy, and the rule of law is called into question, and not only by autocratic regimes. In liberal democracies, nationalist and populist forces on the right and antiglobalist movements on the left target international institutions as well. They are united by their opposition against the liberal intrusiveness of the LIO that curbs popular sovereignty. Forcing states to open their borders to foreign trade, capital, and migrants, liberal international institutions circumscribe the capacities of (elected) governments to redistribute wealth and protect national culture.

While rejecting the liberal authority of international institutions, actors have chosen different strategies to contest the postnational LIO.[48] For reasons of scope, I focus on states that are relevant to the future of the LIO.

Russia and China equally reject the liberal core of the LIO, denouncing the idea of universal values and freedoms as a Western effort to dominate the world.[49] While sharing similar preferences for a less deep LIO, they differ in their power to pursue them. Both are nuclear powers and are permanent members of the United Nations Security Council. But their status as world powers has changed in opposite directions. While China is still on the rise and seeking to upgrade its position in the LIO, Russia has been on an accelerated decline, trying to retain the status of the superpower it once was.[50] Putin has increasingly opted for dissidence, the war of aggression against Ukraine being the most extreme form. Not only does the invasion of Ukraine violate core liberal principles of the LIO with regard to human rights and democracy; the prohibition of violence, collective self-determination, and rule-based multilateralism are central planks of the LIO and the Westphalian order, which have been supported by nonliberal states, including China. Putin's apparent rejection of any international authority puts China in a difficult spot.

Rather than pursuing its destruction or replacement by a nonliberal alternative, China has selectively engaged with the LIO[51] but also used its growing power to push back United States dominance and the liberal intrusiveness of the post–Cold War LIO.[52] Supported by other states, including Russia but also countries from the Global South, Beijing has insisted on the equal sovereignty of states, their territorial integrity, and noninterference in domestic affairs as the core principles of a truly global rule-based international order. It has argued that the liberal universalism of Western states prevents the globalization of the LIO since many states do not accept liberal democracy and market economy as the dominant script. The pushback strategy proved effective. For instance, humanitarian interventions must not only be authorized by the United Nations Security Council but require the consent of the affected sovereign state.[53]

Yet Putin's war of aggression against Ukraine violates precisely the core principles of a less liberal and more global Westphalian international order. China abstained in the vote on the United Nations Security Council resolution demanding an immediate end to Russia's aggression and the withdrawal of its troops from Ukraine. At the same time, China is one of the few countries that have not disavowed Russia over its war of aggression. While calling for an end of violence, Beijing has been highly critical of the unprecedented sanctions Western states are imposing on Russia.[54] It supports Russia's justification of the war[55] as a means to put an end to the U.S.-dominated world order and NATO expansion. While Chinese financial institutions appear to adhere to Western sanctions, China's foreign minister Wang Yi reaffirmed the cooperation framework Presidents Xi and Putin had signed during the Beijing Olympics.

Given its persistent power and liberal imprint, the United States has been the anchor of the LIO. At the same time, there has always been an ambivalence in its commitment. While supporting many reforms of the LIO, U.S. governments have also resorted to pushback, such as when the United States rejected the International Trade Organization already in 1950. The United States had been reluctant to fully commit itself to liberal internationalism.[56] A Wikipedia site lists more than forty international treaties since the end of World War II that the United States has either not signed at all, signed but not ratified, or simply withdrawn from.[57] This selective engagement also applies to the global human rights regime as the cornerstone of international political liberalism. The United States is a treaty partner of only five of the eighteen most important international human rights instruments, which puts it in the same category as China, Cuba, Saudi Arabia, and Iran. The United States is not party to the International Criminal Court either.[58] Withdrawal became the dominant strategy during the first Trump administration and seems to turn into outright dissidence after President Trump won a second term.

U.S. European allies have been grappling with growing contestations of postnational liberalism in their rows. In the early 1990s, France and Germany spearheaded the deepening of the European Union by building the European Community into an economic and monetary union as well as establishing a political union in which member states would at least pool their sovereignty on issues of internal and external security.[59] To prepare the European Union for the "big bang" Eastern enlargement, member states sought to agree on further reforms strengthening the authority of EU institutions by extending majority rule in the Council and by strengthening the role of the European Parliament and the European Court of Justice. This met increasing pushback, not only by the Euroskeptic United Kingdom but also by other member states concerned about their institutional weight in a widened European Union (e.g., Spain), on the one hand, and their sovereignty to decide on social and economic issues, on the other (e.g., France). The Lisbon Treaty of 2009 ultimately strengthened the liberal authority of the European Union by making majority rule, the co-decision powers of the European Parliament, and the judicial review of the European Court of Justice the default, only exempting security and defense and a few other sensitive areas. However, the euro crisis starting in 2009 and the mass influx of refugees in 2015 fueled contestations of the European Union's liberal intrusiveness forcing member states to cut state expenditures and accept refugees.[60] Lacking the power to push back the Maastricht criteria of fiscal austerity and the Schengen rules of non-refoulement, Greece, Italy, Hungary, and others resorted to withdrawal, refusing to comply with their liberal obligations under EU law. In a similar vein, the United Kingdom withdrew from the European Union altogether when it was no longer allowed to opt out of the (future) deepening of European integration. Whether withdrawal will revert to dismissal and dissidence will depend on the electoral success of populist parties. The Western European experience of curbing absolute sovereignty in exchange for peace and prosperity is not only contested by Eastern Europeans who obtained their freedom from socialism by regaining their sovereignty as states; populist left- and right-wing parties in EU founding states (Italy, France, Germany) reject the curbing of popular sovereignty by liberal international institutions as undemocratic and ineffective in reducing social inequality, regulating migration, fighting climate change, and managing pandemics. The war in Ukraine has made a future widening of the European Union more likely. Whether the accession of the Western Balkan and East European countries will be preceded by another deepening of the European Union, for example, by abolishing the unanimity requirement for security and defense policy, is, however, doubtful.

The wave of contestations of the LIO appears to have leveled its deepening and widening in the late 2010s (Figures 10.1 and 10.2). We would need to enlarge the sample of liberal international institutions to corroborate this trend. While membership has stagnated, it has not decreased. This may be an indication that the deepening of the LIO has been stopped by the contestations it caused. These contestations, however, have not (yet) triggered an exodus of states rejecting the growing liberal intrusiveness of the LIO. The United Kingdom (withdrawal from the European Union) and Russia (expulsion from the Council of Europe) are prominent but still isolated cases.[61] While withdrawal can be contagious, states are more reluctant to leave international organizations with a strong democratic membership.[62]

To sum up, the end of the Cold War saw both a deepening and a widening of the LIO. The deepening of the liberal authority of international institutions has been global. The widening of the LIO, in contrast, has been mostly regional, in the Western-dominated parts of the LIO, mostly driven by Eastern European states joining European and transatlantic liberal institutions to lock in their liberal transformation. Former socialist countries account for 20 percent of all new memberships in liberal international institutions since 1990. This may explain why the contestations of the deepening of the LIO in terms of its transformation from liberal multilateralism to postnational liberalism has not negatively affected its widening. While states have not left liberal international institutions in greater numbers, its deepening has not globalized the LIO either. It has become more regionalized and remains Western-dominated. But unlike its predecessor, the postnational LIO is anchored in Europe rather than the United States.[63]

Toward a Postliberal LIO?

The deepening of the LIO gave rise to not one but many contestations.[64] It is too early to tell how the differentiated wave of contestations will affect the globalization of the LIO. But the strategies of China and Russia as two major contestants of the LIO, on the one hand, and of the United States and its European allies as the main protagonists of the LIO, on the other, point to directions in which the LIO might be developing.

If China decided to stand with Russia, then pushing for a return to a less liberal, more Westphalian variety of the LIO would no longer be a credible strategy. At the same time, the liberal international economic order enabled China's rise in the first place. Its economic growth relies on international markets, and Beijing has joined and increasingly engaged with multilateral organizations.[65] China is party to most international agreements, and it arguably complies with them at least as much as the United States does outside of international civil and political rights.[66] Despite debates on decoupling,[67] Beijing has been seeking to move up rather than move out of global value chains.[68] Dissidence still seems too costly. A selective withdrawal is more likely. Similar to President Trump's "America First," Beijing could pull back from international agreements that it perceives as not serving Chinese interests because of their Western dominance or liberal intrusiveness.[69] If its attempts to reshape liberal international institutions, such as the World Trade Organization, the World Health Organization, or the United Nations, fail,[70] China might fall back on its strategy of "contested multilateralism"[71] and "cooperative counter-hegemony."[72] China's withdrawal (from parts of the LIO) could be fueled by the United States and Europe closing ranks to reform the LIO, restoring its Westphalian principles and deepening its liberal content, particularly with regard to democracy and the rule of law. Putin's war of aggression against Ukraine has reminded the West of how fragile liberal institutions can be when attacked by enemies. NATO has been vindicated as a defensive alliance and gained two new members. The European Union has promised membership to Ukraine, Moldova, and Georgia to support their democratization.

The protracted war in Ukraine with refugee flows and rising energy and food prices have fueled authoritarian populism in Europe and the United States. This could eventually bring to power governments pushing back the liberal intrusiveness of the LIO or withdrawing. But would the revoking of the post–Cold War deepening make the LIO more global? A weak(er) variety of the LIO might bring back contestants, including India, South Africa, and Brazil, which accept liberal authority but reject the way it is exercised by Western states and the international institutions they dominate, leading to exclusion and inequality. At the same time, however, a thin or postliberal

LIO 3.0 might lose political support among liberal reformers who seek a stronger protection of individual human rights, democracy, and the rule of law. Growing contestations of its liberal intrusiveness notwithstanding, the European Union appears to be the most likely defender of the current LIO. The majority of its member states are still committed to economic and political liberalism and rule-based multilateralism.[73] Yet to replace the United States as the anchor of the LIO not only takes preference but power to pursue preference. The European Union still lacks strategic autonomy with regard to its military capabilities, its energy security, and, arguably, its economy to act as a real leader of the free world. Moreover, its "soft power"[74] is undermined by the inconsistent adherence to its own liberal principles, both within and outside the European Union.

Rather than a multiplex international order, we might see regional fragmentation. Regional orders do not have to follow the liberal script of free markets and democracy. Yet without liberal internationalism encapsulating a commitment to the peaceful resolution of conflicts, rule-based multilateralism, and the willingness to solve global governance problems cooperatively, it is difficult to see how different orders will coexist peacefully and work together in ensuring peace and stability in the world.

Acknowledgments

I am grateful to Paula Martini, Julian Giera, and Isabel Teixeira Pearce for their research assistance. Research for this chapter is part of the Cluster of Excellence Contestations of the Liberal Script (EXC 2055), funded by the Deutsche Forschungsgemeinschaft (German Research Foundation) under Germany's Excellence Strategy.

Notes

1. Ikenberry 2020.
2. Fukuyama 1992.
3. I am grateful to John Ikenberry, Peter Trubowitz, Charly Kupchan, Mike Mastanduno, Hillary Apple, and Jonathan Kirshner, as well as the participants of the workshop "Rethinking the 1990s: Liberal World Order-Building in the Post–Cold War Era," in Princeton on October 14–15, 2022, for their helpful comments and suggestions.
4. On the concept of the liberal script, see Börzel and Zürn 2021; Börzel and Risse 2023.
5. Mearsheimer 2019.
6. Ikenberry 2011.
7. Johnston 2007.

8. Cf. Kelemen et al. 2014; Börzel et al. 2017.
9. Börzel and Zürn 2021.
10. Acharya 2017, 271.
11. The following draws on Börzel and Zürn 2021.
12. Diamond 2022.
13. Ikenberry and Trubowitz, this volume.
14. Cf. Lake et al. 2021.
15. International organizations are coded 0 when neither trade nor human rights is their primary purpose, 1 when either of them is their primary purpose, and 2 when both human rights and trade are major issues.
16. The International Authority Database uses a comprehensive coding scheme with more than 150 items to empirically capture the autonomy and bindingness dimensions for each policy function for 34 international organizations. The authority score is the weighted product of autonomy, bindingness, and policy scope, with a maximum of 10.25 for each organization. Figure 10.1 depicts the overall level of authority in the international system. The y-axis refers to the sum of authority of all 34 organizations, with 358.75 as the overall maximum. The x-axis describes the development of the values over time. The dotted line adds the authority scores of all coded international organizations (cf. Börzel and Zürn 2021).
17. Cf. Börzel and Zürn 2021.
18. International Authority Database, accessed May 3, 2022, https://www.wzb.eu/en/research/international-politics-and-law/global-governance/projects/international-authority-database.
19. There is a smaller jump after the turn of the millennium when the International Criminal Court resumed its work in 2002.
20. Ruggie 1983.
21. Kentikelenis et al. 2016.
22. The Organization for Economic Cooperation and Development had twenty founding members in 1961, and only four more joined in the three decades that followed.
23. Lake et al. 2021.
24. Narlikar, this volume.
25. Zarakol, this volume.
26. Krasner 1985.
27. Alston 1988.
28. Haas 1997, 19, 20.
29. Cf. Börzel and Peters 2019.
30. Welsh, this volume.
31. Abdelal 2007; Gerstle 2022, 141–188.
32. Cf. Moravcsik 1998, ch. 6; McNamara 1998.
33. For example, Schmidt and Thatcher 2013.
34. Zaun 2017.
35. Börzel and van Hüllen 2015.
36. Drezner, this volume.
37. Cf. Smith 2012.
38. Cf. Pollack and Shaffer 2001.
39. Mearsheimer 2019.
40. Ikenberry 2020.
41. Johnston 2007.
42. Huntington 1991.
43. Pevehouse 2005; Ginsburg 2005.
44. Kazakhstan, Kyrgyzstan, Tajikistan, Turkmenistan, and Uzbekistan.
45. Vachudova 2005.
46. Börzel and Zürn 2021.
47. Cf. Zürn 2018.
48. Cf. Börzel and Zürn 2021.
49. Kupchan 2012; McNally 2012.
50. Cox, this volume.
51. Kahler, this volume.
52. Börzel and Shaffer 2024.
53. Cf. Börzel and Zürn 2021.

54. García Herrero 2022.
55. See, e.g., RT 2022.
56. Eilstrup-Sangiovanni and Hofmann 2020, 1081–1082.
57. Wikipedia, accessed September 7, 2021, https://en.wikipedia.org/wiki/List_of_treaties_unsigned_or_unratified_by_the_United_States.
58. Deitelhoff 2009.
59. Moravcsik 1998.
60. Börzel 2016.
61. States have always withdrawn from international organizations but rarely in greater numbers.
62. Cf. Von Borzyskowski and Vabulas 2019.
63. Kupchan, this volume.
64. Cf. Börzel and Zürn 2021.
65. Chen 2016; Drezner 2019; Yang 2020.
66. Johnston 2019.
67. Wei 2019.
68. Custer et al. 2021.
69. Zhao, M. 2019; Zhao, S. 2022.
70. Kennedy 2017; Börzel and Shaffer 2024.
71. Morse and Keohane 2014.
72. Rodríguez and Rüland 2022; Ikenberry and Lim 2017; Drezner 2019.
73. Drezner, this volume.
74. Blechman 2004.

References

Abdelal, Rawi. 2007. *Capital Rules: The Construction of Global Finance.* Harvard University Press.

Acharya, Amitav. 2017. "After Liberal Hegemony: The Advent of a Multiplex World Order." *Ethics & International Affairs* 31 (3): 271–285.

Alston, Philip. 1988. "Making Space for New Human Rights: The Case of the Right to Development." *Harvard Human Rights Yearbook* 1: 3–40.

Blechman, Barry M. 2004. "Soft Power: the Means to Success in World Politics." *Political Science Quarterly* 119 (4): 680–682.

Börzel, Tanja A. 2016. "From EU Governance of Crisis to Crisis in EU Governance: Regulatory Failure, Redistributive Conflict, and Eurosceptic Publics." *Journal of Common Market Studies: The JCMS Annual Review of the European Union in 2015* 54 (S1): 8–23.

Börzel, Tanja A., Antoaneta Dimitrova, and Frank Schimmelfennig, eds. 2017. "European Union Enlargement and Integration Capacity." Special issue, *Journal of European Public Policy* 24 (2).

Börzel, Tanja A., and Ingo Peters. 2019. "An International Relations Perspective on Strengthening the Legal Framework of the OSCE." In *The Legal Framework of the OSCE*, edited by Mateja Platise Steinbrück, Carolyn Moser, and Anne Peters. Cambridge University Press.

Börzel, Tanja A., and Thomas Risse. 2023. "The Liberal Script between Individual and Collective Self-Determination." Working Paper No. 26. Berlin: Cluster of Excellence 2055 "Contestations of the Liberal Script (SCRIPTS)."

Börzel, Tanja A., and Gregory Shaffer. 2024. "The Transatlantic Community and China in the Age of Disruption: Partners, Competitors, Rivals." In *From Partners to Adversaries: The Transatlantic Community and China in the Age of Great Power Rivalry*, edited by Dan Hamilton and Joe Renouard. Routledge.

Börzel, Tanja A., and Vera van Hüllen, eds. 2015. *Governance Transfer by Regional Organizations: Patching Together a Global Script.* Palgrave Macmillan.

Börzel, Tanja A., and Michael Zürn. 2021. "Contestations of the Liberal International Order from Liberal Multilateralism to Postnational Liberalism." *International Organization* 75 (2): 282–305.

Chen, Zhimin. 2016. "China, the European Union and the Fragile World Order." *Journal of Common Market Studies* 54 (4): 775–792.

Correlates of War Project. 2017. "State System Membership List, v2016." Accessed May 3, 2022. http://correlatesofwar.org.

Custer, Samantha, Justin Schon, Ana Horigoshi, Divya Mathew, Bryan Burgess, Vera Choo, et al. 2021. *Corridors of Power: How Beijing Uses Economic, Social, and Network Ties to Exert Influence along the Silk Road.* AidData; William & Mary.

Deitelhoff, Nicole. 2009. "The Discursive Process of Legalization: Charting Islands of Persuasion in the ICC Case." *International Organization* 63 (1): 33–65.

Drezner, Daniel W. 2019. "Counter-Hegemonic Strategies in the Global Economy." *Security Studies* 28 (3): 505–531.

Eilstrup-Sangiovanni, Mette, and Stephanie C. Hofmann. 2020. "Of the Contemporary Global Order, Crisis, and Change." *Journal of European Public Policy* 27 (7): 1077–1089.

Fukuyama, Francis. 1992. *The End of History and the Last Man.* Avon Books.

García Herrero, Alicia. 2022. "China Can Offer Only an Immediate Respite for the Russian Economy." New Perspectives on Global & European Dynamics, March 30. https://globaleurope.eu/globalization/china-can-only-offer-an-immediate-respite-for-the-russian-economy/.

Gerstle, Gary. 2022. *The Rise and Fall of the Neoliberal Order: America and the World in the Free Market Era.* Oxford University Press.

Ginsburg, Tom. 2005. "Locking in Democracy: Constitutions, Commitment, and International Law." *New York University Journal of International Law & Politics* 38: 707–759.

Haas, Ernst B. 1997. *Nationalism, Liberalism and Progress*: Vol. 1. *The Rise and Decline of Nationalism.* Cornell University Press.

Huntington, Samuel P. 1991. *The Third Wave: Democratization in the Late Twentieth Century.* University of Oklahoma Press.

Ikenberry, G. John. 2011. *Liberal Leviathan: The Origins, Crisis, and Transformation of the American World Order.* Princeton University Press.

Ikenberry, G. John. 2020. *A World Safe for Democracy: Liberal Internationalism and the Crises of Global Order.* Yale University Press.

Ikenberry, G. John, and Darren J. Lim. 2017. *China's Emerging Institutional Statecraft: The Asian Infrastructure Investment Bank and the Prospects for Counter-Hegemony.* Brookings Institution.

Johnston, Alastair Ian. 2007. *Social States: China in International Institutions, 1980–2000.* Princeton University Press.

Kelemen, R. Daniel, Anand Menon, and Jonathan Slapin, eds. 2014. "The European Union: Wider and Deeper?" Special issue, *Journal of European Public Policy* 21 (5).

Kennedy, Scott. 2017. *Global Governance and China: The Dragon's Learning Curve.* Routledge.

Kentikelenis, Alexander E., Thomas H. Stubbs, and Lawrence P. King. 2016. "IMF Conditionality and Development Policy Space, 1985–2014." *Review of International Political Economy* 23 (4): 543–582.

Krasner, Stephen D. 1985. *Structural Conflict: The Third World against Global Liberalism.* University of California Press.

Kupchan, Charles A. 2012. *No One's World: The West, the Rising Rest and the Coming Global Turn.* Oxford University Press.

Lake, David A., Lisa L. Martin, and Thomas Risse. 2021. "Challenges to the Liberal Order: Reflections on International Organization." *International Organization* 75 (2): 225–257.

McNally, Christopher A. 2012. "Sino-Capitalism: China's Reemergence and the International Political Economy." *World Politics* 64 (4): 741–776.

McNamara, Kathleen R. 1998. *The Currency of Ideas: Monetary Politics in the European Union.* Cornell University Press.

Mearsheimer, John J. 2019. "Bound to Fail: The Rise and Fall of the Liberal International Order." *International Security* 43 (4): 7–50.

Moravcsik, Andrew. 1998. *The Choice for Europe: Social Purpose and State Power from Rome to Maastricht.* Cornell University Press.

Morse, Julia C., and Robert O. Keohane. 2014. "Contested Multilateralism." *Review of International Organizations* 9 (4): 385–412.

Diamond, Larry Jay. 2022. "What China Wants." American Purpose. https://www.americanpurpose.com/articles/what-china-wants/.

Pevehouse, Jon C. 2005. *Democracy from Above: Regional Organizations and Democratization.* Cambridge University Press.

Pollack, Mark, and Gregory Shaffer. 2001. *Transatlantic Governance in the Global Economy.* Rowman & Littlefield.

Rodríguez, Fabricio, and Jürgen Rüland. 2022. "Cooperative Counter-Hegemony, Interregionalism and 'Diminished Multilateralism': The Belt and Road Initiative and China's Relations with Latin America and the Caribbean (LAC)." *Journal of International Relations and Development* 25 (2): 476–496.

RT. 2022. "Russia Seeks to End US-Dominated World Order—Lavrov." April 11. https://www.rt.com/russia/553674-lavrov-military-operation-us-dominance/.

Ruggie, John G. 1983. "International Regimes, Transactions, and Change: Embedded Liberalism in the Post-War Economic Order." In *International Regimes*, edited by Stephen D. Krasner. Cornell University Press.

Schmidt, Vivien A., and Mark Thatcher. 2013. *Resilient Liberalism in Europe's Political Economy.* Cambridge University Press.

Smith, Tony. 2012. *America's Mission: The United States and the Worldwide Struggle for Democracy.* Vol. 139. Expanded ed. Princeton University Press.

Vachudova, Milada Anna. 2005. *Europe Undivided: Democracy, Leverage and Integration after Communism.* Oxford University Press.

Von Borzyskowski, Inken, and Felicity Vabulas. 2019. "Hello, Goodbye. When Do States Withdraw from International Organizations." *Review of International Organizations* 14 (2): 335–366.

Wei, Li. 2019. "Towards Economic Decoupling? Mapping Chinese Discourse on the China-US Trade War." *Chinese Journal of International Politics* 12 (4): 519–556.

Yang, Suzanne Xiao. 2020. "Complexity in China's Current Role in Multilateral Orders." *China International Strategy Review* 2 (2): 288–305.

Zaun, Natascha. 2017. *EU Asylum Policies: The Power of Strong Regulating States.* Palgrave Macmillan.

Zhao, Minghao. 2019. "Is a New Cold War Inevitable? Chinese Perspectives on US–China Strategic Competition." *The Chinese Journal of International Politics* 12 (3): 371–394.

Zhao, Suisheng. 2022. "The US-China Rivalry in the Emerging Bipolar World: Hostility, Alignment, and Power Balance." *Journal of Contemporary China* 31 (134): 169–185.

Zürn, Michael. 2018. *A Theory of Global Governance: Authority, Legitimation and Contestation.* Oxford University Press.

11
The Liberal Order Reconsidered
Europe, the United States, and the Missteps of the 1990s

Charles A. Kupchan

The challenges that have of late confronted the liberal international order have their roots in the liberal overreach of the 1990s. In the aftermath of the Cold War, the Western democracies collectively embraced an expansive economic, social, and geopolitical ambition that would eventually come back to haunt them. They placed unwarranted confidence in the staying power of the brand of democratic capitalism that prevailed against communist and autocratic alternatives and in the universal appeal of the West's liberal ideals. As a consequence, the West focused much more heavily on expanding the liberal order than on protecting and deepening its own liberal institutions and practices. In so doing, the Western democracies erred. Not only did the liberal order fail to globalize, but it also eroded from within. While automation and digitalization were undermining the social contract of the industrial era, neoliberal orthodoxy stood in the way of the policies that could have mitigated the economic duress. Automation and digitalization were the product of unstoppable forces of technological advance. But neoliberal orthodoxy was a policy choice. And because it exposed workers to the full brunt of the socioeconomic changes wrought by technological advance, it was a policy choice that ultimately had fateful political consequences. The overreach of the early post–Cold War years set the stage for the illiberal populism that has of late afflicted democratic societies on both sides of the Atlantic.

The United States bears more responsibility for this state of affairs than does Europe. To be sure, the European Union embarked on hugely ambitious projects over the course of the 1990s, encouraged to do so by the collapse of the Soviet Union and the opportunity to extend eastward markets, democratic practices, and collective governance. Yet the grand undertakings aimed at simultaneously deepening and widening the EU, even if ambitious by design, ended up being modest by default. They all ran up against pushback from member states uneasy with the prospect of a union that risked becoming too supranational and too big.

With the advantage of hindsight, it appears to have been a blessing in disguise that member states put the brakes on the EU's grand ambition. A more modest agenda, one that has broadly kept the EU's level of ambition in synch with public attitudes while defending Europe's social contract, has sustained the support of Europe's diverse citizenry. As a result, continental Europe has in critical respects weathered the illiberal turn far more ably than the United States or the United Kingdom. Indeed, if the world still has a reliable bastion of liberal order, it is the EU. While the United States and Britain struggle with polarization, populism, and political dysfunction, the EU's political center has—with notable exceptions in Hungary, Italy, and Poland—held; political centrism dominates decision-making in EU institutions as well as in the governments of most member states. Only time will tell whether Europe's political center will continue to hold; recent elections in France and Germany provide ample cause for concern. But at least for now, the EU remains a steadier defender of a liberal, rules-based international order than its Anglo-American partners.

In the meantime, the United States continues to suffer from the repercussions of the liberal overreach that began in the 1990s. Neoliberal orthodoxy guided the nation's economic policies at home and abroad, with the advance of the digital era and globalization ultimately disadvantaging many working Americans. America's costly "forever wars" in the Middle East produced little good, while Washington's efforts to expand the U.S.-led liberal order, which included hopes of democratizing Russia and China, not only fell far short but also provoked ire in Moscow and Beijing. Along the way, the United States regularly sought to convince Europeans to pursue together expansive ambitions—sometimes succeeding, at other times triggering pushback. The United Kingdom most regularly joined the United States in overreaching, one of the reasons it now joins the United States in suffering some of the most pronounced consequences.

Liberal overreach set the stage for a sharp political backlash in the United States that is manifested in the twin presidencies of Donald Trump. Trump's pivot to an "America First" strategy represented a radical and dangerous shift that fully exposed the domestic vulnerability of the U.S.-led liberal order. President Joe Biden then sought to address the electoral discontent that animated Trump's rise, scaling back neoliberal policies at home, increasing domestic investment and turning to industrial policy to channel both public and private spending. He also pursued a "foreign policy for the middle class" and sought to rebuild domestic support for liberal internationalism, rebuilding alliances and investing in multilateralism. But Biden enjoyed limited success in pulling off his course correction; the nation's deep political divides were on full show during the 2024 presidential campaign—and Trump was back in the Oval Office early in 2025. "America First" 2.0 proved even more disruptive than its earlier version.

This chapter begins by exploring the European side of the equation, chronicling how the EU found its way to more modest ambitions through default, not design. I then widen the aperture to the United States, making the case that Washington was the main driver of the liberal overreach of the transatlantic community that began in the 1990s.

Europe: Overreach by Design, Modesty by Default

The 1990s was a decade of grand visions and grand projects for Europe. In the aftermath of the Cold War and the implosion of the Soviet Union, the EU pursued an ambitious agenda for both deepening and widening the union. The European Community completed the construction of a single market in 1993—formally becoming the EU—and then proceeded to introduce a single currency in 1999. The Schengen Agreement of 1995 secured the free movement of people across the EU's internal borders. The EU opened its doors to Europe's new democracies, in the mid-1990s launching accession negotiations with numerous countries that were once part of the Soviet bloc—a process that guided and incentivized the aspirants' transitions to democracy and capitalism. The union had twelve members when it formally became the EU in 1993; today there are twenty-seven member states, with more in line to join. The EU aimed to enhance its geopolitical heft, developing a European Security and Defense Policy that was to enable member states to aggregate their capability and pursue common foreign and defense policies. This ambitious agenda, and progress in advancing it, led many observers, including this author, to foresee "the rise of Europe" and to claim that the EU is "an emerging pole . . . because it is coming together."[1]

Looking back, that assessment proved to be overly bullish—but also to contain important elements of truth. Europe *has* emerged as an essential anchor of the liberal order. In this second decade of the twenty-first century, Europe is in many respects in better political health, and a more steady defender of the liberal order, than either the United States or the United Kingdom. It was not without good reason that German chancellor Angela Merkel was dubbed "the leader of the free world" while Trump pursued his "America First" agenda and Britain engaged in a stunning act of self-isolation and self-harm by quitting the EU. Germany, aided and abetted by its EU partners, was indeed holding down the liberal fort. Currently under the leadership of Chancellor Friedrich Merz, Germany's center continues to hold – at least for now.

Paradoxically, the EU is in reasonably good shape as an anchor of the liberal order, not because it realized the grand projects of the 1990s but because it fell short. To be sure, the EU did make considerable progress on both deepening and widening. But that progress also produced an incremental political backlash; the EU's ambitious agenda ultimately ran into staunch resistance from member states and their citizens. These "natural" political barriers ultimately forced the EU to curb its ambition and scale back the scope of its vision for a wider, more integrated, and more geopolitical union. This modesty has proved to be a winning formula, endowing the union with a significant measure of political and social resilience.

Yes, illiberal populism and anti-immigrant sentiment have been gaining ground in many member states. Of particular concern is the uncertain prospects for France's political center to continue prevailing against the country's far right. But at least so far, the EU has benefited from the moderation imposed on it by its semi-sovereign member states. Europe did succeed in advancing its four main projects of the 1990s: the introduction of a single currency, the free movement of people within the union (Schengen), the formal enlargement of the union, and the acquisition of geopolitical heft. Notably, however, cautious member states and electorates wary of neoliberal and supranational excesses checked the scope of these projects and their potential for overreach.

The launch of the euro stands out as one of the EU's most notable success stories of the 1990s. The Maastricht Treaty (1988) laid out plans for the introduction of a single currency. The euro was introduced on January 1, 1999, and nineteen of twenty-seven members have since joined the eurozone. The launch of the euro had economic objectives, which included encouraging trade and investment and eliminating exchange rate uncertainty. It also had political objectives: tightening the union and giving it a stronger collective identity. As Chancellor Helmut Kohl put it in 1996 as he made the case for monetary union, "In reality, the policy of European integration comes down to the question of whether we have war or peace in the twenty-first century."[2]

Yet despite its success, the euro came with serious design flaws. Monetary union did not entail fiscal union and the more centralized governing institutions that usually accompany a single currency—and facilitate its smooth functioning. Member states were unwilling to countenance further economic convergence and a level of integration that would have exposed Europe's brand of social democracy to further market liberalization. As discussed below, EU member states have maintained more robust social protections and less pronounced income inequalities than their Anglo-American partners.

Such limitations allowed monetary union to proceed, but they also set the stage for serious disruptions, including the financial crisis that ensued after 2008, which nearly led to the breakup of the eurozone and did lead to lasting political tension between the stronger EU economies of the north and the more vulnerable economies of the southern tier (Greece, Italy, and Spain). Germany and other northern economies were reluctant to deepen union in ways that would have entailed greater taxpayer exposure to collective debt. Populist, Euroskeptic parties (such as Syriza in Greece, the Five Star Movement in Italy, Fidesz in Hungary, Vox in Spain) capitalized on the economic dislocation and have played a role in checking the EU's aspirations of deeper union. The Italian government that took power in 2022 is led by the hard-right Brothers of Italy, a nationalist party determined to push back against what it considers to be the EU's overreach. Europe's success in launching a single currency also set in motion political forces that have arrested the union's further deepening.

The implementation of the Schengen agreement has gone through a similar trajectory of effective implementation—followed by political backlash. The opening of the EU's internal borders advanced the union's commitment to the free flow of goods, capital, services, and people. It was an unequivocal success, clearing the way for the liberalization of migration within the union and producing a substantial relocation of workers. Migration was especially high from the new member states to "Old Europe," where more jobs and higher wages were available. As of 2015, nearly 20 million EU citizens resided in a member state other than the one in which they were born. Countries with the highest number of migrants from other EU members include Germany (5.3 million), the United Kingdom (2.9 million), and

France (2.3 million). Countries with the highest number of migrants to other EU members include Poland (3.5 million) and Romania (3 million).[3]

Yet Schengen's success in facilitating internal migration also produced negative political repercussions, ultimately prompting the EU to scale back its liberalizing ambition. Indeed, the migrant flows prompted by Schengen played a significant role in sinking the EU's efforts to constitutionalize its rules-based order. Beginning in 2001, a European Convention drafted a Constitutional Treaty intended to replace the EU's existing treaties and deepen integration. The text was finalized in 2004, thereafter requiring ratification by member states to take effect.

Eighteen member states ratified the Constitution—but referenda in France and the Netherlands then shot it down. The influx of migrants from new members to old figured prominently in the outcomes of the French and Dutch votes. Public resentment toward the "Polish plumber"—a symbol of the cheap labor allegedly taking jobs from French workers—was arguably the dominant concern convincing the French electorate to vote down the Constitution.[4] The Dutch also rejected the Constitution due in large part to concern about immigration. These votes brought to a close Europe's efforts to constitutionalize its order, demonstrating the limits of popular enthusiasm for ceding more sovereignty to collective governance.

The backlash against Schengen was hardly over with the failure of the Constitution. Popular discontent with immigration rose dramatically in response to the wave of refugees that arrived in the EU during 2015, many of them from Syria and Afghanistan. Berlin pushed the EU to welcome these migrants, with Germany alone hosting over 1 million. But the largess promptly produced a counterreaction and an about-face in policy. Member states temporarily put up internal border controls to manage the flow of migrants and engaged in a bitter dispute about plans for the "fair" distribution of asylum seekers across the EU. A deal on the distribution of migrants failed to materialize. Eventually, the EU effectively turned to an informal brand of bribery—one inconsistent with international norms and its own liberal values—to convince Turkey and Libya to prevent migrants from transiting to the union.

The migrant crisis of 2015 also had quite consequential ripple effects over the longer term. Right-wing populists across Europe have embraced strong anti-immigrant rhetoric and policies. Hard-right parties either have governed or currently govern Hungary, Italy, and Poland, while mainstream parties have adopted more anti-immigrant platforms in many other member states. Discomfort with immigration was arguably the decisive issue enabling the "leave" camp to prevail in the 2016 referendum that led to the United Kingdom's exit from the EU.[5]

In short, Schengen worked so well that it ultimately produced a sharp pullback from the liberalizing ambition of the 1990s. The EU put the brakes on immigration to avert a potentially fatal wave of defections—but not before losing the United Kingdom as a member and contravening its commitment to adhere to a rules-based international regime for managing migration.

The EU's enlargement policy followed a similar trajectory. It was initially an unequivocal success, with the admission of Europe's new democracies beginning in 2004. Meeting the requirements for entry helped aspirant countries undertake onerous economic and political reforms. The allure of entry continues to run strong among numerous European nations that have not yet qualified for entry, augmenting the EU's influence in its eastern neighborhood. In the Balkans, the EU is using the prospect of membership to encourage normalization of relations between Serbia and Kosovo. The EU granted Ukraine candidate status in July 2022 in no small part as a sign of support and a message of encouragement amid the country's efforts to defend itself against Russian aggression.

But as with the EU's other grand projects born in the 1990s, enlargement has produced a political backlash. The inclusion of a large number of new members should have been preceded by institutional reforms aimed at facilitating decision-making; widening necessitated further deepening. As Germany's foreign minister, Joschka Fischer, put it in 2000, a bigger EU creates "the need for decisive, appropriate institutional reform so that the Union's capacity to act is maintained even after enlargement."[6] Nonetheless, the necessary deepening has not been forthcoming—in part because of the popular backlash against the grand ambitions of the 1990s. Accordingly, a larger union has made the union more unwieldy; building consensus among twenty-seven nations at different stages of economic and political development has proved uniquely challenging. In addition, the EU has found it extremely difficult to sanction members that backslide on democracy after joining; Brussels unsuccessfully struggled to address the illiberal practices of governments in Hungary and Poland. So, too, has enlargement contributed to the backlash against internal migration discussed above.

As Hilary Appel notes in her chapter in this volume, enlargement and the process of accession is not the cause of the rise of Euroskeptic and illiberal sentiment among new members in Eastern Europe. However, older members have experienced "enlargement fatigue" and a decided diminishment in political enthusiasm for further enlargement. France, in particular, has begun to slow-roll enlargement, with President Emmanuel Macron effectively putting on indefinite hold enlargement in the Balkans. Although Ukraine now enjoys candidate status, Macron has made clear that it may take "decades" for the country to actually join the EU. Indeed, Paris has advanced the idea of a two-tier Europe that would enable the EU to institutionalize cooperation with European countries that will not be offered membership any time soon—if ever. In October 2022, Macron launched the forty-four-nation European Political Community, his brainchild for pursuing this two-tier structure. The very success of enlargement has effectively brought enlargement to a crawl, if not a halt.

Europe's effort to emerge as a geopolitical heavyweight represents the one arena where the ambitious vision of the 1990s effectively failed to ever get off the ground. Europeans sought to take the diplomatic and military lead as Yugoslavia began its bloody breakup. In 1991, Jacques Poos, the president of the European Council, announced that "the hour of Europe has dawned."[7] But European efforts fell tragically short; it took U.S.-led NATO missions and U.S.-led diplomacy to bring to a close the bloodshed that engulfed the Balkans in the 1990s.

Having failed to meet its own expectations in the Balkans, the EU in 1999 redoubled efforts to build geopolitical muscle, formally launching its European Security and Defense Policy and establishing the high representative for common foreign and security policy—an embryonic EU foreign minister. As France's president Jacques Chirac stated at the time, "The European Union itself [must] become a major pole of international equilibrium, endowing itself with the instruments of a true power."[8] These efforts continued into the next decade. The European Defense Agency was established in 2004 to facilitate defense cooperation among member states. The Lisbon Treaty, which materialized after the failed push for a constitution and took effect in 2009, established the External Action Service, providing the high representative a dedicated diplomatic corps. The Lisbon Treaty also laid the foundation for "structured permanent cooperation," a mechanism that would enable coalitions of the willing within the EU to deepen integration on matters of defense. The European Defense Fund (EDF) was created to support collaboration among member states on defense research and production. Macron has been particularly vocal on the need for Europe to develop "strategic autonomy," with Paris calling for the establishment of a European rapid reaction force.

To be sure, the EU has succeeded in enhancing its collective diplomatic voice. Backed by an External Action Service of some four thousand employees, the high representative has acquired greater influence over time, playing, for example, a prominent role in negotiations over Iran's nuclear program. Progress on defense cooperation, however, has been far more halting. Since Britain is one of Europe's most militarily capable countries, its departure from the union set back the EU's geopolitical aspirations. And even amid the war in Ukraine, many member states have moved slowly to increase defense spending to NATO's 2 percent of GDP benchmark (which was raised to 5 percent at the 2025 NATO summit) or to pool sovereignty on defense procurement and policy. The war in Ukraine, coupled with uncertainty about Trump's commitment to European security, is providing new momentum behind efforts to strengthen Europe's military heft. But national defense remains a redoubt of national sovereignty; the EU's geopolitical ambitions and capabilities will take time to evolve.

Europe has thus fallen far short of realizing the grand visions of the 1990s. European electorates effectively rebuffed the efforts of EU leaders to strengthen supranational governance in the service of building a union that would be deeper, larger, more open, and more geopolitically ambitious. With the advantage of hindsight, however, the setbacks to European aspirations were a blessing in disguise, preventing institutional overreach that ultimately may have been the EU's undoing. Instead, Europe today is the most solid bulwark of the liberal, rules-based order. Member states kept a watchful eye on the political limits of integration, scaling back ambition and protecting their brand of social democracy in order to meet the needs of and safeguard the support of their citizens.

To be sure, the story is not over. Recent elections in Italy, political gyrations in Great Britain, the erosion of the political center in France and Germany, the sustained appeal of illiberal populism across the union—these developments do not augur well, especially against the backdrop of high inflation and energy insecurity, both of which have been exacerbated by the war in Ukraine. Nonetheless, given the self-limiting nature of Europe's liberalizing ambition, the United States emerged as the major driver of the West's overreach during the critical decade of the 1990s.

The United States: The Overconfidence and Overreach of the 1990s

The global setting of the 1990s bred overconfidence and overreach on both sides of the Atlantic—but both were more pronounced in the United States than in Europe. That reaction to end of the Cold War was not without reason. The West had prevailed against the Soviet bloc, which had imploded without the large-scale violence that usually accompanies imperial collapse. After Iraq invaded Kuwait in 1990, a U.S.-led coalition of over thirty nations formed, easily defeating Iraqi forces once Operation Desert Storm began in early 1991. The U.S. economy was booming, fueled in part by a dot-com bubble that produced a 400 percent increase in the technology-heavy Nasdaq index between 1995 and 2000. Democratization proceeded apace not just among countries formerly part of the Soviet bloc but also in the Global South. To be sure, episodes of bloodshed in the Balkans, Rwanda, East Timor, and elsewhere were not infrequent. Nonetheless, the arc of history seemed to be definitively bending toward greater freedom, justice, and prosperity.

The pronouncements of public intellectuals captured the prevailing mood. Francis Fukuyama famously predicted a Hegelian "end of history."[9] Charles Krauthammer pronounced the opening of the "unipolar moment," asserting that "the center of world power is the unchallenged superpower, the United States, attended by its Western allies."[10] Thomas Friedman proclaimed the arrival of new era of commercial peace, with globalization establishing itself as the world's new "North Star": "The free market is the only ideological alternative left. One road. Different speeds. But one road." States that refused to play by the rules of globalization would become "roadkill" on the global investment highway. Those that played by its rules would enjoy the benefits of prosperity and peace. "When a country reaches a level of economic development where it has a middle class big enough to support a McDonald's network, it becomes a McDonald's country. And people in McDonald's countries don't like to fight wars anymore, they prefer to wait in line for burgers."[11]

This political narrative and the accompanying atmosphere of triumphalism contributed to unwarranted belief in the staying power and universal appeal of the liberal order. The United States, along with its Western allies, misjudged the domestic strength of their own liberal institutions and practices; they focused on expanding the liberal order when they should have been protecting and deepening its foundations. Moreover, expanding the liberal order proved far more difficult and elusive than expected. In the end, the liberal order failed to globalize while simultaneously eroding from within. Academic as well as political debate was misled by ideological ambition, producing polices that were insufficiently mindful of the contingent nature of historical development.

Four specific ideological/political dispositions played a particularly important role in fueling the overconfidence and overreach that began in the 1990s: (1) the ascendance of neoliberal orthodoxy, (2) the presumed convergence of modernities, (3) the idealist displacement of realist sobriety, and (4) the neglect of the domestic underpinnings of liberal internationalism.

The Anglo-American Model: The Excesses of Neoliberal Orthodoxy

The West's most consequential misstep during the early post–Cold War era was the failure to foresee the potential erosion of the liberal order from within. The polarization, dysfunction, and illiberalism that have afflicted leading democracies were unthinkable in the 1990s. The success of the free market undergirded the West's triumph—but it also masked the degree to which neoliberal orthodoxy was contributing to the political frailty of liberal democracy.

George Will wrote in 1991, "[T]he Cold War is over, and the University of Chicago won it."[12] Especially in the United States, the end of the Cold War solidified the political consensus behind market orthodoxy. As Jonathan Kirshner details in his chapter in this volume, the ascent of neoliberalism was long in the making, but its dominance of public policy was solidified during the 1990s. Maximizing economic efficiency crowded out concern about the distributional effects of fiscal, monetary, and trade policy. Deregulation fostered competition and lowered prices—but often at the expense of workers. The deregulation of the financial industry may have raised corporate profits, but it also made possible the subprime mortgage crisis that devastated many working families. Free trade increased international commerce, expanded global prosperity, and improved corporate balance sheets and stock prices. But many workers, particularly in the manufacturing sector, have been on the losing end of globalization. The programs needed to buffer workers against automation and globalization were either nonexistent or underfunded. Harold James describes a similar version of this story in his chapter in this volume, noting that the collapse of the Soviet bloc undercut the need for a social democratic alternative to communism, effectively ending the era of class compromise in the United States.

The excesses of neoliberal orthodoxy have been more pronounced in the United States and Britain than in the EU, which has defended its traditional brand of social democracy. The member states of the EU have far more generous social safety nets than do the United States and the United Kingdom. The EU's more extensive welfare systems and higher levels of government spending ease electoral disaffection by cushioning the impact of automation and de-industrialization, financial crises, and pandemic-related economic disruptions. The United States spends around 19 percent of GDP on social welfare, whereas France, Germany, Italy, Sweden, and other large EU countries all spend over 25 percent.[13] In the United States, cash transfers represent 9 percent of national income, whereas Europeans spend 23 percent of national income on cash transfer payments.[14]

Income inequality follows a similar pattern. The average income of the top 10 percent of Americans is seventeen times higher than the bottom 50 percent, whereas in Europe the comparable figure ranges from six to ten times higher.[15] Inequality in the United States has risen dramatically in recent decades. In the 1970s, the top 10 percent of American earners took home 31 percent of real income. In 2016, the top 10 percent took home almost 50 percent of real income.[16] During the industrial boom after World War II, the largest employer in the United States was General Motors, and GM's average hourly wage in current dollars was roughly $30.[17] Today the largest employer in the United States is Walmart, and its average hourly wage is roughly half that.[18] Many working Americans find it hard to make ends meet and face few opportunities for upward mobility. As Daron Acemoglu notes, "In the United States, real (inflation adjusted) incomes at the bottom and middle of the distribution have hardly increased since 1980."[19]

As Britain has scaled back its welfare state and liberalized fiscal, monetary, and trade policy, it has followed a similar socioeconomic trajectory to that of the United States. On basic indicators of social spending and inequality, the United Kingdom generally lies between the United States and the EU. For example, the Gini coefficient (an overall measure of inequality) stands at roughly .31 for the EU, .45 for the United States, and .35 for the United Kingdom.[20]

The EU's greater reliance on economic regulation also contrasts with the Anglo-American preference for minimal regulatory oversight. The EU's General Data Protection Regulation, which was finalized in 2015, represents the world's toughest data regulation legislation. It safeguards personal data and limits corporate collection and sharing of consumers' online activity. In 2022, the EU passed the Digital Markets Act, which targets anticompetition practices among technology companies. The member states also adopted the Digital Services Act, which regulates social media platforms and requires technology companies to delete illicit content, such as hate speech and terrorist propaganda.

In contrast, the United States has not passed a single piece of legislation regulating technology companies. Banking systems in the United States and the United Kingdom are also more lightly regulated than in the EU, enhancing profitability but also making more likely the excesses that can trigger financial crises.

These contrasts between the Anglo-American and European trajectories are reinforced by differences in their political systems. The United States and Britain are dominated by two main parties, meaning that disaffected voters on the left and right pull traditionally centrist parties toward the ideological extremes; the Anglo-American center has not held. In contrast, the EU is dominated by multiparty systems, enabling disgruntled voters to gravitate to antiestablishment parties. Mainstream center-left and center-right have lost market share, but they have stayed in the political center and, for the most part, remained in power; the EU's political center, at least for now, has held.

In addition, the United States and the United Kingdom have strong libertarian traditions and cultures, which can make politically difficult the attenuation of sovereignty and the restrictions on freedom of action that accompany adherence to the norms of liberal multilateralism. The United States was doggedly unilateralist from the founding era until World II; the multilateral turn that began in the 1940s is the exception, not the rule.[21] Indeed, support for institutionalized multilateralism is today much weaker than it was during the second half of the twentieth century. The United Kingdom has followed a similar trajectory, with its departure from the EU in part about a reassertion of sovereignty.

Automation, digitalization, and globalization make for a toxic brew when coupled with the excesses of neoliberal orthodoxy. In both the United States and the United Kingdom, economic insecurity and the perceived status decline of majority populations open the door to identity politics. Illiberal populists tend to rally support through the politics of grievance, which intermixes racial, anti-immigrant, and cultural tropes with promises of material improvement. Unregulated media platforms provide fertile ground for ideological polarization and the mobilization of angry electorates. Divisive debates intensify over social issues, including abortion, gay rights, school curricula, and race relations.

In the United States, ideological polarization and the erosion of the political center have been long in the making, culminating in Trump's combative politics, his efforts to overturn his electoral defeat, the violent siege of the U.S. Capitol on January 6, 2021, and his reelection in 2024. Biden's effort to govern in the center and restore bipartisan comity fell short, doing little to ease deep political cleavage. Helpful remedies are not difficult to identify, but they are mostly out of reach due to the very system of checks and balances put in place to sustain republican freedom. Large-scale investment aimed at improving the lives of working Americans is unable to pass legislative muster. The same goes for electoral reform, including eliminating or revising the Senate filibuster. That option would ease gridlock, but it lacks sufficient support—and could exacerbate the dangers of majoritarian rule. Legal remedies—campaign finance reform, ending gerrymanders, protecting minority voting rights—also appear out of reach in a court system that is itself falling prey to partisan polarization. Ostensibly democratic and legal means are being manipulated to produce manifestly illiberal ends.

Britain has been falling prey to its own brand of dysfunction. Brexit has imposed costly dislocations on the U.K. economy, and ongoing debate over its terms roils British politics and the United Kingdom's relations with the EU. Disaffection with Brexit in Northern Ireland and Scotland have the potential to break up the union. Following three chaotic years with Boris Johnson at the helm, Liz Truss launched a short-lived government whose tax-cutting, neoliberal zealotry produced an economic plan that plunged the value of the pound, triggered bitter divisions in the Conservative Party, and undermined popular support for the new government. Rishi Sunak charted a more moderate course but quickly confronted plunging popularity, setting the stage for Labour's landslide victory in elections in 2024. But within one hundred days of taking office, Keir Starmer's approval ratings had plunged.[22]

The dark side of neoliberal orthodoxy has become readily apparent. But the political dysfunction and paralysis that it has spawned appear to be standing in the way of the remedies needed to redress its harmful impact.

The Presumed Convergence of Modernities

The end of the Cold War and the wave of democratization that followed nurtured a false confidence in the linearity of historical progress. American elites presumed that the West's own pathway to modernity was the world's pathway to modernity—and that the collapse of communism cleared the way for multiple modernities to converge into one. Opening the liberal order to all nations would expand prosperity and fill out the ranks of the middle class, creating stakeholders in representative government, free trade, and international stability. In the parlance of Friedman, the world was poised to be populated by "McDonald's countries."

The developmental trajectory of China offers insight into the glaring fallacies embedded in this outlook. The rise of the West was indeed a story of the ascent of a prosperous middle class that eventually succeeded in wresting political power from monarchs and the church. Political liberalization followed from economic liberalization and the confrontation it produced between the absolutist state and the market-driven rise of empowered commoners. China has followed a different trajectory. Starting with Deng Xiaoping, the one-party state co-opted rather than confronted China's rising middle class. Members of the Chinese Communist Party became business owners and entrepreneurs, and business owners and entrepreneurs became Party members. China's expanding middle class emerged as satisfied stakeholders in the political status quo, not agents of change. Rather than producing political liberalization, China's economic boom and the vast expansion of its middle class have consolidated one-party rule.[23]

American analysts and policymakers also misjudged the impact of the digital/information revolution on the relative performance of different types of political systems. The prevailing wisdom maintained that the more open and free societies were, the better able they would be to take advantage of increasing flows of information, commerce, and capital. Friedman posited that globalization and digital technology would produce a "flat world" in which the fleet-footed would thrive at the expense of states still aspiring to hierarchical control.[24]

Outcomes did not turn out as expected. More state control over finance and commerce proved to have its distinct advantages. China emerged relatively unscathed by the 2008 financial crisis in no small part due to Beijing's tight grip on management of the nation's economy. So too did greater state control over the flow of information prove to have its benefits. Polarization and political dysfunction in the West are in part a product of the free-for-all that takes place across multiple media platforms. In contrast, China, Russia, and other autocracies regularly control their media, censor the internet, and punish dissent, curbing public debate and propagating a uniform political narrative that sustains broad support for the government and its policy decisions.

Many analysts predicted that such constraints on the flow of information, even if effective in suppressing dissent, would come at the expense of innovation and entrepreneurship. That prediction also appears to have been a misjudgment. In the past two decades, China has developed a venture capital and high-tech cluster that is almost on par with America's. Its companies have particular strengths in advanced routers (Huawei), drones (DJI), digital payment systems (Alipay), artificial intelligence (SenseTime), lithium-cobalt batteries for electric vehicles (CATL), and solar panels (the five top manufacturers all come from China). Yes, China's economy is slowing and will be weighed down by domestic debt and demographic decline. But on its current trajectory, the Chinese economy could overtake America's during the next decade. And with a population that is more than four times larger than that of the United States, China may well pull significantly ahead of America in economic output by the second half of the century.[25]

In similar fashion, American elites have tended to overweight the importance of procedural legitimacy while underweighting the salience of performance legitimacy. In the words of the legal scholar Nicholas Bagley, "Legitimacy is not solely, not even primarily, a product of the procedures that agencies follow. Legitimacy arises more generally from the perception that government is capable, informed, prompt and fair."[26] A strong majority of Americans believes their country is on the wrong track. That disaffection stems less from concern about the finer details of electoral and parliamentary procedure than from a perception that the U.S. government is failing to deliver on meeting the material needs of the public. In China, a poll from 2020 revealed that 90 percent of the public believed their country was heading in the right direction.[27] That satisfaction stemmed far less from approval of the Chinese government's decision-making procedures than from its ability to sustain economic growth and improve people's quality of life. In the aftermath of the COVID lockdowns and the slowdown of the Chinese economy, popular satisfaction with the country's direction has no doubt diminished. Yet many Chinese care much more about their standard of living than they do about being able to cast a ballot in a free and fair election. Performance matters.

False expectations of converging versions of modernity also produced missteps in the broader Middle East. The post-9/11 wars are a case in point. "The Iraqi people are deserving and capable of human liberty. . . . [T]hey can set an example to all the Middle East of a vital and peaceful and self-governing nation," President George W. Bush proclaimed just before launching the invasion of Iraq in 2003. But the war resulted in far more bloodshed and chaos than liberty. Notably, while Washington enjoyed British support for the war, many European governments opposed it. German foreign minister Fischer was quite blunt about the likely impact of the proposed invasion: "In addition to the disastrous consequences for long-term stability, we also fear possible negative repercussions for the joint fight against terrorism." French foreign minister Dominique de Villepin agreed: "We think that military intervention would be the worst possible solution."[28]

The U.S. intervention in Afghanistan fell prey to similar delusions. Bush proclaimed in 2004, "[T]he country is changing. There's women's rights. There's equality under the law. Young girls now go to school, many for the first time ever, thanks to the United States and our coalition of liberators."[29] But two decades of exhaustive U.S. efforts to bring stability and democracy to Afghanistan fell far short, and the U.S. withdrawal in the summer of 2021 gave way to Taliban rule and a humanitarian nightmare. The United States tried—and failed—to export to Afghanistan a Western version of modernity.

The U.S. response to the Arab Spring followed the same pattern. Many analysts in the United States understood the Arab Spring to mark the Middle East's overdue embarkation down the path of Western modernity. Observers compared the political turmoil in the region to the French Revolution and the revolutions of 1848, while others welcomed the arrival of an Islamic Reformation.[30] Policymakers followed suit. President Barack Obama affirmed, "[T]here must be no doubt that the United States of America welcomes change that advances self-determination and opportunity. . . . [A]fter decades of accepting the world as it is in the region, we have a chance to pursue the world as it should be."[31]

These expectations were also dashed. NATO intervened in Libya and toppled Muammar Gaddafi to liberate Libya from autocracy, but instead produced a failed state that became a breeding ground for factional rivalry and a haven for extremist groups. Support for the Syrian opposition did not succeed in toppling Bashar al-Assad, but it did help the Islamic State establish a territorial foothold in Syria, triggering a counter-ISIL campaign that eventually succeeded in dismantling the caliphate—but left behind a failed state.

Instead of birthing an Islamic Reformation and a wave of democratization, the Arab Spring produced a surge in political Islam and a paucity of stable democracy. Even Tunisia, which appeared to emerge from the Arab Spring with stable democratic institutions, has of late taken an autocratic turn. Unlike in most Western democracies, where secular power and religious authority were separated after the Wars of the Reformation, the Islamic tradition does not distinguish between mosque and state; more popular will has generally meant more religion in politics. And instead of clearing the way for the practice of pluralism and tolerance, the toppling of strongmen brought to the surface sectarian, tribal, and ethnic cleavages long held in abeyance by coercive rule. The United States spent the better part of two decades spinning its wheels in the Middle East, at a considerable cost in blood and treasure. It is not surprising that Washington has been pulling back from the region and taking a far more sober approach to the prospects for democracy and pluralism in the Arab world.

The Idealist Displacement of Realist Sobriety

Throughout its history, the United States has sought to navigate between foreign-policy idealism and a pragmatic respect for the constraints imposed on the conduct of statecraft by geopolitical realities. The back and forth between idealism and realism can arise from the idiosyncratic preferences of specific U.S. policymakers, irrespective of the global context. But over the broad swath of American history, the United States has generally pursued idealist goals when it could afford to do so and reined them in when strategic circumstances have rendered idealism prohibitively costly or unwise.

Amid the bipolarity of the Cold War, for example, geopolitical expedience guided the U.S. strategy of containment. The Yalta agreement struck by Franklin Roosevelt, Winston Churchill, and Joseph Stalin at the end of World War II was the ultimate realist compromise, providing Russia a buffer zone by leaving much of Eastern Europe under Soviet domination. In contrast, the implosion of the Soviet Union and the geopolitical slack associated with unipolarity allowed the United States to again put lofty ambitions front and center; Washington was confident that the triumph of American power and purpose would usher in the universalization of democracy, capitalism, and a rules-based international order. American statecraft prioritized the promotion of liberty and human rights, free trade, and institutionalized multilateralism.

The ideological bent of U.S. policy has of late crowded out consideration of power realities—with adverse consequences. This bias has manifested on several critical fronts. American analysts and policymakers attached too much weight to the intrinsic ideational appeal of liberal internationalism. To be sure, human dignity and civil and political rights have universal allure. But all ideals, including Western ones, have more pull when they are attached to preponderant power. Unipolarity understandably enhanced the appeal of Pax Americana. The waning of unipolarity understandably does the converse.

Roughly two-thirds of the countries in the world now trade more with China than they do with the United States. It is China rather than the Western democracies that is showing up in the Global South to build infrastructure and provide investment capital. In many parts of the developing world, China is now the lender of first resort. Consider the situation among the island nations of the South Pacific.[32] They might not be yearning to embrace Chinese values and mimic China's autocratic ways, but they are nonetheless deepening their ties to Beijing for instrumentalist reasons. As the *New York Times* recently reported, "With the Chinese foreign minister halfway through an eight-nation tour of the Pacific Islands, China is seeking to bind the vast region together in agreements for greater access to its land, seas and digital infrastructure, while promising development, scholarships and training in return."[33] Ideas matter, but material gain matters more.

The underweighting of power considerations led to a failure to appreciate the important role that unipolarity was playing in promoting geopolitical stability. The absence of great power competition during the first post–Cold War decades was due not to the readiness of Russia and China to join the liberal order and play by its rules but to the West's material preponderance. As power in the international system has diffused, great power competition has returned. China is no longer "biding its time" but is instead intent on augmenting its geopolitical heft and reach. Russia's invasion of Ukraine was a bald act of aggression aimed at blocking what Moscow saw as the West's encroachment in its sphere of influence. The result is likely to be sustained militarized rivalry between the West and an autocratic bloc anchored by Russia and China.

As a further sign of the diffusion of power, more than three-quarters of the world's countries have opted to avoid taking sides in the war in Ukraine, hoping to ride out the disruptive effects on food and energy supplies while avoiding ensnarement in a new round of East-West rivalry. Most of the Global South is staying on the diplomatic sidelines amid the conflict, suggesting that effective nonalignment could be emerging as the policy of choice of most developing nations. The decentralization of power is taking a toll on the reach and appeal of the liberal order.

The United States also erred in failing to appreciate the geopolitical implications of its expansive ambitions—the enlargement of NATO in particular. Moscow objected to NATO enlargement from the outset. As early as 1993, President Boris Yeltsin warned that Russians across the political spectrum "would no doubt perceive this as a sort of neo-isolation of our country in diametric opposition to its natural admission into Euro-Atlantic space." In a face-to-face meeting with President Bill Clinton in 1995, Yeltsin was more direct: "I see nothing but humiliation for Russia if you proceed. . . . Why do you want to do this? We need a new structure for Pan-European security, not old ones! . . . For me to agree to the borders of NATO expanding towards those of Russia—that would constitute a betrayal on my part of the Russian people."[34]

Moscow's discomfort only mounted after Vladimir Putin took power in 1999. At the Munich Security Conference in 2007, Putin declared that NATO enlargement "represents a serious provocation" and asked, "Why is it necessary to put military infrastructure on our borders during this expansion?"[35] In 2008, the Bush administration, although it faced resistance from European allies, convinced NATO to declare that Georgia and Ukraine "will become members of NATO." Soon thereafter, Russia grabbed control of the Georgian regions of Abkhazia and South Ossetia, effectively blocking the country's accession to NATO. Similarly, Putin's invasions of Ukraine in 2014 and 2022 were at least in part to block its pathway to NATO. In his February 24, 2022, address to the nation justifying the beginning of the "special military operation," Putin pointed to "the fundamental threats which irresponsible Western politicians created for Russia. . . . I am referring to the eastward expansion of NATO, which is moving its military infrastructure ever closer to the Russian border."[36]

The United States has largely dismissed Russia's objections. While the Kremlin has been anxiously watching NATO's eastern frontier come its way, Washington has viewed NATO's eastward expansion primarily through the benign lens of America's idealist calling. Enlarging the alliance has been about spreading American values and removing geopolitical dividing lines rather than drawing new ones.

As he launched NATO's open-door policy, President Clinton claimed that doing so would "erase the artificial line in Europe drawn by Stalin at the end of World War II." Madeleine Albright, his secretary of state, affirmed that "NATO is a defensive alliance that . . . does not regard any state as its adversary." The purpose of expanding the alliance, she explained, was to build a Europe "whole and free." And she declared that "NATO poses no danger to Russia." That's the line that Washington has taken ever since, including when it came to Ukraine's potential membership. As Russian troops massed on Ukraine's border in early 2022, President Biden insisted, "[T]he United States and NATO are not a threat to Russia. Ukraine is not threatening Russia."[37] Secretary of State Antony Blinken agreed: "NATO itself is a defensive alliance. . . . And the idea that Ukraine represents a threat to Russia or, for that matter, that NATO represents a threat to Russia is profoundly wrong and misguided." America's allies are mostly on the same page. Jens Stoltenberg, NATO's secretary general, joined the chorus, affirming, "NATO is not a threat to Russia."[38]

The West had noble intentions in opening NATO's doors to Ukraine and other former Soviet republics. But it allowed idealism to dangerously trump realist sobriety in dismissing Russia's legitimate security concerns about NATO setting up shop on the other side of its thousand-plus-mile border with Ukraine. NATO may be a defensive alliance, but it brings to bear aggregate military power that Russia understandably does not want parked near its territory. Geography and geopolitics still matter; major powers, regardless of their ideological bent, don't like it when other major powers stray into their neighborhood.

Indeed, Moscow's objections to NATO membership for Ukraine are very much in line with America's own statecraft, which has long sought to keep other major powers away from its borders. The United States spent much of the nineteenth century ushering Britain, France, Russia, and Spain out of the Western Hemisphere. Thereafter, Washington regularly turned to military intervention to hold sway in the Americas. The exercise of hemispheric hegemony continued during the Cold War, with the United States determined to box the Soviet Union and its ideological sympathizers out of Latin America. When Moscow deployed missiles to Cuba in 1962, the United States issued an ultimatum that brought the superpowers to the brink of war. After Russia recently hinted that it might again deploy its military to Latin America, the U.S. State Department spokesperson Ned Price responded, "If we do see any movement in that direction, we will respond swiftly and decisively."[39] Given its own track record, Washington should have given greater credence to Moscow's objections to bringing Ukraine into NATO.

The Neglect of the Domestic Foundations of Liberal Internationalism

Overconfidence in the durability and appeal of liberal internationalism also contributed to insufficient attention to its domestic foundations in the West—and, in particular, in the United States. Liberal internationalism enjoyed five decades of bipartisan support, from World War II through the end of the Cold War, giving it a taken-for-granted quality. The collapse of the Berlin Wall and implosion of the Soviet Union were interpreted as vindications of U.S. grand strategy, suggesting that the United States should continue on its liberal internationalist course.

Yet the domestic foundations of this brand of U.S. statecraft were not permanent; they rested on a set of historically contingent conditions.[40] The presence of a pressing and formidable external threat engendered political discipline; politics never stopped at water's edge, but it came close during World War II and the Cold War. At home, industrialization produced broadly shared prosperity and fostered mobility and politically diverse regions—both of which contributed to ideological moderation and a stable bipartisan center. Democrats and Republicans alike used to support liberal internationalism because it paid political dividends to do so.

Those conditions have disappeared. America's ideological center has collapsed, fundamentally weakening the bipartisan political foundations of liberal internationalism. Politicians on both sides of the aisle face incentives to defect from the bipartisan compact that emerged under FDR and lasted through the balance of the twentieth century. Republicans have lost interest in institutionalized multilateralism, while both parties have backed away from free trade—a hallmark of U.S. statecraft during the heyday of liberal internationalism. The broadly shared prosperity of the industrial era has been replaced by the economic insecurity and gaping inequality of the digital era. The mobility and demographic heterogeneity fueled by industrialization has also given way to renewed sectionalism, growing tensions across communal boundaries, and sharp partisan divides on social issues.

Today, the post–World War II U.S.-led architecture—the UN, the Bretton Woods institutions, the alliance networks in Europe and East Asia—would have little chance of passing muster in the U.S. Senate. Indeed, President Trump expressed open disdain for that order and took steps to dismantle it. The Democrats may reject "America First" and remain committed to some elements of liberal internationalism. But absent a bipartisan consensus on the contours of U.S. statecraft, American foreign policy swings wildly when power changes hands in Washington. America's democratic partners continue to look to Washington for leadership and protection—a dynamic reinforced by Russian aggression in Ukraine. But America's political inconstancy is fueling global uncertainty, prompting even close partners to hedge their bets when it comes to the future scope and character of U.S. engagement in global affairs.

Conclusion

The revival and defense of the liberal order begins at home. Liberal democracies on both sides of the Atlantic need to renew their social contracts with their electorates, giving up on neoliberal orthodoxy in favor of policies that will meet the needs of their citizens and enable them to prosper in a fast-changing digital economy. Only if the Western democracies are able to deliver for their electorates will they be able to consolidate their political centers and reclaim their full political functionality. Only that outcome will enable the community of liberal democracies to anchor the ongoing transition in the international system. Liberal democracies must compete successfully in the marketplace of ideas and demonstrate that they can outperform autocratic alternatives.

Even if the West recovers its economic competitiveness and political equanimity, it will need to step back from the ideological and strategic excesses that began in the 1990s. Ahead is a world of multiple centers of power and multiple versions of modernity. Given interdependence and a wide range of global challenges, including arresting climate change, promoting public health, and managing a globalized economy, the West will need to work across ideological dividing lines. Perhaps one day the United States and its democratic allies will realize the goal of universalizing a liberal order. But that goal, even if ultimately attainable, is far off. In the meantime, the West can help meet the pressing need for effective global governance only by seeking to work with democracies and non-democracies alike.

Notes

1. Kupchan 2002, 119.
2. Agence France-Presse 1996.
3. Pew Research Center 2017.
4. Sciolino 2005.
5. Goodwin 2017.
6. Fischer 2000.
7. *New York Times* 1991.
8. Chirac 1999.
9. Fukuyama 1989.
10. Krauthammer 1990.
11. Friedman 1999, xviii, 86, 196, 214.
12. Will 1991.
13. OECD n.d.
14. Blanchet et al. 2022.
15. Chancel et al. 2021.
16. Bachman 2017.
17. CNN Money 1960; *New York Times* 1961.
18. Holmes 2022; Repko 2023.
19. Acemoglu 2024.
20. World Bank n.d.
21. See Kupchan 2020.
22. *Washington Post* 2024.
23. See Kupchan 2012, 86–145.
24. Friedman 2005.
25. Daly and Gedminas 2022; OECD 2018.
26. Bagley 2021.
27. Todd et al. 2023.
28. DW News 2003; Kessler and Lynch 2003.
29. White House 2004.
30. Weyland 2012.
31. White House 2011.
32. Dreher et al. 2022.
33. Cave 2022.
34. Blanton and Savranskaya 2018.
35. Putin 2007.
36. Putin 2022.
37. Biden 2022.
38. Carrick 2022.
39. Nicas and Troianovski 2022.
40. See Kupchan and Trubowitz 2007.

References

Acemoglu, Daron. 2024. "US and E.U. Democracy Challenges Reflect Disappointing Economic Growth and Wage Trends." Project Syndicate, June 20. https://www.project-syndicate.org/commentary/us-eu-democracy-challenges-reflect-disappointing-economic-growth-and-wage-trends-by-daron-acemoglu-2024-06.

Agence France-Presse. 1996. "Kohl Issues New Warning to Britain over EU Reform." February 2.

Bachman, Daniel. 2017. "Income Inequality in the United States: What Do We Know and What Does It Mean?" *Issues by the Numbers*. Deloitte University Press, July. https://www2.deloitte.com/content/dam/insights/us/articles/3308_IBTN_income-inequality/DUP_IBTN_Income-inequality.pdf.

Bagley, Nicholas. 2021. "The Procedure Fetish." Niskanen Center, December 7. https://www.niskanencenter.org/the-procedure-fetish/.

Biden, Joseph. 2022. "Remarks by President Biden Providing an Update on Russia and Ukraine." White House, February 15. https://www.whitehouse.gov/briefing-room/speeches-remarks/2022/02/15/remarks-by-president-biden-providing-an-update-on-russia-and-ukraine/.

Blanchet, Thomas, Lucas Chancel, and Amory Gethin. 2022. "Why Is Europe More Equal Than the United States." *American Economic Journal: Applied Economics* 14 (4): 480–518. https://doi.org/10.1257/app.20200703.

Blanton, Tom and Savranskaya, Svetlana. 2018. "NATO Expansion: What Yeltsin Heard." National Security Archive. 621. https://nsarchive.gwu.edu/briefing-book/russia-programs/2018-03-16/nato-expansion-what-yeltsin-heard.

Carrick, Heather. 2022. "Ukraine: What Did NATO Leader Jens Stoltenberg Say—Are There Signs of De-Escalation on Ukrainian Border?" *National World*, February 16. https://www.nationalworld.com/news/world/nato-is-no-threat-to-russia-as-jens-stoltenberg-says-there-is-no-signs-of-russian-de-escalation-in-ukraine-3571697.

Cave, Damien. 2022. "Why China Is Miles Ahead in a Pacific Race for Influence." *New York Times*, May 31. https://www.nytimes.com/2022/05/31/world/australia/china-united-states-pacific.html.

Chancel, Lucas, Thomas Piketty, Emmanuel Saez, and Gabriel Zucman. 2021. "World Inequality Report 2022." World Inequality Lab. https://wir2022.wid.world/www-site/uploads/2023/03/D_FINAL_WIL_RIM_RAPPORT_2303.pdf.

Chirac, Jacques. Speech on the occasion of the 20th Anniversary of the Institute Francais des Relations Internationales, Elysee Palace, November 4, 1999. Text distributed by the French Embassy in Washington, D.C.CNN Money. 1960. "Fortune 500 Archive." https://money.cnn.com/magazines/fortune/fortune500_archive/full/1960/.

Daly, Kevin, and Tadas Gedminas. 2022. "The Path to 2075—Slower Global Growth, but Convergence Remains Intact." Goldman Sachs, December 6. https://www.goldmansachs.com/intelligence/pages/gs-research/the-path-to-2075-slower-global-growth-but-convergence-remains-intact/report.pdf.

Dreher, Axel, Fuchs, Andreas, Parks, Bradley, Strange, Austin, and Tierney, Michael. 2022. *Banking on Beijing*. Cambridge University Press. https://doi.org/10.1017/9781108564496.

DW News. 2003. "Germany Says 'No' to Iraq Involvement." January 21. https://www.dw.com/en/germany-says-no-to-iraq-involvement/a-759857.

European Commission. n.d. "European Defense Fund." https://defence-industry-space.ec.europa.eu/eu-defence-industry/european-defence-fund-edf_en.

Fischer, Joschka. 2000. "From Confederacy to Federation—Thoughts on the Finality of European Integration." Speech at Humboldt University, Berlin, May 12. https://ec.europa.eu/dorie/fileDownload.do?docId=192161&cardId=192161.

Friedman, Thomas L. 1999. *The Lexus and the Olive Tree: Understanding Globalization.* Farrar, Straus and Giroux.

Friedman, Thomas L. 2005. "It's a Flat World, After All." *New York Times*, April 3. https://www.nytimes.com/2005/04/03/magazine/its-a-flat-world-after-all.html.

Fukuyama, Francis. 1989. "The End of History?" *National Interest* 16: 3–18. https://www.jstor.org/stable/24027184.

Goodwin, Matthew. 2017. "Why Immigration Was Key to Brexit Vote." *Irish Times*, May 15. https://www.irishtimes.com/culture/books/why-immigration-was-key-to-brexit-vote-1.3083608.

Holmes, Frank. 2022. "Top 10 Largest Fortune 500 Employers in the US." US Global Investors, October 26. https://www.usfunds.com/resource/top-10-largest-fortune-500-employers-in-the-u-s/.

Kessler, Glenn, and Colum Lynch. 2003. "France Vows to Block Resolution on Iraq War." *Washington Post*, January 21. https://www.washingtonpost.com/archive/politics/2003/01/21/france-vows-to-block-resolution-on-iraq-war/db286647-a77d-48a6-b815-72bf29fc13a3/.

Krauthammer, Charles. 1990. "The Unipolar Moment." *Foreign Affairs* 70 (1): 23–33. https://www.foreignaffairs.com/articles/1990-01-01/unipolar-moment.

Kupchan, Charles A. 2002. *The End of the American Era: US Foreign Policy and the Geopolitics of the Twenty-first Century.* Knopf.

Kupchan, Charles A. 2012. *No One's World: The West, the Rising Rest, and the Coming Global Turn.* Oxford University Press.

Kupchan, Charles A. 2020. *Isolationism: A History of America's Efforts to Shield Itself from the World.* Oxford University Press.

Kupchan, Charles A., and Peter Trubowitz. 2007. "Dead Center: The Decline of Liberal Internationalism in the United States." *International Security* 32 (2), pp. 7–44.

New York Times. 1961. "G.M. Workers' Pay Set Record in 1960." February 19. https://www.nytimes.com/1961/02/19/archives/gm-workers-pay-set-record-in-1960.html.

New York Times. 1991. "Conflict in Yugoslavia; Europeans Send High-Level Team." June 29. https://www.nytimes.com/1991/06/29/world/conflict-in-yugoslavia-europeans-send-high-level-team.html.

Nicas, Jack, and Anton Troianovski. 2022. "A World Away from Ukraine, Russia Is Courting Latin America." *New York Times*, February 15. https://www.nytimes.com/2022/02/15/world/americas/russia-putin-latin-america-bolsonaro.html.

OECD. 2018. "GDP Long-Term Forecast." https://data.oecd.org/gdp/gdp-long-term-forecast.htm.

OECD. n.d. "Social Expenditure Database (SOCX)." https://www.oecd.org/en/data/datasets/social-expenditure-database-socx.html.

Pew Research Center. 2017. "Origins and Destinations of European Union Migrants within the EU." June 19. https://www.pewresearch.org/global/interactives/origins-destinations-of-european-union-migrants-within-the-eu/.

Putin, Vladimir. 2007. "Speech and the Following Discussion at the Munich Conference on Security Policy." February 10. http://en.kremlin.ru/events/president/transcripts/24034.

Putin, Vladimir. 2022. "Address to the Nation Announcing Start of Military Campaign in Ukraine." American Rhetoric, February 24. https://www.americanrhetoric.com/speeches/vladimirputinrussianmilitarycampaignukraine.htm.

Repko, Melissa. 2023. "Walmart Raises Minimum Wage as Retail Labor Market Remains Tight." CNBC, January 24. https://www.cnbc.com/2023/01/24/walmart-raises-minimum-wage-as-retail-labor-market-remains-tight.html.

Rose, Joel, and Liz Baker. 2022. "6 in 10 Americans Say US Democracy Is in Crisis as the 'Big Lie' Takes Root." National Public Radio, January 3. https://www.npr.org/2022/01/03/1069764164/american-democracy-poll-jan-6.

Sciolino, Elaine. 2005. "French Voters Soundly Reject European Union Constitution." *New York Times*, May 30. https://www.nytimes.com/2005/05/30/world/europe/french-voters-soundly-reject-european-union-constitution.html.
Todd, Chuck, Murray, Mark, Kamisar, Ben, Bowman, Bridget, and Marquez, Alexandra. 2023. "Poll Finds 71% of Americans Believe Country Is on Wrong Track." NBC News, January 30. https://www.nbcnews.com/meet-the-press/first-read/poll-finds-71-americans-believe-country-wrong-track-rcna68138.
Washington Post. 2024. "Keir Starmer's First 100 Days as Labour Leader." October 9. https://www.washingtonpost.com/world/2024/10/09/keir-starmer-100-days-labour/.
Weyland, Kurt. 2012. "The Arab Spring: Why the Surprising Similarities with the Revolutionary Wave of 1848?" *Perspectives on Politics* 10 (4): 917–934. https://doi.org/10.1017/S1537592712002873.
White House. 2004. "Rights and Aspirations of the People of Afghanistan." July 8, 2004. https://georgewbush-whitehouse.archives.gov/infocus/afghanistan/20040708.html
White House. 2011. "Remarks by the President on the Middle East and North Africa." May 9. https://obamawhitehouse.archives.gov/thepress-office/2011/05/.
Will, George F. 1991. "Passing of a Prophet." *Washington Post*, December 8. https://www.washingtonpost.com/archive/opinions/1991/12/08/passing-of-a-prophet/c69252cc-2db9-486a-8bfc-f90a72ccfa93/.
World Bank. n.d. "Gini Index." https://data.worldbank.org/indicator/SI.POV.GINI.

12
Mistakes Were Made

Revisiting the 1990s from the EU's Immediate Neighborhood

Ayşe Zarakol

The current discontent with the liberal international order (LIO)[1] is driven by two primary groups, neither fully external to the LIO: "populist" politicians and their voters in the core, and recently antiliberal or illiberal governments on the semiperiphery (yet often technically inside) the order. "Center" or "core" here refers to "societies that feel a strong cultural ownership of both the label and the symbols associated with the term 'West' whereas 'semiperiphery' refers to 'states that could be classified as Western (or have been at times) but could also be classified as non-Western (or have been at times).'" Both groups are "frustrated with their perceived positions in the recognition hierarchy created by the LIO" and are undermining the institutions of the LIO from within. The discontented groups in the core resent the LIO because they believe it to be undermining their privileged global position by promises of expansion and equality, whereas the discontented governments of the semiperiphery resent the LIO because they see it as hardly more than a façade for the business-as-usual political, economic, and social hierarchy between the West and others that has characterized the international order of the twentieth century.[2]

While it is true that large demographic groups in the West have never fully bought into the LIO,[3] it is also true that currently the LIO is more consistently undermined by actors in the semiperiphery:[4] by Russia, but also by Turkey, by Poland, by Hungary, and others. Populist politicians who dislike the LIO may come and go in the core (e.g., United States, Italy), but in the semiperiphery skepticism of the LIO is not limited to only populist politicians and their voters. The question then is this: What caused that widespread skepticism against the LIO in the semiperiphery? And how did these countries in the semiperiphery end up in

Ayşe Zarakol, *Mistakes Were Made*. In: *Rethinking the 1990s*. Edited by: G. John Ikenberry and Peter Trubowitz, Oxford University Press. © Oxford University Press (2025). DOI: 10.1093/9780197813133.003.0012 a situation where they could significantly undermine the LIO to begin with? The 1990s had a lot to do with it.

International Relations (IR) scholarship has attributed the attractiveness of the LIO to non-Western states in the 1990s to one of the following: the investment and commitment of the United States, post–World War II hegemony, the strength of its institutions and rules, the rationality of its economic incentives, the persuasiveness of its normative model and norm entrepreneurs or their cooperative-security practices. However, the LIO also rests on historical (social, economic, and political) hierarchies between the West and the non-West, hierarchies without which it could not come into being. For this reason, it cannot be assumed that non-Western countries sought to join the expanding LIO in the 1990s for entirely "rational" reasons; they have done so because many saw and still see the LIO as another Western status club privileging its members and because they believed membership to offer a way to rise within the international hierarchies of the modern order.[5] Some semiperipheral countries that gained quick acceptance to the LIO in the 1990s have come to undermine it since then (Hungary, Poland), and others who have been jilted by it time after time (until recently) continue to pursue membership (Ukraine). This suggests that resentment against the LIO, where it exists, has deeper and more variable causes than just what happened in the 1990s (same goes for attraction). Domestic political developments within each country are certainly a major part of the story. The inconsistent expansion of the LIO into the semiperiphery in the 1990s also made long-standing grievance dynamics between the Western core and the semiperiphery worse: on the one hand, it increased the status resentments of those who were partially or mostly left out of the LIO clubs; on the other hand, even partial access gave resentful actors the ability to do damage from inside the institutions and organizations of the LIO. Nevertheless, it is important to ask whether there were specific decisions and turning points in the 1990s and early 2000s that might have led to a different pattern of relations between the Western powers and the semiperiphery, and what sorts of mistakes were made by the core actors about inclusion and exclusion.

To answer those questions, this chapter proceeds in three parts, with a focus on two pivotal countries that were mostly left out of the LIO in the 1990s even though they sought to belong: Russia and Turkey.[6] In some ways, these two countries have had the most complicated relationship with the LIO since the 1990s,[7] but the authoritarian evolution (or devolution) of those regimes is not the only reason why that is so. In fact, their interactions with the LIO are at least partly to blame for those domestic outcomes, as this chapter will illustrate.

The section that follows briefly reviews the historical background of the resentments against the LIO, linking these resentments to dynamics of the nineteenth and twentieth century. The next section looks at the 1990s. Here my argument is that Turkey and Russia's trajectory vis-à-vis the LIO converged in this decade: Russia was given a degree of access, whereas Turkey was kept at bay, but after the encouragement of previous decades. To put it another way, Turkey, previously more on track to become an insider, was kept at arm's length while Russia, previously the main rival, was brought into the fold to an extent. In terms of their positioning vis-à-vis the LIO, the end result was the same: both countries ended up neither fully in nor fully out, which fomented resentment. In terms of the themes of this volume, one could thus read the 1990s as a transformative moment for both countries' relationship with the international order, but also one that consolidated long-standing resentments, grievances, and suspicions.

Then I look at the immediate aftermath of the 1990s, when both Russia and Turkey came under new leadership. Both Vladimir Putin and Recep Tayyip Erdoğan were initially welcomed and supported by the West and later buoyed by global economic conditions, giving each regime the maneuvering room to turn more repressive at home while simultaneously pursuing more ambitious foreign policy agendas. From the point of view of the LIO and the home constituencies in Turkey and Russia who wanted their countries to be more integrated with the LIO, these turns look like failures and missed opportunities on the part of the Turkish and Russian regimes. However, from the point of view of Erdoğan and Putin, these choices look to be very much the opposite. After all, they are still in power, whereas their counterparts in the West are not and are blamed for much of what has gone wrong since. History will probably settle on a more midway judgment: that the West's naïve arrogance in dealing with Turkey and Russia in the 1990s and the 2000s aided and abetted the consolidation of antiliberal regimes in both contexts. The outcome was a relational one. Both sides are implicated in this dynamic.

The chapter concludes with some general observations about what the LIO got wrong about Russia and Turkey in the 1990s. Here there are also some lessons to be drawn for the West's current handling of Ukraine. One of the biggest lessons the 1990s offers about Turkey and Russia is that halfway recognition—alternating between inclusion and exclusion—is worse than aloofness because it first creates expectations and then creates resentment when those expectations are not met. Having extended wide-ranging rhetorical (and to a lesser extent material) support for the Ukrainian government since 2022, the West may cause an outcome similar to that of Turkey and Russia there as well if it decides to formally exclude Ukraine down the line.

Russia and Turkey as Historical "Outsiders"

The nineteenth century was pivotal in the creation of the modern international order because, for the first time, economic indicators in "the West" manifestly surpassed those of Asia. Equally important, however, was the emergence during the long nineteenth century of a particular social relationship between the West and the rest of the international system, a relationship that would characterize international relations for the next century and beyond. "The West" came to be seen as the center of the world; its standards (from political to cultural) came to define what was seen as "normal" and started shaping expectations about how international actors should behave (internally and externally). Those who fell short of these expectations were stigmatized, initially formally via the "Standard of Civilization," which deprived states not considered "civilized" of equal legal recognition, and later in the twentieth century through more informal hierarchies such as modern versus traditional or First World versus Third World. As I have argued elsewhere, this dynamic can be thought of as an "established-outsider" relationship: those who are "established" (or early arrivers) in a social setting have the power to set norms, and they look down on those who are "outsiders" (or latecomers) as being anomic even if material differences between them are insignificant. This is a recognition problem, and being considered "less than" actors who define what is "normal" has significant material consequences.[8]

Russia and Turkey have had comparably complicated relationships with the West since the nineteenth century; they were both "outsiders" to the European international order in the sense described above. Throughout the nineteenth century, they were stigmatized. The Ottoman Empire felt the brunt of this treatment more, but it was also a problem for Russia.[9] Prior to the twentieth century, both countries had followed emulation strategies to improve competitiveness, to gain the acceptance of the international society of European states, and to assuage domestic concerns about lagging behind the West. Russia is considered to have taken this step first at the end of the seventeenth century under the leadership of Peter the Great (reigned 1682–1725), followed by his wife Catherine I and, later, under the rule of Catherine the Great (1762–1792). The reform strategy had been revisited most ostensibly again during the reign of Alexander II (1855–1881), who, in 1861, issued the Great Emancipation Statute freeing and elevating a million serfs to equal citizen status. Despite a longer history of participating in European affairs and even borrowing military technology, the first Ottoman sultan to be seriously persuaded of the necessity of comprehensive Westernization was Selim III (1789–1807), but Selim was executed after a rebellion, and serious reforms in line with European demands were not implemented until the reign of Mahmud II (1808–1839) and continued by his son Abdülmecid (1839–1861). In 1839, Abdülmecid issued the Tanzimat Declaration (prepared by his father), which recognized the sanctity of life, liberty, and individual honor of his subjects, and decreed that government should be formed according to fundamental principles. As in Russia (in 1905), these reforms would ultimately culminate in the convening of the first parliament (in 1876).

In the early twentieth century, both countries were taken over by leaders with revisionist agendas. The Russian case is well-known, but in the Ottoman Empire this happened just before the defeat and collapse of the empire: the Committee of Union and Progress (CUP), originally a secret society within the ranks of the Young Turk movement, took de facto control of the empire with a coup in 1913 (following the "Constitutional Revolution" of 1908). Between 1913 and 1918, it followed an aggressively revisionist agenda intended to recapture the Ottoman Empire's glory days and, as a proto-fascist movement, oversaw some of the most brutal actions committed in the name of the empire, including the mass killings of the Armenian population in 1914–1915. The differences do matter, of course: the fact that the Bolsheviks had a more substantive ideology and a domestic reform plan, and the fact that they took power after Russia's near defeat in war, and through a popular revolution, made all the difference in terms of the longevity of their regime, in comparison with the CUP regime in the Ottoman Empire. Both the CUP regime and the Ottoman Empire collapsed via World War I, giving way to the Republic of Turkey, whereas the Bolsheviks created the USSR. Turkey and USSR thus followed different stigma-management strategies during the Cold War years. The new Turkish regime was operating in the aftermath of defeat, which would not come to Russia until the end of the Cold War.[10]

Stigmatized international actors are driven to fix their recognition problem by managing their stigma.[11] The twentieth century gives us examples of two types of stigma-management strategy by the outsiders of the international system. A few countries attempted to embrace their lack of recognition, wearing this as a badge of honor. The Soviet Union was the most high-profile example of this kind, wherein an outsider attempted to create its own normative/ideological universe and get recognition from the leadership of similarly situated states instead. It did succeed to an extent, getting "great power" status and treatment throughout the Cold War. However, the USSR never managed to upend the primary narrative underwriting the social hierarchy of the modern international order, that is, the notion that the East had to "catch up" with the West.

By contrast, many more non-Western states[12] attempted to move up in the social hierarchy of the international system by correcting their stigmatizing attributes and by joining the status clubs of the West, that is, by assimilating into the "Western order." Turkey in the twentieth century is the prime example of this strategy. The Ottoman Empire was defeated in World War I, dismantled, and partially occupied. It took three years of military struggle, domestic chaos, and some stubborn diplomatic maneuvering at the Lausanne Conference for the new Kemalist regime to establish itself. The reincarnated Turkish state was much smaller than the Ottoman Empire and had depleted most of its military and economic resources. Starting in the interwar period, Turkey committed itself to adopting "Western" norms, from seemingly trivial matters such as dress codes to more serious ones such as legal codes, as well as signing treaties and joining international organizations for status-related reasons; for example, Turkey joined the UN as a founding member in 1945, NATO in 1952, the OECD in 1962. In the Cold War years, it became a staunch ally of the United States. But none of these choices brought the full recognition and equal treatment it craved.

Russia and Turkey in the 1990s: Neither In nor Out

Having thus followed different strategies for gaining recognition from the West in the twentieth century, Russia and Turkey saw their fates reconverge to an extent in the 1990s vis-à-vis the LIO. Russia was allowed to come closer compared to where it had been in the twentieth century as a former enemy, whereas Turkey, despite its track record as an ally, was kept at arm's length. This in-between status enflamed historical grievances but also gave enough access later to undermine the LIO from within.

Given the pariah status Russia has now with the LIO, it is very easy to forget that in the initial decades after the collapse of the USSR the Western observers of Russia tended to err on the side of optimism about Russia's receptiveness to international norms and alliance potential. This did not translate into full membership in the LIO but allowed Russia to gain access to some critical institutions in the 1990s. The Conference for Security and Cooperation in Europe, which had been created as a Cold War forum to facilitate interaction between the West and the communist bloc, was transformed into the more formal Organization for Security and Cooperation (OSCE) in Europe in 1995. The OSCE was quite active in the 1990s and the 2000s, especially via the Office for Democratic Institutions and Human Rights. Russia also joined the Council of Europe in 1996. Finally, in 1994, during the early years of Boris Yeltsin's rule, Russia was invited to attend G-7 meetings and, in 1997, was invited to formally join the organization. It is noteworthy that these goodwill gestures from the West followed two moments of crisis in Yeltsin's rule, during the 1993 and 1996 elections. Yeltsin responded to both by taking another step in the nationalist direction, which the West rewarded, interestingly enough, by bringing Russia closer to the inner capitalist club. "The idea was to prop up the flailing Boris N. Yeltsin by making Russia look like a member of the club, even though it didn't qualify based on income or economic growth," remarked an editorial in the *Baltimore Sun*.[13] Russia, however, did not really take advantage of this membership until Putin's presidency.

Turkey, by contrast, saw its importance as an ally get downgraded in the same decade. The path for EU membership was opened for a number of postcommunist countries soon after the fall of the Iron Curtain, in the 1997 Luxembourg Summit, which allowed these countries to jump the queue in front of Turkey. Turkey had been a member of the Council of Europe since 1949. Ankara had applied for formal membership in the European Economic Community in 1987, and Turkey had been an associate member since 1964, but the country's progress stalled in the 1990s, as Central and Eastern Europe took priority. Turkey joined the European Customs Union in 1995, but not until 1999, at the Helsinki Summit, did EU leaders grant Turkey the status of a candidate country, acknowledging its eligibility to potentially join the EU in the future. Accession negotiations with Turkey did not start until 2005, by which point Poland, Hungary, the Czech Republic, Slovakia, Slovenia, Latvia, Lithuania, and Estonia were already full members after the 2004 enlargement (as well as Malta and Cyprus). Romania and Bulgaria acceded in 2007, despite being considered not fully ready. (Croatia joined in 2013.) In other words, Turkey was left in the dust as many others took its place in the queue.

It could be argued that to some extent this treatment was warranted, as the 1990s were politically a tumultuous decade for Turkey. The decade saw a series of coalition governments as no single political party gained a parliamentary majority. These coalitions often faced difficulties in implementing coherent policies and addressing pressing issues. The decade also witnessed a significant escalation of the conflict between the Turkish state and the Kurdistan Workers' Party, which was seeking greater Kurdish rights and autonomy. The conflict led to violence, human rights abuses, and large-scale displacement in predominantly Kurdish areas. Turkey also faced economic difficulties during the 1990s, including high inflation rates, budget deficits, and external debt burdens. Economic reforms were attempted, including liberalization measures and structural adjustments, but their effects were limited. Another major element of Turkish politics in the 1990s was the rise of Islamist politics: the Welfare Party led by Necmettin Erbakan joined a coalition government only to be pushed out in what became known as "the postmodern coup," when the Turkish military issued a memorandum in 1997 pressuring the government to resign due to alleged religious fundamentalist influences. For these reasons, it could be argued that Turkey was not yet ready for full EU membership in the 1990s, as it fell short on indicators of democracy, economy, and human rights. Nevertheless, Turks could not help but feel that Turkey was being held to a higher standard than Eastern European countries. The Turkish state was frequently criticized by Western observers for the quality of its democracy (given frequent interventions by the Turkish military into civilian politics), its human rights record (given its treatment of the Kurdish population especially), and its economic issues (given high rates of inflation and unemployment). In sum, the 1990s were when Turkey was committed to the West only to be told it was not yet deserving of full recognition.

In the early years of the 1990s, Russia too was committed to moving closer to the West. A pro-Western group had considerable influence over the Foreign Ministry in the last years of the USSR and early years of the Russian

Federation under Yeltsin's rule. "International institutionalists" argued that the best option for Russia was political and economic integration. This group saw Russia as a natural member of Western civilization, and the international environment as friendly to Russian security. They argued that Russia's main priority was to liberalize its domestic politics and economy. Under the influence of such "New Thinking" politicians and advisors, Russia made many "unilateral concessions on matters such as UN sanctions on Yugoslavia, Iraq and Libya; the levels and limitations of weapons permitted under START II; controls on missile technology exports to India and arms sales to Iran; the Western position on the rights of Russian minorities in the Baltic; and the dispute with Japan over the South Kurile islands."[14] The Foreign Policy Concept of 1993 stated that "achieving the main civil and economic characteristics associated with the constitutive qualities and values of 'the West'" was among the top priorities of Russia. It declared "the end of the East-West confrontation" and hopefully described a future of collaboration with NATO and support by Western powers. Such Russian overtures were greeted with skeptical relief by the West: "The Western powers were ready to stop considering Russia as a foe, but politely declined the enthusiastic appeals from Yeltsin and [Minister of Foreign Affairs Andrei V.] Kozyrev to instantly become allies."[15] This created a backlash within Russian politics and strengthened the hand of moderate conservatives as well as the nationalists who accused the pro-Western camp of humiliating the country by taking a conciliatory stance that achieved nothing.

Yeltsin himself wavered between the two camps. Electoral and political pressures after 1993 forced him to adopt an awkward middle ground of pro-Western foreign policy abroad, on the one hand, and increasingly authoritarian "Russia first" rhetoric at home, on the other. This shift was very much manifested in the 1997 National Security Concept, which had a remarkably different tone and outlook from the 1993 Foreign Policy Concept. References to democracy and the West were dropped, with the exceptions of a single instance of a "warning against the danger of Russia's 'technological dependence on the leading states of the West' and a mention of discriminatory measures against the Russian goods in the 'developed countries of the West.'"[16] Whereas the 1993 Foreign Policy Concept stated that "achieving the main civil and economic characteristics associated with the constitutive qualities and values of 'the West'" was among the top priorities of Russia, the 1997 National Security Concept took "care to maintain equal distancing in relation to the 'global, European and Asian economic and political actors."[17] The economic crisis of 1998 effectively ended the Yeltsin era, and in 1999 Yeltsin appointed Putin, a political unknown with a KGB background, as his prime minister and, ultimately, successor. Putin quickly gained popularity during his time as prime minister, helped especially by Russian actions in Chechnya. Within a year, his popularity rating had soared from 2 percent to 50 percent.

What Went Wrong after the 1990s: Backing the Wrong Horses

Many Western observers were positively "giddy" about what Putin's presidency meant for Russian capitalism and quite optimistic about what Putin could deliver. Putin believed in a strong, paternalist Russian state and did not reject the legacy of the Soviet period. After taking over from Yeltsin, he argued that Russia could take "its rightful place in the world" by restoring its economic strength. In one of his first public speeches, Putin called for a return of Russia's strong state tradition and insisted that Russia had to look out for its own national interests: "Several years ago, we fell prey to an illusion that we have no enemies. We have paid dearly for this."[18] After he was sworn in, he emphasized his desire for Russia to become "a rich, strong and civilized country of which its citizens are proud and which is respected in the world."[19] Putin soon unveiled a new foreign policy blueprint that attached great importance to the Group of Eight (G-8) and called for closer cooperation with the European Union. In the Foreign Policy Concept of 2000, the referents for defining Russia's interests and objectives were broadened to "include the 'world community' and 'world economy,' 'market economy methods' and 'values of democratic society,' 'international economic organizations,' and the familiar but very rarely mentioned 'leading states of the world' along with a single reference to 'influential developing states,' all complete with thoroughly depersonalized 'foreign states and interstate associations.'"[20] While calling for cooperation and partnership, the document also expressed growing concern about Russia's inability to influence the structural-economic and legal conditions of the international system.

Putin made good on his word by insisting on equal partner treatment at the Japan 2000 summit of the G-8. He made a strong and determined showing there, surprising the other leaders of the group, who were accustomed to dealing with Yeltsin, whose "clownish antics... had only cemented their perception that Russia—notwithstanding its nuclear arsenal—lacked a government that could be taken seriously."[21] Putin came to the summit bearing news from his visit to North Korea and impressed the leaders by not asking for debt relief. He continued his impressive showing in foreign policy by undertaking a whirlwind tour of world capitals in the first year of his tenure, as well as issuing declarations about every possible strategic relationship of Russia. Of course, Putin was very much helped by Russia's economic recovery, which freed his hand to pursue international contacts. He also capitalized quickly on the events of September 11 by supporting American action in Central Asia in return for Western indulgence for Russia's military campaign in Chechnya. This was interpreted as a dramatic pro-Western shift in Putin's foreign policy, both at home and abroad. In 2002, Putin emphasized his desire for Russia to join the World Trade Organization and become a rule-making member of the international economic community. He also made frequent references to Russia's "stronger democracy" and "freer economy." However, if Putin seemed to be inching closer to the West abroad, at home he was doing the opposite, rolling back the political, military, and legal reforms of Yeltsin and ruling in an increasingly authoritarian manner.

Putin resisted joining the Iraq campaign of the United States, however, and in 2003 he put more distance between Russia and the United States. He started promoting the notion of an "arc of stability" stretching from Europe through the Caucasus and Central Asia to China and Southeast Asia, and concluded military alliances with the former Soviet republics of Central Asia and the Caucasus. Following these developments, toward the end of 2003 the United States rediscovered its skepticism about Russia's reliability as a partner. President George W. Bush openly criticized Putin for curtailing basic democratic freedoms, in stark contrast to his earlier statements. Tensions escalated in 2004 and came to a head over developments in Ukraine. However, economically Russia benefited from the instability of the world energy markets: surging demand from China and India, the costliest natural disaster in U.S. history, a global war on terrorism centered on the Middle East and Central Asia, and other events rocked energy markets and pushed Russia into the position of a global energy superpower. As a result, in the 2006 summit of the G-8 nations, Putin put great emphasis on his country's oil and gas exports as a rationale for its inclusion in the club. In the latter part of that decade (and even more so since then) Russia's foreign policy has greatly diverted from the optimistic Western predictions during Putin's early tenure.

Turkey, too, had a new leader in the 2000s. After years of coalition governments, the Justice and Development Party (AKP), which aimed to combine conservative Muslim values with democratic principles and economic liberalization, won a landslide victory in 2002. Erdoğan became prime minister in 2003 and initially pursued a series of political and economic reforms, seemingly including measures to strengthen democracy, promote human rights, and improve economic stability. As in Russia, Turkey's foreign policy trajectory started to shift away from the EU and the West near the end of the decade. Though signs would not be visible to the rest of the world until later, Erdoğan and the AKP also started their slide away from democracy during this time.

Western observers had been similarly optimistic about Erdoğan. A belief emerged in Western policy circles that under the AKP's leadership the country was poised to fix its long-standing economic, political, and social problems: "the AKP governments differed from their predecessors in adopting and promoting a brand approach in Turkish politics, stressing the importance of maintaining a favorable image as a stable investment destination."[22] This approach was especially successful in attracting foreign investment and credit to Turkey. Most of the AKP's much touted economic success (at the time) rested on a domestic infrastructure and housing boom, almost all of it made possible by foreign investment and borrowing.[23] For a brief period, Turkey was seen as one of the closest U.S. allies[24] and as a country with a real chance of EU accession, a feat the previous Kemalist regime had never been able to achieve, despite the lengths they went in order to produce their modernizing vision. That image came crushing down only with the Gezi protests and Turkey's increasingly authoritarian aftermath.

Some General Lessons for the Present: What Went Wrong in the First Decade of LIO Expansion?

As the discussion above makes clear, we cannot reduce the grievances of Russia or Turkey toward the West just to the decisions made by the core actors of the LIO in the 1990s. Many of these grievances have to do with longer-standing social, economic, and political hierarchies of the modern international order that go back to at least the nineteenth century and still influence how more recent decisions are/were interpreted.

This does not absolve LIO decision-making in the 1990s of its responsibility for the mistakes that were made. Nevertheless, it is important realize that international-order making always operates in the shadow of the past.

Second, it hardly needs to be said, but whether a country can act on its anti-LIO grievances and resentments has a lot to do with its material capabilities and institutional maneuvering room. Both Turkey and Russia had much greater interest in working with the LIO and complying with its demands in the 1990s, when they had serious economic and political troubles at home. This changed in the 2000s. The state of the energy markets and the uneven impact of the global financial crisis in 2007 made the economic situation of both Russia and Turkey seem much better than it was, giving Putin and Erdoğan greater maneuvering room in foreign policy.[25]

Third, the LIO can still be blamed for a number of things: for not taking more advantage of the conciliatory attitudes of the 1990s, for extending some recognition (in the form of membership in some LIO organizations) as an encouragement and/or placatory gesture when it was not objectively deserved, for supporting both Erdoğan and Putin in their early years (and continuing to make deals with them later, even when their authoritarian colors showed). In the 1990s, arguably more could have been done to support the Westernizing camps in both countries. Instead, the LIO withheld recognition from both Russia and Turkey for the most part and made the situation even worse by doling it out in partial ways. Russia's admission to G-8 immediately before Putin came to power and Turkey's advancement to EU candidate status immediately after Erdoğan did gave both regimes quite a bit of cover, even before the financial windfalls alluded to above. Simultaneously, the undeserved recognition that other Eastern European countries got in the 1990s increased the perception in both Russia and Turkey that the LIO and the West were not playing fair. Finally, centralizing power moves by each regime (against the oligarchs in the case of Putin and against the army in the case of Erdoğan) were welcomed and even applauded by major actors of the LIO. I would submit that this was partly because there was great optimism in this period about the inevitability of democratization and liberalization, which colored LIO observations of domestic developments within Russia and Turkey with a degree of naïveté. All in all, it was a perfect storm of bad moves. The LIO seemed to always go with the wrong choice in the 1990s and early 2000s when it came to both Russia and Turkey.

The two interesting counterfactuals to consider here are, on the one hand, what would have happened had either Turkey or Russia (or both) (1) been included more in the expansion of the LIO in the 1990s and, on the other, (2) been excluded more obviously. Of course, in both cases we have some real-life examples that come close. The fates of Czechia, Slovakia, Hungary, Bulgaria, Romania, and Poland give us some clues as to how the first path may have unfolded, though most of these countries are too small (less than 10 million population) to be comparable in a meaningful sense to either Turkey (85 million) or Russia (145 million). Only Romania (20 million) and Poland (39 million) come close. However, we could observe that the expansion of the LIO and consolidation of democracy at home has been uneven in even those relatively easier cases, and it is not hard to imagine that the attachment of these countries to the core of the order would be even flimsier had the external threat not grown in the interim. To put it another way, Poland may not be as successful a case of consolidation—to the extent that it even is—in a parallel universe where Russia was more included in the 1990s.

As for the second scenario, there are obviously many countries in the world that were more ignored in the 1990s than both Turkey and Russia, but within their specific neighborhood Ukraine comes closer to this scenario. The comparison once again is not exact because Ukraine's historical relationship with Russia undercuts whatever historical grievances it may have with the West in favor of the West, as it does often other Eastern European countries. Still, this case also supports the argument of this chapter that lack of attention is often better than raising expectations that cannot be met. After all, in the 1990s, apart from the nuclear disarmament agenda, Ukraine was more of an afterthought for the West, receiving encouragement but limited formal engagement. It was not until the 2000s that Ukraine started to feature more prominently in American and European foreign policy agendas, probably due to the emergent relational dynamic with an increasingly more slippery Russia. But it was not until the 2010s—with Euromaidan protests, Russia's annexation of Crimea, and most significantly Russia's 2022 invasion—that Ukraine became priority number one and the most strategic ally in many Western foreign policy agendas.

In other words, the timeline and the trajectory of Ukraine's engagement with the West and the core of the LIO is quite out of sync with Turkey's and Russia's. Unlike in those cases, Ukraine went from being the most ignored and excluded country to being recognized as critical to Western identity and the survival of the LIO. There was not really a case there of raised expectations in the 1990s that were not met later or being passed over for others. However, the way the current war concludes may come to resemble that dynamic. The West's halfway commitment to Ukraine may breed more resentment in the long run than lack of commitment from the start.

Notes

1. Following Adler-Nissen and Zarakol (2021), LIO is understood here to cover not just a specific ordering of international economy, security or politics, but as the combination of practices and visions of "open markets, international institutions, cooperative security. democratic community, progressive change, collective problem solving, shared sovereignty, [and] the rule of law" (Ikenberry 2011, 2). For tensions and debates on the definition of liberal order, see, e.g., Jahn 2018.
2. Adler-Nissen and Zarakol 2021, 612.
3. Adler-Nissen and Zarakol 2021.
4. Though "semiperiphery" is a broad category, for the purposes of this essay, I will limit the discussion of the semiperiphery to countries within the actual *geographic* semiperiphery of Europe where the question of the expansion of the liberal order in the 1990s was most acute and fraught. For more on the semiperiphery, see Lawson and Zarakol 2023.
5. Adler-Nissen and Zarakol 2021.
6. How Russia and Turkey compare to other resentful actors such as Poland and Hungary is an interesting question, but beyond the scope of this chapter. At a minimum, we could observe that the dynamics in those cases were slightly different because both Poland and Hungary gained full formal membership in the LIO. For more on those cases, see especially Appel in this volume.
7. See Aydın-Düzgit and Noutcheva 2022.
8. For more on this, see Zarakol 2011.
9. See Zarakol (2011) for a comparative discussion.
10. Not everyone agrees that the USSR/Russia was defeated in the Cold War; some argue that it self-imploded. Of course, to some extent the debate turns on what we mean by defeat. Here I use in the sense of being able to rival the West.
11. Zarakol 2011, 2013, 2014, 2017, 2019.
12. As explained in *After Defeat* (Zarakol 2011), the choice of coping strategy depends to some extent on material and ideational resources. Most non-Western states lacked the resources to follow any strategy but emulation in the twentieth century (but most did not go as far as Turkey in this regard).
13. *Baltimore Sun* 2006.
14. Arbatov 1993, 23.
15. Kassianova 2001, 829–830.
16. Kassianova 2001, 831.
17. Kassianova 2001, 832.
18. Nicholson 2001, 870.
19. Nicholson 2001, 871.
20. Kassianova 2001, 832.
21. As reported in the *Washington Post* July 24, 2000.
22. Rumelili and Süleymanoğlu-Kurum 2017, 551.
23. Subasat 2014. The author concludes that "Turkey's economy signifies another bubble economy where economic growth is led by domestic demand which is supported by external resources. Turkey's economy is, therefore, neither a 'miracle' nor even a mild success story."
24. Cook et al. 2012.
25. For more on the LIO's relationship with Russia in recent years see e.g. Haukkala 2009, Krastev and Leonard 2015, Morozov 2015, Bechev 2017, Romanova 2018, Schmitt 2020,

Casier 2018, 2021, Kurowska and Reshetnikov 2018, 2021; for Turkey see Bechev 2022, Subasat 2014, Aydin-Düzgit 2018, Kutlay and Onis 2021; for Russia and Turkey see Zarakol 2017, Aydin-Duzgit and Noutcheva 2022, Morozov and Rumelili 2012.

References

Adler-Nissen, Rebecca, and Ayşe Zarakol. 2021. "Struggles for Recognition: The Liberal International Order and the Merger of Its Discontents." *International Organization* 75 (2): 611–634.
Arbatov, Alexei G. 1993. "Russia's Foreign Policy Alternatives." *International Security* 18 (2): 5–43.
Aydın-Düzgit, Senem. 2018. "Legitimizing Europe in Contested Settings: Europe as a Normative Power in Turkey?" *Journal of Common Market Studies* 56 (3): 612–627.
Aydın-Düzgit, Senem, and Gergana Noutcheva. 2022. "External Contestations of Europe: Russia and Turkey as Normative Challengers?" *Journal of Common Market Studies* 1–17.
Baltimore Sun. 2006. Editorial. July 14.
Bechev, Dimitar. 2017. *Rival Power: Russia in Southeast Europe*. Yale University Press.
Bechev, Dimitar. 2022. "A Rival or an Awkward Partner? Turkey's Relationship with the West in the Balkans." *Southeast European and Black Sea Studies* 22 (1): 11–24.
Casier, Tom. 2018. "The Different Faces of Power in European Union–Russia Relations." *Cooperation and Conflict* 53 (1): 101–117.
Casier, Tom. 2021. "Russia and the Diffusion of Political Norms: The Perfect Rival?" *Democratization* 29 (3): 433–450.
Cook, Steven A., Madeleine K. Albright, and Stephen J. Hadley. 2012. "U.S.-Turkey Relations: A New Partnership." Task Force Report. Council on Foreign Relations, May.
Haukkala, Hiski. 2009. "Lost in Translation? Why the EU Has Failed to Influence Russia's Development." *Europe-Asia Studies* 61: 1757–1775.
Ikenberry, G. John. 2011. *Liberal Leviathan: The Origins, Crisis, and Transformation of the American World Order*. Princeton University Press.
Jahn, Beate. 2018. "Liberal internationalism: Historical trajectory and current prospects." *International Affairs* 94 (1): 43–61.
Kassianova, Allia. 2001. "Russia: Still Open to the West? Evolution of the State Identity in the Foreign Policy and Security Discourse." *Europe-Asia Studies* 53 (6): 821–839.
Krastev, Ivan, and Mark Leonard. 2015. "Europe's Shattered Dream of Order: How Putin Is Disrupting the Atlantic Alliance." *Foreign Affairs* 94 (3): 48–58.
Kurowska, Xymena, and Anatoly Reshetnikov. 2018. "Neutrollization: Industrialized Trolling as a Pro-Kremlin Strategy of Desecuritization." *Security Dialogue* 49 (5): 345–363.
Kurowska, Xymena, and Anatoly Reshetnikov. 2021. "Trickstery: Pluralising Stigma in International Society." *European Journal of International Relations* 27 (1): 232–257.
Kutlay, Mehmet, and Ziya Öniş. 2021. "Turkish Foreign Policy in a Post-Western Order: Strategic Autonomy or New Forms of Dependence." *International Affairs* 97 (4): 1085–1104.
Lawson, George and Ayşe Zarakol. 2023. "Recognizing injustice: the 'hypocrisy charge' and the future of the liberal international order." *International Affairs* 99 (1): 201–217.
Morozov, Viacheslav. 2015. *Russia's Postcolonial Identity: A Subaltern Empire in a Eurocentric World*. Palgrave.
Morozov, Viacheslav and Bahar Rumelili. 2012. "The External Constitution of European Identity: Russia and Turkey as Europe-Makers." *Cooperation and Conflict* 47 (1): 28–48.
Neumann, Iver B. 1999. *Uses of the Other: The "East" in European Identity Formation*. University of Minnesota Press.
Nicholson, Martin. 2001. "Putin's Russia: Slowing the Pendulum without Stopping the Clock." *International Affairs* 77 (4): 867–884.

Romanova, Tatiana. 2018. "Russia's Neorevisionist Challenge to the Liberal International Order." *International Spectator* 53 (1): 76–91.

Rumelili, Bahar, and Rahime Süleymanoğlu-Kurum. 2017. "Brand Turkey: Liminal Identity and Its Limits." *Geopolitics* 22 (3): 549–570.

Schmitt, Oliver. 2020. "How to Challenge an International Order: Russian Diplomatic Practices in Multilateral Security Organisations." *European Journal of International Relations* 26 (3): 922–946.

Subasat, Turan. 2014. "The Political Economy of Turkey's Economic Miracle." *Journal of Balkan and Near Eastern Studies* 16 (2): 137–160.

Zarakol, Ayşe. 2011. *After Defeat: How the East Learned to Live with the West*. Cambridge University Press.

Zarakol, Ayşe. 2013. "Revisiting Second Image Reversed: Lessons from Turkey and Thailand." *International Studies Quarterly* 57 (1): 150–162.

Zarakol, Ayşe. 2014. "What Made the Modern World Hang Together: Socialisation or Stigmatisation?" *International Theory* 6 (2): 311–332.

Zarakol, Ayşe. 2017. "Türkiye ve Rusya: Tarihsel Benzerlikler." In *Kuşku ile Komşuluk: Türkiye ve Rusya İlişkilerinde Değişen Dinamikler*, edited by Gencer Özcan, Evren Balta, and Burç Beşgül. İstanbul İletişim Yayınları.

Zarakol, Ayşe. 2019. "Rise of the Rest: As Hype and Reality." In "Reflections on a Century of International Politics." Special issue, *International Relations* 33 (2): 213–228.

13

On Breakthroughs, Deadlocks, and Rose-Gardens Lost in Between

The Failed Promise of North-South Cooperation

Amrita Narlikar

> Footfalls echo in the memory
> Down the passage which we did not take
> Towards the door we never opened
> Into the rose-garden.
> —T. S. Eliot, "Burnt Norton," in *Four Quartets*

Rifts and confrontations between the Global North and the Global South marked several decades of the post–World War II era. The fall of the Berlin Wall and events that followed in the 1990s created a refreshing context, and not for a breakdown of barriers between the East and West alone. New opportunities presented themselves for developed and developing countries to cooperate closely. World leaders signaled their commitment to harness the zeitgeist effectively toward global growth, development, poverty alleviation, and building a sustainable peace worldwide. Fast-forward to the present day, however, and it is clear that the promise of a peaceful, prosperous new world order based on North-South cooperation has fallen short.

On fundamental problems that the world is faced with today—including the weaponization of interdependence, democratic backsliding, the climate emergency, and dramatically reduced biodiversity—developed and developing countries (even among those that share important attributes, such as democracy and pluralism) are far from being on the same page. The persistent reluctance of key states from the Global South to break ties with Russia over its invasion of Ukraine (in spite of Western expectations and insistence) is an illustration of the divergence; polarization over Israel and Palestine is another. Disappointment with the institutions of global governance, which should have been able to address at least some of the current challenges, is rife and comes from many different quarters. In this chapter, I investigate how and why, despite the opportunities of the 1990s and early 2000s, we ended up at this point of distrust, discord, and conflict.

The chapter proceeds in three parts. I start with an empirical overview of North–South relations in the early phases of the post–Cold War era, outlining the early breakthroughs as well as subsequent deadlocks. The next section traces the routes—the *hows*—which brought the system from its promise of success to recurrent and multilayered failures. It further delves into *why* those routes might have been chosen in the first place and identifies three core drivers—located in the realms of policy and scholarship and their interface—that contributed to several unfortunate choices. As a third step, I conduct a thought experiment to highlight one set of might-have-beens, had countries within the Global South and the Global North played their cards differently. I conclude the chapter by developing some policy-relevant ideas on what might still be done to replant the lost rose gardens and nurture new ones.[1]

The Global South and the Post–Cold War Order: The Record

Compare the scale and complexity of problems that afflict our world today against the promise of the post–Cold War era, and the temptation to write off the entire decade as a lost one is high. In this section, I trace both the early highs and the subsequent lows of the 1990s, and thereby make the case for resisting revisionism, on the one hand, and golden-age thinking, on the other.

Credit Where Credit Is Due: Negotiation Breakthroughs across the North-South Divide

Amid the mutual disappointments on the part of the Global North and the Global South today it is sometimes far too easy to dismiss the several successes that characterized the 1990s and early 2000s. Revisionism along such lines needs to be resisted. Actors across the North-South divide had good reason for optimism. Driving the breakthroughs were three mechanisms: the 3Ms of markets, multilateralism, and multipolarity.

The introduction to this volume highlights the role of *markets* in influencing the politics of the 1990s and beyond; as the editors argue, globalization and integration (together with democracy) were the "watchwords" of the post–Cold War "expanded liberal order." Developing countries across the world adopted—and also came to "own"—economic reform programs. The liberalization of markets created new opportunities for growth and development. Importantly, these changes were not simply a case of developing countries making the best of a bad situation, prompted by the collapse of the Soviet Union and correspondingly vanished BATNAs (Best Alternative to a Negotiated Agreement), thereby accepting a wholehearted conversion to the Washington Consensus. Rather, a meaningful back-and-forth got underway between rich and poor countries, which seemed to transcend the "North-South stalemate"[2] of yesteryears and expand the zone of agreement for the negotiation of new norms and rules. Although a new "consensus" was yet to emerge, there was promise that one—more inclusive, more equitable—was in the making.

Multilateral institutions increased dramatically in number.[3] They provided the necessary venues and instruments to facilitate Global North-South conversations, while also ensuring settings where developing countries could work in coalitions. Using this collective agency, developing countries saw new possibilities to regulate certain aspects of the market mechanism about which they had reservations.

Successfully harnessed economic opportunities and multilateral institutions together helped transform the "unilateral moment"[4] of 1990 into a new era of *multipolarity* at the turn of the millennium. The poles in this new world order were not only the usual suspects of middle powers—Germany, Japan, Canada—but a new swath of rising powers from the Global South.[5] Goldman Sachs recognized the growing clout of these emerging markets—Brazil, Russia, India, and China—and also came up with the acronym BRICs in 2001.[6] The four countries embraced the acronym as one of their collective identities and began to engage in global summitry from 2009 onward; South Africa was included in the group in 2010, changing the acronym from BRICs to BRICS. The forum served as a platform to facilitate closer cooperation among the five countries but also to signal the collective clout and bargaining power of emerging markets externally.

State and nonstate actors from both the North and the South were able to harness the mix of the 3Ms to generate multiple achievements. The successes were important in their own right, and also for demonstrating the potential of the system to transform into a more inclusive one. This promise was reflected most clearly in the changing processes and agenda of trade and development issues.

The willingness of the Global North and Global South to work together on a more equal basis in the post–Cold War era was reflected in the changes to the processes of global governance. For instance, developing countries had bitterly described the predecessor of the World Trade Organization (WTO)—the General Agreement on Tariffs and Trade (GATT)—as a "rich man's club." In the aftermath of the critique that the WTO encountered at the Seattle Ministerial Conference, important changes were introduced to facilitate transparency and inclusiveness. Contra consensus-building based on consultations among the old Quad (Canada, EU, Japan, and the United States), new permutations emerged. Brazil, India, and China became regular invitees to the high table of negotiations. Invitation-only Green Room meetings came to be replaced by more open formats to which members could self-select participation. To make up for the small size of their permanent representation in Geneva as well as other constraints that smaller developing countries and Least Developed Countries faced, technical assistance and capacity-building programs were set up. The rising powers became adept in building lasting coalitions with smaller developing countries to facilitate access, legitimacy, and bargaining clout. As a result of these collective efforts and corresponding institutional innovations, developing countries were finally able to transform their theoretical veto power (accorded to each member of the WTO by virtue of the consensus principle) into a genuine veto power that could be used in practice.[7] Reform on its working practices helped increase the internal and external legitimacy of the WTO, promising to create a virtuous cycle of global cooperation.[8]

Other clubs of rich men too were opening up to new players. The G-7 transformed itself into the G-8 by accepting Russia as a member in 1997. Ten years later, the group further expanded its outreach via the Heiligendamm Process and invited Brazil, China, India, Mexico, and South Africa to the summit. The leaders-level G-20 was created in 2008, in recognition of the importance of finding joint solutions to the global financial crisis.[9] These changes in processes facilitated a potential implementation of unprecedented agenda-setting power on the part of the former "Third World."

An important result of the improved inclusiveness of global governance processes was that the political-economic agenda of the Global South finally ceased to be a niche affair, which had been catered to by the United Nations Conference on Trade and Development in the Cold War era. Instead, through the late 1990s and early 2000s, development concerns began to be mainstreamed in an unprecedented way. Bringing together state actors, religious leaders, and celebrities, the Jubilee 2000 initiative was launched in 1996 to seek the cancelation of Third World debt. The first of the UN Millennium Development Goals was chosen to be eradication of extreme poverty and hunger.[10] Activists met at the World Social Forum for the first time, in Porto Allegre in 2001, to advance a different vision of global economic order from the World Economic Forum's, and global citizens marched to Make Poverty History in 2005.[11] Attempts by developed countries to push the Millennium Round at the WTO ended abysmally with the Battle of Seattle in 1999. In place of the aborted Millennium Round, the Doha Development Agenda (DDA) was launched in 2001, which marked a historic first by placing development concerns at the heart of trade multilateralism.

None of these developments happened overnight. They were often a product of tough negotiations across the North-South divide. But breakthroughs thus achieved also had the potential to be longer-lasting and more sustainable, in contrast to rules that parties might have agreed to under duress or due to lack of viable negotiation alternatives. As developed and developing countries created new meeting ground in and across different issue areas (witness the linkage between trade and development, which had been studiously avoided in the GATT era), there was reason to believe that long-held divisions between *us versus them* were finally breaking down in the joint quest for prosperity that globalization afforded.

Unfortunately, neither the momentum nor the optimism lasted for long.

Deadlocks and Failures

Disillusionment and disappointment on both sides began to set in relatively early on, albeit at different rates of speed across different issue areas and regions. Several unambiguous failures followed.[12]

The WTO provides some striking illustrations of such policy failures. Despite the initial promise of sustainable breakthroughs that its reformed decision-making and updated agenda had offered, today the organization is in fundamental disrepair. All three of its core functions—negotiation, transparency, and dispute settlement—are blocked to different degrees. On the negotiation front, the DDA had been scheduled for completion by 2005; even after more than two decades of fraught negotiations, members failed to produce the ambitious package deal that had been envisioned at the launch of the round.[13] The failure of the DDA was not only indicative of a declining faith in multilateralism and globalism but was also emblematic of the souring of North-South relations. After all, this round was the first in the history of the multilateral trading regime to be dedicated to the cause of development, as espoused by developing country members. The costs of its failure included not only the growth and development gains that a successful round would have generated, but also serious dents to the credibility of the WTO as a negotiating forum. Countries turned increasingly to regional alternatives and thereby invested even lesser effort into the multilateral process, creating a downward, damaging spiral for the multilateral trade regime. Post-Doha, too, progress has been slow to negligible, with members neither able to address "traditional" issues (like agriculture and market access) nor update the rules of the organization to address new problems (digital trade, dealing with excess capacity in manufacturing, and national security).[14] The transparency function of the WTO also ran into trouble, its members demonstrating reluctance to share important, requested information (e.g., on general economic support measures).[15] The Dispute Settlement Mechanism—once regarded as the crowning jewel of the regime—was (and remains) paralyzed because the appointment or reappointment of members of the appellate body continues to be blocked by the United States.

On matters of international security, too, global governance institutions and instruments began to lose their luster. Over the past thirty years, rich and poor countries have called for reform of the UN Security Council (UNSC), but this reform has not happened. The reform agenda is not just academic or technocratic. Outside UN headquarters and in the real world it has been increasingly obvious that without major restructuring, the UNSC's credibility deficit will only grow. This was, once again, powerfully illustrated in the case of the Russian invasion of Ukraine and the impotence of the

UNSC to act when a P5 member is involved as an aggressor.[16] The problems of the UNSC, moreover, run deeper than the potential misuse of veto power by a P5 member. Recall, for instance, that on the UNSC Resolution passed on February 25, 2022, besides Russia's use of its veto, three other members (China, India, and the United Arab Emirates) of the fifteen-member council abstained.[17] This pattern has persisted in the UNSC in further resolutions on the issue. The UN General Assembly, while offering the support of a majority of countries (usually over 140) for Ukraine and only a minority of votes against, has also had a significant number of countries abstaining (usually over thirty, including not only China—unsurprisingly so, given that it had declared its "no-limits partnership" with Russia just prior to the invasion—but also two other BRICS countries, India and South Africa).[18] The fault lines on this issue do not reflect a clear North-South divide, but they do reveal that the Western allies may have been overly optimistic in assuming that at least the democracies of the Global South would offer their unambiguous support for Ukraine. Contra Western expectations, major democracies, for instance from the B(R)ICS group, have refrained from imposing sanctions against Russia. And within the G-20—one of the poster-child organizations of the new liberal order—only half of the membership is sanctioning Russia; the other half has either opted out or deepened ties with Russia.[19]

An area where the failures of global governance come together in a very immediate way is the COVID-19 pandemic. Almost 7 million deaths have been recorded thus far, a number perhaps still growing as the virus mutates and long-term effects of the disease become known. This catastrophic outcome is a product of multiple processes of global governance having gone awry, besides the sins of omission and commission by individual governments. Failures by the World Health Organization to hold China to account, its reluctance and delay in declaring COVID to be a global pandemic, and further misleading directives (e.g., an insistence that the infection was not airborne and that masks would not make a difference) form one part of the ignoble story.[20] Following close behind are the problems that occurred in the field of trade politics. Disruptions to supply chains and the demonstrated readiness of some countries to impose export restrictions on lifesaving medicines and other medical supplies—or to use access to those vital supply chains for diplomatic leverage—are examples of failed trade governance in the early part of the pandemic. At least from the perspective of large parts of the Global South, the WTO's agreement on Trade Related Intellectual Property Rights has played a major part in contributing to vaccine inequality as well as lack of access to other treatments.[21] Divisions over and within institutions of global governance are thus rife.

New institutions that were developed in the era of optimism as cooperative endeavors, working in synch with other global institutions while also serving as useful BATNAs for negotiations, have now taken a more competitive (and sometimes even menacing) turn. China's recent attempts to expand the BRICS and turn it into a counterweight to the G-7 is a case in point.[22] In the context of the Asian Infrastructure and Investment Bank (AIIB), Qian Jing, James Crawford, and Jianzhi Zhao similarly argue that even if the institution may have been set up by China with the "ostensible goal" of making up for a shortfall in infrastructure investment in the region and beyond, recent evidence shows that "the World Bank is losing ground to China's AIIB. The AIIB may thus represent a challenge to the political influence the United States has enjoyed over developing countries through its leadership at the World Bank."[23] It is worth pointing out that the observed average reduction in the annual number of World Bank infrastructure projects (22 percent between 2016 and 2019) in developing countries that were founding members of the AIIB is only partly an issue of China-U.S. competition. This behavior pattern reflects the growing dissatisfaction in parts of the Global South with institutions that served as pillars of the liberal economic order (and models of development and governance associated with these institutions) and their openness to alternatives that are on the menu. That said, Chinese power projection via its Belt and Road Initiative and growing dominance in some international organizations have attracted the concern of recipient countries in the Global South in recent years.[24] The Global North is cognizant of these challenges and has attempted to develop their own projects; for example, Europe's Global Gateway and the American Build Back Better World initiatives, however limited, offer potential alternatives to the Chinese Belt and Road Initiative.

These developments add up to a harsher reality of competition, divergence, and polarization, in contrast to the vision of cooperation, convergence, and socialization that had characterized the early phase of the post–Cold War order. The magic of the 3Ms of markets, multilateralism, and multipolarity has been gradually fading over the years.

The Hows and Whys

On both sides of the North-South divide, discontent was brewing, leading politicians and their constituencies to question the gains that had formerly been associated with the 3Ms. In this section, I first outline the *hows* and then identify three drivers that led actors down these altered pathways.

In Western democracies, the "hyperglobalization"[25] of markets was seen to be contributing to increasing income inequality. As John Ikenberry has argued, "Across the western liberal democratic world, liberal internationalism looks more like neo-liberalism—a framework for international capitalist transactions. The 'embedded' character of liberal internationalism has slowly eroded. The social purposes of the liberal order are not what they once were."[26] Economic and political backlash followed, including the rise of populism and right-wing movements.

Multilateral institutions upholding the global order also came under attack in the West. U.S. president Donald Trump's tirades against multilateral organizations during his first term were among the most visceral (e.g., he described the agreement establishing the WTO as "the single worst deal ever made").[27] But the dissatisfaction of the United States with key aspects of multilateralism predated the Trump 1.0 era and has persisted since. The WTO's Dispute Settlement Mechanism is a case in point. The Trump administration's decision to block the appointment or reappointment of appellate body members had precedence in the Barack Obama administration (which had blocked the reappointment of two members and the new appointment of one). Admittedly, under Trump America's dissatisfaction with the Dispute Settlement Mechanism visibly increased: as of December 2019, the appellate body did not have enough members to decide cases, "leaving pending appeals in limbo and threatening to turn every future trade dispute into a mini-trade war."[28] But under President Joe Biden's administration, too, despite the promise "America is back" and reform proposals by several members, the United States stood unrelenting in its position on the blocked appellate body.[29] It is extremely unlikely that the Trump 2.0 administration will help restore the WTO to its former glory, if the returning president's preelection statements are an indicator.[30]

Multipolarity was becoming another irritant for the Global North. Writing an op-ed in the aftermath of the WTO's failed Cancun Ministerial in September 2003, the then U.S. trade representative Robert Zoellick did not disguise his frustration over the role that developing countries had played in the process: "We know well what developing countries are demanding, but have not heard whether more competitive developing economies will cut their high barriers. We do not know whether other developing countries that blocked action in Cancun will now accept packages that ask little or nothing of them. . . . [T]he key division at Cancun was between the can-do and the won't do. As WTO members ponder the future, the US will not wait: we will move towards free trade with can-do countries."[31] U.S. Trade Representative Susan Schwab was even more damning in her indictment of the emerging markets; quoting an African ambassador to the WTO, she likened Brazil, India, China, and South Africa to "elephants hiding behind mice" as they joined forces with other developing countries and refused to open their own markets. The "developed-*versus*-developing-country-framework" was increasingly anachronistic, she argued; a clear differentiation was necessary that required the larger, richer countries of the Global South to take on more responsibility.[32] It further became apparent in subsequent years that the danger posed by multipolarity was not just free-riding. With China's rise, and its ability and willingness to game (and misuse) the system, the challenge to the existing rules—and the values that they were supposed to uphold—became more fundamental, much to the consternation of the United States, the EU, and other Western democracies.

That the cooperative spirit of the 1990s would be difficult to sustain when the very "winners" and guarantors of the system were so disillusioned with it is not surprising. But the Global South—including many of the countries that the Global North claimed were benefiting unfairly from the system—were just as dissatisfied, if not more. This was reflected in the politics of trade and development and the readiness of coalitions from the Global South to hold up the negotiations. (For example, the refrain "No deal is better than this deal" had echoed in the corridors of the Cancun Ministerial Conference as well as outside.) As the years progressed, the frustration of some countries from the Global South on matters of international security too became louder and more pronounced. When India came under criticism for not taking a strong position against Russia on Ukraine, the Indian foreign minister hit back hard with the following response: "Europe has to grow out of the mindset that Europe's problems are the world's problems, but the world's problems are not Europe's problems."[33] Interestingly, even as the mood in the Global North toward China soured, both democracies and authoritarian regimes in the Global South remained reluctant to turn down opportunities coming from China (e.g., infrastructure and investment in critically important sectors). It is further worth noting that India, despite its long history of border disputes and conflict with China, has frequently and in diverse settings ended up in the same corner as its difficult neighbor (e.g., in the WTO, in climate change negotiations, and in seeking a reform of development institutions). And India is not the only democracy from the Global South that has adopted negotiating positions that are out of synch with Western expectations—and shown that they are more comfortable in taking positions that look closer to China's.

Irrespective of their geographical location, political systems, and development levels, countries today are a long way from the optimism and purpose that they shared in the 1990s and early 2000s. I identify three key drivers below, which have led to this state of affairs.

Driver 1: Misjudgments on Norms and Identities

The first and foremost driver that has brought us to this point today was—and remains—misguided strategies on the part of the Global North in dealing with the Global South. Reflexivity further produced unhelpful reactions from the Global South. A downward spiral ensued. Two seemingly contradictory strategies employed by key players in the Global North are outlined in this subsection.

On the one hand, reductionism and underreach...[34]
There has been a tendency to lump together developing countries into groups—from categories such as the "Third World" in the Cold War era to "middle powers" and "swing states" in the post–Cold War era and the "Global South" and "developing world" spanning the decades. This is not a problem per se. Different categories can serve as useful heuristic devices, and developing countries themselves have created and embraced some of them (e.g., the BRICS, or via coalitional identities in international organizations, such as the G-77 in the UN). The problem arises, however, when these categories are reified for policy purposes by the Global North and fundamental differences within the category ignored.

The hyphenation of India and China—exemplified in the creation of the portmanteau word "ChIndia"—serves as a striking "how-not-to" example. Both China and India are ancient civilizations, are located in Asia, and have shared meteoric growth rates in the post–Cold War era; as such, they have been mentioned in the same breath by business leaders, policymakers, and politicians (from the early 2000s to now).[35] The problem with this reductionism, however, is threefold.

First, the two powers, despite their geographic proximity and parallel rise, are fundamentally different—not only in their interests and political systems but also in their civilizational values. Take the example of human rights. It is commonly assumed that together with other countries in the region, China and India share "Asian values" (that stress the importance of family and society) on key issues such as human rights (in contrast to Western, liberal, "universal" values that emphasize the rights of the individual).[36] This broad-brush notion of "Asian" values, however, is misleading. India offers understandings of human rights that are more individual-oriented and more liberal than not only "Asian" interpretations but also Western ones: "human rights," in variants of Indian philosophy, go beyond the human and extend to more-than-human beings.[37] Importantly, these differences between China and India do not rest solely in tomes of ancient philosophy; they form the living traditions of these countries and shape their politics even today. This was reflected, for instance, in India's G-20 presidency, which was built on the uniquely Indian perspective "One Earth, One Family, One Future" and explicitly applied some of the country's ancient traditions to address modern-day problems.[38] Reducing these two fundamentally different powers into one group does not do justice to either.

Second, by bracketing China and India together, countries in the Global North underestimated the extent to which India shared certain liberal values with the West. This, in turn, meant that potential avenues for deepened cooperation—even alliance-building—with the world's largest democracy were lost. The same blind spots in Western perception were also present with reference to other parts of the Global South. Key differences and permutations among the BRICS, and indeed between other Global South members, were missed. Driven by an assumption that *liberal* values were primarily a feature of Western civilization, much of the Global North "underreached." It was wrongly assumed that the Global South was internally more cohesive than it actually was and that it cherished values that were profoundly different from Western, liberal ones. These assumptions were usually not rooted in malicious intent. Often they represented a well-meaning political correctness that tried to avoid testy questions of values, accepted cultural relativism, catered to what were believed to be the interests of the "rest" (which were seen as largely aligned with the North's at the moment when history had supposedly ended), and sometimes also offered new players seats at the high table. But as became all too apparent with the case of the WTO, core differences could not be assumed away, and giving the BRICS a seat at the table was never going to suffice. More fundamental reform was needed, which took into account a far greater diversity of interests that was now being vociferously articulated, underpinned by values that overlapped with Western ones in some cases and clashed in others. By failing to recognize deep-rooted, identity-based differences among the countries of the Global South, the West lost opportunities to win like-minded (liberal) allies and supporters as well as identify potential competitors and rivals in a timely way.

Third, by lumping together divergent—even opposing—parts of the Global South, the West created a self-fulfilling prophecy. The states of the Global South reflexively embraced the labels and identities that were being foisted on them and came to "own" parts of the narrative (e.g., of cohesion within and divergence without), even if sometimes purely for strategic reasons. This, in turn, created feedback loops that reinforced an avoidable essentialization and further entrenched Southern loyalties and North-South differences. A perverse reflexivity was at work, intricately bound up with Western strands of liberalism and the West's colonial baggage. Caught between the conceit of the West being the sole source and preserve of liberal ideas and a subsequent self-flagellation of Western liberalism, given its deep entanglement with colonial projects, Southern players with original and homegrown varieties of liberalism also found themselves cornered into denying their own liberal roots. Instead, developmentalist narratives that drew on shared colonial histories and brought together unlikely bedfellows (liberal and illiberal, democratic and authoritarian) offered safer, more stable ground.

A powerful illustration of this can be found in the example of the BRICS. There were already serious points of difference—on questions of geopolitics, geo-economics, and values—among the five members.[39] In the lead-up to and at the BRICS Summit in South Africa in 2023, China took a clear lead in presenting the group as an alternative to the West.[40] In spite of Brazil's and India's supposed misgivings, the BRICS also decided to expand the group, with six new countries joining in 2024: Argentina, Egypt, Ethiopia, Iran, United Arab Emirates, and Saudi Arabia.[41] That the BRICS grouping has continued to thrive—and, indeed, expand—and that too in the face of many internal differences within the group, should be a wake-up call for the Western allies to reconsider their negotiation behavior and foreign policies toward the Global South.

... on the other hand, blanket rejection of a collective idea and identity?

It seems that some self-reflection has been taking place in policy and think-tank circles amid the global discord and conflict, leading to calls that the term "Global South" be "retired."[42] At the G-7 summit in Tokyo in 2023, an explicit decision was made to avoid using the term on the following grounds: "The term, referring to emerging and developing nations manly in the Southern Hemisphere, may give the impression of lumping together countries with diverse circumstances and is therefore considered inappropriate for such a document."[43] But canceling the term does not address the problems outlined above; if anything, it exacerbates them:

> [S]imply disaggregating the entire Global South into individual actors with whom the West will deal in a hub-and-spoke model is not only intellectually extremely messy, but also looks like an attempt to deprive the Global South of agency. Note also that while Western policy-makers are at pains to disaggregate the Global South, China is pursuing quite the opposite strategy—often rather effectively. It recognizes developing countries as a group, claims belonging to this group, and then offers seemingly cheap infrastructure, investment and even diplomatic support to this group. Perhaps one should then not be surprised that many countries of the Global South are much more receptive to China—with its embrace of their identity and investment towards it—and resistant to European attempts to divide them.[44]

At a time when analysts and governments in the West are trying to discredit the term, developing countries themselves are proudly reclaiming the label, embracing the collective identity associated with it, and further reshaping it. India, for instance, hosted the first Voice of the Global South Summit in January 2023, which saw the participation of 125 countries.[45] The third summit was held within a hundred days of the formation of India's new government, highlighting that the Global South was regarded as a strategic priority. This summit included ten ministerial sessions to cover issues of foreign policy, health, finance, energy, education, and more.[46] The emphasis on the reform of global governance in these summits shows that these diverse countries still share memories and imaginations of colonialism, deprivation, and marginalization. They have long histories of working together, which stand them in good stead as they seek to address current and future challenges.

While failures to recognize their individual experiences and distinctive cultures have made it difficult to discover common ground for cooperation between parts of the Global South and North, trying to deny "the rest" their self-defined collective identities comes across as colonial and paternalistic.[47] Misplaced underreach and overreach on fundamental questions of norms and identities have together turned out to be toxic to the North-South relationship. Negotiating positions and policies that find a balance between these two extremes are needed, as I outline in the final part of this chapter.

Driver 2: Technocratic Overreach

While the West underreached in recognizing like-minded partners in the Global South, it simultaneously overreached in assuming the homogenizing and socializing value of technocratic institutionalism.

Focusing specifically on the multilateral trading system, international lawyer Rob Howse has presented an incisive analysis of a technocratic mindset that came to dominate the WTO, at the expense of political and normative content. Even in the Cold War era, trade governance had come to be entrusted to a "specialized policy elite insulated from, and not particularly interested in, the larger political and social conflicts of the age." This "insider network" comprised "some officials employed in the GATT/WTO Secretariat ... but more important, the larger group of 'experts': former or current government trade officials; GATT-friendly academics who often sat on GATT/WTO dispute settlement panels and were invited to various conferences and meetings of the GATT/WTO; international civil servants in other organizations (particularly the World Bank, the Organization for Economic Cooperation and Development, and the IMF) preoccupied with trade matters; and a few private attorneys, consultants and former politicians." Under the influence of this insider network, "[a] sense of pride developed that an international regime was being evolved that stood above the 'madhouse' of politics ... a regime grounded in the insights of economic 'science.'"[48]

While Howse dates the tendency of the system to (over)rely on "a specialized policy elite" to the Cold War era, the (supposedly) "unabashed victory" of liberalism exacerbated this pattern. Francis Fukuyama had eloquently described the "end of history" as an era when "[t]he struggle for recognition, the willingness to risk one's life for a purely abstract goal, the worldwide ideological struggle that called forth daring, courage, imagination, and idealism, will be replaced by economic calculation, the endless solving of technical problems, environmental concerns, and the satisfaction of sophisticated consumer demands."[49] In such a world, it is hardly surprising that technical expertise was assumed to be paramount in resolving (likely) minor operational disagreements among countries that were now all on the same apolitical page.

The reinforced tendency to downplay political and cultural differences, and instead seek economic and legal solutions, can be seen at work in the technocratic bubbles of Brussels and Geneva even today.[50] By ignoring deep-rooted differences and wishfully assuming (or aiming for) a global homogeneity among diverse actors, negotiators and policymakers underestimated the extent of disagreement that existed between some of the new powers and the incumbents on key principles of order. Multilateral governance—across issue areas—became resistant to a reboot. Restricted reform efforts to bring about changes *within* the system (rather than *of* the system) contributed to the further frustration of countries from the Global South. Additionally, technocratic international institutions were reluctant to engage with urgent political questions of global power shifts and thus found themselves ill-prepared to address new geopolitical and geo-economic threats. One such challenge lies in the phenomenon of "weaponized interdependence."[51]

Recall that an important underlying assumption of the postwar order was that increasing trade (and other forms of economic integration) would contribute not only to prosperity but also to a liberal, Kantian peace. The end of the Cold War further reinforced the belief, especially among Western policymakers, "that extending interdependence and tightening economic integration among nations is a positive development that advances peace, stability, and prosperity."[52] But recent years have seen a structural change in production patterns, which turns this logic on its head: the very same ties of interdependence, which could once be relied on to enhance prosperity and peace, can now be "weaponized." Henry Farrell and Abraham Newman argue that only a few states, by virtue of their privileged positions on network hubs and necessary institutional capacity, are able to exercise control over these closely integrated but highly asymmetric production systems. They can do so either through the "panopticon" ("extract informational advantages vis-à-vis adversaries") or "chokepoint" ("cut adversaries off from network flows") effects.[53] High network externalities make the entry of new players difficult, thereby exacerbating power hierarchies even further in the interests of states already in control of network hubs.

While production patterns create opportunity for some states to weaponize global supply chains, certain institutional characteristics enhance weaponization capacities (such as domestic regulations that ensure effective state control over firms). In contrast to the Cold War era, during which countries of the former Eastern bloc had not formed a part of global economic structures and processes, this time a greater diversity of states with competing political systems and values forms a part of this system. Some of these states have both capacity and intent to weaponize their control over rare earth minerals, energy, and critical infrastructure. But still relying on prior assumptions of the *virtues* of interdependence and unwilling to correct their technocratic overreach, existing multilateral institutions are ill-equipped to deal with the problem of weaponized interdependence.[54] As geo-economic challenges increase, liberal multilateral organizations risk making themselves redundant through their too-little-too-late, lowest-common-denominator reform efforts. Such a development would be suboptimal for a wide range of actors, and perhaps of greatest detriment to countries of the Global South that have little possibility of becoming hub powers themselves.[55]

Driver 3: The Underreach of Positive Narratives

As argued at the start of this chapter, the disillusionment and dysfunctionality that we see today should not take away from the very real successes that the early phase of the post–Cold War era generated. But an important reason why not more was made of the achievements—thereby advancing the strides that had already been made—lay in the disconnect between the worlds of policy and people on the ground. The missing link lay in narratives.[56]

Pro-globalization, pro-multilateralism *narratives* could have clearly communicated to electorates how their prosperity depended on the smooth functioning of an inclusive system of trade rules. The reliance on technocratic institutionalism, as explained under Driver 2, however, allowed—even encouraged—policymakers (and academic experts within the "insider network") to keep their distance from the engaged public. The defenders of the post–Cold War order were, in fact, so convinced about their being on the right side of history that they felt no need to explain their actions to others.[57] In contrast, antiglobalization and anti-multilateralism narratives—even when factually incorrect—did a better job in appealing to the everyday fears and concerns of people. Think, for instance, of the "take back control" narrative of the Leave campaign over the Brexit referendum, in contrast to the solid but dull narrative espoused by the Remainers.[58] China's narrative of offering pro-development and conditionality-free trade, investment, and infrastructure-building opportunities, via the Belt and Road Initiative and other initiatives, similarly managed to convince a range of developing countries, in stark contrast to the Geneva- and Brussels-based debates on trade.

Replanting the Pathways to the Rose-Gardens

Caught between a peculiar mix of hubris of overreach and (sometimes politically correct, sometimes just lazy) underreach, the liberal order of the 1990s would not have survived to the present day. Members from the Global South wanted a fundamental reform of existing organizations (such as the UNSC). Even after they were included at the high table of negotiations (as was the case in the WTO), it became clear that they would not settle for a quiet, compliant, token presence. The pressures from outside the multilateral bubble were even more severe. Failures to engage with key players from the Global South on an eye-to-eye basis (as illustrated in the problems of both underreach and overreach, discussed in the previous section) rendered the presumed 1990s "consensus" unstable, especially as the balance of power shifted toward Asia. Had there been greater engagement with domestic and global publics via convincing, adaptable narratives, the liberal order may have acquired longer-lasting legitimacy. But in the absence of such engagement and feedback loops for updating narratives and embracing new norms of liberalism, the system was unlikely to survive. The great disruption that we are witnessing in global politics today is a product of the limitations of structures, processes, ideas, and narratives that underpinned the 1990s.

Before summarizing the implications of the argument that I have presented in this chapter, I offer a thought experiment on one might-have-been, had North-South relations taken a different tack in the post–Cold War era (Box 13.1). Specifically, would the world have looked different today had Southern varieties of liberalism played—indeed been allowed to play (had there been an absence of the misjudgments, technocratic overreach, and narrational underreach identified in the previous section)—a bigger, shaping role in the 1990s to the early 2000s?

Box 13.1 Thought-Experiment: Environmental Governance with Southern Variants of Liberalism

---

One could imagine a world where the debate on environmentalism and ecologism looks fundamentally different from where it currently stands. In this parallel world, the environmental governance incorporates ideas that challenge Western norms of anthropocentrism. The regime includes ideas from ancient Indian philosophy, which stress the importance of animal rights and do not restrict personhood to human beings.[59] More-than-humans and nature enjoy status and rights equivalent to humans. The resulting global regime governing ecological questions is committed to protecting animals and other species for the preservation of biodiversity, but also seeks to alleviate and prevent the suffering of *individual* animals in their own right. Cognate regimes are also tightening their rules on animal welfare. Trade agreements have far tougher "trade-and" clauses, which are not limited to environmental and labor standards; instead they require compliance with animal protection indices. Trophy hunting faces tougher penalties. Norm cascades follow,[60] deepening the domestic commitment of the countries that are already leading such transspecies initiatives globally (in this case, India and the EU). Material incentives (e.g., better trade deals and aid packages) and norm diffusion are generating parallel movements in several other countries as well, in both the Global South and North. Vegetarianism and veganism are flourishing, with positive implications for addressing the climate crisis. There are also security implications:

Continued

> *Continued*
>
> countries are realigning their supply chains to deepen trade with countries that share these renewed liberal values.
>
> For this parallel world to emerge, only one condition is different from the world that we inhabit: the West is more open to the possibility that parts of the Global South may have their own, indigenous strands of liberalism. This openness allows for mutual learning between parts of the Global North and parts of the Global South. The updated liberal consensus, while founded on an inclusive negotiation process of mutual respect, is also clear in drawing red lines that demarcate the liberal versus the illiberal, the democratic versus the authoritarian, the individual-oriented versus the society-oriented, and the planet-oriented versus the human-oriented.

As the thought experiment suggests, the failure by the West to acknowledge and engage with alternative liberal ideas—together with a diffidence on the part of key actors from the Global South to push for their own liberal variants (rather than conveniently piggyback on sovereignty-oriented, developmentalist ideas)—led to a loss of potential new allies for both sides. It also curtailed the emergence of new imaginaries that could have shaped a more sustainable, more secure, and more equitable world.

Can a renewed liberal order still be achieved?

Under (most likely irreversible) conditions of weaponized interdependence, it is difficult to see how all the opportunities of the 1990s can be re-created today. But the new geo-economic threats also lend an urgency to renewed cooperation between the Global North and at least parts of the Global South (and not only when it comes to voting against Russia over Ukraine). Closer trade agreements will be needed with countries in Africa and Latin America that have rare earth and other critical minerals. Deeper cooperation with India will be necessary to restore balance in the Indo-Pacific and will form an important part of the friends-shoring and diversification strategies of the United States and EU, respectively. Parts of the North will find more like-minded partners in parts of the Global South when it comes to establishing global rules on data protection. The urgency will likely only intensify as the West increases trade barriers on Chinese goods and markets in the Global South find themselves at the receiving end of China's excess production capacity.[61] An emerging wedge between China and developing countries (some of which were already disillusioned by the Belt and Road Initiative) will also create new opportunities for reordering global supply chains, trade rules, and security regimes.

All three drivers identified in the previous section still allow scope for change and reversal of certain negotiation stances and policy positions. Drawing on the errors and misjudgments identified in the previous section, I offer five takeaways for action:

- First, a more balanced approach will have to be found by policymakers and leaders between the two extremes of reductionism and trying to discredit the term "Global South." This balance requires a better understanding of different countries within the Global South on their own terms, while also acknowledging the collective identity that they sometimes share.[62]
- Second, a willingness to work with parts of the Global South at an eye-to-eye level will be especially important. This, in turn, will require acknowledgment of the possibility that there are multiple strands of liberalism on offer and that there are developing countries that can offer novel and complementary liberal ideas. While doing so, politically correct cultural relativism will have to be avoided in order to identify the subsets of Southern states with which parts of the Global North want to build meaningful strategic partnerships. Equally important, countries within the Global South will be well served to "own" their liberal roots if they want to make the most of these new opportunities.
- Third, it is time to bring back the big political and normative questions into global governance. Technical fixes will not solve the fundamental problems of competing political systems and values. Tackling the differences head-on will help identify the red lines of different players, thereby also identifying negotiating space within and outside multilateral institutions more accurately.
- Fourth, one of the major takeaways from the failures of the post–Cold War moment is that even the most promising solutions developed in Brussels, Geneva, or New York will have little buy-in if they do not address and engage with the concerns of real people. Narratives can be a powerful instrument in shaping preferences and legitimizing policies. Democracies as well as multilateral organizations will be well served if they pay at least as much attention to narratives (also on social media) as authoritarian and popular leaders seem to be doing rather effectively.

- Fifth, if the Global North is serious in its desire to engage with parts of the Global South, more expertise will be needed on and from the world regions. Interdisciplinarity will also be key; for instance, if we want to get a better handle on understanding the foreign policies of civilizational states,[63] we need scholarship that is able to combine insights from political science and ancient history and literature. It also means developing an interest in (and providing funding for research on) not only the "problem" countries but also potential allies and friends.

The new rose-gardens will look different from the ones we were promised at the turn of the millennium. They will be smaller, but they will bring together a greater diversity of foliage from both developed and developing worlds. And tended well, they may turn out to be richer, more resilient, and longer-lasting.

Notes

1. I use this T. S. Eliot-inspired imagery deliberately, not solely for a love of poetry but also as a contrast to the EU high representative's (Borrell 2022) ill-chosen, patronizing analogy ("Yes, Europe is a garden. We have built a garden.... [M]ost of the rest of the world is a jungle.") that generated considerable backlash from the Global South in various media outlets and social media.
2. Hansen 1979.
3. See Ikenberry and Trubowitz, this volume.
4. Krauthammer 1990–1991.
5. Narlikar 2010, 2013.
6. O'Neill 2001.
7. Alexandroff and Cooper 2010; Narlikar 2020.
8. Gök and Mehmetchik 2021.
9. Kirton 2013.
10. Notably, extreme poverty was halved by 2015, five years in advance of the target date.
11. Narlikar 2020.
12. I use a definition of policy failures as suggested by Drezner and Narlikar (2022), applying three criteria: policy outcomes are at variance from the ex-ante expectations of instigating actors; a historical revision of their being judged as failures is unlikely over time; and their distributive implications are lose-lose for all players.
13. Blustein 2009; Jones 2009; Narlikar et al. 2012. The deal reached at the Geneva Ministerial in June 2022 was a distant cry from the ambition of the DDA; see, e.g., Beattie 2022; Monicken 2022; Narlikar 2022.
14. The thirteenth Ministerial Conference, held in Abu Dhabi in February 2024, was also widely regarded as a failure (e.g., Global Memo 2024).
15. For example, World Trade Organization 2022.
16. Levy 2022.
17. UN 2022.
18. De la Fuente et al. 2023.
19. Crawford et al. 2022. It is worth noting that "financial sanctions have been imposed on Russia by all ten richest jurisdictions of the Group of Twenty, and by none of the ten poorer G20 countries" (Véron 2023).
20. Applebaum 2020; Kahl and Wright 2021; Saran 2020.

21. Narlikar 2021.
22. Cotterill 2023.
23. Jing et al. 2023, 231–232.
24. These include charges of neocolonialism by China (e.g., Prime Minister Mahathir, cited in Hornby 2018; also see Paszak 2020).
25. Rodrik 2011.
26. Ikenberry 2018, 21.
27. BBC 2018.
28. Hillman 2020.
29. For example, in August 2021, in response to a proposal for reform by a coalition of members, the United States stated that it would not be able to offer its support on the following grounds: "The United States continues to have systemic concerns with the Appellate Body. As Members know, the United States has raised and explained its systemic concerns for more than 16 years and across multiple U.S. Administrations. The United States believes that Members must undertake fundamental reform if the system is to remain viable and credible. The dispute settlement system can and should better support the WTO's negotiating and monitoring functions" (United States 2021).
30. Candidate Trump, for instance, described tariffs as "the most beautiful word in the dictionary" (*Wall Street Journal* 2024).
31. Zoellick 2003.
32. Schwab 2011, 108.
33. PTI 2022.
34. On underreach and overreach in the 1990s, see Ikenberry and Trubowitz, this volume.
35. For example, at the Munich Security Conference in 2022, German chancellor Olaf Scholz had the following to say: "In Asia in particular, it is in any case not a 'rise' that we should speak of, but, if anything, a 'revival.' Being a major power, from the perspective of Beijing or Delhi, is not a historical anomaly but rather a return to the status quo ante. There is nothing wrong with that. Quite the opposite" (German Federal Government 2022).
36. For a thorough debunking of these categories, see Sen 1997.
37. Panikkar 1982; Jalais 2018; Narlikar et al. 2023.
38. Chaturvedi et al. 2025. For more on how India's ancient traditions influence its negotiation behavior, see Narlikar and Narlikar 2014; Jaishankar 2020, 2023; Narlikar et al. 2023.
39. In the group, India probably has the greatest concerns about China. But Brazil and South Africa too have reasons for caution, given the growing presence of Chinese investment in their regions (and the very real risk that trade and investment can be weaponized, especially in strategically important sectors such as 5G technology and surveillance technology).
40. Cotterill et al. 2023; Xi 2023.
41. Republic of South Africa 2023.
42. Stewart and Huggins 2023.
43. Japan Times 2023.
44. For a detailed discussion on the intellectual, logical, political, and ethical reasons why such attempts are counterproductive, and the "Westsplaining" involved in some of these debates, see Kürzdörfer and Narlikar 2023.
45. Indian Ministry of External Affairs 2023. Interestingly, China was not present at the summit.
46. Indian Ministry of External Affairs 2024.
47. Narlikar and Sahni 2025.
48. Howse 2002, 98.
49. Fukuyama 1989, 18.
50. More on this in Narlikar 2022.
51. Farrell and Newman 2019.
52. Wright 2013, 7.
53. Farrell and Newman 2019, 46.
54. On the inadequacies of proposals to address this urgent issue in its most relevant institutional context—the WTO—see Narlikar 2022.
55. On how the Global South has managed to harness aspects of weaponized interdependence to its advantage, see Narlikar 2021.
56. Robert Shiller (2017) defines narratives as "major vectors of rapid change in culture, in zeitgeist, and ultimately in economic behaviour," 972.

57. Narlikar 2022.
58. On the uses and misuses of narratives in international relations and international political economy, and also how winning and sustainable narratives are constructed, see Narlikar 2020.
59. For instance, the *Bhagavad Gita* (13.28) states:

समं सर्वेषु भूतेषु तिष्ठन्तं परमेश्वरम्। विनश्यत्स्व विनश्यन्तं यः पश्यति स पश्यति।।

He who sees the divine in all creatures,

And in all mortal bodies sees the immortal soul, he is the one who truly understands.

This suggests the right to life, respect, and dignity for all beings, irrespective of species, and can also be found in secular texts from ancient India. The G-20's motto वसुधैव कुटुम्बकम् (Vasudhaiva Kutumbakam: "The entire earth is one family") under India's presidency in 2023 exemplifies this. For more on this, see Narlikar et al. 2023; Narlikar 2025.

60. Finnemore and Sikkink 1998.
61. Crabtree 2024.
62. Kürzdörfer and Narlikar 2023. It is worth noting that Japan does this better than other G-7 members; even when the G-7 rejected the term for its communiqué, a Japanese government official stated, "It's a powerful term. We'll use it domestically because it has an established image" (*Japan Times* 2023).
63. Narlikar 2024.

References

Alexandroff, Alan, and Andrew Cooper. 2010. *Rising States, Rising Institutions: Challenges for Global Governance*. Brookings Institution.

Applebaum, Anne. 2020. "When the World Stumbled: Covid and the Failure of the International System." In *COVID-19 and World Order: The Future of Conflict, Competition and Cooperation*, edited by Hal Brands and Francis J. Gavin. Johns Hopkins University Press.

BBC. 2018. "Trump Threatens to Pull US Out of World Trade Organization." August 31.

Beattie, Alan. 2022. "The WTO's Marathon Exercise in Staying Alive." *Financial Times*, June 17.

Blustein, Paul. 2009. *Misadventures of the Most Favoured Nations: Clashing Egos, Inflated Ambitions, and the Great Shambles of the World Trade System*. Public Affairs.

Borrell, Josep. 2022. "European Diplomatic Academy: Opening Remarks by High Representative Josep Borrell at the Inauguration of the Pilot Programme." European Union External Action, October 13. https://www.eeas.europa.eu/eeas/european-diplomatic-academy-opening-remarks-high-representative-josep-borrell-inauguration-pilot_en.

Chaturvedi, Sachin, Seeta Prabhu, and Sabyasachi Saha. 2025. *Well-Being, Values and Lifestyle—Towards a New Development Paradigm*. Springer Verlag.

Crabtree, James. 2024. "The Coming Clash between China and the Global South." *Foreign Policy*, September 11.

Cotterill, Joseph. 2023. "BRICS leaders invite six nations including Saudis and Iran to join bloc," *Financial Times*, 24 August, https://www.ft.com/content/30f96f4c-e5a6-452c-a283-265c558b0cf2.

Cotterill, Joseph, James Kynge, Arjun Neil Alim, and Michael Pooler. 2023. "China Urges Brics to Become Geopolitical Rival to G7." *Financial Times*, August 20.

Crawford, Alan, Jenni Marsh, and Antony Sguazzin. 2022. "The US-Led Drive to Isolate Russia and China Is Falling Short." *Bloomberg*, August 8. https://www.bloomberg.com/news/articles/2022-08-05/the-us-led-drive-to-isolate-russia-and-china-is-falling-short.

De La Fuente, Raquel Alberto, Tess Gibson, and Richard Gowan. 2023. "UN Votes Reveal a Lot about Global Opinion on the War in Ukraine." *World Politics Review*, February. https://www.worldpoliticsreview.com/un-ukraine-resolution-russia-united-nations-vote-putin-war/?share=email&messages%5B0%5D=one-time-read-success.

Drezner, Daniel, and Amrita Narlikar. 2022. "International Relations: The 'How Not To' Guide." *International Affairs* 98 (5): 1499–1513.

Farrell, Henry, and Abraham Newman. 2019. "Weaponized Interdependence: How Global Economic Networks Shape State Coercion." *International Security* 44 (1): 42–79.

Finnemore, Martha, and Kathryn Sikkink. 1998. "International Norm Dynamics and Political Change." *International Organization* 52 (4): 887–917.

Fukuyama, Francis. 1989. "The End of History?" *National Interest* 16: 3–18.

German Federal Government. 2022. "Speech by Olaf Scholz, Chancellor of the Federal Republic of Germany and Member of the German Bundestag, at the Munich Security Conference." February 19. https://www.bundesregierung.de/breg-de/impressum/speech-by-olaf-scholz-chancellor-of-the-federal-republic-of-germany-and-member-of-the-german-bundestag-at-the-munich-security-conference-2006670.

Global Memo by CFR, RSIS, CEPS, ORF and SIIS. 2024. "The WTO at a Crossroads: What the Failed Ministerial Conference Means." Council of Councils, March 6. https://www.cfr.org/councilofcouncils/global-memos/wto-crossroads-what-failed-ministerial-conference-means.

Gök, Gonca Oğuz, and Hakan Mehmetcik, eds. 2021. *The Crises of Legitimacy in Global Governance*. Routledge.

Hansen, Roger. 1979. *Beyond the North-South Stalemate*. McGraw Hill.

Hillman, Jennifer. 2020. "A Reset of the World Trade Organization's Appellate Body." Greenberg Center for Geoeconomic Studies & Renewing America: Council on Foreign Relations, January 14. https://www.cfr.org/report/reset-world-trade-organizations-appellate-body.

Hornby, Lucy. 2018. "Mahathir Mohamad Warns against 'Neo-Colonialism' during China Visit: Free Trade Should Also Be Fair Trade, Malaysian Prime Minister Stresses." *Financial Times*, August 20.

Howse, Robert. 2002. "From Politics to Technocracy—and Back Again: The Fate of the Multilateral Trade Regime." *American Journal of International Law* 96 (1): 94–117.

Ikenberry, John. 2018. "The End of Liberal International Order?" *International Affairs* 94 (1): 7–23.

Indian Ministry of External Affairs. 2023. "Voice of Global South Summit." January 12–13. https://mea.gov.in/voice-of-global-summit.htm.

Indian Ministry of External Affairs. 2024. "Chair's Summary: 3rd Voice of the Global South Summit (17 August 2024)." August 20. https://www.mea.gov.in/bilateral-documents.htm?dtl/38186/Chairs+Summary+3rd+Voice+of+Global+South+Summit+August+17+2024.

Jaishankar, Subramanyam. 2020. *The India Way: Strategies for an Uncertain World*. Harper Collins.

Jaishankar, Subramanyam. 2023. *Why Bharat Matters*. Rupa Publications.

Jalais, Annu. 2018. "Reworlding the Ancient Chinese Tiger in the Realm of the Asian Anthropocene." *International Communication of Chinese Culture* 5: 121–144.

Japan Times. 2023. "G7 Hiroshima Communique Will Not Use Term 'Global South.'" May 13. https://www.japantimes.co.jp/news/2023/05/13/national/politics-diplomacy/g7-global-south-term-communique/.

Jing, Qian, James Crawford, and Jianzhi Zhao. 2023. "The Impact of China's AIIB on the World Bank." *International Organization* 77 (1): 217–237.

Jones, Kent. 2009. *The Doha Blues: Institutional Crisis and Reform in the WTO*. Oxford University Press.

Kahl, Colin, and Thomas Wright. 2021. *Aftershocks: Pandemic Politics and the End of the Old International Order*. St Martin's.

Kirton, John. 2013. *G20 Governance for a Globalized World*. Routledge.

Krauthammer, Charles. 1990–1991. "The Unipolar Moment." *Foreign Affairs* 70 (1): 23–33.

Kürzdörfer, Nora, and Amrita Narlikar. 2023. "Was Ist Schon Ein Name." *Internationale Politik* 5 (23): 110–113. Republished in English as "A Rose by Any Other Name: In Defence of the Global South." *Global Policy Blog*, August 29. https://www.globalpolicyjournal.com/blog/29/08/2023/rose-any-other-name-defence-global-south.

Levy, Ivan. 2022. "The United Nations (In)Security Council: Time for Reform in a Post-Ukraine War World?" *Journal of International Affairs* 75 (1): 169–176.

Narlikar, Amrita. 2010. *New Powers: How to Become One and How to Manage Them*. Oxford University Press.

Narlikar, Amrita. 2013. (ed.) "Negotiating the Rise of New Powers." Special issue, *International Affairs* 89 (3).

Narlikar, Amrita. 2020. *Poverty Narratives and Power Paradoxes in International Trade Negotiations and Beyond*. Cambridge University Press.

Narlikar, Amrita. 2021. "Holding Up a Mirror to the World Trade Organization: Lessons from the COVID19 Pandemic." *Global Perspectives* 2 (1): 24069.

Narlikar, Amrita. 2021. "Must the Weak Suffer What They Must? The Global South in a World of Weaponized Interdependence." In *The Uses and Abuses of Weaponized Interdependence*, edited by Daniel Drezner, Henry Farrell, and Abraham Newman. Brookings Institution.

Narlikar, Amrita. 2022. "How Not to Negotiate: The Case of Trade Multilateralism." *International Affairs* 98 (5): 1553–1573. https://academic.oup.com/ia/article/98/5/1553/6686642.

Narlikar, Amrita. 2024. "India and the World: Civilizational Narratives in Foreign Policy." In *Foreign Policy: Theories, Actors, Cases*, 4th ed., edited by Steve Smith, Tim Dunne, Amelia Hadfield and Nicolas Kitchen. Oxford University Press.

Narlikar, Amrita. 2025. "One Earth, One Family, One Future: Unpacking the Theme of India's G20 Presidency." In *Well-being, Values and Lifestyle—Towards a New Development Paradigm*, edited by Sachin Chaturvedi, Seeta Prabhu, and Sabyasachi Saha. Springer Verlag.

Narlikar, Amrita and Aruna Narlikar. 2014. *Bargaining with a Rising India: Lessons from the Mahabharata*. Oxford University Press.

Narlikar, Amrita, and Gokul Sahni. 2025. "Renewing the EU-India Strategic Compact: Doing Better, Doing More, and Key How-Not-Tos." Observer Research Foundation, January 7. https://www.orfonline.org/english/research/renewing-the-eu-india-strategic-compact-doing-better-doing-more-and-key-how-not-to-s.

Narlikar, Amrita, Martin Daunton, and Robert Stern, eds. 2012. *The Oxford Handbook on the World Trade Organization*. Oxford University Press.

Narlikar, Aruna, Amitabh Mattoo, and Amrita Narlikar. 2023. *Strategic Choices, Ethical Dilemmas: Stories from the Mahabharat*. Penguin Random House India.

O'Neill, Jim. 2001. "Building Better Global Economic BRICs." Goldman Sachs, November 30. https://www.goldmansachs.com/intelligence/archive/building-better.html.

Panikkar, Raimundo. 1982. "Is the Notion of Human Rights a Western Concept?" *Diogenes* 30 (120): 75–102.

Paszak, Pawel. 2020. "China's Growing Influence in International Organizations." *China Monitor*, Warsaw Institute, October 14.

Patrick, Stewart, and Alexandra Huggins. 2023. "The Term 'Global South' Is Surging: It Should Be Retired." Commentary: Carnegie Endowment for International Peace, August 15. https://carnegieendowment.org/2023/08/15/term-global-south-is-surging.-it-should-be-retired-pub-90376.

PTI. 2022. "'Europe Has to Grow out of Mindset That Its Problems Are World's Problems': Jaishankar." *The Wire*, June 3. https://thewire.in/government/europe-has-to-grow-out-of-mindset-that-its-problems-are-worlds-problems-jaishankar.

Republic of South Africa. 2023. XV BRICS Summit, Johannesburg II Declaration BRICS and Africa: Partnership for Mutually Accelerated Growth, Sustainable Development and Inclusive Multilateralism. Sandton, Gauteng, South Africa, August 23. https://www.thepresidency.gov.za/content/xv-brics-summit-johannesburg-ii-declaration-24-august-2023.

Rodrik, Dani. 2011. *The Globalization Paradox: Democracy and the Future of the World Economy*. W. W. Norton.

Saran, Samir. 2020. "Dr WHO Gets the Prescription Wrong." Observer Research Foundation, March 25. https://www.orfonline.org/expert-speak/covid19-dr-who-gets-prescription-wrong-63708.

Schwab, Susan. 2011. "After Doha: Why the Negotiations Are Doomed and What We Should Do about It." *Foreign Affairs*, May–June.

Sen, Amartya. 1997. "Human Rights and Asian Values." Sixteenth Annual Morgenthau Memorial Lecture on Ethics and Foreign Policy, Carnegie Council for Ethics in International Affairs, May 25. https://media-1.carnegiecouncil.org/cceia/254_sen.pdf.

Shiller, Robert. 2017. "Narrative Economics." *American Economic Review* 107 (4): 967–1004.

United States. 2021. "Statements by the United States Delivered at the Meeting of the Dispute Settlement Body, Geneva, August 30." https://uploads.mwp.mprod.getusinfo.com/uploads/sites/25/2021/08/Aug30.DSB_.Stmt_.as_.deliv_.fin_.public.pdf.

Véron, Nicolas. 2023. "Much of the Global South Is on Ukraine's Side." Bruegel, March 13. https://www.bruegel.org/first-glance/much-global-south-ukraines-side.

Wall Street Journal. 2024. "Trump Calls Tariffs 'The Most Beautiful Word.'" October 16. https://www.wsj.com/livecoverage/harris-trump-election-10-16-2024/card/trump-calls-tariffs-the-most-beautiful-word-YMVPAupw4EjBRp6yobOy.

World Trade Organization. 2022. "Report on G20 Trade Measures: Mid-May 2022 to Mid-October 2022." November 14. https://www.wto.org/english/news_e/news22_e/report_trdev_nov22_e.pdf.

Wright, Thomas. 2013. "Sifting through Interdependence." *Washington Quarterly* 36 (4): 7–23.

Xi Jinping. 2023. "Full Text: Xi Jinping's Speech at the 15th BRICS Summit." August 23. https://news.cgtn.com/news/2023-08-23/Full-text-Xi-Jinping-s-speech-at-the-15th-BRICS-Summit-1mvxFMvuFLW/index.html.

Zoellick, Robert. 2003. "America Will Not Wait for the Won't Do Countries." *Financial Times*, September 22. https://ustr.gov/archive/Document_Library/Op-eds/2003/America_will_not_wait_for_the_won't-do_countries.html.

Index

For the benefit of digital users, indexed terms that span two pages (e.g., 52–53) may, on occasion, appear on only one of those pages.

Tables, figures, and boxes are indicated by an italic *t*, *f*, or *b*.

Abdelal, Rawi, 49–50, 63
Abe, Shinzo, 98
Abkhazia, 300–301
accountability *see* individual accountability
Acemoglu, Daron, 292
ad hoc tribunals, 126; *see also* International Criminal Tribunal for Rwanda (ICTR); International Criminal Tribunal for the Former Yugoslavia (ICTY)
Afghanistan, 217
  refugees from, 286
  U.S. intervention in, 11, 297
African Charter on Human and Peoples' Rights, 268–269
African Union, 268–269
agency, legal concept of, 122
al-Assad, Bashar, 298
Albright, Madeleine, 183–185, 189, 246, 301
"America First", 83, 203, 282–284
American Convention on Human Rights, 268–269
American Service Members Protection Act, 128–129
Ames, Aldrich, 179
Annan, Kofi, 112–113
antiglobalism, 14–15
anti-immigrant sentiment, 284
anti-neoliberal consensus, 230–231
Appel, Hilary, 288
Arab Spring, 297–298
Arbour, Louise, 129
Argentina, 339–340
Aron, Raymond, 53
ASEAN Regional Forum, 203, 214
Asian financial crisis, 67, 99, 207–208
Asian Infrastructure Investment Bank (AIIB), 43 n.19, 334
Asia-Pacific Economic Cooperation forum, 4, 29–30, 203

Association of Southeast Asian Nations, 268–269
atrocity crimes, 126
  intensification of, 126
automation, 281, 291–292, 293–294
Azerbaijan, 143

Babiš, Andrej, 150–151
backlash
  against EU enlargement, 287–288
  against liberal order, 282–283
  against Schengen Agreement, 285–286
Badinter Commission, 118
Bagley, Nicholas, 296–297
Baker, James, 87–88, 172, 174, 232–233
Barings Bank, 56
Barkin, Samuel, 112
Bartel, Fritz, 230–231
Belarus, 143
Bell, Daniel, 230
Belt and Road Initiative, 334
  and neocolonialism, 349 n.24
Berlin, Isaiah, 250
Bezos, Jeff, 63
Bhagwati, Jagdish, 67
Biden, Joe, 282–283, 294, 301
Biden administration
  policy toward China, 218
  and WTO, 335
Blair, Tony, 236–237, 246
  Doctrine of the International Community, 129–130
  and "Third Way", 38–39
Blinder, Alan, 55, 66
Blinken, Antony, 301
Blyth, Mark, 49–50, 69 n.15
Bodin, Jean, 115–116
Bohlen, Celestine, 183
Bolton, John, 133 n.58
Bonner, Yelena, 187

Born, Brooksley, 56–57
Bosco, David, 128
Bosnia
    conflict in, 243–246
    recognition of, 118–119
    UN peacekeeping mission in, 5
    and U.S. foreign policy, 175–176
    U.S. involvement in, 84
Bosnia-Herzegovina, 112
Brazil, 275–276, 330–331, 335–336, 349 n.38
Bretton Woods institutions, 28, 32–33, 36, 264
    expansion, 29–30
Brexit, 274, 283–284, 287, 294
BRICS, 329, 339–340
Brown, Jerry, 83
Brzezinski, Zbigniew, 179–180
Buchanan, Allen, 112
Buchanan, Pat, 83, 203
Budapest Memorandum, 177
Bulgaria, 322
    EU accession, 242, 315–316
Bush, George H. W., 49, 52, 83, 87–88, 174
    and "common European house", 251
    and intervention in Somalia, 121
    and U.S.-China relationship, 198
Bush, George W., 297
    critical of Putin, 319
Bush administration, 85, 87
    1992 defense guidance strategy, 84
    and China's admission into WTO, 215
    and European integration, 89–90
    policy toward China, 197–199, 207
    and U.S. exceptionalism, 128–129
Buzan, Barry, 110

Cancun Ministerial Conference, 335–337
capitalism; *see also* crony capitalism;
        shareholder value capitalism; state-led
        capitalism
    new culture of, 61–62
    twenty-first-century, 63
Carrère d'Encausse, Hélène, 234–235
change through trade (*Wandel durch
        Handel*), 213, 247–248
Chechnya, 181–182, 186, 317–319
checkbook diplomacy, 98
Chen Shui-bian, 208–209
Cheney, Dick, 173–174
Cherkesov, Viktor, 187
China
    acceptance into global economy, 30–31
    Belt and Road Initiative, 334
    and BRICS, 339–340
    developmental trajectory of, 295, 296–297, 299–300
    engagement with, 4, 19, 196–197, 203–204, 205–206, 207–209, 212–217, 220, 272, 330–331
    European policies toward, 204–205
    and future world order, 217–220
    and global order at turn of century, 209–213
    and India, 337–339
    and Japan, 198, 215
    and LIO, 271, 274–275
    membership of Nuclear Suppliers Group, 36
    as partner, 205
    repression of pro-democracy movement, 197–198
    rise of, 40–41, 217, 269–271
    and Russia, 272
    and Taiwan, 201–202
    and UNSC, 332–333
    and U.S. hegemony, 93, 101
    U.S. policy toward, 195–201, 203–204, 205–206, 207–209
    WTO accession, 25–26, 39–40, 207–209
"China shock", 30, 39–40, 216
China-Taiwan conflict (1995), 97, 196, 202–203
Chirac, Jacques, 237, 288–289
Christensen, Thomas, 203
Christopher, Warren, 175–176, 200
Churchill, Winston, 40, 298–299
CitiGroup, 55, 64
civil society, 231–233
Clark, Ian, 80–81
Clark, Phil, 127–128
Clinton, Bill, 18–19, 49–50, 53–54, 65–66, 82, 84
    on Bosnia-Herzegovina, 244–245
    and car seatbelts, 233
    and Chechnya, 186
    and China's admission into WTO, 30
    engagement with China, 210
    engagement with Russia, 172, 175–181
    and ICC, 126
    and NATO expansion, 92–93, 300–301
    and Rome Statute, 128–129
    and Russian crisis, 181–182
    and Rwandan genocide, 121–122
    and "Third Way", 38–39
Clinton administration, 99–100
    bilateral alliance system in Asia, 203
    and European integration, 89–90

and NATO, 89
policy toward China, 198–201, 208–209
policy toward Russia, 175–181
and Taiwan, 202
Cohen, Benjamin, 90–91
Cohen, Jean, 132 n.27
Cold War
aftermath of, 6, 18–19
end of, 5–6, 13–14, 17–18, 32–33
Commodity Futures Modernization Act, 56–57
conditionality, 145; *see also* membership conditionality
as tool of recognition policy, 118–119
Conference for Cooperation and Security in Europe (CSCE), 35, 108, 266–267, 315
containment, 209–210, 212, 213–214, 298–299
Convention on the Law of the Sea, 128–129
Cook, Robin, 246
Council of Europe, 142, 268–269
expansion, 270
counter-institutionalization, 260–261
COVID-19 pandemic, 333–334
Cox, Michael, 93
Crawford, Beverly, 87
credit-default swaps, 56–57
crimes against humanity, 122–123
Croatia
EU accession, 315–316
recognition of, 118
war with Serbia, 243–244
crony capitalism, 187–188
CSCE *see* Conference for Cooperation and Security in Europe
Csehi, Robert, 152
Cuban Missile Crisis, 301–302
Cunliffe, Philip, 109–110
currency crises, 241
Cyprus, 242, 315–316
Czech Republic, 142
EU accession, 146, 242, 315–316
and Euroskepticism, 150–151
NATO accession, 149, 159–160, 181, 239–240
populism in, 158–159
public opinion on EU, 157
Czechoslovakia, 148, 159–160

D'Amato, Alfonse, 179
Darfur, 121–122
DDA *see* Doha Development Agenda
de Villepin, Dominique, 297

Del Ponte, Carla, 129
Delors, Jacques, 238
democratic deficit, 242
democratization, 5–6, 290
third wave, 41–42, 125, 269–270
Deng, Francis, 111, 112–113, 114–116, 131
Deng Xiaoping, 295
deregulation, 51–52, 54, 68, 291–292; *see also* financial deregulation
derivatives, 55–57
digitalization, 281, 293–294
and "flat world", 295
dissidence, against LIO, 260–261, 271
distributive injustice, 126
Doha Development Agenda (DDA), 331–332
dollar, postwar dominance of, 90–91

East Timor, 246–247, 290
UN peacekeeping mission in, 5
ecologism, 345–346
Economic Community of West African States, 268–269
economic liberalism, 82, 261–262, 264
international, 82
economic nationalism, 81
efficient markets hypothesis, 53
Egypt, 339–340
Eichengreen, Barry, 51
embedded liberalism, 50, 58, 61, 264
engagement
aftermath of, 217–220
with China, 4, 19, 196–197, 203–206, 207–209, 210, 212–217, 220, 272, 330–331
Chinese view of, 212–213
defining, 209–213
political backlash, 215–216
redefining, 215
with Russia, 3–4, 36, 172, 175–181
as term, 203–204
with Ukraine, 322–323
Enron, 56
entanglement strategy, 210–211
environmentalism, 345–346
Erbakan, Necmettin, 316
Erdoğan, Recep Tayyip, 311, 320
and LIO, 321
Estonia, 146, 242, 315–316
Ethiopia, 339–340
ethnic cleansing, 244
in Kosovo, 129
EU *see* European Union
EU Stability Pact, 242

euro
  emergence of, 90–91
  introduction of, 268, 284–285
European Convention on Human Rights, 268–269
European Defence Agency, 288–289
European integration, 88–91
  and Bush administration, 89–90
  and Clinton administration, 89–90
  and France, 88–89, 273–274
  and Germany, 88–89, 240, 273–274
  and Hungary, 285
  and Spain, 285
  and UK, 240, 273–274; *see also* Brexit
European Monetary System, 240–241
European monetary union, 90, 239, 285
European single market, 89–90, 268, 283
European Union (EU), 32–33, 36, 259
  accession, 144, 146–148, 159–160
  enlargement, 158–159, 242, 273–274, 283, 287
Euroskepticism, 158
  and national chauvinism, 150–152

Farage, Nigel, 249
Faroohar, Rana, 30
Farrell, Henry, 342–343
Federal Reserve, 52
Feldstein, Martin, 68
Fico, Robert, 142–143, 156
financial deregulation, 50, 53, 54–58, 69
financial liberalization, 50–51, 65, 68, 100
  campaign for, 54
  promotion of, 54–55
financial services sector, 57–58, 60
  increasing size of, 59–60
Finland, 157
Fischer, Joschka, 246, 287, 297
Food and Agriculture Organization, 265
Ford Motor Company, 57–58
France
  and contestation of globalization, 229–230
  and currency fluctuations, 241
  and enlargement fatigue, 288
  and European integration, 88–89, 273–274
  and European monetary union, 241
  and European security, 240
  and immigration, 286
  social welfare spending, 292
free markets, 145
free trade, 82, 291–292
  agreements (FTAs), 4

freedom, 249
Friedberg, Aaron, 77–78
Friedman, George, 182–183
Friedman, Thomas, 290, 295
Fukuyama, Francis, 13–14, 182–183, 233, 290, 342

G-7, 330–331
  July 1990 summit, 203–204
G-8, 330–331
  and Russia, 318–319
G-20, 330–331
Gaddafi, Muammar, 298
Garton Ash, Timothy, 235
Gates, Robert, 173–174
General Agreement on Tariffs and Trade (GATT), 29, 264, 330
General Data Protection Regulation (GDPR), 293
General Motors, 292
genocide, 244
  in Rwanda, 84, 112–113, 121–122, 246–247; *see also* International Criminal Tribunal for Rwanda (ICTR)
Georgia, 92–93, 158, 270, 275, 300–301
Germany, 78–79
  and European integration, 88–89, 240, 273–274
  and introduction of euro, 90–91
  and migration, 285–286
  and normalization, 233–234
  reunification, 87–89
  social welfare spending, 292
Gerstle, Gary, 230–231
Gilpin, Robert, 78–79
Glass-Steagall Act, 51–52
  repeal of, 55, 64
global financial crisis, 64–65, 217
global governance
  1990s-era, 27
  choices, 26–27, 31, 35
Global South, as term, 340–341
globalization, 42, 229–235, 247, 250–251, 293–294
  challenges to, 237–238
  domestic politics of, 38
  and "flat world", 295
  and human rights, 247–248
  and LIO, 260–274
  politicians' promises, 249
  tension in discourse, 249

use of term in English-language
    newspapers, 230f
  and workers, 291–292
Goddard, Stacie, 41
Godemont, François, 204–205
Goldstein, Judith, 37
Gorbachev, Mikhail, 28, 87–88, 171–175
  and "common European house", 251
Gore, Al, 176–177
governance, 232; *see also* global governance
  multilateral, 342
Gramm, Phil, 54, 56–57, 63–64
Gramm-Leach-Bliley Act, 55
Gray, John, 229
Great Depression, 51
great power wars, 31–32
  end of, 32
Greece, 240, 260–261, 273–274, 285
Greenspan, Alan, 52–57, 60–61, 63–64, 66–69
Gregor, Milos, 161 n.37
Grotius, Hugo, 110
guilt, individualization of, 126
Gulf War (1990–1991), 83–84, 98

Haas, Ernest B., 266–267
Haas, Richard, 113
Haiti, 112
  UN peacekeeping mission in, 5
Harkin, Tom, 83
Havel, Václav, 148
Hegel, Georg Wilhelm Friedrich, 231–232
hegemonic orders, 80, 85–86
hegemonic relationships, 85
hegemonic stability theory, 258–259
hegemons, 37–38
hegemony, 78–79, 84, 100–101
  definitions, 79–80
  liberal, 81, 85
  maintaining in Europe, 86–93
  reasserting in East Asia, 93–99
  U.S., 90–93, 99
Hillman, Jennifer, 215, 218
Hobbes, Thomas, 115–116, 117, 132 n.39
Hombach, Bodo, 236–237
Hong Kong, 201, 204–205, 214
Howe, Geoffrey, 238
Howse, Rob, 341–342
Hu Jintao, 215–216
human rights, 338; *see also* international human rights
  in China, 197–201
  as constitutional rights, 267–268
  and globalization, 247–248
  idea of, 107–108
  individual, 108
  and sovereignty, 112
  violations, 122
human security, discourse of, 130–131
humanitarian intervention, 119–122
Hungary, 142–143, 148, 158–160, 237, 273–274, 322
  and backlash against migration, 286–287
  and discontent with LIO, 309–310
  EU accession, 242, 315–316
  and European integration, 285
  Euroskepticism in, 151–152, 282
  illiberal practices in, 152–153, 287
  mortality rates, 248–249
  NATO accession, 149–150, 181, 239–240
  public opinion on EU, 157
  rapprochement with Russia, 154–156
hyperglobalization, 42
  of markets, 335

ICC *see* International Criminal Court
ICISS *see* International Commission on Intervention and State Sovereignty
ICTR *see* International Criminal Tribunal for Rwanda
ICTY *see* International Criminal Tribunal for the Former Yugoslavia
identity politics, 293–294
IDPs *see* internally displaced persons
IGOs *see* intergovernmental organizations
Ikenberry, G. John, 31–32, 34, 37, 92–93, 335
IMF *see* International Monetary Fund
immigration *see* migration
impunity from prosecution, 122
income inequality, 292
India, 275–276, 329–331
  and China, 337–339
  and Global South as term, 340–341
  importance of cooperation with, 346–347
  and international security, 332–333, 336–337
  and international trade, 335–336
individual accountability, 110–111, 131
  early post-Cold War practices, 123–126
  origins of idea, 122–123
  and war in Kosovo, 129
inequality, 292; *see also* income inequality
  soaring levels of, 63

institutionalism, 34; *see also* rationalist institutionalism; sociological institutionalism; technocratic institutionalism
institutionalist approach, 26
institutions; *see also* international institutions
  modal realist perspective, 33–34
interdependence, weaponized, 342–343, 346–347
intergovernmental organizations (IGOs), 35
internally displaced persons (IDPs), 112–113, 115
International Authority Database, 277 n.16
international business, 234–235
International Commission on Intervention and State Sovereignty (ICISS), 112–113, 116, 130–131
International Criminal Court (ICC), 110–111, 126–129, 134 n.94
International Criminal Tribunal for Rwanda (ICTR), 123–124, 125–126
International Criminal Tribunal for the Former Yugoslavia (ICTY), 123–124, 125–126, 129, 243, 245
international human rights, 110–111, 264–265
  doctrine of, 108–109
  norms, 112
international institutions, 4, 33
International Monetary Fund (IMF), 144–145, 230–231, 234, 264
  expansion, 29
interoperability, 89
intervention; *see also* humanitarian intervention
  as ally of sovereignty, 116
Iran, 181–182, 339–340
Iraq, 11
  invasion of Kuwait (1990), 28, 290
  U.S. intervention in, 120, 190, 217, 297
Islamic State, 298
Ismay, Lord, 87
isolationism, 83
Italy, 237, 282
  and backlash against migration, 286–287
  and EU Stability Pact, 242
  and European Monetary System, 241
  and Euroskepticism, 273–274, 285
  social welfare spending, 292
Ivanov, Igor, 185
Ivanov, Sergei, 187

Jackson Hole Symposium, 60–61
Jacoby, Wade, 149, 161 n.29
James, Harold, 291–292

Japan, 77–79
  and China, 198, 215
  security relationship with U.S., 97–99
  and U.S. hegemony, 93–97, 100
Jentleson, Bruce, 27
Jiang Shigong, 222 n.99
Jiang Zemin, 207–208
Jin Canrong, 212–213
Johnson, Boris, 294
Johnston, Alastair, 205, 211–212
Johnston, Iain, 41
Jospin, Lionel, 237
Jubilee 2000, 331
Judt, Tony, 250
Juncker, Jean-Claude, 242
Junichiro, Koizumi, 203–204

Kaczyński, Jarosław, 152–154
Kaczyński, Lech, 153 154
Kampala Process, 114–115, 132 n.30
Karadžić, Radovan, 126, 245
Kellogg-Briand Pact (1928), 133 n.71
Kennedy, Paul, 78–79
Keynes, John Maynard, 50, 58–60, 63
Keynesianism, 53
Kindleberger, Charles, 65
King, Mervyn, 247
Kiriyenko, Sergei, 182
Kirshner, Jonathan, 291–292
Klaus, Václav, 150–151, 161 n.37
Kohl, Helmut, 87–88, 204–205, 284–285
Konno, Hidehiro, 95–96
Korea, 68; *see also* North Korea; South Korea
Kosovo, 287
  use of force in, 120
  war in, 129–130
Krastev, Ivan, 157–158
Krauthammer, Charles, 290
Kurdish population, 316
Kuwait, 28, 243, 290

Lampton, David, 196, 199, 213
Latvia, 146, 242, 315–316
Lawson, Nigel, 242
Le Pen, Jean-Marie, 237
Le Pen, Marine, 152, 249
League of Nations, 32
Lee Teng-hui, 202
Leebaw, Bronwyn, 126
legitimacy, 296–297
Levy, Philip, 215
liberal international order (LIO), 257–258, 323 n.1
  contesting, 260–261

deepening and widening, 258–259, 263f–263f
discontent with, 309–310
and end of Cold War, 266–267
and engagement with China, 213–217
lessons for present, 320–323
liberal multilateralism of, 264–265
mapping, 261–264
postliberal, 274–276
postnational liberalism of, 267–269
liberal internationalism, 261–262, 335
  neglect of domestic foundations, 302–303
liberal legalism, 123–124
liberal order
  durability in Eastern Europe, 156–158
  expansion, 145
  possibilities for renewal, 346–348
liberal overreach, 282–283
liberalism, 170, 266–267; *see also* economic liberalism; embedded liberalism
liberalization, 52–53; *see also* financial liberalization; trade liberalization
Libya, 121–122
  and migration, 286
  NATO intervention in, 190, 298
LIO *see* liberal international order
Lisbon Treaty, 273–274, 288–289
Lithuania, 242, 315–316
Long-Term Capital Management, 56
Lord, Winston, 198–199, 200–204
Luban, David, 133 n.66
Lucas, Robert, 53
Lugar, Richard, 179

Maastricht Treaty, 4, 238–241, 284–285
Macedonia, 118
Macková, Alena, 161 n.37
Macron, Emmanuel, 288–289
Maizière, Lothar de, 233–234
Major, John, 244–245
Make Poverty History, 331
Malaysia, 29–30, 68–69, 182
Malcolm, Noel, 244–245
Malia, Martin, 182–183
Malta, 242, 315–316
Mandelson, Peter, 236–237
markets, 236–237, 329, 334; *see also* efficient markets hypothesis; free markets
  hyperglobalization of, 335
Martin, Lisa, 37
Marx, Karl, 231–232
McNamara, Kate, 90–91

Mearsheimer, John, 30–31, 40–41, 77–78, 169–170, 195–196
Mečiar, Vladimir, 146–147, 149–150
membership conditionality, 146–147, 160
Merkel, Angela, 283–284
Merz, Friedrich, 283–284
Mexico, 4, 81, 330–331
middle way, 58–59
migration, 285–287
military withdrawal, 83
Millennium Round, 331
Milošević, Slobodan, 129, 244–246
minority rights, 108
Mitsotakis, Konstantinos, 240
Mitterrand, François, 244–245
Mladić, Ratko, 126, 243–244
modernities, convergence of, 295–298
Moldova, 158, 270, 275
morality, global, 243–247
mortality rates, 248–249
multilateralism, 329, 334–335
multipolarity, 77–79, 329, 334–336
Musgrave, Paul, 38

NAFTA *see* North American Free Trade Agreement
narratives, 347, 349 n.56, 350 n.58
  positive, 340–341
  of U.S. decline, 78–79
national chauvinism, 150–152
National Economic Council, 53–54
National Security Strategy (2002), 100
national sovereignty, 267–268
nationalism, 151–152
nation-states, 234–235
nativism, 160
NATO, 32–33, 77–78
  enlargement, 5, 19, 91–93, 158–160, 270, 300–301
  expansion, 28–29, 85–93, 100, 181–182, 239–240
  joining, 144, 148–150
  and war in Kosovo, 129
neoliberal turn, 20
neoliberalism, 100
  economic logic behind, 38
  excesses, 291–295
  policies, 40

neoliberalism (*Continued*)
  spread of, 145
New Forum, 107–108
new interventionism, 121
New Keynesians, 53
"new middle", 236–237
Newman, Abraham, 342–343
Nixon, Richard, 177
Nölke, Andreas, 150
nonimpunity norm, 122, 125–126
non-inflationary continuing expansion (NICE), 247–248
nonintervention, principle of, 116
normalization, 233–234
  in politics, 235–242
norms and identities, misjudgments on, 337–341
North American Free Trade Agreement (NAFTA), 4, 36, 81, 89–90
North Korea, 97–98, 214, 217
North-South cooperation
  deadlocks and failures, 331–334
  failed promise of, 327
  negotiation breakthroughs, 328–331
  reasons for failure, 335–344
nostalgia, 234–235, 238
Nuclear Non-Proliferation Treaty, 36, 205
Nuremberg tribunal, 122–123, 133 n.73
Nye, Joseph, 33

Obama, Barack, 297
Obama administration
  engagement with China, 216
  and WTO, 335
OECD *see* Organisation for Economic Co-operation and Development
Operation Desert Storm, 290
Orbán, Viktor, 151–153, 154–156, 161 n.42
Organisation for Economic Co-operation and Development (OECD), 264, 277 n.16
Organization for Security and Cooperation in Europe (OSCE), 35, 108, 315
  expansion, 270
Organization of American States, 268–269
Ornstein, Norman, 81–82
Ottoman Empire, 312–314
overconfidence, 14
  of United States in 1990s, 290–303
overreach, 14, 100, 281; *see also* liberal overreach
  strategic, 100
  technocratic, 337–340

oversight and supervision
  renunciation of, 54
  withdrawal of, 55–56

Pakistan, 205–206
Patel, Dev, 42
Patrushev, Nikolai, 187
Peace of Westphalia (1648), 250
People's Republic of China (PRC) *see* China
perestroika, 173–174
permanent normal trade relations (PNTR), for China, 208–209
Perot, Ross, 81–82, 203
Perry, William, 180
personality, legal concept of, 122
Pickering, Thomas, 187–188
Pinochet, Augusto, 125–126
Plaza Agreement (1985), 95–96
Poland, 142–143, 148, 159–160, 237, 322
  EU accession, 315–316
  illiberal practices in, 152–153, 287
  and migration, 285–286
  NATO accession, 149–150, 181, 239–240
  and populism, 152, 158–159, 286–287
  public opinion on EU, 157
  and Russia-Ukraine War, 153–154, 156–157
  "shock therapy" programs in, 145
Polanyi, Karl, 58–59
policy failures, definition, 348 n.12
political liberalism, 261–262, 264–265, 267–268
Poos, Jacques, 88–89, 288
populism, 159; *see also* right-wing populists
  American, 81
  in Czech Republic, 158–159
  illiberal, 284, 293–294
  leaders, 143
  in Poland, 152, 158–159, 286–287
  rise of, 160, 281
  in Slovakia, 142–143
postnational liberalism, 269–274
  of LIO, 267–269
PRC *see* China
Price, Ned, 301–302
primacy, strategy of, 84–85
Primakov, Yevgeni, 183–184
Prodi, Romano, 242
protectionism, 82
pushback, against LIO, 260–261
Putin, Vladimir, 155, 170–172, 311, 317–319
  and dissidence against LIO, 271–272
  emergence of, 172–173, 185–190

and LIO, 321
and NATO enlargement, 300–301
and pushback against LIO, 260–261
and Russia-Ukraine War, 169–170

Quinton-Brown, Patrick, 116

Rachman, Gideon, 42
Rajan, Raghuram G., 60–61
rationalist institutionalism, 258–259, 269
Reagan, Ronald, 173–174
realist sobriety, idealist displacement of, 298–302
redistribution, 238
regulation, 52–53
  minimal, 293
Regulation Q, 69 n.5
responsible sovereignty, 131
  early post-Cold War practices, 117–122
  origins of idea, 111–113
  unpacking, 113–117
  and war in Kosovo, 129
restraint, 83–84
revolutionism, 109
  soft, 110–111, 127, 130
right-wing populists, 286–287
risk *see* systemic risk
Rodrik, Dani, 40
Rohatyn, Felix, 66
Romania, 322
  EU accession, 242, 315–316
  and migration, 286
  mortality rates, 248–249
Romano, Flavio, 38–39
Rome Statute, 126, 128–129
Roosevelt, Franklin, 298–299
Rubin, Robert, 53–55, 64, 66–68
Ruggie, John, 50, 58, 61
rules-based international order, erosion of, 25
Russia, 189–190; *see also* Putin, Vladimir
  in 1990s, 314–318
  and China, 272
  and Clinton administration, 175–181
  in crisis, 181–184
  and democracies of Global South, 332–333
  engagement with, 3–4, 36, 172, 175–178
  fear of, 148
  and G-8, 318–319
  as historical "outsider", 312–314
  and LIO, 258, 271, 274, 310–312, 320–323
  and NATO enlargement, 10–11, 19, 85–86, 92–93, 149, 300–302

nostalgia for communist past, 238
and Western liberalism, 170–172
Russia-Ukraine War, 141–142, 153–157, 169–170, 272, 275–276, 288, 299–300
and NATO enlargement, 159–160
Rwanda
  genocide in, 84, 112–113, 121–122, 246–247; *see also* International Criminal Tribunal for Rwanda (ICTR)

Salvini, Matteo, 152, 249
sanctions, 198, 205–206; *see also* United Nations: economic sanctions
Sandefur, Justin, 42
Sarotte, Mary, 28–29
Saudi Arabia, 339–340
Scheffer, David, 128–129, 134 n.74
Schengen Agreement, 283, 285–287
Schimmelfennig, Frank, 161 n.20
Scholz, Olaf, 349 n.35
Schröder, Gerhard, 236–237, 246
Schwab, Susan, 335–336
Scowcroft, Brent, 198
securitization, 55–56
self-determination, 116, 132 n.37
semiperiphery, 323 n.4
Sen, Amartya, 249
Serbia, 143, 158, 287
  ethnic cleansing in, 129
  war with Croatia, 243–244
shareholder value capitalism, 61–63, 64–65
Shifrinson, Joshua, 28–29
Shirk, Susa, 216
shock therapy, 145
Sikkink, Kathryn, 125
Simpson, Gerry, 132 n.27
Single European Act (1986), 88–89
Skidelsky, Robert, 53
Slovakia, 156, 159–160
  EU accession, 146–147, 242, 315–316
  NATO accession, 149–150
  populism in, 142–143
  public opinion on EU, 157
Slovenia, 248–249
  EU accession, 242, 315–316
  recognition of, 118
social welfare, 292
socialism, 269
sociological institutionalism, 258–259, 269
solidarity, 110–111
Solow, Robert, 59–60
Somalia

Somalia (*Continued*)
   U.S. involvement in, 84, 121
   use of force in, 119
South Africa, 275–276, 329, 330–331, 335–336
   and Russia-Ukraine War, 332–333
South Korea, 98–99, 203–204
South Ossetia, 300–301
sovereignty
   as responsibility, 109–111; *see also* responsible sovereignty
Soviet Union, 174, 247–248, 314; *see also* Gorbachev, Mikhail; Yeltsin, Boris
   collapse of, 13–14, 17, 28, 32–33, 174–175, 234–235, 240, 266, 269, 283
   and LIO, 257, 265
   and UNSC, 35, 243
Spain
   and arrest of General Pinochet, 125–126
   and European integration, 285
   and European Monetary System, 241
Srebrenica massacre, 243–244
Stalin, Joseph, 298–299
Starmer, Keir, 294
START I, 177
START II, 186
state model of accountability, 122
state recognition, 118–119
state-led capitalism, 94–95
Steinberg, James, 196, 210, 214–215
stigma-management strategies, 314
Stoltenberg, Jens, 301
Structural Impediments Initiative, 95–96
Subramanian, Arvind, 42
subsidiarity, 232, 238–239
Suettinger, Robert, 208
Sullivan, Jake, 39
Summers, Lawrence, 43 n.19, 54–55, 56–57, 60–61, 63–64, 66–69
Sunak, Rishi, 294
Sweden
   NATO accession, 157
   social welfare spending, 292
Syria, 298
   and migration, 286
systemic risk, 60–61

Tadić, Duško, 245
Taiwan, 97, 201–202, 203–204, 206, 208–209, 219
   conflict with China (1995), 97, 196, 202–203
Talbott, Strobe, 176–178, 179–182, 184, 188

technocratic institutionalism, 341
Teitel, Ruti, 112
Teltschik, Horst, 87–88
Tenet, George, 186
tequila effect, 30
terrorism, 217
Teson, Fernando, 112
Thatcher, Margaret, 87–88, 173–174, 238
There Is No Alternative (TINA), 227–228
Third Way, 38–39
Thucydides trap, 214–215
Tiananmen, 196–201
Tobin, James, 59–60
Tokyo tribunal, 122–123
Toyota, 95–96
Track 1.5 Northeast Asian Cooperation Dialogue, 203
trade liberalization, 100
transitional justice for wrongdoing, 125
transitional recessions, 145
treaty ratification, U.S. ranking for, 34
tribunal fatigue, 126
triumphalism, of West, 290–291
Trotsky, Leon, 250
Trubowitz, Peter, 31
Trump, Donald, 272–273, 282–284, 294, 303
   and WTO, 335
Truss, Liz, 294
Tunisia, 298
Turkey, 311–312
   in 1990s, 314–316
   in 2000s, 320
   as historical "outsider", 312–314
   and LIO expansion, 320–323

Ukraine, 270
   engagement with the West, 322–323
   EU membership, 275, 287–288
   independence, 180
   and NATO enlargement, 190, 300–302
UN *see* United Nations
unipolarity, 299–300
United Arab Emirates, 332–333, 339–340
United Kingdom
   and European integration, 240, 273–274; *see also* Brexit
   and European Monetary System, 241
   excesses of neoliberal orthodoxy, 291–295
   and financial deregulation, 236–237
   inequality, 292
   and intervention in Kosovo, 120
   and liberal overreach, 282

and migration, 285–286
mortality rates, 248
social welfare spending, 292
United Nations (UN), 265
  economic sanctions, 35–36, 44 n.55
  General Assembly, 116
  Military Staff Committee, 28
  Office of the High Commissioner for Human Rights, 108
  peacekeeping, 5
  Security Council (UNSC), 28, 35–36, 205, 332–333
United States; *see also* Biden administration; Bush administration; Clinton administration; hegemony; Obama administration
  alliance system in Asia, 203–204
  excesses of neoliberal orthodoxy, 291–295
  intervention in Afghanistan, 11, 297
  narrative of decline, 78–79
  overconfidence in 1990s, 290–303
  policy toward China, 195–201, 203–204, 205–206, 207–209
  policy toward Japan, 93–97
  security relationship with Japan, 97–99
  treaty ratification, 34
UNSC *see* United Nations: Security Council
Uruguay Round, 82, 89–90
U.S. Government Accountability Office, 56–57
use of force, for humanitarian purposes, 119–121
USSR *see* Soviet Union
Uzbekistan, 143

Vershbow, Alexander, 185–186
Visegrad states, 142
Vliegenthart, Arjan, 150
Volcker, Paul, 52, 60
Volkswagen, 247–248
von Eichendorff, Joseph, 228

Wałęsa, Lech, 148
Wall Street, 57–58
Wallander, Celeste, 34
Walmart, 292
Walt, Steve, 169–170

Waltz, Kenneth, 77–78
Wang Jisi, 214–215
Warsaw Summit of Conservative Leaders of Europe, 162 n.46
Washington Consensus, 25–26, 82, 144–145
Weber, Steven, 27
Weinberger, Caspar, 96
Wen Jiaobo, 215–216
Westphalian system, 113
Wight, Martin, 109, 130
Will, George, 291–292
Wolf, Martin, 64–65
World Bank, 234, 264
  expansion, 29
World Health Organization (WHO), 265
  and COVID-19 pandemic, 333–334
World Trade Organization (WTO), 82, 89–90, 142, 330
  China's entry into, 25–26, 39–40, 207–209
  expansion, 29
  policy failures, 332
  U.S. dissatisfaction with, 335

Xi Jinping, 216

Yakovlev, Alexander, 230–231
Yalta agreement, 298–299
Yeltsin, Boris, 148, 173, 175–176, 177–179, 181, 234–235, 317–319
  in crisis, 182
  and emergence of Putin, 185
  and G-7, 315
  and NATO expansion, 181–182, 300
  relationship with Bill Clinton, 172
yen, revaluation of, 95–96
Yugoslavia; *see also* International Criminal Tribunal for the Former Yugoslavia (ICTY)
  collapse of, 243, 288

Zeman, Miloš, 150–151
Zgut, Edit, 152
Zhirinovsky, Vladimir, 176–177
Zhu Rongji, 207–208
Ziuganov, Genadii, 148
Zoellick, Robert, 335–336

www.ingramcontent.com/pod-product-compliance
Ingram Content Group UK Ltd.
Pitfield, Milton Keynes, MK11 3LW, UK
UKHW041135230426
470302UK00016B/89